T0212430

Lecture Notes in Computer Science 11500

More information about this series at http://www.springer.com/series/7407

Ezio Bartocci · Rance Cleaveland ·
Radu Grosu · Oleg Sokolsky (Eds.)

From Reactive Systems to Cyber-Physical Systems

Essays Dedicated to Scott A. Smolka
on the Occasion of His 65th Birthday

 Springer

Editors
Ezio Bartocci [ID]
Technische Universität Wien
Vienna, Austria

Radu Grosu [ID]
Technische Universität Wien
Vienna, Austria

Rance Cleaveland
University of Maryland
College Park, MD, USA

Oleg Sokolsky [ID]
University of Pennsylvania
Philadelphia, PA, USA

ISSN 0302-9743   ISSN 1611-3349   (electronic)
Lecture Notes in Computer Science
ISBN 978-3-030-31513-9   ISBN 978-3-030-31514-6   (eBook)
https://doi.org/10.1007/978-3-030-31514-6

LNCS Sublibrary: SL1 – Theoretical Computer Science and General Issues

This Springer imprint is published by the registered company Springer Nature Switzerland AG
The registered company address is: Gewerbestrasse 11, 6330 Cham, Switzerland

Scott A. Smolka

Courtesy of Computer Science Department, Stony Brook University, USA.
Picture taken by Tony Scarlatos. Used with permission.

Preface

This Festschrift is dedicated to Scott A. Smolka on the occasion of his 65th birthday that was celebrated on August 1, 2019. This book contains the papers written by his closest friends and collaborators. These papers were presented during a two-day workshop organized in his honor that was held during August 1–2, 2019, at Stony Brook University, NY, USA.

Scott joined the Department of Computer Science of Stony Brook University in 1982, and was promoted to full professor in 1995. In 2016 he was appointed to the rank of Distinguished Professor in the same university.

He has made fundamental research contributions in a number of areas, including process algebra, model checking, probabilistic processes, runtime verification, and the modeling and analysis of cardiac cells and neural circuits. He is perhaps best known for the algorithm he and Paris Kanellakis invented for checking bisimulation. Scott's research in these areas has resulted in over 200 publications, generating more than 9,000 citations.

He has been principal investigator and co-principal investigator on grants totaling more than $23 million, and he is the lead principal investigator of CyberCardia, a $4.3-million National Science Foundation (NSF) multi-institutional grant, "Compositional, Approximate, and Quantitative Reasoning for Medical Cyber-Physical Systems." He served as Deputy Director of a $10-million NSF multi-institutional grant on "Computational Modeling and Analysis of Complex Systems." Scott is also a director and co-founder of Reactive Systems, Inc., a company selling tools and services for embedded-software testing and validation.

In 2016, Scott was recognized as a Fellow of the European Association for Theoretical Computer Science for his "fundamental contributions in formal modeling and analysis." He is the recipient of the President and Chancellor's Award for Excellence in Scholarship and Creative Activities, and the Department of Computer Science's Research Excellence Award.

The title of this volume, *From Reactive Systems to Cyber-Physical Systems*, reflects Scott's main research focus throughout his career. The contributions, which went through a peer-review process, cover a wide spectrum of the topics related to Scott's research scientific interests, including model repair for probabilistic systems, runtime verification, model checking, cardiac dynamics simulation, and machine learning.

Dear Scott, on behalf of all your friends, students, and collaborators, we wish you all the best!

June 2019

Ezio Bartocci
Rance Cleaveland
Radu Grosu
Oleg Sokolsky

CyberCardia Team
Courtesy of Rahul Mangharam, University of Pennsylvania, USA.
Used with permission.

Personal Notes for Scott

From Ezio Bartocci - I met Scott for the first time twelve years ago, while I was pursuing my PhD in Italy. My former advisor, given my background in both computer science and biology, suggested me to spend three months in Stony Brook to visit Scott. During that period, Scott and Radu were working on computational modelling and analysis of cardiac dynamics. Starting that collaboration was of key importance to my life, with a clear impact on my future academic career - and not only. Scott has been a wonderful teacher, nurturing motivation, ideas and new exciting problems to be solved, beyond my stay in Stony Brook. I am extremely indebted to Scott. I consider him not only a scientific father, but also a dear friend and I am very happy to organize this event.
Scott I wish you all the best for your 65th birthday!!

From Samir Das, Chair of the Department of Computer Science, Stony Brook University - Scott is a leading expert in formal methods for the analysis of computing systems and has an outstanding track record for making foundational technical contributions and applications to real-world problems. He is inspiring to both our faculty and students. His visibility and high-impact research bring significant recognition to our department.

From James Glimm - Congratulations Scott! I have learned so much from the CyberCardia project and benefited from your leadership of it. I have met with many new colleagues and renewed an ancient collaboration with Flavio Fenton. You have made all of this possible. My deepest thanks for this.

From Radu Grosu - It is my great pleasure and honor to write a Laudation for Scott Smolka with the occasion of his 65-birthday celebration, highlighting some of my memories with him. Scott has become over the years not only a mentor but also a true friend of mine.

In order to do justice to my recollections with Scott, I would have to write volumes. The first would be about our countless hours of joint research, which are continuing to this day. The second would be about our common passion for tennis, and the countless hours spent together on the tennis courts. The third would be about our countless dinners together, where we both enjoyed wonderful conversations and delicious food. Finally, the fourth would have to be about the miraculous way he overcame a serious illness, such that we still have the privilege to be with him today. Since I will not have the space required for these volumes, I will just mention the way I would probably like to start the first volume.

One of the most distinguished aspects of Scott's work is his extraordinary ability to identify very relevant and exciting research problems, by giving an often-unexpected twist to a mainstream research topic. One of the problems he came up with happened during the time I still was in Stony Brook. Together with our systems colleague, Erez Zadok, we were looking at various verification problems for the Linux OS. As we soon realized that scaling up model checking to the extensive Linux-OS code was still problematic, we started to consider cheaper and faster ways to achieving results. Runtime verification (RV) seemed to be the right way to go, as it allowed us to regard the OS as a black box. However, we needed to instrument the code with monitors, which introduced in some cases considerable overhead. While looking for ways to reduce this overhead, by selectively enabling and disabling some of the monitors, Scott spent a sabbatical at NASA JPL working together with Klaus Havelund. When he came back, he posed us the following research problem: What happens to RV if one misses observations? This problem took us by surprise, but we immediately realized its importance. Formalizing observation uncertainty required either the use of nondeterminism, leading to a logical approach to the problem, or probabilities, leading to a stochastic approach. Since in the former one learns pretty large automata models (and thus monitors), we opted for the latter, and at the suggestion of Scott Stoller, we settled to Hidden Markov Models (HMM). During our discussions, I realized that Scott's problem, was strongly related to the state-estimation problem in control theory and we dubbed our paper as "Runtime Verification with State Estimation". Ezio Bartocci, a Post- doctoral student at that time, took over the implementation aspects, by using the Baum-Welch algorithm to learn the appropriate HMMs from corresponding partial traces. This allowed us to successfully compute the probability that a desired property of a system was violated or not during blackout periods, that is, while the systems was running without being observed. Our synergistic work resulted in a paper that was later distinguished with the best paper award at the RV'11 conference. Scott triggered it all.

Another scientific problem posed by Scott using his above-mentioned ability is Flocking in V-Formation. We are still working on it today. It touches even more aspects of (possibly distributed) machine learning, verification, and control. The origins of this work have a very interesting story, too, but I leave this for another occasion.

From Panagiotis Katsaros - On the occasion of celebrating the 65th birthday of Scott Smolka I would like to express my best wishes, along with my joy for having the honour to collaborate with Scott during the last decade of his amazing research career. Many colleagues will remind Scott's seminal contributions in an impressively wide range of research problems on formal modeling and verification. I will recall the man who always leads his group to pioneering research ideas, the man with the strength to collaborate with his fellows from the beginning to the last moment of a research by overcoming any durability limitations, the man who inspires the younger researchers with his attitude and human potential, our good friend, our own Scott. Happy birthday Scott! I wish having the chance to work with you for many more years yet.

From Shan Lin - Dear Scott, I really appreciate all your help for me to start my research career at Stony Brook. You've always been there, providing guidance and advise since I joined Stony Brook. You have inspired me to work on my new projects and explore new directions. I am very grateful for your support and looking forward to continuing to work together.

From Emanuela Merelli - When I met Scott for the first time, it was at Sunny. We went for a meeting; during my talk about BioAgent modeling, Scott asked me if the behavior of an agent in the multi-agent system was deterministic and how to analyze the evident non-deterministic behavior emerging from the interactions of biological entities whose compositional rules are unknown. He was speaking with his long vision about of Aristotle's "the whole cannot be decomposed as the sum of its parts". Many years passed, I'm happy to take this opportunity to thank Scott for helping me foster a critical sense in going towards new intriguing science for Computer Science. It is unbelievable how a person, even if met for some hours, can change your mind; this is my experience in meeting Scott. For these reasons, I'm honored to take part in Scott's Festschrift contribution.

From Oleg - I arrived at Stony Brook for my Ph.D. studies without, as it quickly turned out, a reasonable understanding of how computer science research works or even what computer science, as a discipline, is about. Running into Scott at one of the department's Friday donut hours during my first semester turned out to be my lucky break, which helped me find direction both in my doctoral work and later in my career. He encouraged me to attend group meetings to learn more about the topic and later invited me to join the group.

I had a lot of fun working a number of challenging problems while at Stony Brook and learned much about formal verification. Still, probably the most important things I learned were the ones you cannot pick up from technical papers. Scott was very generous with sharing his insights into what it means to do good research, how to choose problems to attack, and how to derive pleasure from solving them.

I would like to share a memory, which at the time has significantly influenced my decision to stay in academia after completing my Ph.D. We had a weekly project meeting that involved Scott, Gene Stark, and several of their students, including myself. One day I showed up for the meeting, expecting students to give the usual progress reports, followed by guidance from professors. Instead, Scott came in a very bright mood and said that he had proved a new result and wanted to share it with the group. The lively discussion that followed showed me that, first, it is possible to make good technical progress without relying on graduate students. And second, maybe even more importantly, I saw how excited Scott was and how much he enjoyed doing it. I clearly remember thinking: if this is really as much fun as it seems, I want it, too. I did stick with academic research and never regretted it. Thanks, Scott, for setting me (and your many other students) on the right track!

From Shoji Yuen, Nagoya University, Japan - Dear Scott, Congratulations on your 65th birthday!! In Japanese, "65-sai no Otanjobi, Omedetou-Gozaimasu". It's been a long time since my last visit to Stony Brook. I cannot believe how fast time passed and how quickly things have been changing. Because of your great help and kindness, I have been able to stay in academia till now. I do wish you stay well and take good care of yourself. Hope you visit Japan again.

From Erez Zadok, Professor and Graduate Academic Adviser - In my PhD work I had to write and debug lots of difficult kernel code. When I joined the department in 2001, I found out that Scott worked on verification. Knowing very little about verification, I approached Scott with a "simple" request that I hoped would ease my work—to verify all five million or so lines of Linux kernel code. Scott smiled, took a deep breath, and carefully explained to me why this task is "not as simple" as I had thought, especially for complex operating system code written in C. Boy, that was an understatement! Knowing what I know now, Scott could have easily burst in laughter at my naiveté. Instead, we began to collaborate towards that goal—a highly fruitful and rewarding collaboration that continues to this day. Here's hoping for many more years of learning from Scott's wisdom.

Contents

Scott Smolka and Me

Rance Cleaveland$^{(\boxtimes)}$

University of Maryland, College Park, MD 20742, USA
rance@cs.umd.edu

Abstract. Scott Smolka and I have been colleagues for over 30 years. In this note I reminisce about our history as collaborators, colleagues and friends.

Keywords: Process algebra · Model checking · Cyber-physical systems

1 Introduction

Scott Smolka and I have known each other since 1988, although I first encountered him several years earlier through a ground-breaking paper [1] that he co-authored with his PhD adviser, Paris Kanellakis. Throughout the decades of our collaboration and friendship we have co-authored papers; written grant proposals; co-supervised research projects, students and postdocs; met each other's families; played basketball and tennis; and shared meals all over the world, from our own kitchens, to restaurants in our respective cities as well as locales both American and European. We have also started a company, Reactive Systems Inc., and have shared in each other's personal and professional lives.

Given this wealth of shared experience, my conundrum in writing this *laudatio* is, where do I start? And what do I include? My decision has been to focus primarily on our professional, and personal, relationship, as Scott has had one of the most profound influences on my career of anyone.

2 My First Encounter with Scott

I first encountered Scott in the spring of 1984. At the time I was PhD student at Cornell University, finishing my coursework and preparing to start my dissertation research. I was taking a class on Distributed Algorithms that semester, and one of the requirements each student had to fulfill was to present a published paper on some algorithmic aspects of distributed systems. I was nonplussed by most of the material, which was heavily focused on consensus protocols of various sorts, and sought advice from the professor about a paper that I could present that was related to the course topic but also was more related to my interests. To his great credit, the professor asked me what these interests were (I struggled to explain, beyond saying that I wished the models of distributed computing we were studying were more precisely specified) and then suggested a paper that had been published the previous year in the 1983 ACM Principles of Distributed Computing (PODC) conference. The paper was by Scott Smolka and Paris Kanellakis, and it addressed algorithmic issues in the computation of

© Springer Nature Switzerland AG 2019
E. Bartocci et al. (Eds.): From Reactive Systems to Cyber-Physical Systems, LNCS 11500, pp. 1–6, 2019.
https://doi.org/10.1007/978-3-030-31514-6_1

semantic equivalences over finite-state systems. There was reference to Milner's Calculus of Communication Systems (CCS), composition and congruence, process algebra, and other concepts that I had no earthly idea about. However, I could see that what I had found off-putting in some of the other work we studied in the class was completely and definitively absent in this new theory.

I was hooked, and became obsessed with understanding every detail in the paper! I devoted at least six weeks to preparing for my presentation. I read most of the papers referenced in Scott's and Paris' article, and in doing so I encountered Robin Milner's original CCS notes [2], which was a complete revelation. I then gave what I am sure, in retrospect, was a thoroughly incomprehensible hour-long presentation on process algebra, CCS, bisimulation, observational equivalence, and the Kanellakis-Smolka algorithm.

That was not all, however. I wound up being so intrigued by CCS that I wrote my PhD thesis [3] on formalizing CCS in the NuPRL proof-development system [4]. I then went to the University of Sussex to work as a postdoctoral research associate with Matthew Hennessy on the Concurrency Workbench project [5], which was devoted to developing an automated suite of routines for checking equivalences between, and properties of, CCS processes. A major theme of my research career has subsequently involved process-algebraic modeling and verification techniques. All of this work I can trace back to 1984, when I was first exposed to CCS, and process algebra, as I read Scott's and Paris' paper.

3   Our First Meeting

As I mentioned in the previous section, after I finished my PhD in 1987 I went to the University of Sussex for a two-year postdoc. We had a number of interesting speakers who came through Sussex during my stay, including Jean-Yves Girard and Richard Stallman, and in the summer of 1988 Scott came to Brighton, where the University of Sussex is located, to give a talk. I was thrilled, but also a little intimidated, when I heard about this; after all, Scott had (indirectly) introduced me to what was becoming one of my main research topics, and I had "lived" his and Paris' paper during that fateful spring four years previously. In addition to inspiring me, that paper had inspired others as well; indeed, Robin Milner, who was a co-leader of the Concurrency Workbench project, had told me during one of my visits to Edinburgh that a main driver behind the conception of the Workbench was that same paper that had drawn me in as well.

Despite feeling a bit star-struck, and after consulting with my wife, I nevertheless offered to put Scott up in our apartment during Scott's visit to Sussex, and he stayed with us for a couple of nights. I was expecting a god of concurrency: I got something even better, a personable, engaging scholar who was a delight to be around! He was interested in what I was doing and asked a lot of questions, as I did of him, and although I did not think of it in those terms then, I realize in hindsight that during this visit Scott morphed from a hero of mine to a colleague.

4 1989–1998 BSB (Before Stony Brook)

After I finished my postdoc in 1989 I returned to the US to become a university professor. Stony Brook, where Scott was (and is!), was very attractive to me, but there were no positions available there, so I wound up on the faculty at North Carolina State University (NCSU). At the time NCSU did not have a PhD program in Computer Science, although one was started a couple of years later, and I was feeling a little lonely, research-wise, although I made a couple of life-long friends on the faculty and felt generally well-treated by the university.

During this time Scott's and my professional relationship really blossomed. We wrote papers and grant proposals together, and saw each other relatively frequently at conferences and workshops. I also traveled to Stony Brook several times during this period, to visit Scott, give talks and serve on PhD committees. (Indeed, one of these students was Oleg Sokolsky!) I would usually stay with Scott when I came to Stony Brook, and these frequent visits felt like a lifeline professionally to me then; they were also very enjoyable. Scott was, and is, a great host, not least because he opens himself up to visitors in a way that makes them feel welcome and engaged. I also learned several things about Scott that helped cement our personal as well as our professional relationship.

- Scott loves good food. Every time we have gotten together meals are a big topic, and I always ate well when I visited Stony Brook.
- Scott loves basketball and tennis. This jibes with my interests also, especially basketball.
- Scott loves New York professional sports teams, and in particular the Knicks, Mets and Jets.
- Scott loves New York City.
- Scott loves music.
- Scott loves dogs, and indeed all animals, but especially dogs.

These topics have been fodder for any number of stimulating conversations over the years, not least because Scott is so open. I also got to engage with Scott at a personal level: I have been to a Passover seder at Scott's sister's house, attended Scott's wedding, walked his dogs with him, cooked out with him, played basketball, and gone to innumerable restaurants. I had the good fortune to meet his parents and see his stepdaughter Zoe grow up. Scott's friendship and professional interaction with me during this time is something I treasured at the time, and it continues to inspire me to this day.

5 I Go to Stony Brook, and We Start a Company

In 1997 Scott approached me about the possibility of moving to from NCSU to Stony Brook. We had a couple of joint grants at the time, and were working on a patent application and a very large grant proposal to the NSF. We had also started talking about the possibility of starting a company, something Scott had long had an interest in.

My response? "Of course I would be interested!" One thing led to another, and in late summer of 1998 my family and I moved to Long Island so that I could join the Stony Brook faculty.

The changes were numerous, of course, but universities are universities, and I soon fell into the familiar rhythm of teaching and research. The large NSF grant alas did not pan out. The company, however, did: Reactive Systems Inc. (RSI) was started by Scott and me in 1999, and is celebrating its 20th birthday this year.

The RSI story is an interesting one to me, because left to my own devices, I never would have thought of founding a company. Scott however had that vision, and the confidence to pursue it, so we started working on developing a strategy and business plan with the idea of obtaining venture capital to launch our business, which we originally anticipated would sell formal modeling and verification tools to telecommunications companies.

Early one we also recruited one of my former PhD students, Steve Sims, to join the team, and the three of us put obtained a grant from the NSF to help commercialize our technology, which was based on the Concurrency Factory [6]. We soon changed direction, however, because early feedback from a potential customer, and pivoted towards making a test-generation tool, called Reactis®[1], for MATLAB®/ Simulink®/Stateflow®[2] models. Reactis, and tools derived from it, have been the mainstay of RSI ever since.

One of the things I quickly realized as we launched RSI was that starting a company is vastly different from running a research group at a university. In particular, the open flow of information so prized in academe is largely absent in the commercial sector, where information is money, and issues involving sales and marketing, not to mention finance and governance, attain tremendous importance. I have to admit to feeling overwhelmed on more than one occasion, especially with the courting of investors, and confessed to Scott that I felt ill-suited to the task. He told me that from his perspective, I was actually doing very well. This gave me pause: could he be right, or was he just being encouraging? I looked inside myself and asked whether I enjoyed the work I was doing in looking for investors. Somewhat surprisingly, the answer was yes, I did! It was tiring, but rewarding, even if we did not in the end "go the venture capital route" (we had a couple of offers, but we turned them down). It is still interesting to me that an off-hand remark by Scott led me to a realization about myself that I had not previously had; this realization has helped shape the trajectory of my professional life ever since, as I understood I had a knack for interacting with other people.

Anyway, we eventually obtained a second, and then a third, government grant to develop Reactis, and in 2001 I took a leave of absence from Stony Brook to move to the Washington DC area and work full-time for RSI. The company slowly found its bearings and become profitable. In the mean time, I had a decision to make: return with my family to Long Island and resume my position at Stony Brook, or leave Stony Brook and stay in the Washington DC area?

---

[1] Reactis® is a registered trademark of Reactive Systems, Inc.

[2] MATLAB®, Simulink® and Stateflow® are registered trademarks of The MathWorks, Inc.

6 The Big Project Era

As I was thinking about these matters in late 2004 I received a call from the University of Maryland about a professorial position there that would also involve me heading a research center on software engineering. Taking that position would mean leaving Stony Brook and remaining in Washington – close to the company, but remote from Scott. After talking the matter over, my wife and I decided to stay in DC, and I have been on the faculty at Maryland since 2005.

Scott and I managed to continue our collaboration, however, with the great bulk of the credit for this going to his invitations to me to join multi-university research proposals that he helped put together and lead. We had one project with 19 co-investigators on formal methods for various cyber-physical systems, then another with 13 co-investigators on cardiac assistive devices. Scott's research interests had broadened during this time to include biological cyber-physical systems, a topic I was not expert in but knew about from a more applied perspective because of work I had done with a couple of medical-device companies. While Scott and I were not collocated anymore we have managed to interact fairly extensively in the context of these projects, as well as through our ongoing involvement as board members for RSI. I continue to appreciate Scott's judgment, and his ability to focus on big-picture ideas, even if we no longer have as many opportunities for those fine meals and conversations that we enjoyed earlier in our careers.

7 Coda

So what has Scott meant to me? The question is so large, it is hard for me to formulate a concise answer. He started off as a hero, as a co-author of a paper that would literally change my career. He became a colleague, and a mentor, and a friend, as well as a collaborator in some of the most consequential undertakings I have been part of. With his optimism and creativity, he has pointed my personal research efforts in directions I would not have imagined on my own. He has had among the deepest impacts of anyone on my professional life, and I am profoundly grateful to him for that. On the occasion of his 65th birthday, and as I reflect back on our 30+ years of our interactions, I thank him, and also say that I am eager and impatient to see what happens next.

References

1. Kanellakis, P., Smolka, S.: CCS expressions, finite state processes, and three problems of equivalence. Inf. Comput. **86**(1), 43–68 (1990). A preliminary version of this paper appeared in 2nd ACM Symposium on Principles of Distributed Computation (PODC), 1983
2. Milner, R. (ed.): A Calculus of Communicating Systems. LNCS, vol. 92. Springer, Heidelberg (1980). https://doi.org/10.1007/3-540-10235-3
3. Cleaveland, R.: Type-theoretic models of concurrency. Ph.D. dissertation, Cornell University, Ithaca, NY (1987)

4. Constable, R.L., et al.: Implementing Mathematics with the Nuprl Proof Development System. Prentice-Hall, Inc., Upper Saddle River (1986)
5. Cleaveland, R., Parrow, J., Steffen, B.: The concurrency workbench: a semantics-based tool for the verification of concurrent systems. ACM Trans. Program. Lang. Syst. **15**(1), 36–72 (1993). https://doi.org/10.1145/151646.151648
6. Cleaveland, R., Lewis, P.M., Smolka, S.A., Sokolsky, O.: The concurrency factory: a development environment for concurrent systems. In: Alur, R., Henzinger, Thomas A. (eds.) CAV 1996. LNCS, vol. 1102, pp. 398–401. Springer, Heidelberg (1996). https://doi.org/10.1007/3-540-61474-5_88

Analysis of Complex Biological Systems

A Comprehensive Comparison of GPU Implementations of Cardiac Electrophysiology Models

Abouzar Kaboudian[1]([✉]), Hector Augusto Velasco-Perez[1], Shahriar Iravanian[2], Yohannes Shiferaw[3], Elizabeth M. Cherry[1,4], and Flavio H. Fenton[1]

[1] Georgia Institute of Technology, Atlanta, GA 30332, USA
`abouzar.kaboudian@physics.gatech.edu`
[2] Emory University, Atlanta, GA 30322, USA
[3] California State University, Northridge, CA 91330, USA
[4] Rochester Institute of Technology, Rochester, NY 14623, USA

Abstract. Cardiac disease is the leading cause of death in developed countries, and arrhythmias, which are disorders in the regular generation and propagation of electrical waves that trigger contraction, form a major class of heart diseases. Computational techniques have proved to be useful in the study and understanding of cardiac arrhythmias. However, the computational cost associated with solving cardiac models makes them especially challenging to solve. Traditionally, hardware available on personal computers has been insufficient for such models; instead, supercomputers have been employed to overcome the computational costs of cardiac simulations. However, in recent years substantial advances in the computational power of graphics processing units (GPUs), combined with their modest prices and widespread availability, have made them an attractive alternative to high-performance computing using supercomputers. With greater use of GPUs, however, new challenges have emerged. GPUs must be programmed using their own languages or extensions of other languages, and, at present, there are a number of languages that support general-purpose GPU codes with substantial differences in programming ease and available levels of optimization. In this work, we present the implementation of cardiac models in several major GPU languages without language-specific optimization and compare their performance for different levels of model complexity and domain sizes.

Keywords: Cardiac electrophysiology · GPU · MATLAB · OpenACC · Python · Numba · TensorFlow · WebGL · Abubu.js · NVIDIA CUDA

1 Introduction

Cardiac disease remains the leading cause of death worldwide [1]. Ventricular fibrillation (VF), a life-threatening arrhythmia, is associated with disruption of

© Springer Nature Switzerland AG 2019
E. Bartocci et al. (Eds.): From Reactive Systems to Cyber-Physical Systems, LNCS 11500, pp. 9–34, 2019.
https://doi.org/10.1007/978-3-030-31514-6_2

the ventricular electrophysiological signalling that controls the contraction of the heart muscle. Such disruption manifests as spatiotemporally disorganized electrical waves [2–5] that require immediate intervention. Another form of arrhythmia that can last for years and impair the quality of life of patients is atrial fibrillation (AF). It is estimated that over 2.7–6.1 million Americans suffer from AF [1]. If untreated for prolonged periods, AF can lead to more problematic arrhythmias or even stroke.

It is possible that VF and AF treatment could be improved by designing patient-specific prevention, control and/or therapy using new computational tools that are fast, accessible and easy to use [6]. In fact, numerical simulations of cardiac dynamics are becoming increasingly important in addressing patient-specific interventions [7] and evaluating drug effects [8]. It is noteworthy that the Food and Drug Administration recently sponsored a new Cardiac Safety Research Consortium initiative (CiPA) [8,9] that specifies the use of mathematical models of cardiac cells to aid pro-arrhythmic drug risk assessment. However, as the mathematical models incorporate more detailed and sophisticated biophysical mechanisms, they are becoming extremely complex mathematically, with some of them requiring the solution of 50–100 nonlinear ordinary differential equations (ODEs) per computational cell [10]. Such ODEs typically are stiff and thus require a small temporal discretization, which is further complicated by the spatial discretization size imposed by the size of the cardiac cells. These complicating factors make cardiac dynamic simulations too large for traditional serial CPU-based computing. While some efforts have been made to create programs to aid with cardiac cell simulations in PCs [11,12], in general, scientists have used supercomputer-based high-performance implementations of cardiac models to study cardiac electrophysiology, especially for large two- and three-dimensional tissues. However, supercomputers are expensive to acquire and hard to maintain, and even when such resources are managed by individuals other than the end users, users typically are required to submit their programs for execution as batch jobs, which can be inconvenient.

Substantial advances in the computational power of graphic processing units (GPUs) have made them an attractive alternative to traditional high-performance computing. Currently available GPUs are equipped with thousands of powerful computational cores, and they can be acquired at affordable prices sometimes as low as a few hundred US dollars. As such, they can provide high-performance computing on personal computers at merely a fraction of the cost of traditional CPU-based supercomputers. However, GPUs require machine code that is prepared for the specific target GPU hardware. Thus, computer codes either need to be implemented in a special language that is intended for GPU programming or should be modified such that they become suitable for execution on GPUs. At present, there are several languages and programming solutions that enable implementation of GPU applications. As might be expected, each solution and programming language has certain benefits and may perform differently for different applications. Therefore, a comprehensive study focused on comparing the ease of programming and performance of such programming languages and solutions when applied to cardiac models can be beneficial to help researchers in the cardiac community choose the appropriate approach.

In this study, we investigate some of the major languages and solutions in cardiac GPU computing. Specifically, we consider (1) GPU computing solutions available in MATLAB, (2) the pragma-based approach of OpenACC, (3) Python-Numba, (4) TensorFlow, (5) WebGL 2.0, and (6) NVIDIA CUDA together with the Abubu.js library. Our comparisons will be based on implementations without any substantial program-specific optimization. Of course, we expect that applying language-specific optimizations could improve performance. However, it is fair to assume that most cardiac researchers are not necessarily experts in GPU programming, so that in many cases the solution that would provide the best performance with minimal effort would be ideal. Nevertheless, our comparisons will help users with a broad range of programming expertise make informed choices about GPU implementations for cardiac models.

2 Methods

2.1 Models

We will compare performance using three different models with different complexity. The FitzHugh-Nagumo (FHN) model [13,14] is a two-variable model used as a generic excitable media model and in some cases as a cardiac model. Tuning the model's parameters can change features like the trajectory of the spiral wave tip [15].

The Minimal Model (MM) [16] is a four-variable model developed to reproduce many important properties of cardiac cells while also prioritizing computational tractability. The model includes a variable representing voltage as well as three gating variables that govern the dynamics of summary sodium and calcium currents; a time-independent potassium current also is included. Different parameterizations of the MM have been shown to reproduce the dynamics of other models with good fidelity [6,16–18].

The Beeler-Reuter (BR) model [19] is an eight-variable model that includes sodium, calcium, and potassium currents. It was the first model developed to simulate ventricular tissue and the first to include an intracellular calcium concentration. We made modifications to the BR model by speeding up the τ_f and τ_d in the model to 50% of their original value to prevent the model from breakup [20]. If the original model was used with the default parameter set, it would gives rise to spiral wave breakup in two dimensions [20,21]. This is also the first model for which it was shown that reaction-diffusion equations for cardiac cells can produce spiral waves in 2D [21].

2.2 Numerical Methods

The cardiomyocytes' membrane potential (V) propagation through gap junctions (and in neurons through synapses) can be modeled by a cable equation [22], which is given by

$$\partial_t V(\boldsymbol{x}, t) = \nabla \cdot (\tilde{D} \nabla V) - \frac{I_{total}}{C_m}. \tag{1}$$

Here, the membrane potential diffuses with a diffusion coefficient $\tilde{D}$ (which represents the fiber orientation of the heart [23,24] and, in general, is anisotropic and heterogeneous), while the ionic concentrations are local in cardiac as well as neuronal tissues. The transmembrane currents for all ions as well as the ion pumps and exchangers are included in $I_{total} = \sum I_i(V, y_i)$. The most general form of a transmembrane current I_i permeable to ion i is simply $I_i = g_i(V - E_i)$, where g_i is a conductance term, V is the membrane potential or voltage, and E_i is the Nernst potential for ion species i. Often, the conductance is calculated using gates following the Hodgkin-Huxley [22] formalism, in which the conductance term is decomposed into the product of a maximal conductance term and one or more separate normalized variables that represent the probability of finding the channel open, which typically depends on the membrane potential or an ion concentration. These variables follow first-order differential equations of the form

$$\frac{dy_i(t)}{dt} = \alpha_{y_i}(V)(1 - y_i) - \beta_{y_i}(V)y_i \tag{2}$$

where α_{y_i} is the probability that the channel gate y_i will transition from closed to open and β_{y_i} is the probability it will transition from open to closed; both probabilities are a function of voltage. An alternative representation used in some models is achieved through Markov chains, where each state s_p follows a differential equation of the form

$$\frac{ds_p(t)}{dt} = \sum_{q=1, q \neq p}^{n} (k_{qp} s_q - k_{pq} s_p), \tag{3}$$

where k_{qp} is the transition rate from state s_q to s_p. With either formulation, the ordinary differential equations become partial differential equations once a spatially extended system, rather than a single cell, is considered. More details on how to numerically integrate these equations including convergence and boundary conditions can be found in Ref. [25].

In all cases, we used a domain size of 20×20 cm. The diffusion coefficient $\tilde{D}$ was assumed to be isotropic and homogeneously defined over the domain. Finite differences were used for numerical simulations. To discretize the spatial term in Eq. (1), a second-order central difference scheme was used both in the x and y directions. All ODEs were solved using the forward Euler time-stepping scheme for most variables. As an exception, the time-integration of the Hudgkin-Huxley-type gates in Eq. (2) used the Rush-Larsen time-stepping scheme [26]. In all cases, a uniform Cartesian grid was employed. The grid sizes used were 256×256, 512×512, 1024×1024, and 2048×2048. This implies that for smaller grid sizes, the solution was not fully numerically resolved. However, we emphasize that our objective was to compare the same solution obtained under different conditions. This would guarantee that for the same model, we deal with the same loading conditions on the GPU cores. The time step was chosen as $\Delta t = 0.05$ ms up to a grid size of 2048×2048, where $\Delta t = 0.01$ ms was employed instead to satisfy the CFL condition. Our initial conditions were set to the resting state of the cells everywhere in the domain, except for nodes with $x < 1$ cm to create a traveling wave toward the right-hand side of the domain. Later, at $t = 600$ for the FHN model and at $t = 370$ ms for the MM and BR models, a depolarizing wave is applied at the bottom half of the domain where $y < 10$ cm by changing the transmembrane potential to a higher depolarizing potential. This voltage was set to 1.0 for the FHN and MM model and 30 mV for the BR model. For more information on the implementation details, see the computer codes that can be downloaded from http://abouzar.net/SmolkaFest2019/codes.zip (Fig. 1).

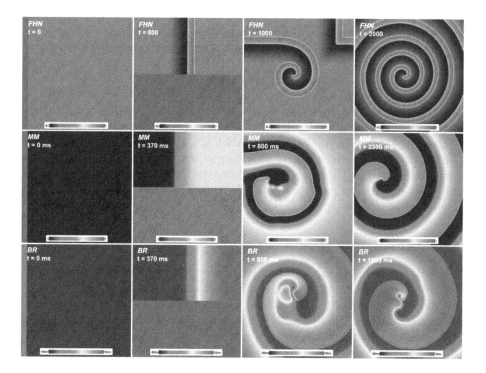

Fig. 1. Membrane potential for the FHN (first row), MM (second row), and BR (third row) models at the initial time (first column), application of the depolarizing voltage from the bottom half of the domain (second column), transient spiral wave dynamics (third column), and after the spiral wave stabilizes (fourth column).

Because the details of GPU programming are closely connected with the different implementations studied, this information is provided below in the next section.

3   Comparison of GPU Implementations

Below, we describe six different GPU implementations of the three models (FHN, MM, and BR). In some cases, we also compare additional options available for a particular configuration. Along with measurements of speedup as a function of the number of grid points, we also comment on ease of programming.

First, we implemented a serial version of all three models in the C programming language. The PGI-C compiler was used to generate the machine code. This serial version was used in all speedup calculations. The speedup was defined as follows:

$$\text{Speedup} = \frac{\text{wall-time of single-core serial CPU C-program}}{\text{wall-time of GPU implementation}}, \qquad (4)$$

where wall-time is the measured time of execution of the program that an ordinary wall-clock would measure, albeit here, we used the computer's clock for measurements.

All measurements were carried out on a Linux Manjaro operating system with Kernel version 4.19.34. The system had an AMD® Ryzen threadripper 2990wx 32-core processor that was used for CPU time measurements (although only one core was used in the CPU case). The graphics card that was used for GPU measurements was a NVIDIA TITAN V/PCIe/SSE2.

In this study, all measurements were carried out in double precision, except for the WebGL 2.0 and TensorFlow cases. For the CUDA and OpenACC implementations, we tried single-precision calculations and the speedups did not change more than 10% on this GPU.

3.1   MATLAB

MATLAB, originally meaning matrix laboratory, is a proprietary programming language developed by MathWorks. MATLAB allows for easy matrix operations and is equipped with several linear solvers, as well as built-in plotting and visualization features, that together make it very popular for general programming in academic settings. MATLAB's easy-to-learn programming syntax makes it attractive to novice programmers, and its feature-rich environment makes it attractive to seasoned programmers, for both prototyping algorithms and research. Additionally, MATLAB has an interactive user interface that combined with MATLAB's interpreter removes the hurdles of compiling, running, and visualization of the data. As such, MATLAB has been adopted as the companion language or the language of choice in several books [27–35]. MATLAB is also widely used in several research fields, including but not limited to, fluid mechanics [36,37], geophysical studies [38–40], volcanology [41–44], astrophysics [45–48], chemical engineering [49–52], image analysis [53–57], neural networks [58–60], cell modeling [61–64], and cardiac studies [65–71]. MATLAB also provides GPU parallelism through fully automated GPU acceleration, the arrayfun command which applies a function to each element of arrays, and CUDA kernel calls.

Here, we implemented the arrayfun and CUDA kernel call options for each of the three models. The arrayfun function applies a MATLAB function to all elements of an array. After sending the arrays to the GPU using the gpuArray() function, calling the arrayfun function for each time step allows the function to be run on the GPU. MATLAB's interpreter recognizes that it can run the function independently for each element of the array on the GPU and it will do so. Since this approach still relies on automatic detection of the parallelizable section and acceleration of the code, it is expected to be less than "ideal". The second approach in MATLAB is to manually write the GPU code as a CUDA kernel and run the CUDA kernel. This approach is supposed to result in the best observed performance since there is no "guess-work" necessary by the MATLAB interpreter and the GPU code is already parsed. The upside is that all MATLAB visualizaton and data analysis tools still can be used, and the CUDA kernel will only be in charge of running the accelerated code in an optimum way. However, writing CUDA kernels requires familiarity with the NVIDIA CUDA C language in addition to familiarity with MATLAB. Hence, it is expected that a smaller number of MATLAB users will be comfortable programming CUDA kernels. Speedup is assessed for problems sizes of 2^{16}, 2^{18}, 2^{20}, and 2^{22} grid points. By default, all implementations in MATLAB use double-precision variables.

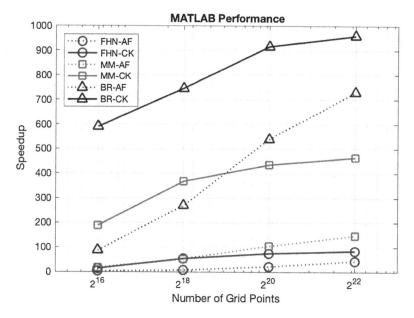

Fig. 2. Speedup of models vs. grid size for the FHN, MM, and BR models using MATLAB with array functions (dashed lines) and with CUDA kernels (solid lines).

Figure 2 shows that in all cases, as expected, the use of CUDA kernels provided more substantial speedup than the corresponding arrayfun implementations by as much as a factor of six. The largest speedup was found for the BR model, which is not surprising given that it has the most equations and thus the most potential for concurrency within a given time iteration. Correspondingly, the FHN model attained the smallest speedups, but it still achieved a speedup of nearly two orders of magnitude for the largest grid size using CUDA kernels. The MM achieved speedups more than twice that of the FHN model, most likely because although it has twice the number of ODEs, it has a significant number of additional algebraic equations evaluated during each time step, thus allowing greater potential for performance increase through greater parallelization over each time step.

3.2 OpenACC

OpenACC is a programming standard that developed as a joint effort between Cray, CAPS, NVIDIA and PGI as an alternative to low-level CUDA programming. OpenACC, similar to OpenMP, uses a pragma-based approach to identify the computer code regions that can be parallelized on the GPU. The pragma directives, together with environment variables and library calls, facilitate accelerating regions of the serial C/C++ or FORTRAN CPU codes that can benefit from parallelization, typically loops, and in this case support use of GPGPU computing. As a result, OpenACC provides an approach that can accelerate mature CPU C/C++ or FORTRAN codes with minimal effort. This feature has made OpenACC an attractive choice to a large group of researchers in various fields including but not limited to fluid mechanics [72–76], earthquake modeling [77], deep neural networks [78,79], astrophysics and data mining [80], cardiovascular [81] and cardiac electrophysiology [82,83].

First, we implemented a serial version of all three models in the C programming language. This serial version was used in all speedup calculations. OpenACC pragmas were added to the serial code to achieve parallelism. After initializing the solution we used the OpenACC's "data in" pragmas to copy the data to the GPU. Then in the parallel loops these arrays were marked as present on the GPU to avoid unnecessary copy of the arrays in and out of the GPU. The data was copied out to CPU memory only on the time-steps that we intended to write data to disk. This was achieved through the "update self" pragma. The data was written to disk only for debugging and during performance measurements no data was written to disk. Both single-precision and double-precision implementations were tested and the variations in performance were limited to less than 10% on this particular GPU. The results presented here were generated using double-precision variables.

Figure 3 shows the resulting speedups, which are quite similar to the speedups obtained using MATLAB with CUDA kernels. Again, the BR model benefited the most from acceleration, with speedups of up to three orders of magnitude due to the fact that, for the BR model, the computational cost of the reaction operations is much more than for the diffusion term. This suggests that the more complicated models of cardiac dynamics can benefit even further from the use of OpenACC implementations.

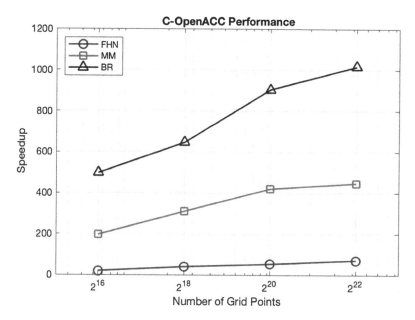

Fig. 3. Speedup of models vs. grid size for the FHN, MM, and BR models using OpenACC directives in the C programming language.

3.3 Python Numba Implementation

Python is an interpreted general-purpose language created in the early 1990s by Guido van Rossum at Stichting Mathematisch Centrum in the Netherlands as a successor of ABC [84]. Python supports multiple programming paradigms, including functional, object-oriented, and procedural programming. Due to its feature-rich environment and its approachable learning curve, Python is widely popular as a language for teaching [85, 86] and research in various field such as astrophysics [87–89], machine learning [90, 91], neural networks [92], and business [93]. Similarly, Python is also used in cardiovascular [94–101], cardiac electrophysiology [102–107], and arrhythmia detection [108] studies. Python's popularity is evident in the large number of conferences that are held each year dedicated to Python programming including DjangoCon Europe, EuroPython, EuroSciPy, Kiwi PyCon, O'Reilly Open Source Convention, Plone Conference, PyCon conferences held in different regions of the world, PyData, PyGotham, SiPy and many more [109]. Project Jupyter has also contributed significantly to the popularity of the Python language by providing a web application that allows users to create and share documents that contain live interactive Python codes, equations, visualization and narrative text [110].

The widespread popularity of Python has resulted in a broad range of Python libraries that can be used for various different applications. One very popular library is NumPy, which provides support for definition of multi-dimensional array objects and array operations [111], which can be very useful in scientific computing. Numba is an open-source Just-In-Time (JIT) compiler that translates a subset of Python and NumPy code into accelerated machine code [112]. The Numba compiler can provide acceleration through multicore CPUs or GPGPU. Numba has a very simple approach to accelerating Python code. In fact, the Numba website provides a tutorial that teaches Python programmers to start accelerating their Python code in as little as five minutes [113]. This small learning curve makes Numba an attractive choice for cardiac modeling.

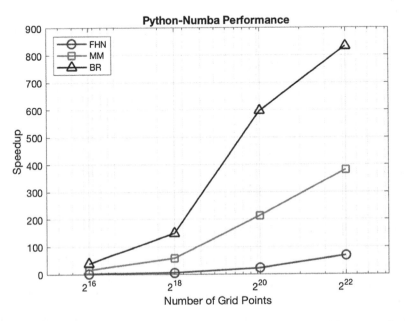

Fig. 4. Speedup of models vs. grid size for the FHN, MM, and BR models using Python Numba.

Figure 4 shows speedup results using Python-Numba. All measurements were carried out using double-precision variables. As expected, the BR model achieves the greatest speedup and the FHN model the least. Most notable is that large performance gains do not appear until grid sizes of 2^{20}, which may be due to the fact that for each time step there is a certain overhead time imposed for launching a parallel code on the GPU. However, that effect becomes less important when we keep the GPU busy for longer periods before advancing to the next time step.

3.4   TensorFlow Implementation

TensorFlow is a free and open-source software library primarily designed by the Google Brain team [114,115] for internal use. It was released for public use later under Apache 2.0 open-source licence on November 9, 2015 [116]. It has been used by a number of companies, including Airbnb, AIRBUS, Coca-Cola, Google, Intel, PayPal and Qualcomm [117] in both research and production. TensorFlow can be used on single as well as multiple CPUs and GPUs. Once the target device is chosen, the parallelization is carried out automatically by the TensorFlow engine. TensorFlow provides extensive features to be used for machine learning and deep neural network applications [114,115,118]. Hence, it can be considered an attractive choice for model-based machine-learning environments where machine-learning algorithms can be trained using a dynamical numerical model. A number of groups in the cardiac community have embraced TensorFlow [119–127].

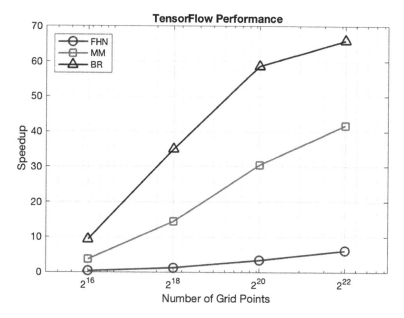

Fig. 5. Speedup of models vs. grid size for the FHN, MM, and BR models using TensorFlow.

Speedup results for the three models using Tensor-flow are given in Fig. 5. The measurements for TensorFlow were made using single-precision variables, as some of the functions did not have a double-precision implementation for GPU parallelism at the time of coding the TensorFlow programs. In this case, speedup is quite limited compared to the other approaches considered, with the maximum speedup (attained for the BR model on the largest grid) still well below 100. The speedups are the result of just choosing the target device to be the GPU. No optimization such as using convolutions was used here. We would say the effort required for parallelism on the GPU was minimal compared to other languages. Given the minimal effort required for achieving parallelism, programmers are encouraged to use the GPU as their target device for all models, especially more complex ones.

3.5   WebGL and Abubu.js Implementation

WebGL or the Web Graphics Library is a royalty-free JavaScript application programming interface standard that provides low-level 2D and 3D rendering capabilities in modern web browsers without the need to install any plug-ins through the HTML5 canvas element [128]. This means that WebGL applications can run on any modern web browser and on any major operating system (such as Microsoft Windows, macOS, Linux, Android, or even iOS), and at the same time harness the computational power of the available GPU on that device. WebGL applications are automatically compiled at run-time for the particular user's graphic cards. Therefore, the WebGL applications do not need to be compiled by the developers for all the intended GPUs and operating systems. This also means that WebGL applications are capable of harnessing the computational power in various GPU devices from various vendors, unlike some of the languages such as NVIDIA CUDA, which can only run on specific hardware.

The heart of the WebGL applications is written in OpenGL Shading Language (GLSL), which is a high-level programming language with a syntax based on the C programming language [129]. GLSL supports most of the C/C++ familiar structural components, such as if statements, for loops, etc. It also has a number of built-in functions for mathematical, vector, and matrix operations as well as texture access [130]. The only drawback for using WebGL is that currently it only supports single-precision variables and textures. Therefore, for applications that must use double-precision floats, WebGL is not suitable at present. When using WebGL for parallelism, usually texture memory is utilized as the basic data structure for the input and output of the programs [131]. However, the WebGL language can have a high learning curve for novice programmers or those who are not well versed in graphics programming. The Abubu.js programming library is used to address this issue and remove the hurdles of GPGPU programming with WebGL [6]. Using Abubu.js, WebGL has been shown to be capable of solving a wide range of problems from studying fractals, solitons and chaos [132] to cardiac dynamics, fluid mechanics, and crystal growth [6].

In this work, we followed the methods proposed in [6] to implement the FHN, the MM, and the BR model in WebGL using Abubu.js. Figure 6 shows performance gains using our WebGL implementation, which generally outperforms all other implementations. In particular, the speedup for the MM is now above 1000 for the largest grid size, and for the BR model speedup exceeds 2000 for a grid size of 2^{20}. However, performance for the BR model is more variable, with a dropoff in speedup at the largest grid size in contrast to monotonic increases with grid size in all other cases. In addition, WebGL performance for the smallest grid size is typically no greater than that seen in OpenACC and MATLAB with CUDA kernels. That is due to the fact that there is a minimum overhead time to launch the WebGL applications in each time step. The performance drop in the BR model for larger grid sizes could be due to memory access bottlenecks and how the data is stored on the GPU. It should be noted that even with the performance drops, the WebGL applications outperform all other implementations by a large margin for larger domains.

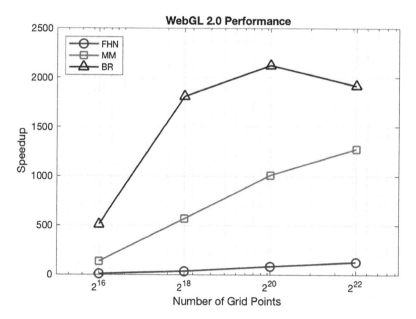

Fig. 6. Speedup of models vs. grid size for the FHN, MM, and BR models using WebGL together with the Abubu.js library.

3.6 NVIDIA CUDA Implementation

One of the most popular platforms to solve PDEs in parallel using GPUs is CUDA. CUDA is a parallel platform developed by NVIDIA that allows the user to execute programs on the GPU of a personal computer. This allows faster processing and visualization of large data sets that fulfill certain characteristics that will be discussed below. Since its launch in 2007, CUDA has helped to extend the use of GPU technology to the scientific community. Specifically, the CUDA platform has been applied in several scientific and engineering fields such as fluid dynamics [133,134], machine learning and neural networks [135–138], astrophysics [139–142], the Lattice Boltzmann method [143–145], molecular dynamics [146–148], clinical applications [149,150], and recently in the cardiac modeling community [151–155]. CUDA has also been successfully used for teaching purposes, including in undergraduate workshops [156]. Like all computational tools, it has advantages and disadvantages.

The CUDA platform is an extension of other programming languages, i.e., it is a set of functions added to a preexisting platform that allows the user to communicate with the GPU. This implies that most of the base language characteristics and logic will be inherited by the parallel functions. There are several versions of CUDA, mainly C/CUDA (CUDA for the C language), PyCUDA (CUDA for Python) and CUDA Fortran. We decided to develop our solvers in C/CUDA because it is the most supported version. The description below is valid regardless of the version chosen.

In some cases, CUDA is able to launch millions of processing threads simultaneously, which can increase the speed of computations and save many hours and possibly days of processing time (). The speedup depends mainly on the type of algorithm implemented to process the data and the structure of the data. To understand better how these factors affect the speed of the computations, it is important to understand the interaction between the software and hardware, particularly the interaction between the CPU (commonly referred to as the host) and the GPU (commonly referred to as the device). All programs start at the host level, meaning that they are all managed by the host and all the data is held in CPU RAM or the hard drive. Meanwhile, sections of memory in the GPU are reserved to hold the data that needs to be processed. Once everything is ready, the CPU calls specific functions to be executed on the GPU. After the GPU processes the data, it must be sent back to the CPU so that it can be post-processed by the user. In most programs, there is a constant exchange of data between host and device. As a rule of thumb, the programmer should try to reduce the number of memory transactions between both ends mainly due to bandwidth limitations. Other factors to be considered are the GPUs memory capacity and frequency of kernel calls (functions called by the CPU that execute on the GPU and hold the bulk of the processing algorithm). In addition to adequately controlling the data flow, the program must manage the data in a parallel-friendly arrangement, specifically, we must determine the way that data will be read and written. As commonly observed in programming languages with arrays of two or more dimensions, the data layout and memory access patterns need to be aligned to achieve maximum performance. More specifically, CUDA requires the data layout to adapt to a single instruction multiple data processing structure, which means that all processing threads must be performing the same instructions simultaneously to avoid thread divergence.

In addition to the memory transactions and layout mentioned above, CUDA requires the programmer to adapt the data to a specific hierarchical structure of threads. In general, threads are organized into blocks, which can be one-, two-, or three-dimensional. Sets of blocks are then organized in a grid. Again, the grid can be arranged in all three dimensions. More information can be found in [157] and [158]. The dimension of these objects refers to how they will be accessed, not how they are physically stored in memory. The user can adapt this structure to increase the performance of their computations. In our particular case, two-dimensional blocks and grid resemble very well the 2D domains in which we are solving the PDEs. Still, different memory access patterns will influence the speed of our computations. Other factors to be considered when building a CUDA program are coalesced memory patterns, in which multiple threads can receive data through a single combined memory access, and the use of the various types of internal memories and the interaction among them. These are just some of many considerations that are important to keep in mind. It is also worth noting that if a task is not inherently parallelizable due to dependencies across loop iterations without substantial work within each iteration (such as a Fibonacci sequence calculation) or if the number of threads is small (typically on the order of hundreds or lower), CUDA will perform worse than most standard serial implementations due to overhead associated with launching kernels and moving data between the host and device.

In our implementations, we used global memory. Both single- and double-precision implementations were tested and the variations in performance were limited to less than 10% on this particular GPU. The results presented here are generated using double-precision variables. One-dimensional arrays were used to represent the 2D domain. The data could be arranged in either a row-major or a column-major fashion in the one-dimensional arrays. In the row-major structure, the matrix is stored in the 1D array one row after another until the entire matrix is stored. In the column-major order, the same procedure is followed for the matrix columns. Both versions were tested to observe the performance differences. The row-major version of the data-structures performed consistently better than the column-major structures. This could be due to the fact that the row-major structure was more compatible with hardware, possibly due to the way that warps are organized on this GPU. Different results might be expected for different GPUs and the users should be aware of such differences. It should be noted that this should not be confused with the loop access of multi-dimensional arrays in CPUs. Here, in both cases, the data structures are one-dimensional and the central difference algorithm for the diffusion term imposes a symmetry condition on both directions.

We also decided against using shared-memory implementations such as those suggested in earlier studies [152]. The use of shared memory requires copying the variables from the global memory into shared memory, performing calculations from shared memory in registered memory (implicit), then writing data into shared memory, and then to global memory. These steps are required in each time step as no data can be retained between time steps. However, the use of global memory would require bringing the data to register for calculations and writing the data back to global memory. It is evident that using global memory for this type of problems involves fewer memory transactions compared to the shared memory implementations but the same number of global memory accesses and thus is expected to be faster. Additionally, our goal in this study is to compare the simplest implementations in each language as the targeted programmers are scientists whose primary expertise is not GPU programming. The use of texture memory instead of one-dimensional arrays could also change the performance of the applications. However, any performance improvements could be hardware-dependent and would also depend on the problem size and complexity. In favor of simplicity, we chose the use of a global memory implementation.

We used a 16×16 thread size for the CUDA implementations, and each direction was then divided by 16 to get the block size. Smaller thread sizes led to lower performance and larger thread sizes did not improve the performance on our particular GPU.

Figure 7 shows the speedup achieved for each of the three models using our CUDA implementation. CUDA slightly outperforms MATLAB with CUDA kernels and OpenACC, especially for smaller grids, but overall the performance

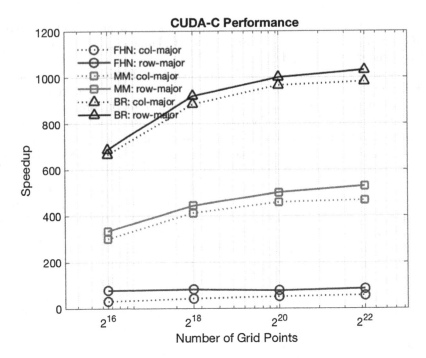

Fig. 7. Speedup of models vs. grid size for the FHN, MM, and BR models using CUDA with column-major data structures in dashed lines and row-major data structures in solid lines.

is fairly comparable for these three implementations. WebGL maintains better performance for all grid sizes. Note that speedup seems to have saturated for the FHN model and appears to be close to saturating for the other models. In addition, it should be noted that we could potentially observe a performance saturation similar to those observed in WebGL implementations. Moreover, due to the limitations in the GPU memory size, there is a limit to the problem size that can be handled on a single GPU so that using multiple GPUs for larger problems becomes inevitable. While using multiple GPUs can be useful for handling larger domains due to memory constraints, it should be noted the required communication between the multiple GPUs will impose performance penalties on the parallel GPU codes.

4   Discussion and Conclusion

Figure 8 shows the comparison between the speedup gains for each of the GPU implementations of the three different models with different grid sizes. It can be seen that the WebGL applications outperform all other implementations for all cases except for the smallest grid sizes and the FHN model. As soon as the workload on the GPU is "large" enough to take full advantage of concurrency, WebGL provides the best performance. All implementations performed

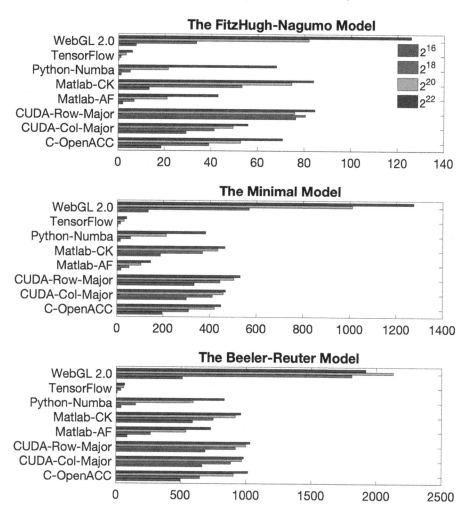

Fig. 8. Speedup comparison for various implementations of the FHN, MM, and BR models. Each color corresponds to a different grid size.

better with larger grid sizes and more complicated models, with the BR model implementations providing the best performances among all models. Another notable observation is that almost all GPU implementations provided performance comparable to that of the NVIDIA CUDA implementations with minor differences with the exception of TensorFlow. Therefore, we can conclude that almost all languages considered in this study are ready to make effective use of GPU hardware to reduce program runtimes. The least effort for achieving parallelism in the languages was required by TensorFlow, C-OpenACC, MAT-LAB arrayfun, and then Python Numba implementations. However, writing the serial code in TensorFlow was the most convoluted of all the approaches tested.

Nevertheless, moving from the serial code to the accelerated GPU code was as simple as just choosing the target device. C-OpenACC was the most natural for a novice programmer, which could provide the best performance with the least programming effort. However, MATLAB and Python Numba provide built-in visualization tools.

Acknowledgements. This work was supported in part by the National Science Foundation under grants CNS-1446312(EMC) and by CMMI-1762553 (FHF and AK). EMC, AK, YS, and FHF, also collaborated while at Kavli Institute for Theoretical Physics (KITP) and thus research was also supported in part by NSF Grant No. PHY-1748958, NIH Grant No. R25GM067110, and the Gordon and Betty Moore Foundation Grant No. 2919.01.

References

1. Benjamin, E.J., et al.: Heart disease and stroke statistics-2017 update: a report from the American Heart Association. Circulation **135**(10), e146–e603 (2017)
2. Winfree, A.: Electrical turbulence in three-dimensional heart muscle. Science **266**(5187), 1003–1006 (1994)
3. Gray, R.A., et al.: Mechanisms of cardiac fibrillation. Science **270**(5239), 1222–1226 (1995)
4. Gray, R.A., Pertsov, A.M., Jalife, J.: Spatial and temporal organization during cardiac fibrillation. Nature **392**(6671), 75 (1998)
5. Fenton, F.H., Cherry, E.M., Glass, L.: Cardiac arrhythmia. Scholarpedia **3**(7), 1665 (2008)
6. Kaboudia, A., Cherry, E.M., Fenton, F.H.: Real-time interactive simulations of large-scale systems on personal computers and cell phones. Sci. Adv. **5**, eaav6019 (2019)
7. Zahid, S., et al.: Feasibility of using patient-specific models and the "minimum cut" algorithm to predict optimal ablation targets for left atrial flutter. Heart Rhythm **13**(8), 1687–1698 (2016)
8. Dutta, S., et al.: Optimization of an in silico cardiac cell model for proarrhythmia risk assessment. Front. Physiol. **8**, 616 (2017)
9. Cavero, I., Holzgrefe, H.: CiPA: ongoing testing, future qualification procedures, and pending issues. J. Pharmacol. Toxicol. Methods **76**, 27–37 (2015)
10. Fenton, F.H., Cherry, E.M.: Models of cardiac cell. Scholarpedia **3**(8), 1868 (2008)
11. Fenton, F.H., Cherry, E.M., Hastings, H.M., Evans, S.J.: Real-time computer simulations of excitable media: JAVA as a scientific language and as a wrapper for C and FORTRAN programs. Biosystems **64**(1–3), 73–96 (2002)
12. Barkley, D.: EZ-spiral: a code for simulating spiral waves (2002). https://homepages.warwick.ac.uk/~masax/. Accessed 29 Apr 2019
13. FitzHugh, R.: Impulses and physiological states in theoretical models of nerve membrane. Biophys. J. **1**(6), 445–466 (1961)
14. Nagumo, J., Arimoto, S., Yoshizawa, S.: An active pulse transmission line simulating nerve axon. Proc. IRE **50**(10), 2061–2070 (1962)
15. Winfree, A.T.: Varieties of spiral wave behavior: an experimentalist's approach to the theory of excitable media. Chaos Interdisc. J. Nonlinear Sci. **1**(3), 303–334 (1991)

16. Bueno-Orovio, A., Cherry, E.M., Fenton, F.H.: Minimal model for human ventricular action potentials in tissue. J. Theor. Biol. **253**(3), 544–560 (2008)
17. Cherry, E.M., Ehrlich, J.R., Nattel, S., Fenton, F.H.: Pulmonary vein reentry–properties and size matter: insights from a computational analysis. Heart Rhythm **4**(12), 1553–1562 (2007)
18. Lombardo, D.M., Fenton, F.H., Narayan, S.M., Rappel, W.-J.: Comparison of detailed and simplified models of human atrial myocytes to recapitulate patient specific properties. PLoS Comput. Biol. **12**(8), e1005060 (2016)
19. Beeler, G.W., Reuter, H.: Reconstruction of the action potential of ventricular myocardial fibres. J. Physiol. **268**(1), 177–210 (1977)
20. Courtemanche, M.: Complex spiral wave dynamics in a spatially distributed ionic model of cardiac electrical activity. Chaos Interdiscip. J. Nonlinear Sci. **6**(4), 579–600 (1996)
21. Courtemanche, M., Winfree, A.T.: Re-entrant rotating waves in a beeler-reuter based model of two-dimensional cardiac electrical activity. Int. J. Bifurc. Chaos **1**(02), 431–444 (1991)
22. Hodgkin, A.L., Huxley, A.F.: A quantitative description of membrane current and its application to conduction and excitation in nerve. J. Physiol. **117**(4), 500–544 (1952)
23. Streeter Jr., D.D., Spotnitz, H.M., Patel, D.P., Ross Jr., J., Sonnenblick, E.H.: Fiber orientation in the canine left ventricle during diastole and systole. Circ. Res. **24**(3), 339–347 (1969)
24. Peskin, C.S.: Fiber architecture of the left ventricular wall: an asymptotic analysis. Commun. Pure Appl. Math. **42**(1), 79–113 (1989)
25. Ji, Y.C., Fenton, F.H.: Numerical solutions of reaction-diffusion equations: application to neural and cardiac models. Am. J. Phys. **84**(8), 626–638 (2016)
26. Rush, S., Larsen, H.: A practical algorithm for solving dynamic membrane equations. IEEE Trans. Biomed. Eng. **4**, 389–392 (1978)
27. Halpern, D., Wilson, H.B., Turcotte, L.H.: Advanced Mathematics and Mechanics Applications using MATLAB. Chapman and Hall/CRC, Boca Raton (2002)
28. Pozrikidis, C.: Introduction to Finite and Spectral Element Methods Using MATLAB. CRC Press, Boca Raton (2005)
29. Quarteroni, A., Saleri, F., Gervasio, P.: Scientific Computing with MATLAB and Octave, vol. 2. Springer, Heidelberg (2006). https://doi.org/10.1007/978-3-642-45367-0
30. Strang, G.: Computational Science and Engineering, vol. 791. Wellesley-Cambridge Press, Wellesley (2007)
31. Aarnes, J.E., Gimse, T., Lie, K.-A.: An introduction to the numerics of flow in porous media using MATLAB. In: Hasle, G., Lie, K.A., Quak, E. (eds.) Geometric Modelling, Numerical Simulation, and Optimization, pp. 265–306. Springer, Heidelberg (2007). https://doi.org/10.1007/978-3-540-68783-2_9
32. Li, J., Chen, Y.-T.: Computational Partial Differential Equations Using MATLAB. Chapman and Hall/CRC, Boca Raton (2008)
33. Anderson, D., Tannehill, J.C., Pletcher, R.H.: Computational Fluidmechanics and Heat Transfer. CRC Press, Boca Raton (2016)
34. Elsherbeni, A.Z. Demir, V.: The finite-difference time-domain method for electromagnetics with MATLAB simulations. The Institution of Engineering and Technology (2016)
35. Kwon, Y.W., Bang, H.: The Finite Element Method Using MATLAB. CRC Press, Boca Raton (2018)

36. Martin, N., Gorelick, S.M.: MOD_FreeSurf2D: a Matlab surface fluid flow model for rivers and streams. Comput. Geosci. **31**(7), 929–946 (2005)

37. Gholami, A., Bonakdari, H., Zaji, A.H., Akhtari, A.A.: Simulation of open channel bend characteristics using computational fluid dynamics and artificial neural networks. Eng. Appl. Comput. Fluid Mech. **9**(1), 355–369 (2015)

38. Irving, J., Knight, R.: Numerical modeling of ground-penetrating radar in 2-D using MATLAB. Comput. Geosci. **32**(9), 1247–1258 (2006)

39. Tzanis, A., et al.: MATGPR: a freeware MATLAB package for the analysis of common-offset GPR data. In: Geophysical Research Abstracts, vol. 8 (2006)

40. Xuan, C., Channell, J.E.: UPmag: MATLAB software for viewing and processing u channel or other pass-through paleomagnetic data. Geochem. Geophys. Geosyst. **10**(10), 1–12 (2009). https://doi.org/10.1029/2009GC002584

41. Lesage, P.: Interactive MATLAB software for the analysis of seismic volcanic signals. Comput. Geosci. **35**(10), 2137–2144 (2009)

42. Battaglia, M., Cervelli, P.F., Murray, J.R.: dMODELS: a MATLAB software package for modeling crustal deformation near active faults and volcanic centers. J. Volcanol. Geoth. Res. **254**, 1–4 (2013)

43. Charpentier, I., Sarocchi, D., Sedano, L.A.R.: Particle shape analysis of volcanic clast samples with the MATLAB tool MORPHEO. Comput. Geosci. **51**, 172–181 (2013)

44. Valade, S., Harris, A.J., Cerminara, M.: Plume ascent tracker: interactive MATLAB software for analysis of ascending plumes in image data. Comput. Geosci. **66**, 132–144 (2014)

45. Ofek, E.O.: MATLAB package for astronomy and astrophysics. Astrophysics Source Code Library (2014)

46. Ahmad, I., Raja, M.A.Z., Bilal, M., Ashraf, F.: Bio-inspired computational heuristics to study lane-emden systems arising in astrophysics model. SpringerPlus **5**(1), 1866 (2016)

47. Loredo, T., Scargle, J.: Time series exploration in Python and MATLAB: unevenly sampled data, parametric modeling, and periodograms. In: AAS/High Energy Astrophysics Division, vol. 17 (2019)

48. Kamel, N.A., Selman, A.A.-R.: Automatic detection of sunspots size and activity using MATLAB. Iraqi J. Sci. **60**(2), 411–425 (2019)

49. Guo, G.: Electromechanical feed control system in chemical dangerous goods production. Chem. Eng. Trans. **71**, 1039–1044 (2018)

50. Esche, E., Bublitz, S., Tolksdorf, G., Repke, J.-U.: Automatic decomposition of nonlinear equation systems for improved initialization and solution of chemical engineering process models. Comput. Aided Chem. Eng. **44**, 1387–1392 (2018)

51. Fitzpatrick, D., Ley, S.V.: Engineering chemistry for the future of chemical synthesis. Tetrahedron **74**(25), 3087–3100 (2018)

52. Eastep, C.V., Harrell, G.K., McPeak, A.N., Versypt, A.N.F.: A MATLAB app to introduce chemical engineering design concepts to engineering freshmen through a pharmaceutical dosing case study. Chem. Eng. Educ. **53**(2), 85 (2019)

53. Svoboda, T., Kybic, J., Hlavac, V.: Image Processing, Analysis and Machine Vision-A MATLAB Companion. Thomson Learning, Toronto (2007)

54. Dhawan, A.P.: Medical Image Analysis, vol. 31. Wiley, Hoboken (2011)

55. Schneider, C.A., Rasband, W.S., Eliceiri, K.W.: NIH image to imagej: 25 years of image analysis. Nat. Methods **9**(7), 671 (2012)

56. Rodríguez-Cristerna, A., Gómez-Flores, W., de Albuquerque-Pereira, W.C.: BUSAT: a MATLAB toolbox for breast ultrasound image analysis. In: Carrasco-Ochoa, J.A., Martínez-Trinidad, J.F., Olvera-López, J.A. (eds.) MCPR 2017. LNCS, vol. 10267, pp. 268–277. Springer, Cham (2017). https://doi.org/10.1007/978-3-319-59226-8_26

57. Cho, J.I., Wang, X., Xu, Y., Sun, J.: LISA: a MATLAB package for longitudinal image sequence analysis. arXiv preprint arXiv:1902.06131 (2019)

58. Vedaldi, A., Lenc, K.: MatConvNet: convolutional neural networks for MATLAB. In: Proceedings of the 23rd ACM international conference on Multimedia, pp. 689–692. ACM (2015)

59. Novikov, A., Podoprikhin, D., Osokin, A., Vetrov, D.P.: Tensorizing neural networks. In: Advances in Neural Information Processing Systems, pp. 442–450 (2015)

60. Vardhana, M., Arunkumar, N., Lasrado, S., Abdulhay, E., Ramirez-Gonzalez, G.: Convolutional neural network for bio-medical image segmentation with hardware acceleration. Cogn. Syst. Res. **50**, 10–14 (2018)

61. Molitor, S.C., Tong, M., Vora, D.: Matlab-based simulation of whole-cell and single-channel currents. J. Undergrad. Neurosci. Educ. **4**(2), A74 (2006)

62. Cardin, J.A., et al.: Driving fast-spiking cells induces gamma rhythm and controls sensory responses. Nature **459**(7247), 663 (2009)

63. Kirkton, R.D., Bursac, N.: Engineering biosynthetic excitable tissues from unexcitable cells for electrophysiological and cell therapy studies. Nat. Commun. **2**, 300 (2011)

64. Kodandaramaiah, S.B., Franzesi, G.T., Chow, B.Y., Boyden, E.S., Forest, C.R.: Automated whole-cell patch-clamp electrophysiology of neurons in vivo. Nat. Methods **9**(6), 585 (2012)

65. Prassl, A.J., et al.: Automatically generated, anatomically accurate meshes for cardiac electrophysiology problems. IEEE Trans. Biomed. Eng. **56**(5), 1318–1330 (2009)

66. O'Hara, T., Virág, L., Varró, A., Rudy, Y.: Simulation of the undiseased human cardiac ventricular action potential: model formulation and experimental validation. PLoS Comput. Biol. **7**(5), e1002061 (2011)

67. Cusimano, N., Bueno-Orovio, A., Turner, I., Burrage, K.: On the order of the fractional laplacian in determining the spatio-temporal evolution of a space-fractional model of cardiac electrophysiology. PLoS ONE **10**(12), e0143938 (2015)

68. Elshrif, M.M., Shi, P., Cherry, E.M.: Representing variability and transmural differences in a model of human heart failure. IEEE J. Biomed. Health Inform. **19**(4), 1308–1320 (2015)

69. Passini, E., et al.: Human in silico drug trials demonstrate higher accuracy than animal models in predicting clinical pro-arrhythmic cardiotoxicity. Front. Physiol. **8**, 668 (2017)

70. Cusimano, N., del Teso, F., Gerardo-Giorda, L., Pagnini, G.: Discretizations of the spectral fractional laplacian on general domains with Dirichlet, Neumann, and Robin boundary conditions. SIAM J. Numer. Anal. **56**(3), 1243–1272 (2018)

71. Handa, B.S., et al.: Interventricular differences in action potential duration restitution contribute to dissimilar ventricular rhythms in ex-vivo perfused hearts. Front. Cardiovasc. Med. **6**, 34 (2019)

72. Kraus, J., Schlottke, M., Adinetz, A., Pleiter, D.: Accelerating a C++ CFD code with OpenACC. In: 2014 First Workshop on Accelerator Programming using Directives, pp. 47–54. IEEE (2014)

73. Blair, S., Albing, C., Grund, A., Jocksch, A.: Accelerating an MPI lattice Boltzmann code using OpenACC. In: Proceedings of the Second Workshop on Accelerator Programming Using Directives, p. 3. ACM (2015)

74. Huismann, I., Stiller, J., Fröhlich, J.: Two-level parallelization of a fluid mechanics algorithm exploiting hardware heterogeneity. Comput. Fluids **117**, 114–124 (2015)

75. Lou, J., Xia, Y., Luo, L., Luo, H., Edwards, J.R., Mueller, F.: OpenACC directive-based GPU acceleration of an implicit reconstructed discontinuous Galerkin method for compressible flows on 3D unstructured grids. In: 54th AIAA Aerospace Sciences Meeting, p. 1815 (2016)

76. Raj, A., Roy, S., Vydyanathar, N., Sharma, B.: Acceleration of a 3D immersed boundary solver using OpenACC. In: 2018 IEEE 25th International Conference on High Performance Computing Workshops (HiPCW), pp. 65–73. IEEE (2018)

77. Gallovic, F., Valentova, L., Ampuero, J.-P., Gabriel, A.-A.: Bayesian dynamic finite-fault inversion: 1. Method and synthetic test (2019)

78. Kan, G., He, X., Ding, L., Li, J., Liang, K., Hong, Y.: A heterogeneous computing accelerated SCE-UA global optimization method using OpenMP, OpenCL, CUDA, and OpenACC. Water Sci. Technol. **76**(7), 1640–1651 (2017)

79. Liu, C., Yang, H., Sun, R., Luan, Z., Qian, D.: SWTVM: exploring the automated compilation for deep learning on Sunway architecture. arXiv preprint arXiv:1904.07404 (2019)

80. Cavuoti, S., et al.: Astrophysical data mining with GPU. A case study: genetic classification of globular clusters. New Astron. **26**, 12–22 (2014)

81. Rosenberger, S., Haase, G.: Pragma based GPU parallelizations for cardiovascular simulations. In: 2018 International Conference on High Performance Computing and Simulation (HPCS), pp. 1022–1027. IEEE (2018)

82. Campos, J., Oliveira, R.S., dos Santos, R.W., Rocha, B.M.: Lattice boltzmann method for parallel simulations of cardiac electrophysiology using GPUs. J. Comput. Appl. Math. **295**, 70–82 (2016)

83. Canal Noguer, P.: Modeling human atrial electrodynamics and arrhythmias through GPU parallel computing: from cell to tissue. B.S. thesis, Universitat Politècnica de Catalunya (2016)

84. History and license. https://docs.python.org/3/license.html. Accessed 28 Apr 2019

85. Fangohr, H.: A comparison of C, MATLAB, and Python as teaching languages in engineering. In: Bubak, M., van Albada, G.D., Sloot, P.M.A., Dongarra, J. (eds.) ICCS 2004. LNCS, vol. 3039, pp. 1210–1217. Springer, Heidelberg (2004). https://doi.org/10.1007/978-3-540-25944-2_157

86. Goldwasser, M.H., Letscher, D.: Teaching an object-oriented CS1-: with Python. ACM SIGCSE Bull. **40**, 42–46 (2008)

87. Vallisneri, M., Kanner, J., Williams, R., Weinstein, A., Stephens, B.: The LIGO open science center. J. Phys. Conf. Ser. **610**, 012021 (2015)

88. Rodriguez, C.L., Morscher, M., Pattabiraman, B., Chatterjee, S., Haster, C.-J., Rasio, F.A.: Binary black hole mergers from globular clusters: implications for advanced LIGO. Phys. Rev. Lett. **115**(5), 051101 (2015)

89. Aasi, J., et al.: Advanced LIGO. Class. Quantum Gravity **32**(7), 074001 (2015)

90. Pedregosa, F., et al.: Scikit-learn: machine learning in Python. J. Mach. Learn. Res. **12**, 2825–2830 (2011)

91. Raschka, S.: Python Machine Learning. Packt Publishing Ltd., Birmingham (2015)

92. Goodman, D.F., Brette, R.: Brian: a simulator for spiking neural networks in Python. Front. Neuroinform. **2**, 5 (2008)

93. Yen, D.C., Huang, S.-M., Ku, C.-Y.: The impact and implementation of XML on business-to-business commerce. Comput. Stand. Interfaces **24**(4), 347–362 (2002)
94. Lehmann, G., et al.: Towards dynamic planning and guidance of minimally invasive robotic cardiac bypass surgical procedures. In: Niessen, W.J., Viergever, M.A. (eds.) MICCAI 2001. LNCS, vol. 2208, pp. 368–375. Springer, Heidelberg (2001). https://doi.org/10.1007/3-540-45468-3_44
95. Lehmann, G., Habets, D., Holdsworth, D.W., Peters, T., Drangova, M.: Simulation of intra-operative 3D coronary angiography for enhanced minimally invasive robotic cardiac intervention. In: Dohi, T., Kikinis, R. (eds.) MICCAI 2002. LNCS, vol. 2489, pp. 268–275. Springer, Heidelberg (2002). https://doi.org/10.1007/3-540-45787-9_34
96. Azaouzi, M., Makradi, A., Petit, J., Belouettar, S., Polit, O.: On the numerical investigation of cardiovascular balloon-expandable stent using finite element method. Comput. Mater. Sci. **79**, 326–335 (2013)
97. Herman, W.H., et al.: Early detection and treatment of type 2 diabetes reduce cardiovascular morbidity and mortality: a simulation of the results of the Anglo-Danish-Dutch study of intensive treatment in people with screen-detected diabetes in primary care (addition-Europe). Diabetes Care **38**(8), 1449–1455 (2015)
98. Itani, M.A., et al.: An automated multiscale ensemble simulation approach for vascular blood flow. J. Comput. Sci. **9**, 150–155 (2015)
99. Ramachandra, A.B., Kahn, A.M., Marsden, A.L.: Patient-specific simulations reveal significant differences in mechanical stimuli in venous and arterial coronary grafts. J. Cardiovasc. Transl. Res. **9**(4), 279–290 (2016)
100. Updegrove, A., Wilson, N.M., Merkow, J., Lan, H., Marsden, A.L., Shadden, S.C.: Simvascular: An open source pipeline for cardiovascular simulation. Ann. Biomed. Eng. **45**(3), 525–541 (2017)
101. Kuo, S., Ye, W., Duong, J., Herman, W.H.: Are the favorable cardiovascular outcomes of empagliflozin treatment explained by its effects on multiple cardiometabolic risk factors? A simulation of the results of the EMPA-REG OUTCOME trial. Diabetes Res. Clin. Pract. **141**, 181–189 (2018)
102. Myers, C.R., Sethna, J.P.: Python for education: computational methods for nonlinear systems. Comput. Sci. Eng. **9**(3), 75–79 (2007)
103. Niederer, S.A., et al.: Verification of cardiac tissue electrophysiology simulators using an N-version benchmark. Philos. Trans. R. Soc. A Math. Phys. Eng. Sci. **369**(1954), 4331–4351 (2011)
104. Burton, R.A., et al.: Optical control of excitation waves in cardiac tissue. Nat. Photonics **9**(12), 813 (2015)
105. Hurtado, D.E., Castro, S., Gizzi, A.: Computational modeling of non-linear diffusion in cardiac electrophysiology: a novel porous-medium approach. Comput. Methods Appl. Mech. Eng. **300**, 70–83 (2016)
106. Cherubini, C., Filippi, S., Gizzi, A., Ruiz-Baier, R.: A note on stress-driven anisotropic diffusion and its role in active deformable media. J. Theor. Biol. **430**, 221–228 (2017)
107. Gizzi, A., et al.: Nonlinear diffusion and thermo-electric coupling in a two-variable model of cardiac action potential. Chaos Interdiscip. J. Nonlinear Sci. **27**(9), 093919 (2017)
108. Mane, R.S., Cheeran, A., Awandekar, V.D., Rani, P.: Cardiac arrhythmia detection by ECG feature extraction. Int. J. Eng. Res. Appl. **3**, 327–332 (2013)
109. Conferences and workshops. https://www.python.org/community/workshops/. Accessed 28 Apr 2019

110. Project jupyter. https://jupyter.org/. Accessed 29 Apr 2019
111. Numpy. https://www.numpy.org/. Accessed 29 Apr 2019
112. Numba. http://numba.pydata.org/. Accessed 29 Apr 2019
113. 1.1. a 5 minute guide to Numba. http://numba.pydata.org/numba-doc/latest/user/5minguide.html. Accessed 29 Apr 2019
114. Abadi, M., et al.: TensorFlow: a system for large-scale machine learning. In: 12th USENIX Symposium on Operating Systems Design and Implementation (OSDI 2016), pp. 265–283 (2016)
115. Girija, S.S.: TensorFlow: large-scale machine learning on heterogeneous distributed systems (2016). Software tensorflow.org
116. Google just open sourced TensorFlow, its artificial intelligence engine. https://www.wired.com/2015/11/google-open-sources-its-artificial-intelligence-engine/. Accessed 29 Apr 2019
117. Case studies and mentions. https://www.tensorflow.org/about/case-studies/. Accessed 29 Apr 2019
118. Cheng, H.-T., et al.: Wide & deep learning for recommender systems. In: Proceedings of the 1st Workshop on Deep Learning for Recommender Systems, pp. 7–10. ACM (2016)
119. Lieman-Sifry, J., Le, M., Lau, F., Sall, S., Golden, D.: FastVentricle: cardiac segmentation with ENet. In: Pop, M., Wright, G.A. (eds.) FIMH 2017. LNCS, vol. 10263, pp. 127–138. Springer, Cham (2017). https://doi.org/10.1007/978-3-319-59448-4_13
120. Warrick, P., Homsi, M.N.: Cardiac arrhythmia detection from ECG combining convolutional and long short-term memory networks. In: 2017 Computing in Cardiology (CinC), pp. 1–4. IEEE (2017)
121. Biswas, S., Aggarwal, H.K., Poddar, S., Jacob, M.: Model-based free-breathing cardiac MRI reconstruction using deep learned & storm priors: MoDL-storm. In: 2018 IEEE International Conference on Acoustics, Speech and Signal Processing (ICASSP), pp. 6533–6537. IEEE (2018)
122. Kamaleswaran, R., Mahajan, R., Akbilgic, O.: A robust deep convolutional neural network for the classification of abnormal cardiac rhythm using single lead electrocardiograms of variable length. Physiol. Meas. **39**(3), 035006 (2018)
123. Iravanian, S.: fib-tf: a TensorFlow-based cardiac electrophysiology simulator. J. Open Source Softw. **3**(26), 719 (2018)
124. Kang, S.-H., Joe, B., Yoon, Y., Cho, G.-Y., Shin, I., Suh, J.-W.: Cardiac auscultation using smartphones: pilot study. JMIR mHealth uHealth **6**(2), e49 (2018)
125. Savalia, S., Emamian, V.: Cardiac arrhythmia classification by multi-layer perceptron and convolution neural networks. Bioengineering **5**(2), 35 (2018)
126. Teplitzky, B.A., McRoberts, M.: Fully-automated ventricular ectopic beat classification for use with mobile cardiac telemetry. In: 2018 IEEE 15th International Conference on Wearable and Implantable Body Sensor Networks (BSN), pp. 58–61. IEEE (2018)
127. Bello, G.A., et al.: Deep-learning cardiac motion analysis for human survival prediction. Nat. Mach. Intell. **1**(2), 95 (2019)
128. WebGL overview. https://www.khronos.org/webgl/. Accessed 29 Apr 2019
129. OpenGL shading language. https://www.khronos.org/opengl/wiki/OpenGL_Shading_Language. Accessed 29 Apr 2019
130. WebGL 2.0 API quick reference guide. https://www.khronos.org/files/webgl20-reference-guide.pdf. Accessed 29 Apr 2019
131. Owens, J.D., et al.: A survey of general-purpose computation on graphics hardware. Comput. Graph. Forum **26**-1, 80–113 (2007)

132. Kaboudian, A., Cherry, E.M., Fenton, F.H.: Large-scale interactive numerical experiments of chaos, solitons and fractals in real time via GPU in a web browser. Chaos Solitons Fractals **121**, 6–29 (2019)

133. Jacobsen, D., Thibault, J., Senocak, I.: An MPI-CUDA implementation for massively parallel incompressible flow computations on multi-GPU clusters. In: 48th AIAA Aerospace Sciences Meeting Including the New Horizons Forum and Aerospace Exposition, p. 522 (2010)

134. Ladický, L., Jeong, S., Solenthaler, B., Pollefeys, M., Gross, M.: Data-driven fluid simulations using regression forests. ACM Trans. Graph. **34**(6), 1–9 (2015)

135. Jang, H., Park, A., Jung, K.: Neural network implementation using CUDA and OpenMP. In: 2008 Digital Image Computing: Techniques and Applications, pp. 155–161. IEEE (2008)

136. Nageswaran, J.M., Dutt, N., Krichmar, J.L., Nicolau, A., Veidenbaum, A.V.: A configurable simulation environment for the efficient simulation of large-scale spiking neural networks on graphics processors. Neural Netw. **22**(5–6), 791–800 (2009)

137. Sierra-Canto, K., Madera-Ramirez, F., Uc-Cetina, V.: Parallel training of a back-propagation neural network using CUDA. In: 2010 Ninth International Conference on Machine Learning and Applications, pp. 307–312. IEEE (2010)

138. Ciresan, D.C., Meier, U., Masci, J., Gambardella, L.M., Schmidhuber, J.: Flexible, high performance convolutional neural networks for image classification. In: Twenty-Second International Joint Conference on Artificial Intelligence (2011)

139. Nylons, L.: Fast n-body simulation with CUDA (2007)

140. Belleman, R.G., Bédorf, J., Zwart, S.F.P.: High performance direct gravitational n-body simulations on graphics processing units II: an implementation in cuda. New Astron. **13**(2), 103–112 (2008)

141. Glinskiy, B.M., Kulikov, I.M., Snytnikov, A.V., Romanenko, A.A., Chernykh, I.G., Vshivkov, V.A.: Co-design of parallel numerical methods for plasma physics and astrophysics. Supercomput. Front. Innov. **1**(3), 88–98 (2015)

142. Hamada, T., Narumi, T., Yokota, R., Yasuoka, K., Nitadori, K., Taiji, M.: 42 TFlops hierarchical N-body simulations on GPUs with applications in both astrophysics and turbulence. In: Proceedings of the Conference on High Performance Computing Networking, Storage and Analysis, pp. 1–12. IEEE (2009)

143. Obrecht, C., Kuznik, F., Tourancheau, B., Roux, J.-J.: A new approach to the lattice Boltzmann method for graphics processing units. Comput. Math. Appl. **61**(12), 3628–3638 (2011)

144. Rinaldi, P.R., Dari, E., Vénere, M.J., Clausse, A.: A lattice-Boltzmann solver for 3D fluid simulation on GPU. Simul. Model. Pract. Theory **25**, 163–171 (2012)

145. Obrecht, C., Kuznik, F., Tourancheau, B., Roux, J.-J.: Scalable lattice Boltzmann solvers for cuda GPU clusters. Parallel Comput. **39**(6–7), 259–270 (2013)

146. Anderson, J.A., Lorenz, C.D., Travesset, A.: General purpose molecular dynamics simulations fully implemented on graphics processing units. J. Comput. Phys. **227**(10), 5342–5359 (2008)

147. Liu, W., Schmidt, B., Voss, G., Müller-Wittig, W.: Accelerating molecular dynamics simulations using graphics processing units with CUDA. Comput. Phys. Commun. **179**(9), 634–641 (2008)

148. Stone, J.E., Vandivort, K.L., Schulten, K.: GPU-accelerated molecular visualization on petascale supercomputing platforms, pp. 1–8 (2013)

149. Reichl, T., Passenger, J., Acosta, O., Salvado, O.: Ultrasound goes GPU: real-time simulation using CUDA. In: Medical Imaging 2009: Visualization, Image-Guided Procedures, and Modeling, vol. 7261, p. 726116, International Society for Optics and Photonics (2009)

150. Alsmirat, M.A., Jararweh, Y., Al-Ayyoub, M., Shehab, M.A., Gupta, B.B.: Accelerating compute intensive medical imaging segmentation algorithms using hybrid CPU-GPU implementations. Multimedia Tools Appl. **76**(3), 3537–3555 (2017)

151. Dawes, T.J.W., et al.: Machine learning of three-dimensional right ventricular motion enables outcome prediction in pulmonary hypertension: a cardiac MR Imaging Study. Radiology **283**(2), 161315 (2017)

152. Bartocci, E., Cherry, E.M., Glimm, J., Grosu, R., Smolka, S.A., Fenton, F.H.: Toward real-time simulation of cardiac dynamics. In: Proceedings of the 9th International Conference on Computational Methods in Systems Biology, pp. 103–112. ACM (2011)

153. Berg, S., Luther, S., Parlitz, U.: Synchronization based system identification of an extended excitable system. Chaos **21**(3), 033104 (2011)

154. Sato, D., Xie, Y., Weiss, J.N., Qu, Z., Garfinkel, A., Sanderson, A.R.: Acceleration of cardiac tissue simulation with graphic processing units. Med. Biol. Eng. Comput. **47**(9), 1011–1015 (2009)

155. Landoni, M., Genoni, M., Riva, M., Bianco, A., Corina, A.: Application of cloud computing in astrophysics: the case of Amazon web services. In: Software and Cyberinfrastructure for Astronomy V, vol. 10707, p. 107070G. International Society for Optics and Photonics (2018)

156. Bartocci, E., et al.: Teaching cardiac electrophysiology modeling to undergraduate students: laboratory exercises and GPU programming for the study of arrhythmias and spiral wave dynamics. Adv. Physiol. Educ. **35**(4), 427–437 (2011)

157. Fallis, A.: CUDA by example, vol. 53 (2013)

158. NVIDIA: NVIDIA CUDA C Programming Guide Version 4.2, p. 173 (2012)

From Automated MRI Scan to Finite Elements

James Glimm[1], Hyunkyung Lim[1(✉)], Martin Bishop[2], and Soojin Kim[1]

[1] Stony Brook University, Stony Brook, NY 11794, USA
hyun-kyung.lim@stonybrook.edu
[2] King's College, London, UK

Abstract. We present algorithms for the automated transition from scanned MRI images to finite element simulations. The algorithms are designed for the reconstruction of fine scale blood vessels as possibly important to defibrillation studies in electrocardiac physiology. The automated nature of the transition is essential for practical usage, as the otherwise necessary human intervention is prohibitive. The automated software relies on a mixture of public domain algorithms and new algorithms developed specifically for the current purpose. The problem of transitions from MRI images to accurate physiology is important in many medical applications, and much of our work will be helpful in more general cases. The definitive nature of the blood vessel problem which makes the entire analysis feasible is a conceptual model of the final geometry, as the connected branches of veins and arteries together with the inner and outer cardiac surface.

Keywords: MRI scan · Defibrillation · Cardiac blood vessels

1 Introduction

Heart failure is a leading cause of death in the industrial world [1,2]. Understanding the normal and abnormal behaviors of the heart has been studied actively [10]. Ventricular fibrillation is a significant aspect of heart failure. It is fatal if not treated promptly, by an electrical shock to reset the cardiac conditions and to allow resumption of a normal heart beat. As an alternative to the traditional method of a single high voltage defibrillation shock, the method of Low Energy Action Potential (LEAP) [29] offers advantages, but details in its mode of operation remain to be clarified. The effectiveness of both LEAP and the strong shock method depend on localized discontinuities in the cardiac electrical conductivity to generate charges, known as virtual electrodes as a response to the electrical shock. These virtual electrodes interfere with the chaotic fibrillating state and bring about its termination, allowing resumption of a normal heart beat. The electrical discontinuities are located at the cardiac surfaces are of primary importance. The blood vessel walls are also a source of electrical discontinuity. They play a helpful but secondary role [3]. In a quantitative study

© Springer Nature Switzerland AG 2019
E. Bartocci et al. (Eds.): From Reactive Systems to Cyber-Physical Systems, LNCS 11500, pp. 35–48, 2019.
https://doi.org/10.1007/978-3-030-31514-6_3

of defibrillation [4], it was shown that both the shock strength and the minimum blood vessel size were important in determining which blood vessels were significant. Here a threshold of perhaps $50\,\mu$ radius was identified. In [5], the interplay between applied voltage and blood vessel diameter is examined, with most of the effect occurring at voltages larger than typical LEAP protocols or only for large blood vessels. Our aim here is to refine our understanding of this secondary role, especially as a function of the blood vessel size, and in a model of the full ventricle, beyond the thickened slab previously considered.

With high resolution $25\,\mu$ MRI data of a rabbit ventricle, we have an opportunity to assess the roles of blood vessels of various sizes in the formation of virtual electrodes. This is where the automated analysis of this paper is important. Starting with the high resolution MRI data, we transition from segmentation (black-white stair step images) to finite element surface meshes to full volume finite elements meshes, to fiber orientation within the mesh to finite element fibrillation and defibrillation simulations. The main thrust of the present paper is the automated procedure, with the fibrillation and defibrillation studies not considered here. The automation is nearly complete, and remaining manual steps are sufficiently minor to allow systematic use of this technology. As the later stages of this suite of algorithms were developed in [6], our focus here is on the surface mesh and its construction from the segmented (stair steps) image.

In emphasizing an automated procedure, our goal is feasibility of the analysis. The decision to be made, fragment by fragment, is whether it is included in the analysis (radius above $50\,\mu$) or excluded from analysis. The number of such variables in the rabbit ventricle is of the order of tens of tens of thousands, and for a human heart, approximately $3^3 = 27$ larger, this number approaches million.

The human effort to manage the automated software is also a complicated and time consuming undertaking. Thus we allow instances where human judgement is less burdensome than the addition of a new software tool to the suite of analysis programs.

The governing equations for the electrical activity within the heart consist of a diffusion equation and a reaction source term depending on ionic currents. The equations and a finite element algorithm based on the CHASTE simulation platform (Cancer, Heart and Soft Tissue Environment) [7–9], for their solution are described in [6]. We solve the bidomain equations, representing the cardiac tissue at overlapping intracellular and extracellular domains [10], as is needed for the duration of the electrical shock. In the bidomain equations, a distinguished orientation within each mesh cell describes the direction of the fibers in that cell.

Computational resource requirements for this automated pipeline are a linux cluster or equivalent supercomputer access, both for computation and memory usage.

Finite elements are a form of discretization of the cardiac equations. In this technology, all of space is divided into tetrahedra, and the equations are solved on this basis, with the voltages defined as having values in each tetrahedra, As we use them here, they are adaptive, with the cardiac surfaces (inner and outer walls and blood vessels) lying on the boundary of the finite elements. With this framework, the surface mesh is the set of surface elements (triangles) that define the conductivity discontinuity boundaries (i.e. the heart walls and the blood vessel (inner) surfaces). For some purposes, there are not one but two voltages defined in each cell, one representing the average of the voltages of the individual cardiac cells and the other the voltage on the average of the extracellular space. This is called a bidomain model, and is needed during the passage of the electrical shock as part of the defibrillation treatment. In the bidomain equations, the orientation of the cardiac fibers is important, and must be added to the equations to specify it. The standard bidomain equations for cardiac electro physiology [7] consist of a diffusion equation for the voltages (in the intra cellular and extracellular cardiac tissue and non cardiac tissue called bath) coupled to an ordinary differential equation for the ionic currents. The extracellular voltage and the bath voltage are solved as a single continuous potential, with no flux (Neumann) boundary conditions for the external bath boundary and a discontinuous diffusion tensor across the heart-bath boundary. The solution domain is denoted by $\Omega = H \cup B$, where H is the heart tissue and B is the bath. The boundaries of the heart tissue and bath are denoted by ∂H and ∂B respectively. The governing bidomain equations with the boundary conditions can be written as [32]

$$\chi(C_m \frac{\partial v}{\partial e} + I_{ion}(v, w)) - \nabla \cdot (D_i \nabla v) - \nabla \cdot (D_i \nabla v_e) = 0, \quad in \; H \tag{1}$$

$$\nabla \cdot (D_i \nabla v) + \nabla \cdot ((D_i + D_e) \nabla v_e) = 0, \quad in \; H \tag{2}$$

$$\frac{\partial w}{\partial t} + g(v, w) = 0, \quad in \; H \tag{3}$$

$$\nabla \cdot (D_b \nabla v_e) = 0, \quad in \; B \tag{4}$$

$$\mathbf{n} \cdot (D_i \nabla v) + n \cdot (D_i \nabla v_e) = 0, \quad on \; \partial H \tag{5}$$

$$n \cdot (D_e \nabla v_e) = n \cdot (D_b \nabla v_e), \quad on \; \partial H \tag{6}$$

$$n \cdot (D_e \nabla v_e) = I_e, \quad on \; \partial B \backslash \partial H \tag{7}$$

where χ is the surface to volume ratio of the membrane, C_m is the electrical capacitance of the cardiac tissue per unit area, I_{ion} is the ionic current over the membrane per unit area, which is calculated by the transmembrane potential v and the gate variable w. The gate function g and I_{ion} are determined by the cell ionic model, including the electroporation current I_{ep} [33–35]. The intra cellular and extracellular potentials and intra and extra conductivity tensors, denoted by v_i, v_e, D_i and D_e respectively, are defined in the heart tissue H. The extracellular potential is also defined in the bath B with the bath conductivity D_b. The unit normal vector at the cardiac surface, n, is oriented outward while I_e represents the electrical current across $\partial B \backslash \partial H$.

For both the surface and the volume mesh, mesh quality is important, of the numerical solution method will fail. Mesh quality is assessed in terms of approximate equal volumes of the mesh elements, areas of the surface mesh triangles and in both cases of the size of the vertex angles. The finite element equations are a linear system of equations, which cannot be solved explicitly. The solution is iterative and involves successive approximations. It is a general lore for such solutions that poor mesh quality makes the resulting iterative equations poorly conditioned. This means excessive computation time as the most favorable outcome, and more likely, failure of the iteration to converge. As there are many time steps and many such iterative solution steps, a high degree of reliability is essential, and this reliability requirement imposes a mesh quality condition.

The paper is organized as follows. The main thrust of the paper is contained in Sect. 2, where the automated algorithm is constructed. While many aspects of the algorithm can be used for the interpretation of a variety of MRI image data, we observe that its full force depends on high resolution data and on a clear conceptual understanding of the answer: an inner and an outer surface and connected branching networks of blood vessels (the veins and the arteries). Sect. 3 describes the ionic model of the equations and Sect. 4 contains a discussion of the model construction.

To complete the finite element equations in their bidomain form, we specify a fiber orientation in every mesh cell. This is constructed from an algorithm [11], as detailed experimental data is missing. We show a schematic diagram of the model construction for defibrillation studies in Figs. 1 and 2.

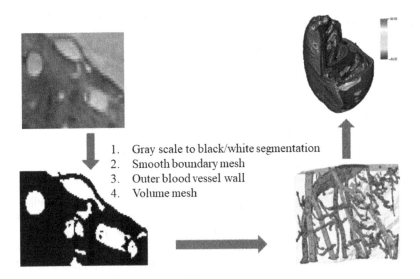

1. Gray scale to black/white segmentation
2. Smooth boundary mesh
3. Outer blood vessel wall
4. Volume mesh

Fig. 1. Automated Construction of Whole Heart from MRI

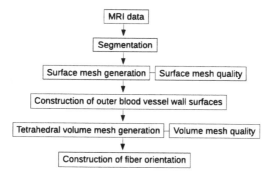

Fig. 2. A schematic diagram of the model construction for defibrillation studies.

2   The Automated Algorithm

We emphasize the large increase in automation achieved here vs. [4]. The [4] level of automation allowed detailed construction of a slice only from a rabbit ventricle. In contrast, we address detailed vascular resolution of the full ventricle with possible extension to the human ventricle.

Our approach is a combination of the use of existing tools and the skilled of new ones. Often, especially with our emphasis on public domain tools, their tools are immature and require additional effort to become useful. The tools are designed for use in a stand alone fashion, and these integration and interoperability is a further problem. As examples of new algorithms and developments, we mention several issues. Identification of which intermediate sized structure contain a segment of greater than $50\,\mu$ is not contained in any software package. The algorithm for growing the outer wall of a blood vessel from its inner wall, which are previously used in a hand corrected version is now fully automated [6]. The step of surface mesh quality was not previously considered, and we did not find a suitable public domain algorithm for [6].

2.1   Segmentation

The segmentation algorithm is described in detail in [5,12]. We only summarize a few of the highlights from this algorithm, which as given in these references is not fully automated. We only make use of the initial step of the method described in detail below. Our main trust is to by pass all but the initial step fully automated.

The methods of tissue preparation are described in detail in [5]. Initial segmentation only attempts to differentiate between tissue and non-tissue, with the further segmentation into distinct tissue classes (vessel walls vs. blood) accomplished later. In contrast to [12], the full resolution MR dataset was segmented, with no prior down-sampling. The heart of the method is an iterative use of level set technology, to identify a smooth surface separating distinct regions. Here the Insight Toolkit library, ITK, www.itk.org and several other software packages played an important role. A segmentation pipeline involving threshold, geodesic and Laplacian level-set algorithms was employed in an automated manner, with specific parameter combinations for each filter obtained by visual inspection, as described in [12]. Following automated segmentation, due to poor MR contrast at some tissue boundaries, minor manual adjustments were needed throughout the dataset, again based on visual inspection.

For our present purposes, we take only the first pass segmentation version of the [5,12] segmentation protocol, which is fully automated. This algorithm leads to subsequent data problems which we address here.

2.2   Surface Mesh

The surface mesh is constructed from the stair step segmented image of Sect. 2.1 by a level surface algorithm. The level surface algorithm finds an interpolating surface between the stair steps. At each point, its distance to the nearest black-white boundary is noted. This is a signed distance, and the 0 (mid) value of the interpolation is by definition the level surface. The level surface is triangulated via the marching cubes template based formula [13].

Blood Vessel Surface Mesh Data Cleaning. The blood vessel surface mesh constructed in Sect. 2.2 can be divided topologically into distinct connected components (i.e. isolated fragments of the surface mesh). The decision variable is made for the component as a whole, to retain in the final model or to eliminate, on the basis of a size criteria. These components are the primary decision variables for subsequent analysis. There are 9642 of these components. The algorithm for the identification of the individual components is a marching front method, with the key decision criteria based on the fact that each triangle knows (has pointers to) each of the three triangles which it borders.

The mesh is of low quality. The many artifacts to be removed are mainly obvious to a human eye, but due to the large number of decision variables, an automated method is required. A fully resolved cardiac blood vessel model might have two components, one consisting of arteries and the other of veins, with possible exceptions due to the ventricle only nature of the data.

Our goal is to resolve only the blood vessels of radius $50\,\mu$ or larger. Studies conducted by [5,12] indicated that a significant role for blood vessels of inner radius smaller than $50\,\mu$ appears to be excluded. These studies were conducted in idealized geometries. This conclusion appears to be accepted by most workers in this field. As the resolution is $25\,\mu$, we divide the problem into three parts, large, intermediate and small sized components. The automated decision used to govern this separation is based on a count of the number of triangles in each component. The border between the sizes is adjusted by visual inspection. The large ones are components which are to be retained, the small ones are ones to be eliminated and the intermediate ones require a more careful analysis. The point of this division is to reduce the number of intermediate components as their detailed analysis is more expensive. Of the 9642 total components, we find 8246 small components and 142 large ones, leaving 1250 intermediate ones, about 15% of the total number of components. By numbers of surface triangles, the proportions is quite different, with 33,053,937 surface triangles assigned as 208,41,658 (about 2/3) to the large components, 7,467,308 (about 1/5) to the intermediate and 4,744,971 (about 1/7) to the small components.

Large Components

We search among the blood vessels for regions with a large volume. These are located within the large blood vessels. This search depends on the software package meshlab, http://www.meshlab.net/. Its use is manual, but not onerous in difficulty, as it is used to determine the full connected component of the blood vessels after manual identification of a large blood region starting point, with a relatively modest number of manual choices made. This algorithm brings along with the large starting blood vessel the many smaller ones branching off of it. The triangles identified in this manner are a preponderance of the total triangles of the surface. In Fig. 3 we show the five largest components identified in this manner.

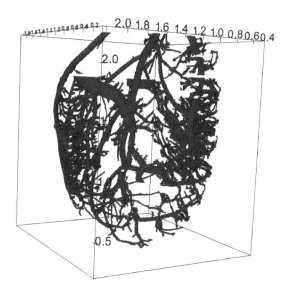

Fig. 3. We display the five largest blood vessel connected component networks. Each is identified starting from a large volume branching point and with the aid of a visualization tool finding all multiple smaller blood vessels connected to it. The units on the coordinate axes are in cm.

Intermediate Components

The most difficult case is the intermediate one. An example is shown in Fig. 4. By adjustment of parameters, we place most of the components into the large or small categories. The remaining intermediate sized components represent in blood vessels of a marginal size, near the $50\,\mu$ radius criteria for elimination.

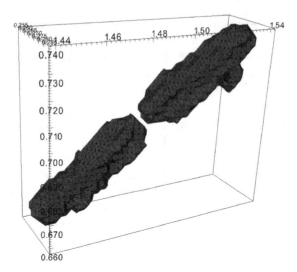

Fig. 4. We show an example of the intermediate sized blood vessel with two components. The components could be joined, but this seems to be a minor change in terms of surface triangles involved, which is where the virtual electrodes are located. Units in cm. On the coordinate axis indicate a radius of 100 μ, indicating that these components are to be retained in the final model.

We consider 1254 components of this category, a reduction 15% from the total number of components. Because of the borderline nature of the intermediate cases, these cases require a more careful and detailed analysis.

The detail analysis is based on the medial axis algorithm, is available from Matlab under the program name Skeleton3D. Public domain medial axis software is available from http://www.ams.sunysb.edu/~lindquis/3dma/3dma_rock/3dma_rock.html with technical description in [14]. The medial axis finds a precisely defined centerline for any component. It may have multiple branching points. We apply it only away from its branching points. As such, the medial axis defines a centerline of an extended 1D object. We form a normal plane to the centerline and intersect the blood vessel surface with this normal plane. The result is a curve in the normal plane, changing as one moves along the medial axis. This curve, if approximated by an ellipse, has a major and a minor radius. The major radius is of interest here. If anywhere along the medial axis, the maximum radius exceeds 50 μ, then (at least this fragment of) the component is to be retained.

The medial axis technology also offers the opportunity to join disconnected components, as the two components in question will appear as gaps in a single line or curve. We expect for the current purposes, this step will not be important, as the blood vessels joined in this manner will often be below the threshold of (50 μ) radius. See Fig. 4. The medial axis (not shown in the figure) runs down the centerline of the two segments. Direct determination of the maximum radius within a component is also possible, avoiding use of the medial axis.

Small Components

The small components (which we might refer to as "fly specks") are regarded as segmentation artifacts and are removed from further analysis. Some of these represent small but under resolved blood vessels and that a more accurate reconstruction would "connect the dots" to yield an intact blood vessel. If this level of data analysis were achieved, the reconstructed blood vessels would be mainly below our target threshold, and after this careful reconstruction, would be removed from the analysis.

The number of components within the small category is 8246, by far a large fraction of the total number of components. Thus we see that the fly specks algorithm is a crucial first step in reducing the human complexity of the algorithm.

We show typical "fly specks" in Figs. 5 and 6

Surface Mesh Quality. Next we eliminate edges too small or too large. The large/small edge elimination is through a queue of large and small edges. The small edges are collapsed to a point, thereby reducing two triangles with this common edge to become edges themselves. Similarly, the edges too large are bisected by the insertion of a new point at the edge midpoint, thereby replacing two triangles having a common edge with four triangles having two common edges. These two operations are the inverse of one another, and in combination, will keep the side length ratios between triangles or within a single triangle within the range $[0.5, 2]$. Thus bad aspect ratios are also eliminated. The algorithm is similar to the volume mesh quality algorithm, previously described [6], so we omit further details.

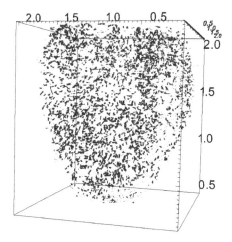

Fig. 5. The totality of all small components shows only low levels of coherent structure, and is regarded as "noise" in the present context. Units in cm.

Surface Mesh Verification. The first check for surface quality is to ensure that the surface has no non-manifold edge. These are edges which border three or more triangles. The non-manifold search is automated, but repair is manual. An absence of holes in the cardiac surfaces is ensured by the same marching front algorithm discussed above.

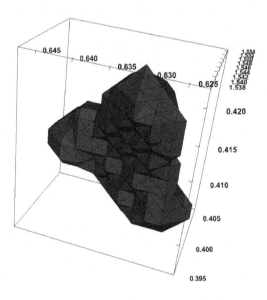

Fig. 6. A typical small component is shown.

We require that the entire cardiac surface consists of inner and outer wall, each without gaps and multiple fragments of artery and vein networks. Nonmanifold segments have been removed.

2.3   Vessel Wall Thickness

The segmentation yields the inner wall of the blood vessel only. Experimental correlations establish a vessel wall thickness according to its diameter and whether it is a vein or an artery. For the 142 large components, the distinction is based on expert knowledge.

As discussed in [6], the outer blood vessel wall surface is constructed as the solution of a dynamic equation

$$\frac{dx(t)}{dt} = -\mathbf{n} \tag{8}$$

to "grow" the inner surface in the direction $-\mathbf{n}$. The $\mathbf{n}$ is oriented outward relative to the cardiac tissue and so $-\mathbf{n}$ is outward relative to the blood vessel. $x(0)$ is some node of a triangle on the inner blood vessel wall, as initial conditions for (8), and the final time for this equation is set by the wall thickness. The dynamics of (8) are stable for outward growth of convex surface which is the normal case for the construction of the outer blood vessel wall from the inner wall. At branching points, where the veins divide, the inner surface is concave and the outward dynamics is unstable. Conceptually, consider a closed polygon in 2D to be propagated inward. If some of the vertex angles are sharp as with an elongated diamond shape, the points on the short axis can self intersect under inward propagation with a finite step size. Locations generating self intersections are characterized sharp surface angles and vertices or small triangles. The self intersections are resolved incrementally within the algorithm. If the local surface is concave, the stable version of this algorithm forces the outward growing surface to be single valued in infinitesimal steps.

2.4   Volume Mesh

The public domain algorithm TetGen will construct a volume mesh which respects a given surface mesh [15]. However the mesh quality can be poor and the resulting discretized equations cannot be solved by the finite element method. Our mesh quality improvement algorithm was discussed in [6]. To improve the mesh quality, we make a list of problem mesh volume elements, and introduce an algorithm which will improve the local mesh in each of the several cases.

As with the surface mesh quality algorithm, the volume mesh quality is based on a queue of bad element edges. The bad edges are either too large or too small, and are eliminated by addition of a midpoint with two new triangle facets of four new tetrahedrons or the inverse operation, by collapse of an edge, combining two facing facets into an edge and four tetrahedrons into a single tetrahedron. As in the case of the edge mesh quality algorithm, the resulting edge ratios are consistent within a factor of 2. Because this edge ratio criterion has already been enforced for the surface mesh, the volume mesh will never divide an edge which is part of the surface mesh. Thus the surface mesh is not modified as part of the volume mesh quality algorithm.

2.5   Fiber Orientation

At least during the application of the shock, a bidomain conductivity model is needed, in which the electrical currents occur simultaneously within the fibers defining the cardiac cells and in the extracellular space that surrounds the fibers. The fibers are much finer that any feasible mesh resolution, so that within any mesh cell, both regions will occur. The resulting diffusion tensor then has distinguished properties along a single direction (the fiber direction). Thus to complete the specification of the equations, the fiber orientation must be specified in every mesh cell. The limited experimental data for the fibers will establish general properties of the fiber orientation, but not its cell by cell orientation. Thus a software model, informed by the limited experimental data, is used to fill in the required fiber orientation at the mesh cell level [16]. The wrapping of fibers around and not terminating at blood vessels is discussed in [11].

3   Ionic Model

A number of models of the ionic currents have been proposed at differing levels of completeness and complexity [17,18]. The canine ventricular cell model of Flaim et al. [19] includes as many as 87 variables, the Bondarenko et al. model [20] involves more that 100 variables. Although these complex models reproduce existing experimental results through careful selection of parameters, high parameter numbers often affect model robustness and introduce inconsistencies between models of the same animal species and specific regions of the heart [21], not to mention their computational expenses. Several reduced models have been proposed [22–25]. In the Fenton-Karma (FK) model [24],

$$I_{\text{ion}}\left(\phi, \mathbf{y}\right) = I_{\text{fi}}\left(\phi, v\right) + I_{\text{so}}\left(\phi\right) + I_{\text{si}}\left(\phi, w\right), \tag{9}$$

where I_{fi}, I_{so} and I_{si} denote the fast-inward, slow-outward, and slow-inward ionic currents respectively, and $\mathbf{y} = (v, w)$ is the vector of gate variables controlling the fast- and slow-inward components. The FK three-variable model is widely used, due to its capability to maintain most of the quantitative properties of the more complicated models, while reducing the computational complexity significantly [17]. These properties have made the FK model popular in a wide range of studies, including vortex dynamics in the myocardium [24], mechanisms for discordant alternate [26], temperature effects [27,28] and the promising field of low-energy defibrillation [29,30]. These models and the more complicated Mahajan model [31], which has been calibrated to experimental data for the rabbit, are known not to allow a sustained fibrillation state. For this reason, following [3], we introduce an enhanced CA^{++} channel, with a parameter denoted R into into the model [31], which is believed to allow sustained fibrillation and a more accurate model of defibrillation.

4   Discussion

A combination of publicly available software tools with new algorithms described here and in [6] allow the construction of a detailed cardio-vascular mesh and finite element software model. The main point of the construction is to avoid prohibitive levels of human involvement in the construction. For this purpose, manual aspects of the construction are kept to a minimum.

The detailed mesh allows definitive studies of the importance (or not) of small features in the LEAP defibrillation protocol. The current data is for a rabbit. The authors believe that the same methods allow finite element models of a human heart, based on high resolution MRI data.

The optimal balance between efforts assigned to the various software stages remains to be explored. For example, automated but stronger segmentation algorithms appear to be a possibility.

Acknowledgements. This work is supported in part by the National Science Foundation grant NSF CPS-1446832.

References

1. Centers for Disease Control and Prevention: State-specific mortality from sudden cardiac death-united states, 1999. MMWR Morb. Mortal. Wkly. Rep. **51**(6), 123 (2002)
2. Cherry, E.M., Fenton, F.H., Gilmour, R.F.: Mechanisms of ventricular arrhythmias: a dynamical systems-based perspective. Am. J. Physiol. Heart Circ. Physiol. **302**(12), 2451–2463 (2012)
3. Bishop, M., Plank, G.: The role of fine-scale atonomical structure in the dynamics of reentry in computational models of the rabbit ventricles. J. Physiol. **18**, 4515–4535 (2012)
4. Bishop, M.J., Plank, G., Vigmond, E.: Investigating the role of coronary vasculature in the mechanisms of defibrillation. Circ. Arrthymia Electrophysiol. **5**(1), 210–219 (2012)
5. Bishop, M., Boyle, P.M., Plank, G., Walsh, D.G., Vigmond, E.: Modeling the role of the cornary vasclature during external field simulation. IEEE Trans. Biomed. Eng. **10**, 2335–2345 (2010)
6. Lim, H., Cun, W., Wang, Y., Gray, R., Glimm, J.: The role of conductivity discontinuities in design of cardiac defibrillation. Chaos **28**, 013106 (2018)
7. Mirams, G.R., Arthurs, C.J., Bernabeu, M.O., et al.: Chaste: an open source C++ library for computational physiology and biology. PLoS Comput. Biol. **9**(3), e1002970 (2013)
8. Pathmanathan, P., Gray, R.A.: Verification of computational models of cardiac electro-physiology. Int. J. Numer. Methods Biomed. Eng. **30**(5), 525–544 (2014)
9. Pathmanathan, P., et al.: A numerical guide to the solution of the bidomain equations of cardiac electrophysiology. Int. Prog. Biophys. Mol. Biol. **102**(2–3), 136–155 (2010)
10. Clayton, R.H., et al.: Models of cardiac tissue electrophysiology: progress, challenges and open questions. Int. Prog. Biophys. Mol. Biol. **104**(1), 22–48 (2011)
11. Bishop, M., Boyle, P., Plank, G., Vigmond, E.: Modeling the role of coronary vasculature during external field stimulation. IEEE Trans, Biomed. Eng. **57**, 2335–2345 (2010)
12. Bishop, M.J., Plank, G., Burton, R.A.B., Schneider, J.E., Gavaghan, D.J., Grau, P.K.V.: Development of an anatomically detailed mri-derived rabbit ventricular model and assessment of its impact on simulations of electrophysiological function. Am. J. Physiol. Heart Circ. Physiol. **298**(2), H699–H718 (2010)
13. Lorensen, W.E., Cline, H.E.: Marching cubes: a high resolution 3D surface construction algorithm. Comput. Graph. **21**(4), 163–169 (1987)
14. Lindquist, W.B., Lee, S.-M., Coker, D.A., Jones, K.W., Spanne, P.: Medial axis analysis of void structure in three-dimensional tomographic images of porous media. J. Geophys. Res. **101B**, 8297–8310 (1996)
15. Si, H.: TetGen, a Delaunay-based quality tetrahedral mesh generator. ACM Trans. Math. Softw. **41**(2), 11:1–11:36 (2015)
16. Bayer, J.D., Blake, R.C., Plank, G., Trayanova, N.A.: A novel rule-based algorithm for assigning myocardial fiber orientation to computational heart models. Ann. Biomed Eng. **40**(10), 2243–2254 (2012)
17. Fenton, F., Cherry, E.: Models of cardiac cell. Scholarpedia **3**(8), 1868 (2008)
18. Lloyd, C.M., Lawson, J.R., Hunter, P.J., Nielsen, P.F.: The CellML model repository. Bioinformatics **24**(18), 2122–2123 (2008)

19. Flaim, S.N., Giles, W.R., McCulloch, A.D.: Contributions of sustained INa and IKv43 to transmural heterogeneity of early repolarization and arrhythmogenesis in canine left ventricular myocytes. Am. J. Physiol. Heart. Circ. Physiol. **291**(6), 2617–2629 (2006)
20. Bondarenko, V.E., Bett, G.C.L., Rasmusson, R.L.: A model of graded calcium release and L-type Ca2+ channel inactivation in cardiac muscle. Am. J. Physiol. Hear. Circ. Physiol. **286**(3), 1154–1169 (2004)
21. Cherry, E.M., Fenton, F.H.: A tale of two dogs: analyzing two models of canine ventricular electrophysiology. Am. J. Physiol. Heart Circ. Physiol. **292**(1), 43–55 (2007)
22. Mitchell, C.C., Schaeffer, D.G.: A two-current model for the dynamics of cardiac membrane. Bull. Math. Biol. **65**(5), 767–793 (2003)
23. Duckett, G., Barkley, D.: Modeling the dynamics of cardiac action potential. Phys. Rev. Lett. **85**(4), 884 (2000)
24. Fenton, F., Karma, A.: Vortex dynamics in three-dimensional continuous myocardium with fiber rotation: filament instability and fibrillation. Chaos **8**(1), 20–47 (1998)
25. Karma, A.: Electrical alternans and spiral wave breakup in cardiac tissue. Chaos Interdiscip. J. Nonlinear Sci. **4**(3), 461–472 (1994)
26. Watanabe, M.A., Fenton, F.H., Evans, S.J., Hastings, H.M., Karma, A.: Mechanisms for discordant alternans. Comput. Fluids **12**(2), 196–206 (2001)
27. Fenton, F.H., Gizzi, A., Cherubini, C., Pomella, N., Filippi, S.: Role of temperature on nonlinear cardiac dynamics. Phys. Rev. E **87**(4), 042717 (2013)
28. Filippi, S., Gizzi, A., Cherubini, C., Luther, S., Fenton, F.H.: Mechanistic insights into hypothermic ventricular fibrillation: the role of temperature and tissue size. Europace **16**(3), 424–434 (2014)
29. Chebbok, M., et al.: Low-energy anti-fibrillation pacing (LEAP): a gentle, non traumatic defibrillation option. Eur. Hear. J. **33**, 381 (2012)
30. Fenton, F.H., et al.: Termination of atrial fibrillation using pulsed low-energy far-field stimulation. Circulation **120**(6), 467–476 (2009)
31. Mahajan, A., Shiferaw, Y., Sato, D., et al.: A rabbit ventricular action potential model replicating ardiac dynamics at rapid heart rates. Biophys J. **94**, 392–410 (2008)
32. Xue, S., Lim, H., Glimm, J., Fenton, F.H., Cherry, E.M.: Sharp boundary electro-cardiac simulations. SISC **38**, B100–B117 (2016)
33. Krassowska, W.: Effects of electroporation on transmembrane potential induced by defibrillation shocks. Pacing Clin. Electrophysiol. **18**, 1644–1660 (1995)
34. Cheng, D.K., Tung, L., Sobie, E.A.: Nonuniform responses of transmembrane potential during electric field stimulation of single cardiac cells. Am. J. Physiol. Heart Circ. Physiol. **277**, H351–H362 (1999)
35. Ashihara, T., Trayanova, N.A.: Asymmetry in membrane responses to electric shocks: insights from bidomain simulations. Biophys. J. **87**, 2271–2282 (2004)

Program Analysis

Formalizing Requirements Is ◊□ Hard

Gerard J. Holzmann[✉]

Nimble Research, Monrovia, CA 91016, USA
gh@nimbleresearch.com

Abstract. The use of formal methods in software engineering requires that the user adopt a suitable level of precision in the description of both design artifacts and the properties that should hold for those artifacts. The level of precision must be sufficiently high that the logical consistency of the design and the logic properties can be verified mechanically.

The source code of any well-defined program is itself a formal object, although it typically contains more detail than desirable for effective analysis. But, practitioners often have no problem producing or recognizing an abstracted version of the key features of a design, expressed in the modeling language of a verification tool.

The real problem preventing a broader acceptance of formal methods is that there are no intuitive formalisms that practitioners can use to express logic requirements at the level of precision that is required for formal verification. That problem is the focus of this paper.

Keywords: Software verification · Logic model checking ·
Temporal logic · Rule based specification

1 Introduction

Some claim that all defects in software products find their root cause in misstated requirements, e.g., [1]. Industrial software development processes typically start with a requirements elicitation process, with requirements captured in English prose documents. The requirements are meant to be understood with some ease by software developers, who can fill in gaps and resolve cases of ambiguity by using common sense and experience. But, as we know, this process can lead to problems.

A formal methods based process requires us to make things sufficiently precise that requirements and a suitably abstract representation of the code can be checked for their logicall consistency by purely mechanical means: by an algorithm. We will side-step the question here what the best way is to produce this magical "suitably abstract representation" of the code, and for convenience consider this a solved problem for now. What we would like to focus on is the difficulty of turning ambiguously and incompletely stated requirements into precise logic statements that can be verified mechanically.

E. Bartocci et al. (Eds.): From Reactive Systems to Cyber-Physical Systems, LNCS 11500, pp. 51–56, 2019.
https://doi.org/10.1007/978-3-030-31514-6_4

2   The Charm of Informality

"When you pick up the phone, you get a dialtone". Unfortunately, the relevance of this informal requirement is familiar only to a rapidly shrinking audience, but for those of us with longer memories, the meaning of the statement will be clear. The English text, though, is not precise enough for use in any formal verification tool.

Pnueli was the first to point out, in 1977 [2], that statements like these can be stated more precisely in temporal logic. A first attempt to do so can then look as follows:

offhook → ◇ dialtone

where the right arrow → stands for logical implication, and the diamond operator ◇ is pronounced "eventually." But that formalization needs quite a bit more work before it could be considered correct.

The statement has precisely defined semantics that can roughly be summarized as saying: "either the phone is not offhook now (i.e., in the *initial* state of the system we are considering) or it must be true that now or at some point in the future a dialtone will be present." And, that's not what we meant.

A first improvement is to make it clear that the property should not just hold when coincidentally the phone happens to be offhook in the initial state, but it should hold at any time. That leads to this version:

□ (offhook → ◇ dialtone)

This is better, but still not quite right. Note that the property will be satisfied even if the dialtone is already present in the very state that the phone goes offhook. That takes away the cause and effect that we would like to verify, so we have to separate the effect from the cause. That leads to this version:

□ (offhook → X ◇ dialtone)

where we used the X symbol to represent the "next" operator, as we do in the Spin model checker [4].

Are we done now? No, not really. For a more complete statement we may also have to state that the dialtone should *not* be generated unless there was an offhook event first, and it also need not be generated if the offhook event is followed by an onhook event before the dialtone appears. Then we haven't said anything about the requirement that the dialtone should be generated within the first few milliseconds after the offhook event, and it should disappear after the first digit is dialed.

Once we are done with a precise statement of this still relatively simple requirement, any user uninitiated in the use of temporal logic is unlikely to recognize the statement, nor would that user be likely to produce it.

2.1 Visualizing Requirements

One way to address these problems is to build tools that can visualize requirements in a more intuitive way, leaving it to a tool to synthesize the correct
formalization of the requirement with all subtleties properly addressed.

One such tool that we experimented with long ago is the timeline editor [3].
The editor allowed users to place events of interest on a timeline, and to annotate
that timeline with various types of constraints that can span overlapping periods
of time. The tool could convert the specifications into Büchi automata, which
could then be used directly in a logic model checking tool such as Spin [4].
A specification of the dialtone property is illustrated in Fig. 1.

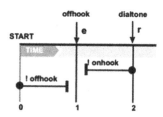

Fig. 1. Visual formalism for specifying temporal logic properties from [3].

The use of a visual formalism as shown here does still have limitations. One
main drawback is, for instance, that the visual formalism is not expressive enough
to specify everything that can be specified in temporal logic.

But then again, also temporal logic is not expressive enough to formalize all
types of requirements that may be encountered in practice. The next section will
give an example.

3 Graphs and Sets

The following example property is inspired by [6].

Consider a graph where each node represents a lock. There is an edge in
the graph from node a to node b if at any time during an execution a thread
holds lock a while it acquires lock b. If this graph contains a cycle, there is a
potential for a deadlock scenario. Two events are of interest: $acquire(t, a)$, which
represents the acquisition of lock a by thread t, and $release(t, a)$, which represents
the release of lock a by thread t.

The property of interest is that in any given run of the system, the lock graph
as defined above is acyclic. How can we express this formally?

The first problem we have is that basic temporal logic does not have variables,
and it does not allow us to *bind* variables to symbols. If, for instance, we wanted
to state that every time lock a is acquired it is also released, we have to be able
to correlate the a from the *release* event with the a from the corresponding
acquire event. We may not know a priori which lock names might be used.

There have been a few attempts to explore extensions of temporal logic in model checkers, but the restrictions are usually non-trivial, cf. [5]. But even if we allow for variable binding, and add quantification, it is still very hard to talk about the existence of a cycle in a graph of unknown size.

It is possible to state a highly simplified version of the problem, if we restrict the problem to two threads and two locks only, by saying:

$$\forall t_1, t_2, l_1, l_2 \cdot$$

$$\square \left(\left(\text{ aquire}(t_1, l_1) \wedge \left(\neg \text{ release}(t_1, l_1) \text{ U aquire}(t_1, l_2) \right) \right) \rightarrow$$
$$\square \neg \left(\text{ aquire}(t_2, l_2) \wedge \left(\neg \text{ release}(t_2, l_2) \text{ U aquire}(t_2, l_1) \right) \right) \right)$$

The formalization is very limited, but already relies on powerful features that are not present in most systems.

A very similar specification problem would be to formalize the type of check that is performed by the Eraser algorithm [7] for detecting data races in a multithreaded program. In this case we want to maintain a lockset for every shared data object, and on every write access take the intersection of the lockset that is currently held by the writer with previous locksets. If the stored set every becomes empty we know there is a problem.

Here too the check asks us to track and update data, this time not in the form of a graph but as a set of sets (one for each shared data object). Temporal logic is clearly not equipped to handle this, but the question is: what type of formal specification could do so elegantly?

One method, described in the context of runtime verification tools, in an early draft of [6], is to use rule-based checks. We then minimally need the basic operations to insert or remove items from sets, and to check for set membership. Basic events like *aquire* and *release* then trigger set operations. Next we can define a set of rules to deduce facts of interest from the stored sets, e.g. using the Rete algorithm [8].

Writing properties in this way requires a change in perspective. Rather than a logic-based approach we now have a more operational view. Basically, we are writing a program to perform the checks we are interested in, though at a relatively high level of abstraction.

The deadlock problem we started this section with can be formalized in the following five rules (with minor edits, from the draft of [6]):

1. $\text{acquire}(t, l) \rightarrow \text{insert}(\text{Locked}(t, l))$
2. $\text{release}(t, l) \rightarrow \text{remove}(\text{Locked}(t, l))$
3. $\text{Locked}(t, l_1) \wedge \text{acquire}(t, l_2) \rightarrow \text{insert}(\text{Edge}(l_1, l_2))$
4. $\text{Edge}(l_1, l_2) \wedge \text{Edge}(l_2, l_3) \wedge \neg\text{Edge}(l_1, l_3) \rightarrow \text{insert}(\text{Edge}(l_1, l_3))$
5. $\text{Edge}(l, l) \rightarrow \text{error}$

This is a remarkably succinct specification, though, like specifications written in temporal logic, it may still require a substantial effort to create.

The last two rules perform what is basically term rewriting on the generated sets. Clearly, the computation of transitive closure in rule 4 and the indirect check for cycles in rule 5 could be computationally demanding. To use this approach in a model checker, e.g., integrated with a depth-first search algorithm, we'd need to make arrangements for backtracking of changes to the constructed sets.

3.1 Rule-Based Model Checking

In principle, one could write an entire logic model checking procedure as a rule based system. After all, in standard explicit state model checking we merely construct a graph and check for the existence of specific types of cycles in that graph. There have been several attempts already to implement model checkers as rewrite systems, starting more than two decades ago, e.g. [9].

Yet, we are left with the question if rule based specification formalisms, or rewrite systems in general, are any easier to use than logic based formalisms?

4 Conclusion

There may be two factors that can explain the continuing reticence of software developers and software development organizations to adopt formal methods as a routine part of software design, even for safety critical applications as used, for instance, in cars and in medical devices. One factor is certainly the unpredictability of the demands on both human and computer time that a formal verification approach can impose. Cloud-based solutions may be able to change at least some of these trade-offs [10].

A more serious factor is that writing formal specifications is not just perceived to be hard, it actually is hard. Even expert users can be misled by the exact meaning of complex formulae stated in temporal logic. It is perhaps also telling that semi-formal methods based tools, such as static source code analyzers, that make use of predefined specifications have indeed found broad acceptance, and are routinely used in industrial software development. Routine use of these tool could be boosted still further with the advent of interactive code exploration algorithms for large code bases [11].

Logic model checking and formal program analysis techniques though seem stuck at the hurdle of making formal specification human friendly. What can we do to make formal requirements specification □◊ Easy?

References

1. Lutz, R.R.: Analyzing software requirements errors in safety-critical embedded systems. In: Proceedings IEEE International Symposium on Requirements Engineering, pp. 126–133. San Diego, CA, January (1993)
2. Pnueli, A.: The temporal logic of programs. In: Proceedings 18th FOCS, pp. 46–57. Providence, RI, November (1977)
3. Smith, M.H., Holzmann, G.J., Etessami, K.: Events and constraints a graphical editor for capturing logic properties of programs. In: Proceedings 5th International Symposium on Requirements Engineering, pp. 14–22. Toronto Canada, August (2001)

4. Holzmann, G.J.: The Spin Model Checker - Primer and Reference Manual. Addison-Wesley, Mass (2004)
5. Bohn, J., Damm, W., Grumberg, O., Hungar, H., Laster, K.: First-order-CTL model checking. In: Arvind, V., Ramanujam, S. (eds.) FSTTCS 1998. LNCS, vol. 1530, pp. 283–294. Springer, Heidelberg (1998). https://doi.org/10.1007/978-3-540-49382-2_27
6. Havelund, K., Reger, G., Thoma, D., Zălinescu, E.: Monitoring events that carry data. In: Bartocci, E., Falcone, Y. (eds.) Lectures on Runtime Verification. LNCS, vol. 10457, pp. 61–102. Springer, Cham (2018). https://doi.org/10.1007/978-3-319-75632-5_3
7. Savage, S., Burrows, M., Nelson, G., Sobalvarro, P.: Eraser: a dynamic data race detector for multithreaded programs. ACM Trans. Comput. Syst. **15**(4), 391–411 (1997)
8. Rete algorithm. https://en.wikipedia.org/wiki/Rete_algorithm
9. Clavel, M., Eker, S., Lincoln, P., Meseguer, J.: Principles of maude. In: 1st International Workshop on Rewriting Logic and its Applications. Electronic Notes in Theoretical Computer Science, vol. 4 (1996)
10. Holzmann, G.J.: Cloud-based verification of concurrent software. In: Jobstmann, B., Leino, K.R.M. (eds.) VMCAI 2016. LNCS, vol. 9583, pp. 311–327. Springer, Heidelberg (2016). https://doi.org/10.1007/978-3-662-49122-5_15
11. Holzmann, G.J.: Cobra: a light-weight tool for static and dynamic program analysis. Innov. Syst. Softw. Eng. NASA J. **13**(1), 35–49 (2017). http://spinroot.com/cobra

Invisible Invariants Are Neither

Lenore D. Zuck[1](✉) and Kenneth L. McMillan[2]

[1] University of Illinois at Chicago, Chicago, USA
lenore@cs.uic.edu
[2] Microsoft Research, Redmond, USA
kenmcmil@microsoft.com

Abstract. The method of Invisible Invariants was conceived to verify properties of parameterized systems, for any instantiation, in one fell swoop. Given a deductive proof rule for the desired property, the method calls for two steps: (1) An heuristic to generate the hypothesis of the proof rule, and (2) a method to validate the premises of the proof rule once an hypothesis is generated.

At the time of its conception, the method was carried out by model checkers based on BDDs, and both steps were performed without ever having to explicitly generate the hypotheses, which rendered them "Invisible". Moreover, initially the method was applied to generate invariants, but shortly after its introduction, it was used to generate other types of hypotheses. Nowadays, the method can be applied without BDDs, which renders Invisible Invariants to be neither invisible nor invariants.

In this paper we attempt to shed light on the fundamental ideas of the method and to argue for its applicability for a large class of infinite-state systems.

Prologue

This paper is a *Formal Method Offering* (rather than an "Invisible Offering") to Scott Smolka for his seminal contributions to the area. While the connection to Scott's work may be indirect, we hope that it is aligned in spirit.

1 Introduction

The method of *Invisible Invariants* was conceived almost two decades ago [13] to automatically verify safety of *parameterized systems* – systems consisting of unbounded many instantiations of some finite-state systems. In this paper, we would like to revisit that method in the light of subsequent developments. Our goal is to gain a clearer understanding of the principles involved and to separate these from aspects of the method that were contingent upon technologies available at the time.

The work of the first co-author was partially funded by NSF award CCF-1563393.

E. Bartocci et al. (Eds.): From Reactive Systems to Cyber-Physical Systems, LNCS 11500, pp. 57–72, 2019.
https://doi.org/10.1007/978-3-030-31514-6_5

The Invisible Invariants method falls in the general category of *deductive* proof techniques. It begins with a proof schema or rule which contains a place-holder ϕ for an unknown hypothesis. It also contains symbols for given facts, such as the initial condition Θ and transition relation $\mathcal{T}$ of a transition system. To infer the conclusion of the rule, the would-be prover must accomplish two tasks:

1. *Discover* a suitable hypothesis ϕ.
2. *Discharge* the premises of the rule by proving them valid over the system defined by Θ, $\mathcal{T}$, and the hypothesis ϕ.

For example, the proof rule INV, in Fig. 1, is a schema to show that some state property p holds over all reachable states of a system defined by the initial condition Θ and the transition relation $\mathcal{T}$. The hypothesis ϕ is an inductive strengthening of p. A good ϕ should hold at the initial state (I1), be inductive (I2), and strengthen p (I3). If such a ϕ is found, then the invariance of p over the system ($\Box\, p$) is established.

$$
\begin{array}{l}
\text{I1.}\ \Theta\ \rightarrow\ \phi \\
\text{I2.}\ \phi \wedge \mathcal{T}\ \rightarrow\ \phi' \\
\text{I3.}\ \phi\ \rightarrow\ p \\
\hline
\quad\ \Box\, p
\end{array}
$$

Fig. 1. The invariance rule INV.

The idea of instantiating a general proof schema with particular facts is at the foundation of logic. What remains elusive is the *method* to discover the unknown hypothesis ϕ and to discharge the resulting premises.

While the first task, that of divining a good hypothesis, is hard for all types of systems, the second task, of discharging the premises, is more challenging for parameterized systems, since these have to be discharged on all possible instantiations of the system. *Invisible invariants* provide a method to accomplish both tasks by resorting to finite models:

1. *Discovering* a candidate for ϕ by considering only a single finite model (for example, a system of exactly k finite-state processes, or a program with a heap containing exactly k objects). This aspect of the method is heuristic in nature. The intuition is that what works for one model *may* generalize to all models.
2. *Discharging* the premises by considering only finite models of up to a certain cardinality. This step is justified by the syntactic form of the premises and a corresponding *small model theorem* which is proved once for all cases.

The motivating advantage of this method is that both tasks can be accom-plished by well-developed finite-state methods. In the original work, the focus was on finding a strengthening inductive invariant ϕ for rule INV of Fig. 1. Both phases of the discovery of the invariant and the discharging of the premises were accomplished by BDD-based symbolic model-checking techniques. Moreover, the two phases were combined in such a way that the formula ϕ was never actually constructed. For this reason, the method was named "Invisible Invariants".

In retrospect, this technicality, of the invisibility, was perhaps the least salient aspect of the method. There was no reason in principle why the invariants should be "invisible".

In the case of INV, the unknown hypothesis ϕ is an inductive invariant. However, the general method sketched above applies to other proof rules and other sorts of hypotheses. For example, the conclusion of the rule might be a liveness property and ϕ a well-founded order on states. So it appears that invisible invariants are not only possibly visible, but possibly not invariants as well.

1.1   The Problem of Generalization

In our current view, the most important aspect of the Invisible Invariants method is the generalization from one model to all models. In fact it is far from clear that such a method is justified. The best we can do is to appeal to examples in which hypotheses derived from particular cases do work in the general case[1]. Moreover, as pointed out by Goodman [6], the generalizations we make depend on the language we speak.

In practice, our success at generalization depends on the space from which we draw our hypotheses. This is a familiar phenomenon in the domain of machine learning, where the hypothesis space is sometimes referred to as an *inductive bias* [11]. In the Invisible Invariants work, the inductive bias was carefully chosen to abstract away from the size of the model. For example, for a system of N processes, we may restrict ourselves to statements about all pairs or triples of processes. This bias reflects an intuition that, for large enough N, the feasible states of process pairs or triples are unaffected by N. In fact, for finite-state processes this is true, but it is still not enough to guarantee that a ϕ that is inductive for models of size N will be inductive for models of size $N + 1$. Our inductive bias may reflect our general knowledge or experience of proofs of protocols, but it cannot guarantee a correct generalization.

Coming back to Goodman's point, our hypothesis space is defined by the *syntax* of the assertion ϕ. For example, we may express ϕ in the form $\forall i, j.\ \psi(i, j)$ where i and j represent process identifiers and $\psi(i, j)$ is a quantifier-free formula in a suitable theory. This form provides an inductive bias. Amongst all such formulas satisfying the proof rule premises, we must choose one. We might choose the strongest, which is another inductive bias.

The form of ϕ also has a strong bearing on the problem of discharging the proof rule premises. That is, for some classes of formulas we may find that the

---

[1] That is, we justify induction by appeal to induction, a method called into question by David Hume [7].

premises lie within a decidable logic (perhaps admitting a small model theorem). This is an important consideration apart from the heuristic question of inductive bias. It is not strictly necessary for the premises to be in a known decidable fragment, since they may still be proved valid in any given instance. However, it is important to be able to determine when some premise is *invalid* in order to try a new generalization using a different model.

This framework bears a strong similarity to supervised learning (for an overview see, e.g., [16]). We have a *learner* whose job is to select a hypothesis from a given space based on observations (finite models). The *teacher* determines whether the learner's hypothesis is acceptable (the rule premises are valid) and if not provides the learner with addition data (addition models).

The original Invisible Invariants work proposed one approach to generalization. For proving safety properties, this relied on the symmetry of a set of processes and involved projecting the reachable state space onto a tuple of arbitrarily chosen processes and then generalizing onto all tuples. This approach captures the intuition of using finite models as a guide, but is not guaranteed to satisfy the proof rule premises even for a fixed finite model, since the result may not be inductive.

In this paper, we will try to present the Invisible Invariants approach in a way that brings out its full generality, and also its relation to other methods that generalize from finite models.

A difficulty in doing this is to present examples that are both realistic and concrete. Proofs of realistic systems, especially of liveness properties, would involve us in formidable technicalities that can obscure the underlying principles. For this reason, we will confine ourselves to toy examples that illustrate certain principles, with the hope that these will equip the reader to understand more substantial examples worked in the literature.

2 Modeling Systems

A proof rule such as the invariance rule INV of Fig. 1 is sound relative to a particular process formalism and allows to infer a temporal behavior of a transition system whose initial states are characterized by Θ and whose transitions are characterized by $\mathcal{T}$. In principle, the Invisible Invariants method applies to instances of proof rules, and we need not be concerned with the syntax of the process whose semantics is captured in the rule. Nonetheless, it is useful to have some process model in mind in order to understand the origin of the proof rules, and to describe examples, bearing in mind that the method is not tied to any particular process model.

We present below a model of transition systems used in various works on Invisible Invariants. The model allows us to compose processes in parallel, which will be useful for describing protocols and also certain proof constructions. The model also enables to easily define temporal properties of computations. Later we will extend the model to deal with fairness properties when reasoning about non-safety properties.

The model is based on standard many sorted first-order logic with equality. We can extend the logic with various background theories as needed to express the behavior of systems. We assume a collection $\mathcal{S}$ of primitive sorts, and a signature Σ of symbols representing constants, functions and predicates over these sorts. A Σ-structure assigns a non-empty range to each primitive sort and values of appropriate type to each symbol in Σ. A structure M is said to be a *model* of a theory T if every formula in T is true under M. Given a Σ-structure and set V of sorted first-order variables, we say an M-*interpretation* of V is a map assigning to each variable $v \in V$ a value of the appropriate sort in M. We write $\varphi(V)$ to indicate that the free variables of formula φ are contained in V. Given a Σ-structure M and an M-interpretation s of V we write $s \models_M \varphi(V)$ to indicate that φ is true in structure M, assigning $s(v)$ to every variable $v \in V$. If M is understood, we write just $s \models \varphi$. For each variable v, we assume a distinct successor variable v', and we write V' for the set of successors of variables in V. If s is an interpretation of V, then s' is the corresponding interpretation of V'.

2.1 A Basic Transition System

In the following, we fix a signature Σ, a theory T and model M of T. Similar to [10], a *transition system* is described by:

- V—a *finite* set of sorted first-order variables. We say a *state* is an interpretation of V, and denote the set of all states by Π. A first order formula $\varphi(V)$ is called an *assertion*, and a state s such that $s \models \varphi$. is a φ-*state*.
- $\Theta(V)$—The *initial condition*: An assertion characterizing the initial states. A state is called *initial* if it is a Θ-state.
- $\mathcal{T}(V, V')$—A transition relation between states expressed as a *bi-assertion* over the systems variables V and corresponding successor variables V'. A *transition* of the system is a pair of states $\langle s, t \rangle$ such that $s \cup t' \models \mathcal{T}$.

It is convenient to represent the transition relation $\mathcal{T}$ as a disjunction of *labeled transitions* of the form $\tau : \mathcal{T}_\tau(V, V')$, where τ is a label and $\mathcal{T}_\tau$ is a corresponding transition relation, and the labels occurring in $\mathcal{T}$ are distinct. We say that label τ is *enabled* at state s if for some state t, $(s \cup t') \models \mathcal{T}_\tau$. Let $\sigma : s_0, s_1, s_2, \ldots$, be an infinite sequence of states. We say that σ is a *computation* of the system if it satisfies the following requirements:

- *Initiality*—s_0 is initial, that is, $s_0 \models \Theta$.
- *Consecution*—For each $\ell = 0, 1, \ldots$, $\langle s_\ell, s_{\ell+1} \rangle$ is a transition.

For a set $U \subseteq V$, we define $pres(U) = \bigwedge_{u \in U}(u' = u)$ as an abbreviation asserting that the variables of U remain unchanged in a transition. We usually assume an idle transition $\tau_{idle} : pres(V)$ that leaves all state variables unchanged.

For the purpose of examples, we will introduce useful sorts such as integers, integer ranges and arrays as needed, without formally defining their theories. Their definitions should be easily understood from context and are not generally needed for the results we will obtain here. Where they are needed for the proof of small model theorems, we will point this out and refer to the appropriate literature.

We use $\parallel$ to denote asynchronous (interleaving) composition of transition systems. We will dispense with the definition of this operator (see [10] for details) and instead give examples of the resulting transition systems using formulas.

Example 1. Consider program SIMPLE in Fig. 2, which is a simple mutual exclusion algorithm that guarantees deadlock-free access to the critical section for any N processes. Here, N is a constant of natural number sort in the signature Σ. The constraint $N > 1$ is part of the background theory T. Thus, any model of T fixes a number of processes greater than one.

In this version of the algorithm, location 0 constitutes the non-critical section which a process may non-deterministically exit to the trying section at location 1. Location 1 is the waiting location where a process waits until the semaphore (sem) is available and then sets it to 0. Location 2 is the critical section, and location 3 is the exit section where the process releases the semaphore. As we show, the program guarantees that at each given point in time there is at most one process in the critical section (location 2).

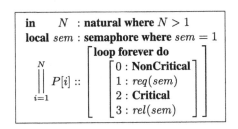

Fig. 2. Program SIMPLE

To model the system induced by the algorithm as a transition system, we define:

$$V : \begin{cases} \pi : & \textbf{array } [1..N] \textbf{ of } [0..3] \qquad / \text{ the \textbf{program counter}}/ \\ sem : \textbf{boolean}; \end{cases}$$

$\Theta : \forall i : \pi[i] = 0 \ \wedge \ sem = 1$

$T : \ \vee \ \exists i \in 1..N.$

$$\begin{pmatrix} \tau_{idle} : pres(V) & \vee \\ \tau_0[i] : \pi[i] = 0 \wedge \pi'[i] \in \{0,1\} \wedge \forall j \neq i. \ pres(V \setminus \{\pi[j], sem\}) & \vee \\ \tau_1[i] : \pi[i] = 1 \wedge sem = 1 \wedge \pi'[i] = 2 \wedge sem' = 0 \wedge pres(V \setminus \{\pi[i], sem\}) & \\ \quad \vee \ \pi[i] = 1 \wedge sem' = 0 \wedge \pi'[i] = 1 \wedge pres(V) & \vee \\ \tau_2[i] : \pi[i] = 2 \wedge \pi'[i] = 3 \wedge \forall j \neq i. \ pres(V \setminus \{\pi[j], sem\}) & \vee \\ \tau_3[i] : \pi[i] = 3 \wedge \pi'[i] = 0 \wedge sem' = 1 \wedge \forall j \neq i. \ pres(V \setminus \{\pi[j]\}) & \end{pmatrix}$$

The interleaving concurrency of the N processes is represented by the existential quantifier in the transition formula T. We explicitly include an idle transition τ_{idle}, though when it is taken, it cannot be distinguished from any $\tau_1[i]$ when the semaphore is not available. Also, note that we use a sort $1..N$ as the index of array π, where N is a parameter in Σ. This is interpreted in the background theory T, which restricts the sort $1..N$ to have exactly N elements.

2.2   Accommodating Fairness

Establishing non-safety properties or reasoning about parameterized systems require some infinitary assumptions on computations. Most notable among them are "fairness" properties that rule out some computations. Traditional fairness properties are *justice* (weak fairness) and *compassion* (strong fairness). Justice restricts to computation in which some property has to occur infinitely many times, such as "every process attempts to take infinitely many steps".

Justice can be incorporated by adding to the system a "just set" $\mathcal{J}$ of labeled transitions that cannot be enabled indefinitely and never taken. For the system of Example 1, these are all the transitions but for the idle one.

Sometimes justice is too weak to allow progress in the system. In Example 1, this is illustrated by τ_1: having this transition in the justice set would only guarantee that if the semaphore is always available it will eventually be granted. Since there are several processes competing for this resource, even if it's available infinitely many times, justice would only grant that one of the processes will get it infinitely many times, but not that each of them will.

To avoid such a "discrimination" amongst the processes, a stronger type of fairness, called *compassion*, requires that a transition is either infinitely many times taken or finitely many times enabled. We define a set $\mathcal{C}$ of compassionate labeled transitions. For Example 1, we may as well include in $\mathcal{C}$ all the non-idle transitions. For non-τ_1 transition, being "upgraded" to $\mathcal{C}$ from $\mathcal{J}$ makes no difference since, once enabled, they can only be disabled if taken.

The two types of fairness are usually kept distinct because the proof rules handling liveness under them are different, with those that have only justice being considerably simpler computation-wise. In fact, semaphore is one of the few cases where compassion is needed, and most systems can be dealt with using only justice.

While justice and compassion are the most common fairness properties, others can be defined, in particular those describing probabilistic systems [1,14,17].

Here we do not give examples of liveness properties. Yet, many liveness properties are, by nature, "bounded safety" ones. For example, a liveness property "always eventually p" may be reduced, in some systems, into "always, once every process takes k steps, p holds," which is a bounded safety property assuming, of course, that every process is always guaranteed to eventually take k steps. Then, the proof of liveness can split into two parts, one establishing a bounded-safety property assuming a particular fairness assumption, say f, and one establishing that the fairness assumption f follows from the fairness requirements. What makes this method attractive is that the fairness assumption f is often trivially implied by the justice assumptions, thus the second step is straightforward.

3   Discharging the Premises

As mentioned in Sect. 1, the Invisible Invariants method consists of two tasks, discovering an hypothesis (initially, an invariant) and discharging the premises of a proof rule using the discovered hypothesis. In this section we focus on the second task.

To discharge the premises on *BDD-based tools*, the Invisible Invariants methods calls for the hypothesis to be constructed in a language that renders the premises to be in a logical fragment with a small model property. That is, that the validity of the premises, once the hypothesis is embedded in them, can be established by checking small instantiations of the system.

In order to obtain a small model result, some restrictions on the sorts and operators used are generally required. Typically, the variable sorts are restricted to be Booleans, bounded scalars, index types $1..N$, Boolean arrays (maps from index variables to Booleans or other finite sorts) or data arrays (map from index types to other index types). The data arrays are required to be stratified (that is, the graph where each scalar sort is a node and each array induces an edge from its index sort to its value sort is acyclic).

The quantifier structure of formulas must also be restricted. Consider for example Rule INV in Fig. 1. Assume that the initial condition Θ is a $\forall$ formula, which is often the case in parametrized systems. Moreover, assume that the transition relation is a $\exists\forall$ formula in prenex normal form, and that the only operations on the bound variables are equality and inequality. (Note that all these assumptions hold for the case of Example 1).

If then an hypothesis consists of a boolean combination of $\forall$ and $\exists$ formulae (assuming prenex normal form), then the premisses of INV all have a small model property. We sketch the intuition of the proof of the existence of a small model property on the inductive premise I2 of INV, which has the most complex structure.

Suppose there is a large model that is a counterexample to I2. Then this offending model satisfies the negation of the $\forall\exists$ formula, which is an $\exists\forall$ formula. Here's a smaller model that also violates the formula: Consider the set of values the (big) model assigns to the existentially quantified variables and all values assigned to variables that are bound to them. All other values are removed. The resulting model is a smaller one that also satisfies the $\exists\forall$ formulae.[2]

The size of the small model depends on the number of quantified variables, the number of constants, and the structures allowed. For example, if i and j are index variables in the scope of an existential quantifier, then having a comparison of the type $a[i] < a[j]$ will "cost" with a larger model than if all comparisons are between i and j directly.

The small model property was generalized from equalities and inequalities to more involved relations (e.g., $i = j + 1$) and transitive closures [2–4], at a cost in the size of the resulting small model. It can even be generalized to

---

[2] This process is akin to Alice's rule in the "Mock Turtle's Story": Take care of the sense, and the sounds will take care of themselves.

some premises that are of the form $\exists\forall$ [5]. These extensions allow the method of Invisible Invariants to be applied to infinite state systems that are not necessarily parameterized such as various heap structures.

The main role of the small model property in the Invisible Invariants method is that it reduces the problem of checking validity of an application of a deductive proof rule for parameterized systems to that of checking the validity of the premises in small instantiations. The need for the small model property is rooted in the restriction to BDD-based techniques. Now, almost 20 years later, with the vast progress in automatic theorem proving and in particular SMT solving, this is no longer necessary and any tool that can establish the validity of the premises can be applied.

4   Hypotheses Discovery: Classical Invisible Invariants

As stated in the introduction, the discovery of hypotheses in Invisible Invariants has an inductive bias: that hypotheses are of a certain structure. Moreover, that they can be derived from small instantiations of the system, and generalized into larger ones. This bias is justified in the case of systems such as the one in Example 1 which is of the form $\|_{i=1}^{N}P_i$, where the P_i's differ only in their indices (i), and we want to prove some property that should hold for every $N > 1$.

Such systems have a "basic" *symmetry*: The processes behave similarly to one another. The nature of the symmetry depends on the details of the transition relation. In Example 1 the symmetry is perfect. This, however, is not generally the case. Often, the guards of the transition relation of each P_i refer to states or variables of other processes, as in containing expressions like $\forall j \neq i.\pi[j] = \ell$ or $\exists j.a[j] > a[i]$, which allows for a uniform (and symmetric) syntactic description while not a perfect semantic one.

The basic idea to discover hypotheses introduced by Invisible Invariants is to:

1. Instantiate the system to some small number of processes, say k;
2. *Project* the resulting reachable set of states onto fewer processes, say $m < k$. The projection is the strongest formula that can be constructed from the formula describing the reachable states for the k-process system restricting the vocabulary to the m chosen processes. In the simple case such as Example 1, where we have only bounded scalars (*sem*) and arrays from indexed variables to scalars (π whose range is $[0..3]$), this amounts to removing mention of any $\pi[j]$ for an index j outside of the chosen m indices. In the general case, this may be a harder task that depends on the stratification of the data structures. Modulo equivalence, there are finitely many formulas that can be constructed over the allowed vocabulary, the one which is constructed is bound to be the *strongest* over the m processes;
3. *Generalize* the projection onto arbitrary processes. The generalization is achieved by replacing the references to the concrete processes, say $p_1, \ldots, p_m$ by symbols, say $i_1, \ldots, i_m$, and adding a universal quantifier over $i_1, \ldots, i_m$

to the formula. Usually, the quantification has to be explicit about the i_j's being mutually distinct. At times, there is some ordering imposed on them.

We refer to steps (1)–(3) as *Project & Generalize*.

Example 2. Consider Example 1 and the mutual exclusion property

$$\square \, \forall i, \forall j \neq i. \; \neg(\pi[i] = 2 \, \wedge \, \pi[j] = 2)$$

we wish to prove for every N. Using the above recipe, we perform:

Step 1: We first instantiate the system to $N = 3$. The set of reachable states can be described by

$$reach : \left(\sum_{i=1}^{3} \pi[i] \in \{2,3\} \right) + sem = 1$$

that is, the number of processes in locations 2 or 3, plus the value of *sem*, is always 1. The formula we chose for *reach* is a manually obtained shorthand of what an automated tool can produce. There are many equivalent representation of *reach*, but since there are finitely many reachable states, there are only finitely many potential candidates (again, modulo equivalence).

Step 2: We next project *reach* onto a single process, say P_2. That is, we start with *reach* (or an equivalent formula describing the set of reachable states), remove references to $\pi[1]$ and $\pi[3]$, and leave the references to $\pi[2]$ and *sem* intact. For example, a state described by $\pi[1] = 0 \wedge \pi[2] = 3 \wedge \pi[3] = 1 \wedge sem = 0$ is projected onto the state described by $\pi[2] = 3 \, \wedge \, sem = 0$. The result of this projection on *reach* can be summarized by the formula $\pi[2] \in \{2,3\} \rightarrow sem = 0$. This projection is also a representation of a finite set of states and could have been written in many different (and equivalent) ways.

Step 3: To generalize the projection, we replace the index 2 by a generic i, to obtain $\pi[i] \in \{2,3\} \rightarrow sem = 0$, and add a universal quantifier to obtain

$$\phi_1 : \quad \forall i. \pi[i] \in \{2,3\} \rightarrow sem = 0$$

While invariant, when this hypothesis is used in INV, both premises I2 and I3 are not valid, implying ϕ_1 is neither inductive nor does is it strengthen the property.

The hypothesis for INV has to be an inductive over-approximation of the reachable states. The project & generalize technique attempts to discover the strongest hypothesis that over-approximates the reached states (which is not always inductive), regardless of the property whose invariance one has to prove (the p in the "$\square \, p$"). In Example 2, the derived invariant, ϕ_1, is neither inductive nor does it imply p. Yet, it is an over-approximation of the reachable states.

When a candidate hypothesis derived from the project & generalize technique is not inductive, a projection to a larger number of processes results in a smaller hypothesis that is still includes the reachable state. As a rule of thumb, it makes sense to project on at least as many processes that appear under universal quantification in the property p.

Example 3. Since the mutual exclusion property has 2 processes under universal quantification, we can attempt to compute an invariant from a projection to 2 processes, say P_2 and P_3. The projection is just like the one in Example 2, only here we ignore every variable in the reachability set that refers to P_1, namely, $\pi[1]$. We then generalize the result by replacing 2 and 3 by i and j (in whichever order), to obtain the hypothesis

$$\phi_2: \quad \forall i, \forall j \neq i. \; \pi[i] \in \{2,3\} \to (\pi[j] \notin \{2,3\} \land sem = 0)$$

which turns out to be a good hypothesis that suffices to prove the mutual exclusion property using INV.

An alternative method of narrowing a non-inductive candidate hypothesis is conjuncting it with a formula that rules out some unreachable states: Let ϕ be an non-inductive invariant and let $rest = reach \land \neg\phi$. We can then apply project & generalize to $rest$ to obtain another $\forall$-formula, say χ, and take $\phi \land \neg\chi$ as the next candidate. Note that $\neg\chi$ is a $\exists$-formula, and the small model theorem outlined in Sect. 3 still holds over the new hypothesis.

In our running example, which is somewhat trivial, this "trick" yields nothing interesting, yet, it did help in other cases. Another obvious idea we can employ is to add (conjunct) the property p to the hypothesis and test this as a new candidate hypothesis.

Example 4. Recall the property p whose invariance we want to establish and the (bad) hypothesis ϕ_1 from Example 2. Their conjunction is:

$$\phi_3: \quad \underbrace{\forall i, \forall j \neq i. \; \neg(\pi[i] = 2 \land \pi[j] = 2)}_{p} \quad \land \quad \underbrace{\forall i.\pi[i] \in \{2,3\} \to sem = 0}_{\phi_1}$$

The hypothesis ϕ_3 does render the premises of INV valid.

While the restrictions of the hypothesis in the previous two examples can be fully automated, sometimes some human intervention helps: As been observed at the dawn of formal verification, (e.g., [9,12]) history variables can make things simpler.

Example 5. A common version of the program in Fig. 2 is one where a fresh variable, say *last*, whose values in the range $[1..N]$, is added. Whenever a process enters the critical section it sets *last* to its own id. This doesn't alter the normal execution of the system since no guard depends on *last*. Its only role is to remember "the last process to have entered the critical section." With this variable, the set of reachable states is:

$$(\sum_{i=1}^{N} \pi[i] \in \{2,3\}) + sem = 1 \quad \land \quad \forall i. \; (\pi[i] \in \{2,3\} \to last = i)$$

Applying project & generalize now to a single process results in the candidate hypothesis

$$\phi_4: \quad \forall i. \; \pi[i] \in \{2,3\} \to (sem = 0 \land last = i)$$

which is a good hypothesis for INV.

For all above examples, the small model property implies that it suffices to check the premises of INV for instantiations up to size 4 to conclude the mutual exclusion property.

5   An Abstract Interpretation Discovery

The project & generalize operation can be viewed as the abstraction function α for a particular abstract domain. This abstract domain is that of *Indexed Predicate Abstraction* [8], consisting of a set of universally quantified formulas, using a set of atomic predicates built from the state variables and the operators of the background theory. We can think of the approach to hypothesis generation in the previous section as a particular strategy to arrive at the strongest inductive invariant in this domain. This view gives us alternatives to project & generalize for inferring hypotheses from finite instances, and also allows us to continue refining our hypothesis when the first attempt at generalization fails to yield an inductive predicate.

Suppose M is a model of the background theory T. This model determines the value of the system parameters. We let $\mathcal{S}_M$ stand for the finite set of M-interpretations of the state variables V. That is, $\mathcal{S}_M$ is the set of states of the system for the parameter values in M. We will say that $\mathcal{K}$, the set of *configurations* of the system, is the set of pairs $\langle M, s \rangle$ where M is a model of T and $s \in \mathcal{S}_M$. In other words, a configuration captures a parameter valuation and also a system state. We define the concrete domain $\mathcal{D}$ as the powerset lattice over $\mathcal{K}$. Let $\mathcal{L}$ be a finite collection of formulas that is closed under conjunction. For any set of configurations $K \in \mathcal{D}$, we define its *abstraction* $\alpha(K)$ as the conjunction of all the $\mathcal{L}$-formulas that are valid over K. That is,

$$\alpha(K) \;=\; \bigwedge \{\phi \in \mathcal{L} \;:\; \forall \langle M, s \rangle \in K. \; s \models_M \phi\}$$

Conversely, the *concretization* $\gamma(\phi)$ of a formula $\phi \in \mathcal{L}$ is the set of its models:

$$\gamma(\phi) = \{\langle M, s \rangle \in \mathcal{K} \;:\; s \models_M \phi\}$$

We also define a *collecting semantics* $\tau : \mathcal{D} \to \mathcal{D}$. Let the initial configurations I be the set of configurations $\langle M, s \rangle$ that satisfy the initial condition Θ. For two configurations $c_s = \langle M, s \rangle$ and $c_t = \langle M, t \rangle$, we say that $c_s \leadsto c_t$ if $\langle s, t \rangle \models_M \mathcal{T}$. Then

$$\tau(K) = K \cup I \cup \{c_t \in \mathcal{K} : \exists c_s \in K. \; c_s \leadsto c_t\}$$

The collecting semantics is defined so that its least fixed point is the set of reachable configurations.

We next generalize from a finite set of reachable system states to an inductive hypothesis using α. We fix a model M (hence fixing the parameter values) and define the concrete domain $\mathcal{D}_M$ to be the powerset lattice over $\mathcal{S}_M$. We define corresponding abstraction and concretization functions $\alpha_M(S) = \alpha(\{\langle M, s\rangle : s \in S\})$ and $\gamma_M(\phi) = \{s \in S : \langle M, s\rangle \in \gamma(\phi)\}$. We define a corresponding collecting semantics $\tau_M : \mathcal{D}_M \to \mathcal{D}_M$. Define the initial states $I_M = \{s \in \mathcal{S}_M : s \models_M \Theta\}$ and say that $s \leadsto_M t$ when $(s \cup t') \models_M \mathcal{T}$. Then we have:

$$\tau_M(S) = S \cup I_M \cup \{t \in \mathcal{S}_M : \exists s \in S.\; s \leadsto_M t\}$$

The set of reachable states of model M is the least fixed point of τ_M, which we will also write as $\tau_M^*(\emptyset)$. Our first guess at an inductive hypothesis is the abstraction of reachable states of M, that is, $\alpha_M \circ \tau_M^*(\emptyset)$. This is the strongest formula in our abstract domain that is true of all the reachable states for the particular parameter valuation defined in M. Assuming our abstract domain contains "false" ($\perp$), we can rewrite the above as $\rho_M(\perp)$, where $\rho_M = \alpha_M \circ \tau_M^* \circ \gamma_M$.

Remarkably, this is often sufficient to obtain a hypothesis that satisfies the premises of INV. The intuition behind this is that M represents some measure of the size or complexity of a uniformly defined system. Because the abstraction can capture only a finite amount of information about the system, at some point it loses the ability to distinguish the reachable states of system M from the reachable states of any larger system. That is, the abstraction must saturate for sufficiently large instances of the system.

This does not *guarantee*, however, that the hypothesis we obtain will be inductive. It may be the case that our hypothesis abstracted from the reachable states is not even inductive for the given fixed model M. In this case, we know that there is a strongest ϕ in the abstract domain that is inductive and that our guess under-approximates it. We thus continue by concretizing our guess using γ_M, producing a larger set of concrete states, and continue the reachability computation, producing a new guess $\rho_M^2(\perp)$. Continuing this process we obtain a sequence of undera-pproximations of the strongest invariant that is guaranteed to converge, since the abstract domain is of finite height.

Having obtained an inductive invariant for model M does not guarantee it being inductive for other models, that is, premise I2 may still fail. In this event, the original invisible invariants method would give up on M and move on to a larger model. The abstract interpretation view gives us an alternative: Since the abstract domain is closed under conjunction, there exists a best abstract transformer $\tau^\sharp = \alpha \circ \tau \circ \gamma$. The strongest hypothesis satisfying I2 is the least fixed point of $\tau^\sharp$. Since our guess under-approximates it, we can make progress towards the strongest inductive invariant by applying $\tau^\sharp$ to it. This gives us the following fixed point computation:

$$(\tau^\sharp \circ \rho_M^*)^*(\perp) \tag{1}$$

We alternately take ρ_M to a fixed point, and apply $\tau^\sharp$, until a fixed point is reached. This gives the same final result as if we had computed the least fixed point of $\tau^\sharp$, but may require us to apply $\tau^\sharp$ fewer times (in fact, in the best cases, zero times). This can be a major advantage, since available techniques for computing $\tau^\sharp$ require an exponential number of calls to a theorem prover [8].

For example, the method of indexed predicate abstraction as implemented in [8] computes $\tau^\sharp$ by using an eager transformation of the consecution test I2 into propositional logic and then applying ALL-SAT methods. This has two weaknesses. First, the eager encoding is incomplete, since it uses a fixed set of instantiations of the universal quantifiers. Moreover, the ALL-SAT computation may be very expensive. An alternative method introduced in [15] relies on a finite model finder to discover counterexamples to consecution and computes the abstract meet over these counterexamples until no counterexamples remain. This process may diverge in the finite model finder (if the logic does not have a finite model property) and when it terminates may be very costly, since the number of calls to the model finder is exponential in the worst case. By contrast, in the Invisible Invariants approach, it is sufficient to under-approximate $\tau^\sharp$ with a single counterexample to consecution and still make progress towards the strongest inductive invariant on the domain. Moreover, if we have a small model property, we can use it to obtain a complete reduction to SAT of the consecution test. We do not need to rely on an incomplete heuristics for quantifier instantiation.

The Invisible Invariant approach, extended as in Formula (1), can be seen as a way to use finite-state model checking techniques to make the computation of the least fixed point of $\tau^\sharp$ more efficient, by minimizing the number of calls to a theorem prover. In addition, we can also easily extend this approach from parameterized finite-state systems to infinite-state systems, as long as we can identify a suitable finite subset of the states. For example, given a program with an unbounded heap, we could arbitrarily restrict the state space to states with up to k objects in the heap, and use this finite-state system in place of τ_M.

In the Invisible Invariants method, the abstract domain $\mathcal{L}$ is finite. However, the general approach outlined above applies as well to domains of infinite height, for which a widening might be required to obtain finite convergence. Note that widening is only required in the outer iterations of Formula (1) above.

From the point of view of abstract interpretation it is interesting to note that we have computed an over-approximation (the least fixed point of $\tau^\sharp$) from an under-approximation (the reachable states for a fixed model M). Somehow we have computed the fixed point of the abstract transformer before ever actually applying it. In practice this approach often does converge to the abstract least fixed point and suggests an alternative approach to computing abstract fixed points that might greatly reduce the computational cost when the abstract transformer is computationally expensive. The only requirement for this is that we have a meaningful way to divide the infinite concrete state space into finite subsets of increasing size or complexity.

Obviously, one doesn't have to choose between the two approaches, but can use a hybrid approach, where, the classic Invisible Invariants uses symbolic techniques to generate the concrete reachability and some of the computations of α_M, γ_M, or $\tau^\sharp$.

Finally, note that the hypothesis we obtain from the abstract interpretation approach is not invisible, yet, the way it is obtained is consistent with the project

& generalize approach, which is the heart of the generation in the Invisible Invariants method.

6 Epilogue

The method of Invisible Invariants was conceived to verify properties of parameterized systems, for any instantiation, in one fell swoop. Given a deductive proof rule for the desired property, the method calls for two steps: (1) A heuristic to generate the hypothesis of the proof rule, and (2) a method to validate the premises of the proof rule once an hypothesis is generated. Any language that allows for the above conditions can be used to obtain invisible invariants.

At the time of its conception, BDD-based model checking was at its peak, and, at the time, both steps were performed by such. To that end, the systems were restricted to be expressible in (a variety) of specific languages, and the validation was heavily dependent on a small model property of the derived premises. In fact, having both generation and validation performed by BDD-based model checking allowed both steps to be carried out without ever having to explicitly generate the hypotheses, which rendered them "invisible". This was considered a great quality since, being generated by BDD-techniques, they were rather unsightly and their invisibility was part of their appeal.

Soon after its introduction, the method of Invisible Invariants was applied to other non-invariant hypothesis, yet maintaining the "Invariant" part of its name. Later it was applied so that the constructs obtained (invariant or not) by the heuristics employed were no longer invisible. In fact, the advent of SMT solving offered validating of the premises with non-BDD methods, thus alleviating the allure of their initial invisibility. We are thus left with Invisible Invariants that are neither invisible nor invariant.

Although its name is no longer accurate, the method is still appealing. It can be viewed as a case of supervised learning, where the learner suggests hypotheses and a teacher who checks whether they render the premises valid, with the learner having an bias towards a certain shape of the hypotheses that, once plugged into the premises, results the premises being decidable and checkable by the teacher. In particular, the language we chose to specify the system and the hypotheses is justified by the following considerations:

- To generate a candidate hypothesis we want to obtain a finite set of states for each instantiation of the system.
- To project, we need the abstract domain to have a finite height so to guarantee that the α computation (see below) is finite. The restrictions we chose result in a finite set of expressible predicates, thus guaranteeing an finite abstract domain, and therefore can be generalized (concretized.).
- The premises of the rules should be in a decidable logic so they can be verified.

We gave two examples of viewing the method – the "classical" one that is most often referred to, and one based on abstract interpretation that in fact generalizes the classical approach and offers new application areas.

We hope that the paper sheds light on the fundamental ideas of Invisible Invariants and will encourage their use in new cases of infinite-state systems.

References

1. Pnueli, A., Zuck, L.: Parameterized verification by probabilistic abstraction. In: Gordon, A.D. (ed.) FoSSaCS 2003. LNCS, vol. 2620, pp. 87–102. Springer, Heidelberg (2003). https://doi.org/10.1007/3-540-36576-1_6
2. Balaban, I., Pnueli, A., Sa'ar, Y., Zuck, L.D.: Verification of multi-linked heaps. J. Comput. Syst. Sci. **78**(3), 853–876 (2012)
3. Balaban, I., Pnueli, A., Zuck, L.D.: Shape analysis by predicate abstraction. In: Cousot, R. (ed.) VMCAI 2005. LNCS, vol. 3385, pp. 164–180. Springer, Heidelberg (2005). https://doi.org/10.1007/978-3-540-30579-8_12
4. Balaban, I., Pnueli, A., Zuck, L.D.: Shape analysis of single-parent heaps. In: Cook, B., Podelski, A. (eds.) VMCAI 2007. LNCS, vol. 4349, pp. 91–105. Springer, Heidelberg (2007). https://doi.org/10.1007/978-3-540-69738-1_7
5. Fang, Y., McMillan, K.L., Pnueli, A., Zuck, L.D.: Liveness by invisible invariants. In: Najm, E., Pradat-Peyre, J.-F., Donzeau-Gouge, V.V. (eds.) FORTE 2006. LNCS, vol. 4229, pp. 356–371. Springer, Heidelberg (2006). https://doi.org/10.1007/11888116_26
6. Goodman, N.: Fact Fiction and Forecast, 4th edn. Harvard University Press, Cambridge (1983)
7. Hume, D.: Treatise of Human Nature. Clarendon Press, Oxford (1888). Edited by L. A Selby Bigge. Originally published 1739–1740
8. Lahiri, S.K.: Ubounded system verification using decision procedure and predicate abstraction. Ph.D. thesis, Carnegie Mellon University (2004)
9. Lamport, L.: Proving the correctness of multiprocess programs. IEEE Trans. Softw. Eng. **SE-3**, 2:125–143, 3 (1977)
10. Manna, Z., Pnueli, A.: Temporal Verification of Reactive Systems: Safety. Springer, New York (1995). https://doi.org/10.1007/978-1-4612-4222-2
11. Mitchell, T.M.: The need for biases in learning generalizations, Technical report (1980)
12. Owicki, S., Gries, D.: Verifying properties of parallel programs: an axiomatic approach. Commun. ACM **19**(5), 279–285, 5 (1976)
13. Pnueli, A., Ruah, S., Zuck, L.: Automatic deductive verification with invisible invariants. In: Margaria, T., Yi, W. (eds.) TACAS 2001. LNCS, vol. 2031, pp. 82–97. Springer, Heidelberg (2001). https://doi.org/10.1007/3-540-45319-9_7
14. Pnueli, A., Zuck, L.D.: Probabilistic verification by tableaux. In: Proceedings of the Symposium on Logic in Computer Science (LICS 1986), Cambridge, Massachusetts, USA, 16–18 June 1986, pp. 322–331 (1986)
15. Reps, T., Sagiv, M., Yorsh, G.: Symbolic implementation of the best transformer. In: Steffen, B., Levi, G. (eds.) VMCAI 2004. LNCS, vol. 2937, pp. 252–266. Springer, Heidelberg (2004). https://doi.org/10.1007/978-3-540-24622-0_21
16. Russell, S.J., Norvig, P.: Artificial Intelligence: A Modern Approach, 3rd edn. Pearson Education Limited, London (2014)
17. Zuck, L., Pnueli, A., Kesten, Y.: Automatic verification of probabilistic free choice. In: Cortesi, A. (ed.) VMCAI 2002. LNCS, vol. 2294, pp. 208–224. Springer, Heidelberg (2002). https://doi.org/10.1007/3-540-47813-2_15

A Refinement Proof
for a Garbage Collector

Klaus Havelund[1(✉)] and Natarajan Shankar[2]

[1] Jet Propulsion Laboratory, California Institute of Technology, Pasadena, USA
`klaus.havelund@jpl.nasa.gov`
[2] Computer Science Laboratory, SRI International, Menlo Park, USA

Abstract. We describe how the PVS theorem prover has been used to verify a safety property of a widely studied garbage collection algorithm. The safety property asserts that *"nothing but garbage is ever collected"*. The garbage collection algorithm and its composition with the user program can be regarded as a concurrent system with two processes working on a shared memory. Such concurrent systems can be encoded in PVS as state transition systems using a model similar to TLA [16]. The safety criterion is formulated as a refinement and proved using refinement mappings. Russinoff [19] originally verified the algorithm in the Boyer-Moore prover, but his proof was not based on refinement. Furthermore, the safety property formulation required a glass box view of the algorithm. Using refinement, however, the safety criterion makes sense independent of the garbage collection algorithm. As a by-product, we encode a version of the theory of refinement mappings in PVS. The paper reflects substantial work that was done over two decades ago, but which is still relevant.

1 Introduction

Russinoff [19] used the Boyer-Moore theorem prover to verify a safety property of a *mark–and–sweep* garbage collection algorithm originally suggested by Ben-Ari [3]. The garbage collector and its composition with a user program is regarded as a concurrent system with both processes working on a common shared memory. The collector uses a colouring (marking) technique to iteratively colour all accessible nodes *black* while leaving garbage nodes *white*. When the colouring has stabilized, all the white nodes can be collected and placed in the free list.

An initial version of the algorithm was first proposed by Dijkstra, Lamport, Martin, Scholten, and Steffens [6] as an exercise in organizing and verifying the cooperation of concurrent processes. Their solution involved three colours. Ben-Ari improved this algorithm so as to use only two colours while simplifying

K.Havelund – The research performed by his author was carried out at LITP, Paris 6, France (supported by an HCM grant); SRI International, California, USA; Aalborg University, Denmark; and Jet Propulsion Laboratory, California Institute of Technology, under a contract with the National Aeronautics and Space Administration.

E. Bartocci et al. (Eds.): From Reactive Systems to Cyber-Physical Systems, LNCS 11500, pp. 73–103, 2019.
https://doi.org/10.1007/978-3-030-31514-6_6

the resulting proof. All of these proofs were informal *pencil and paper* exercises. As pointed out by Russinoff [19], these informal proofs ran into difficulties of one sort or another. Dijkstra et al. [6] explained (as an example of a "logical trap") how they originally proposed a minor modification to the algorithm. This claim turned out to be wrong, and was discovered by the authors just before the proof reached publication. Ben-Ari later proposed the same modification to his algorithm and argued for its correctness without discovering its flaw. Counterexamples were later given by Pixley [18] and van de Snepscheut [20]. Furthermore, although Ben-Ari's algorithm is correct, his proof of the safety property was found to be flawed. This flaw was essentially reproduced by Pixley [18] where it again survived the review process, and was only discovered ten years later by Russinoff during the course of his mechanical verification [19]. Ben-Ari also gave a flawed proof of a liveness property (*every garbage node will eventually be collected*) that was later observed and corrected by van de Snepscheut [20].

Russinoff's correctness property is formulated as a state predicate P, which is then proven to be an invariant, i.e., true in all reachable states. In gross terms, this invariant predicate is formulated as follows. The garbage collector can at any time be in one of 9 different locations. In one of the locations, here called APPEND, the *append* operation representing garbage collection is applied to a certain memory node X, but only when this node is white. The safety predicate P is then formulated as: *"if the control of the garbage collector is at location* APPEND *and* X *is white then* X *is garbage"*. However, this formulation of the safety property does not really tell us whether the program is correct. We have to additionally ensure that the *append* operation is only invoked in location APPEND, and only on white nodes. Hence, the safety property of the garbage collector follows from both the invariance of P and an operational understanding of the garbage collection algorithm.

This observation motivated us to carry out a proof in the PVS[1] theorem prover [1] using a refinement approach, presented in this paper, where the safety property itself is formulated as an abstract algorithm, and the proof is based on refinement mappings as suggested by Lamport [16]. This approach has the advantage that the safety property can be formulated more abstractly without considering the internal structure of the final implementation. Here a *black box* view of the algorithm is sufficient. This yields a further contribution in terms of the formalization of refinement mappings in PVS. In order better to make a comparison, we also carried out a proof in PVS using the same technique as in [19]. This work was documented in [11]. In [12] we verified a distributed communication protocol using similar techniques for representing state transition systems. Our key conclusion is that techniques for strengthening invariants are of major importance also in refinement proofs, and that refinement does not remove this burden. The proof presented here was carried out over two decades ago, but was only published as a (substantial) technical report [13]. Since we still consider the work relevant, and even cited, we decided to finally publish this work.

---

[1] PVS stands for Prototype Verification System.

The paper is organized as follows. Section 2 outlines additional related work. In Sect. 3, a formalization of state transition systems and refinement mappings is provided in an informal mathematical style that is later formalized in PVS. The garbage collection algorithm is described in Sect. 4. Sections 5 and 6 present the successive refinements of the initial algorithm in three stages. This presentation is based on an informal notation for transition systems. Section 7 lists some observations on the entire verification exercise. Appendices A and B formalize the concepts introduced in Sects. 3, 5 and 6 in PVS.

2 Additional Related Work

Our proof was performed in 1996. In the same year, Gonthier [10] verified a detailed implementation of a realistic concurrent garbage collector [7] using TLP, a prover for the Temporal Logic of Actions. Gonthier's proof demonstrates that the implementation preserves a complex safety invariant with about 22,000 lines of proof. Since 1996, there have been a number of verification efforts aimed at the verification of garbage collectors. Jackson [15] used an embedding of temporal logic in PVS to verify both safety and liveness properties for an abstract mutator/allocator/collector model of the tricolor algorithm of Dijkstra *et al.* This abstract model is then refined to a lower-level heap-based implementation. Burdy [4] formalized our refinement argument in both B and Coq for the purpose of comparing the two formal systems. In Burdy's formalization, the abstract mutator already colors the target of a pointer assignment. Gammie, Hosking, and Engelhardt [9] describe the Isabelle/HOL formalization and verification of the tricolor concurrent garbage collector (similar to the one verified by Gonthier) for an x86-TSO memory model in a multi-mutator setting as an invariance proof. Many of the proofs build the cooperative marking by the mutator into the specification. When this marking by the mutator alternatively is viewed as a refinement, as in our proof, it is important to demonstrate that the refinement has not restricted the mutator so that it does not generate any garbage. It can do this, for example, by never redirecting a pointer so as to leave a node orphaned. Such a mutator would satisfy the refinement with an idle garbage collector. A correct refinement must preserve the nondeterminism of the mutator and therefore must simultaneously witness a simulation relation on the collector and a bisimulation relation on the mutator.

Several efforts cover non-concurrent garbage collectors. McCreight, Shao, Lin, and Li [17] use Coq to verify the safety of the implementation of several stop-the-world and incremental garbage collectors in an assembly language. Coupet-Grimal and Nouvet [5] embed temporal logic in Coq to verify an incremental garbage collection algorithm. Hawblitzel and Petrank [14] verify stop-the-world garbage collectors using Boogie exploiting the quantifier instantiation capability of the Z3 SMT solver. Ericsson, Myreen, and Pohjola [8] describe the verification of the CakeML generational garbage collector in HOL4.

3 Transition Systems and Refinement Mappings

In this section, we establish the formal theory for using an abstract non-deterministic program as a safety specification so that any behaviour is safe as long as it is generated by the abstract program. An implementation is then defined as a refinement of this program. The basic concepts are those of *transition systems*, *traces*, *invariants*, *observed transition systems*, *refinements*, and *refinement mappings*. The theory presented is a minor modification of the theory developed by Abadi and Lamport [2]. We first introduce the basic concept of a transition system. Specifications as well as their refinements are written as transition systems.

Definition 1 (Transition System). *A transition system is a triple (Σ, I, N), where*

- *Σ is a state space*
- *$I \subseteq \Sigma$ is the set of initial states.*
- *$N \subseteq \Sigma \times \Sigma$ is the next-state relation. Elements of N are denoted by pairs of the form (s, t), meaning that there is a transition from the state s to the state t.*

An *execution trace* is an infinite sequence of states, where the first state satisfies the initiality predicate and every pair of adjacent states is related by the next-state relation. A sequence σ is just an infinite enumeration of states $\langle s_0, s_1, s_2, \ldots \rangle$. We let σ_i denote the i'th element s_i of the sequence. The traces of a transition system can be defined as follows.

Definition 2 (Traces). *The traces of a transition system are defined as follows:*

$$\Theta(\Sigma, I, N) = \{\sigma \in \Sigma^{\omega} \mid \sigma_0 \in I \wedge \forall i \geq 0 \cdot N(\sigma_i, \sigma_{i+1})\}$$

We shall need the notion of a transition system invariant, which is a state predicate true in all states reachable from an initial state by following the next-state relation.

Definition 3 (Invariant). *Given a transition system $S = (\Sigma, I, N)$, then a predicate $P : \Sigma \to \mathcal{B}$ is an S invariant iff.*

$$\forall \sigma \in \Theta(S) \cdot \forall i \geq 0 \cdot P(\sigma_i)$$

Since we want to compare transition systems, and decide whether one transition system refines another, we need a notion of *observability*. For that purpose, we extend transition systems with an *observation function*, which when applied to a state returns an observation in some domain.

Definition 4 (Observed Transition System). *An observed transition system is a five-tuple $(\Sigma, \Sigma_o, I, N, \pi)$ where*

- (Σ, I, N) *is a transition system*
- Σ_o *is a state space, the observed one*
- $\pi : \Sigma \rightarrow \Sigma_o$ *is an* observation function *that extracts the observed part of a state.*

Typically (at least in our case) a state $s \in \Sigma$ consists of an observable part $s_{obs} \in \Sigma_o$ and an internal part s_{int}, hence $s = (s_{obs}, s_{int})$ and π is just the projection function: $\pi(s_{obs}, s_{int}) = s_{obs}$. We adopt the convention that a projection function π applied to a trace $\langle s_1, s_2, \ldots \rangle$ results in the projected trace $\langle \pi(s_1), \pi(s_2), \ldots \rangle$.

The central concept in all this is the notion of refinement: that one observed transition system S_2 refines another observed transition system S_1. By this we intuitively mean that every observation we can make on S_2, we can also make on S_1. Hence, if S_1 behaves safely so will S_2 since every projected trace of S_2 is a projected trace of S_1. This is formulated in the following definition.

Definition 5 (Refinement). *An observed transition system*
$S_2 = (\Sigma_2, \Sigma_o, I_2, N_2, \pi_2)$ *refines an observed transition system* $S_1 = (\Sigma_1, \Sigma_o, I_1, N_1, \pi_1)$ *iff for every trace of S_2 there exists a trace of S_1 with the same observed states (note that they have the same observed state space Σ_o):*

$$\forall \sigma_2 \in \Theta(S_2) \cdot \exists \sigma_1 \in \Theta(S_1) \cdot \pi_1(\sigma_1) = \pi_2(\sigma_2)$$

We have thus established what it means for one observed transition system to refine another, but we still need a practical way of showing refinement. Note that refinement is defined in terms of traces which are infinite objects so that reasoning about them directly is impractical. We need a way of reasoning about states and pairs of states. A *refinement mapping* is a suitable tool for this purpose. A refinement mapping from a lower level transition system S_2 to a higher-level one S_1 is a mapping from the state space Σ_2 to the state space Σ_1, that when applied statewise, maps traces of S_2 to traces of S_1. This is formally stated as follows.

Definition 6 (Refinement Mapping). *A* refinement mapping *from an observed transition system* $S_2 = (\Sigma_2, \Sigma_o, I_2, N_2, \pi_2)$ *to an observed transition system* $S_1 = (\Sigma_1, \Sigma_o, I_1, N_1, \pi_1)$ *is a mapping* $f : \Sigma_2 \rightarrow \Sigma_1$ *such that there exists an S_2 invariant P (representing reachable states in S_2), where:*

1. $\forall s \in \Sigma_2 \cdot \pi_1(f(s)) = \pi_2(s)$
2. $\forall s \in \Sigma_2 \cdot I_2(s) \Rightarrow I_1(f(s))$
3. $\forall s, t \in \Sigma_2 \cdot P(s) \wedge P(t) \wedge N_2(s, t) \Rightarrow N_1(f(s), f(t))$

Property 1 says that the observation of a state in S_2 is the same as that of its image in S_1 obtained by applying the refinement mapping. Property 2 says that an initial state in S_2 is mapped to an initial state in S_1. Property 3 says that if two *reachable* states (satisfying the invariant P) in S_2 are connected via S_2's next-state relation, then their images in S_1 are correspondingly connected via S_1's next-state relation.

We can now state the main theorem (which is stated in [2], and which we have proved in PVS for our slightly modified version):

Theorem 1 (Existence of Refinement Mappings). *If there exists a refinement mapping from an observed transition system S_2 to an observed transition system S_1, then S_2 refines S_1.*

We shall show how we demonstrate the existence of refinement mappings in PVS, by providing a *witness*, that is: defining a particular one. Defining the refinement mapping turns out typically to be easy, whereas showing that it is indeed a refinement mapping (the properties in Definition 6) is where the major effort goes. Especially finding and proving the invariant P is the bulk of the proof.

We differ from Abadi and Lamport [2] in two ways. First, we allow general observation functions, and not just projection functions that are the identity map on a subset of the state space. Second, in Definition 6 of refinement mappings, we assume that states s and t satisfy an implementation invariant P, which is not the case in [2]. We have thus weakened the premises of the refinement rule. Whereas the introduction of observation functions is just a nice (but not strictly necessary) generalization, the use of invariants is of real importance for practical proofs.

4   The Algorithm

In this section we informally describe the garbage collection algorithm. As illustrated in Fig. 1, the system consists of two processes, the *mutator* and the *collector*, working on a shared *memory*.

4.1   The Memory

The memory is a fixed size array of *nodes*. In Fig. 1 there are 5 nodes (rows) numbered 0–4. Associated with each node is an array of uniform length of *cells*. Figure 1 shows 4 cells numbered 0–3 per node. A cell is identified by a pair of integers (n,i) where n is a node number and where i is called the *index*. Each cell contains a pointer to a node, called the *son*. In the case of a LISP implementation,

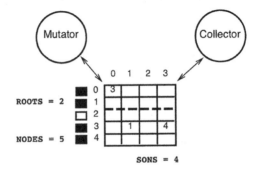

Fig. 1. The mutator, collector and shared memory

there are, for example, two cells per node. In Fig. 1, we assume that all empty cells contain the *NIL* value 0, and hence point to node 0. In addition, node 0 points to node 3 (because cell (0,0) does so), which in turn points to nodes 1 and 4. Hence the memory can be thought of as a two-dimensional array, the size of which is determined by the positive integer constants NODES and SONS. Each node has an associated *colour*, black or white, that is used by the collector in identifying garbage nodes.

A pre-determined number of nodes, defined by the positive integer constant ROOTS, are designated as the *roots*, and these are kept in the initial part of the array (they may be thought of as static program variables). In Fig. 1, there are two such roots shown separated from the rest with a dotted line. A node is *accessible* if it can be reached from a root by following pointers, and a node is *garbage* if it is not accessible. Nodes 0, 1, 3, and 4 in Fig. 1 are therefore accessible, and node 2 is garbage.

There are only three operations by which the memory structure can be modified:

- Redirect a pointer towards an accessible node.
- Change the colour of a node.
- Append a garbage node to the free list.

In the initial state, all pointers are assumed to be 0, and nothing is assumed about the colours.

4.2   The Mutator

The mutator corresponds to the user program and performs the main computation. From an abstract point of view, it continuously changes pointers in the memory; the changes being arbitrary except for the fact that a cell can only be set to point to an already accessible node. In changing a pointer the "previously pointed-to" node may become garbage, if it is not accessible from the roots in some alternative way. In Fig. 1, any cell can hence be modified by the mutator to point to a node other than 2. Only accessible cells can be modified, but as shown below, the algorithm can in fact be proved safe without this restriction. The algorithm is as follows:

1. Select a node n, an index i, and an accessible node k, and assign k to cell (n,i).
2. Colour node k black. Return to step 1.

Each of the two steps is regarded as an atomic instruction.

4.3   The Collector

The collector collects garbage nodes and puts them into a *free list*, from which the mutator may then remove them as they are needed during dynamic storage allocation. Associated with each node is a *colour* field, that is used by the collector during its identification of garbage nodes. Basically, it colours accessible nodes *black*, and at a certain point it collects all *white* nodes, which are then garbage, and puts them into the free list. Figure 1 illustrates the situation at such a point: only node 2 is white since it is the only garbage node. The collector algorithm is as follows:

1. Colour each root black.
2. Examine each pointer in succession. If the source is black and the target is white, colour the target black.
3. Count the black nodes. If the result exceeds the previous count (or if there was no previous count), return to step 2.
4. Examine each node in succession. If a node is white, append it to the free list; if it is black, colour it white. Then return to step 1.

Steps 1–3 constitute the *marking* phase where all accessible nodes are blackened. Each of these steps involves an iteration involving a smaller step that is executed atomically. For example, step 3 consists of several atomic instructions, each counting (or not) a single node.

5   The Specification

We now present the initial specification of the garbage collector. It is presented as a transition system using an informal notation. In Appendix A it is described how we encode transition systems in PVS.

We shall assume a data structure representing the memory. The number of nodes in the memory is defined by the constant NODES. The type Node defines the numbers from 0 to NODES − 1. The constant SONS defines the number of cells per node. The type Index defines the numbers from 0 to SONS − 1. Hence, the memory can be thought of a two-dimensional array, and can be declared as in Fig. 2[2].

```
var M : array[Node,Index] of Node;
```

Fig. 2. Specification state

The memory will be the observed part of the state (Σ_o – see Definition 6) throughout all refinements. For example, the node colouring structure and other auxiliary variables that we later add will be internal. Recall that an initial segment of the nodes are roots, the number being defined by the constant ROOTS. A number of functions (e.g., for reading the state) and procedures (e.g., for modifying the state) are assumed, see Fig. 3.

---

[2] The actual PVS specification shown on page 23 is more abstract and does not specify the memory as being implemented as an array. We use an array implementation here for clarity of presentation.

```
function   accessible(n:Node):bool;
function   son(n:Node,i:Index):Node;
procedure set_son(n:Node,i:Index,k:Node);
procedure append_to_free(n:Node);
```

Fig. 3. Functions and procedures used in the specification

The function **accessible** returns true if its argument node is accessible from one of the roots by following pointers. The function **son** returns the contents of cell (n,i). The procedure **set_son** assigns k to the cell identified by (n,i). Hence after the procedure has been called, this cell now points to k. The procedure **append_to_free** appends its argument node to the list of free nodes, assuming that it is a garbage node. The specification consists of the parallel composition of the mutator and the collector. The mutator is shown in Fig. 4.

```
MODIFY :
    [1] choose n,k:Node; i:Index where accessible(k) ->
            set_son(n,i,k);
            goto MODIFY
        end
```

Fig. 4. Specification of mutator

A program at any time during its execution is in one of a finite collection of locations that are identified by program labels. The above mutator has one such location named **MODIFY**. Associated with each location is a set of numbered ([1], [2], ...) rules, typically of the form p -> s, where p is a pre-condition on the state and s is an assignment statement. When the program execution is at this location, all rules where the condition p is true in the current state are enabled, and a non-deterministic choice is made between them, resulting in the next state being obtained by applying the s statement of the chosen rule to the current state. The "choose x:T where p(x) -> s end" construct represents a set of such rules, one for each choice of x within its type T. Hence, the mutator repeatedly chooses two arbitrary nodes n,k:Node and an arbitrary index i:Index such that k is accessible. The cell (n,i) is then set to point to k. The collector is shown in Fig. 5.

```
COLLECT :
    [1] choose n:Node where not accessible(n) ->
            append_to_free(n);
            goto COLLECT
        end
```

Fig. 5. Specification of collector

It repeatedly chooses an arbitrary inaccessible node which is then appended to the free list of nodes. Since the node is not accessible it is a garbage node, hence only garbage nodes are collected (appended), and this is the proper specification of the garbage collector. This yields an abstract specification of the behavior of the collector that is not yet a reasonable implementation. We need to somehow implement the selection of an inaccessible node.

6   The Refinement Steps

In this section we outline how the refinement is carried out in three steps, resulting in the garbage collection algorithm described informally in Sect. 4. Each refinement is given an individual subsection, which again is divided into a *program* subsection presenting the new program, and a *proof* subsection outlining the refinement proof. According to Theorem 1 a refinement can be proved by identifying a refinement mapping from the concrete state space to the abstract state space, see Definition 6. Hence, each *proof* section will consist of a definition of such a mapping together with a proof that it is a refinement mapping, focusing on the simulation relation required in item (3) of Definition 6. The PVS encoding of the programs is described in Appendix A, while the PVS encoding of the refinement proofs is described in Appendix B.

6.1   First Refinement : Introducing Colours

6.1.1   The Program

In the first step, the collector is refined to base its search for garbage nodes on a colouring technique. The type `Colour` is defined as `bool`, the set of Booleans, assumed to represent the colours *black* (true) and *white* (false). The global state must be extended with a colouring of each node in the memory (not each cell), and a couple of extra auxiliary variables Q and L used for other purposes. The extended state is shown in Fig. 6.

```
var
  M : array[Node,Index] of Node;
  C : array[Node] of Colour;
  Q : Node;
  L : nat;
```

Fig. 6. First refinement state

Three extra operations on this new data structure are needed, shown in Fig. 7.

```
procedure set_colour(n:Node,c:Colour);
function   colour(n:Node):Colour;
function   blackened():bool;
```

Fig. 7. Additional functions and procedures used in first refinement

The procedure set_colour colours a node either white or black by updating the variable C. The function colour returns the colour of a node. Finally, the function blackened returns true if *all accessible nodes are black*. The mutator is now refined into the program which was informally described in Sect. 4, see Fig. 8.

```
MUTATE :
    [1] choose n,k:Nodes; i:Index where accessible(k) ->
           set_son(n,i,k);
           Q := k;
           goto COLOUR;
         end
COLOUR :
    [1] true -> set_colour(Q,true); goto MUTATE;
```

Fig. 8. Refinement of mutator

There are two locations, MUTATE and COLOUR. In the MUTATE location, in addition to the mutation, the target node k is assigned to the global auxiliary variable Q. Then in the COLOUR location, Q is coloured black. *Note that the mutator will not be further refined, it will now stay unchanged during the remaining refinements of the collector.* The collector is defined in Fig. 9.

```
COLOUR :
    [1] choose n:Nodes ->
           set_colour(n,true);
           goto COLOUR;
         end;
    [2] blackened() -> L := 0; goto TEST_L;
TEST_L :
    [1] L = NODES -> goto COLOUR;
    [2] L < NODES -> goto APPEND;
APPEND :
    [1] not colour(L) -> append_to_free(L); L := L + 1; goto TEST_L;
    [2] colour(L) -> set_colour(L,false); L := L + 1; goto TEST_L;
```

Fig. 9. First refinement of collector

It consists of two phases. While in the COLOUR location, nodes are coloured arbitrarily until all accessible nodes are black (blackened()). The style in which colouring is expressed may seem surprising, but it is a way of defining a post condition: *colour at least all accessible nodes.*[3] In the second phase at locations TEST_L and APPEND, all white nodes are regarded as garbage nodes, and are hence collected (appended to the free list). The auxiliary variable L is used to control the loop: it runs through all the nodes. After appending all garbage nodes to the free list, the colouring phase is restarted.

6.1.2 The Refinement Proof

The refinement mapping, call it *abs*, from the concrete state space to the abstract state space maps M to M. Note that such a mapping only needs to be defined for each component of the abstract state, showing how it is generated from components in the concrete state. Hence, the concrete variables C, Q and L are not used for this purpose. This is generally the case for the refinement mappings to follow: they are the identity on the variables occurring in the abstract state. Also program locations have to be mapped. In fact, each program (mutator, collector) can be regarded as having a program counter variable, and we have to show how the abstract program counter is obtained (mapped) from the concrete. Whenever the concrete program is in a particular location l, then the abstract program will be in the location $abs(l)$. In the current case, the concrete mutator locations MUTATE and COLOUR are both mapped to MODIFY, while the concrete collector locations COLOUR, TEST_L and APPEND all are mapped to COLLECT. This completes the definition of the refinement mapping.

In order to prove Property (3) in Definition 6, we associate each transition in the concrete program with a transition in the abstract program, and prove that: "if the concrete transition brings a state s_1 to a state s_2, then the abstract transition brings the state $abs(s_1)$ to the state $abs(s_2)$". We say that the concrete transition, say t_c, *simulates* the abstract transition, say t_a, and write this as $t_c \ll t_a$. Putting all these sub-proofs together will yield a proof of (3). Some of the concrete transitions just simulate a stuttering step (no state change) in the abstract system. This will typically be some of the new transitions associated with *new location names* added to the concrete program. Other concrete transitions have exact counterparts in the abstract program. These are typically transitions associated with *same location names* as in the abstract program. In the following, we will only mention cases that deviate from the above two; i.e., where we add *new location names*, and where the corresponding *new* transitions do *not* simulate a stuttering step in the abstract program.

Hence in our case, MUTATE.1 $\ll$ MODIFY.1, and APPEND.1 $\ll$ COLLECT.1 (APPEND.2 simulates stuttering). In the proof of APPEND.1 $\ll$ COLLECT.1, an invariant is needed about the concrete program:

---

[3] By formulating this colouring as an iteration, we can avoid introducing a history variable at a lower refinement level. Note that any node can be coloured, not only accessible nodes. This allows a later refinement to colour nodes that originally were accessible, but later have become garbage.

collector@APPEND ∧ accessible(L) ⟹ colour(L)

It says that whenever the concrete collector is at the APPEND location, and node L is accessible, then L is also black. From this we can conclude that the append_to_free operation is only applied to garbage nodes, since it is only applied to white nodes. Hence, we need to prove an invariant about the concrete program in order to prove the refinement. In general, the proof of these invariants is what really makes the refinement proof non-trivial. To prove the above invariant, we do in fact need to prove a stronger invariant, namely that in locations TEST_L and APPEND: $\forall n \geq L \cdot \text{accessible}(n) \implies \text{colour}(n)$. This invariant strengthening is typical in our proofs.

6.2 Second Refinement : Colouring by Propagation

6.2.1 The Program

In this step, accessible nodes are coloured through a propagation strategy, where first all roots are coloured, and next all white nodes which have a black father are coloured. The state is extended with an extra auxiliary variable K used for controlling the iteration through the roots. The extended state is shown in Fig. 10. Two additional functions are needed, shown in Fig. 11.

The function bw returns true if n is black and son(n,i) is white. The function exists_bw returns true if there exists a black node, say n, that via one of its cells, say i, points to a white node. That is: bw(n,i). The collector becomes as shown in Fig. 12.

The COLOUR location from the previous level has been replaced by the two locations COLOUR_ROOTS and PROPAGATE (while the append phase is mostly unchanged). In the COLOUR_ROOTS location all roots are coloured black, the loop being controlled by the variable K. In the PROPAGATE location, either there exists no black node with a white son (i.e. not exists_bw()), in which case we start collecting (going to location TEST_L), or such a node exists, in which case its son is coloured black, and we continue colouring.

```
var
  M : array[Node,Index] of Node;
  C : array[Node] of Colour;
  Q : Node;
  K, L : nat;
```

Fig. 10. Second refinement state

```
function bw(n:Node,i:Index):bool;
function exists_bw():bool;
```

Fig. 11. Additional functions used in second refinement

```
COLOUR_ROOTS :
  [1] K = ROOTS -> goto PROPAGATE;
  [2] K < ROOTS -> set_colour(K,true); K := K+1; goto COLOUR_ROOTS;
PROPAGATE :
  [1] choose n:Node; i:Index where bw(n,i) ->
          set_colour(son(n,i),true);
          goto PROPAGATE;
      end;
  [2] not exists_bw() -> L := 0; goto TEST_L;
TEST_L :
  [1] L = NODES -> K := 0; goto COLOUR_ROOTS;
  [2] L < NODES -> goto APPEND;
APPEND :
  [1] not colour(L) -> append_to_free(L); L := L + 1; goto TEST_L;
  [2] colour(L) -> set_colour(L,false); L := L + 1; goto TEST_L;
```

Fig. 12. Second refinement of collector

6.2.2   The Refinement Proof

The refinement mapping, besides being the identity on identically named entities (variables as well as locations), maps the collector locations COLOUR_ROOTS and PROPAGATE to COLOUR. Hence concrete root colouring as well as concrete propagation are just particular kinds of abstract colourings.

Concerning the transitions, COLOUR_ROOTS.2 ≪ COLOUR.1, PROPAGATE.1 ≪ COLOUR.1, and PROPAGATE.2 ≪ COLOUR.2. In the proof of PROPAGATE.2 ≪ COLOUR.2, an invariant is needed about the concrete program:

$$\text{collector@PROPAGATE} \implies \forall r : \text{Root} \cdot \text{colour}(r)$$

It states that in location PROPAGATE all roots must be coloured. This fact combined with the propagation termination condition not exists_bw(): "there does not exist a pointer from a black node to a white node", will imply the propagation termination condition in COLOUR.2 of the abstract specification: blackened(), which says that "all accessible nodes are coloured".

6.3   Third Refinement : Propagation by Scans

6.3.1   The Program

In the last refinement, the propagation, represented by the location PROPAGATE above, is refined into an algorithm, where all nodes are repeatedly scanned in sequential order, and if black, their sons coloured; until a whole scan does not result in a colouring. The state is extended with auxiliary variables BC (*black count*) and OBC (*old black count*), used for counting black nodes; and the variables H, I, and J for controlling loops, see Fig. 13.

```
var
  M    : array[Node,Index] of Node;
  C    : array[Node] of Colour;
  Q    : Node;
  H, I, J, K, BC, OBC : nat;
```

Fig. 13. Third refinement state

The collector is described in Fig. 14, where transitions have been divided into 4 steps corresponding to the informal description of the algorithm on page 8. Two loops interact (steps 2 and 3). In the first loop, TEST_I, TEST_COLOUR and COLOUR_SONS, all nodes are scanned, and every black node has all its sons

```
- Step 1 : Colour roots
  COLOUR_ROOTS :
     [1] K = ROOTS -> I := 0; goto TEST_I;
     [2] K < ROOTS -> set_colour(K,true); K := K + 1; goto COLOUR_ROOTS;
- Step 2 : Propagate once
  TEST_I :
     [1] I = NODES -> BC := 0; H := 0; goto TEST_H;
     [2] I < NODES -> goto TEST_COLOUR;
  TEST_COLOUR :
     [1] not colour(I) -> I := I + 1; goto TEST_I;
     [2] colour(I)    -> J := 0; goto COLOUR_SONS;
  COLOUR_SONS :
     [1] J = SONS -> I := I + 1; goto TEST_I;
     [2] J < SONS -> set_colour(son(I,J),true); J := J + 1;
         goto COLOUR_SONS;
- Step 3 : Count black nodes
  TEST_H :
     [1] H = NODES -> goto COMPARE;
     [2] H < NODES -> goto COUNT;
  COUNT :
     [1] not colour(H) -> H := H + 1; goto TEST_H;
     [2] colour(H) -> BC := BC + 1; H := H + 1; goto TEST_H;
  COMPARE :
     [1] BC = OBC -> L := 0; goto TEST_L;
     [2] BC /= OBC -> OBC := BC; I := 0; goto TEST_I;
- Step 4 : Append garbage nodes
  TEST_L :
     [1] L = NODES -> BC := 0; OBC := 0; K := 0; goto TEST_I;
     [2] L < NODES -> goto APPEND;
  APPEND :
     [1] not colour(L) -> append_to_free(L); L := L + 1; goto TEST_L;
     [2] colour(L) -> set_colour(L,false); L := L + 1; goto TEST_L;
```

Fig. 14. Third and final refinement of collector

coloured. The variables I and J are used to "walk" through the cells. In the second loop, TEST_H, COUNT and COMPARE, it is counted how many nodes are black. This amount is stored in the variable BC, and if this amount exceeds the old black count, stored in the variable OBC, then yet another scan is started, and OBC is updated. The variable H is used to control this loop.

6.3.2   The Refinement Proof

The refinement mapping is the identity, except for six of the locations of the collector. That is, the collector locations TEST_I, TEST_COLOUR, COLOUR_SONS, TEST_H, COUNT, and COMPARE are all mapped to PROPAGATE. Concerning the transitions, COLOUR_SONS.2 ≪ PROPAGATE.1 whereas COMPARE.1 ≪ PROPAGATE.2. In the proof of COLOUR_SONS.2 ≪ PROPAGATE.1, the following invariant is needed:

$$\text{collector@COLOUR\_SONS} \implies \text{colour(I)}$$

This property implies that the abstract PROPAGATE.1 transition pre-condition bw(I,J) will be true (in case the son is white) or otherwise (if the son is also black), the concrete transition corresponds to a stuttering step (colouring an already black son is the identity function). Correspondingly, in the proof of COMPARE.1 ≪ PROPAGATE.2, the following invariant is needed:

$$\text{collector@COMPARE} \wedge \text{BC} = \text{OBC} \implies \neg \text{ exists\_bw()}$$

It states that when the collector is in location COMPARE, after a counting scan where the number of black nodes have been counted and stored in BC, if the number counted equals the previous (old) count OBC then there does not exist a pointer from a black node to a white node. Note that BC = OBC is the propagation termination condition, and this then corresponds to the termination condition not exists_bw() of the abstract transition PROPAGATE.2. The proof of these two invariants is quite elaborate, and does in fact compare in size and "look" to the complete proofs in [11] as well as in [19].

7   Observations

It is possible to compare the present proof (PVS_{ref}-proof) with two other mechanized proofs of exactly the same algorithm: the proof in the Boyer-Moore prover [19], from now on referred to as the BM_{inv}-proof; and the PVS proof [11], referred to as the PVS_{inv}-proof. Instead of being based on refinement, these two proofs are based on a statement of the correctness criteria as an invariant to be proven about the implementation (the third refinement step). The PVS_{inv}-proof follows the BM_{inv}-proof closely. Basically the same invariants were needed.

The PVS_{ref}-proof has the advantage over the two other proofs, that the correctness criteria can be appreciated without knowing the internal structure of the implementation. That is, we do not need to know for example that the append operation is only applied in location APPEND to node X, and only if X is white. Hence, from this perspective, the refinement proof represents an improvement. The PVS_{ref}-proof has approximately the same size as the PVS_{inv}-proof, in that basically the same invariants and lemmas about auxiliary functions need to be proven (19 invariant lemmas and 57 function lemmas). The proof effort took a couple of months. Hence, one cannot argue that the proof has become any simpler. On the contrary in fact: since we have many levels, there is more to prove. Some invariants were easier to discover when using refinement, especially at the top levels. In particular nested loops may be treated nicely with refinement, only introducing one loop at a time. In general, loops in the algorithm to be verified are the reason why invariant discovery is hard, and of course nested loops are no better. The main lesson obtained from the PVS_{inv}-proof is the importance of invariant discovery in safety proofs. Our experience with the PVS_{ref}-proof is that refinement does not relieve us of the need to search for invariants. We had to come up with exactly the same invariants in both cases, but the discovery process was different, and perhaps more structured in the refinement proof. Automated or semi-automated discovery of invariants remains a challenging research topic.

A   Formalization in PVS

This appendix describes how in general transition systems and refinement mappings are encoded in PVS, and in particular how the garbage collector refinement is encoded.

A.1   Transition Systems and Their Refinement

Recall from Sect. 3 that an observed transition system is a five-tuple of the form: $(\Sigma, \Sigma_o, I, N, \pi)$ (Definition 4). In PVS we model this as a theory with two type definitions, and three function definitions.

```
ots : THEORY
BEGIN
  State   : TYPE = ...
  O_State : TYPE = ...

  proj : [State -> O_State] = ...
  init : [State -> bool] = ...
  next : [State,State -> bool] = ...
END ots
```

The correspondence with the five-tuple is as follows: $\Sigma = $ State, $\Sigma_o = $ O_State, $\pi = $ proj, $I = $ init and $N = $ next. The init function is a predicate on states, while the next function is a predicate on pairs of states. We shall formulate the specification of the garbage collector as well as all its refinements in this way. It will become clear below how in particular the function next is defined. Now we can define what is a trace (Definition 2) and what is an invariant (Definition 3). This is done in the theory Traces.

```
Traces[State:TYPE]  :  THEORY
BEGIN
  init : VAR pred[State]
  next : VAR pred[[State,State]]
  sq   : VAR sequence[State]
  n    : VAR nat
  p    : VAR pred[State]

  trace(init,next)(sq):bool =
    init(sq(0)) AND FORALL n: next(sq(n),sq(n+1))

  invariant(init,next)(p):bool =
    FORALL (tr:(trace(init,next))): FORALL n: p(tr(n))
END Traces
```

The theory is parameterized with the State type of the observed transition system. The VAR declarations are just associations of types to names, such that in later definitions, axioms, and lemmas, these names are assumed to have the corresponding types. In addition, axioms and lemmas are assumed to be universally quantified with these names over the types. Note that pred[T] in PVS is short for the function space [T -> bool]. The type sequence[T] is short for [nat -> T]; that is: the set of functions from natural numbers to T. A sequence of States is hence an infinite enumeration of states. Given a transition system with initiality predicate init and next-state relation next, a sequence sq is a trace of this transition system if trace(init,next)(sq) holds. A predicate p is an invariant if invariant(init,next)(p) holds. That is: if for any trace tr, p holds in all positions n of that trace. Note how the predicate trace(init,next) (it is a predicate on sequences) is turned into a type in PVS by surrounding it with parentheses – the type containing all the elements for which the predicate holds, namely all the program traces.

The next notion we introduce in PVS is that of a refinement between two observed transition systems (Definition 5). The theory `Refine_Predicate` below defines the function `refines`, which is a predicate on a pair of observed transition systems: a low level implementation system as the first parameter, and a high level specification system as as the second parameter.

```
Refine_Predicate[O_State:TYPE, S_State:TYPE, I_State:TYPE] : THEORY
BEGIN
  IMPORTING Traces
  s_init : VAR pred[S_State]
  s_next : VAR pred[[S_State,S_State]]
  s_proj : VAR [S_State -> O_State]
  i_init : VAR pred[I_State]
  i_next : VAR pred[[I_State,I_State]]
  i_proj : VAR [I_State -> O_State]

  refines(i_init,i_next,i_proj)(s_init,s_next,s_proj):bool =
    FORALL (i_tr:(trace(i_init,i_next))):
      EXISTS (s_tr:(trace(s_init,s_next))):
        map(i_proj,i_tr) = map(s_proj,s_tr)
END Refine_Predicate
```

The theory is parameterized with the state space `S_State` of the high level specification theory, the state space `I_State` of the low level implementation theory, and the observed state space `O_State`, which we remember is common for the two observed transition systems. Refinement is defined as follows: *for all traces* `i_tr` *of the implementation system, there exists a trace* `s_tr` *of the specification system, such that when mapping the respective projection functions to the traces, they become equal.* The function map has the type `map : [[D->R] -> [sequence[D] -> sequence[R]]]` and simply applies a function to all the elements of a sequence. Finally, we introduce in the theory `Refinement` the notion of a refinement mapping (Definition 6) and its use for proving refinement (Theorem 1). The theory is parameterized with a specification *observed transition system* (prefixes S), an implementation *observed transition system* (prefixes I), an abstraction function `abs`, and an invariant `I_inv` over the implementation system.

```
Refinement [
  O_State  : TYPE,
  S_State  : TYPE,
  S_init   : pred[S_State],
  S_next   : pred[[S_State,S_State]],
  S_proj   : [S_State -> O_State],
  I_State  : TYPE,
  I_init   : pred[I_State],
  I_next   : pred[[I_State,I_State]],
  I_proj   : [I_State -> O_State],
  abs      : [I_State -> S_State],
  I_inv    : [I_State -> bool]] : THEORY
BEGIN
  ASSUMING
    IMPORTING Traces
    s      : VAR I_State
    r1,r2  : VAR (I_inv)
    proj_id : ASSUMPTION FORALL s: S_proj(abs(s)) = I_proj(s)
    init_h  : ASSUMPTION FORALL s: I_init(s) IMPLIES S_init(abs(s))
    next_h  : ASSUMPTION I_next(r1,r2) IMPLIES S_next(abs(r1),abs(r2))
    invar   : ASSUMPTION invariant(I_init,I_next)(I_inv)
  ENDASSUMING
  IMPORTING Refine_Predicate[O_State,S_State,I_State]

  ref : THEOREM refines(I_init,I_next,I_proj)(S_init,S_next,S_proj)
END Refinement
```

The theory contains a number of assumptions on the parameters and a theorem, which has been proven using the assumptions. Hence, the way to use this parameterized theory is to apply it to arguments that satisfy the assumptions, prove these, and then obtain as a consequence, the theorem which states that the implementation refines the specification (corresponding to Theorem 1). This theorem has been proved once and for all. The assumptions are as stated in Definition 6. We shall further need to assume transitivity of the refinement relation, and this is formulated (and proved) in the theory Refine_Predicate_Transitive.

```
Refine_Predicate_Transitive[
  O_State:TYPE, State1:TYPE, State2:TYPE, State3:TYPE] : THEORY
BEGIN
  IMPORTING Refine_Predicate
  init1 : VAR pred[State1]
  next1 : VAR pred[[State1,State1]]
  proj1 : VAR [State1 -> O_State]
  init2 : VAR pred[State2]
  next2 : VAR pred[[State2,State2]]
  proj2 : VAR [State2 -> O_State]
  init3 : VAR pred[State3]
  next3 : VAR pred[[State3,State3]]
  proj3 : VAR [State3 -> O_State]

  transitive : LEMMA
    refines[O_State,State2,State3]
      (init3,next3,proj3)(init2,next2,proj2) AND
    refines[O_State,State1,State2]
      (init2,next2,proj2)(init1,next1,proj1)
      IMPLIES
    refines[O_State,State1,State3]
      (init3,next3,proj3)(init1,next1,proj1)
END Refine_Predicate_Transitive
```

A.2   The Specification

In this section we outline how the initial specification from Sect. 5 of the garbage collector is modeled in PVS. We start with the specification of the memory structure, and then continue with the two processes that work on this shared structure.

A.2.1   The Memory

The memory type is introduced in the theory Memory, parameterized with the memory boundaries. That is, NODES, SONS, and ROOTS define respectively the number of nodes (rows), the number of sons (columns/cells) per node, and the number of nodes that are roots. They must all be positive natural numbers (different from 0). There is also an obvious assumption that ROOTS is not bigger than NODES. These three memory boundaries are parameters to all our theories. The Memory type is defined as an abstract (non-empty) type upon which a constant and collection of functions are defined. First, however, types of nodes, indexes and roots are defined. The constant null_array represents the initial memory containing 0 in all memory cells (axiom mem_ax1). The function son returns the pointer contained in a particular cell. That is, the expression son(n,i)(m) returns the pointer contained in the cell identified by node n and index i. Finally, the function set_son assigns a pointer to a cell. That is, the expression `set_son(n,i,k)(m)` returns the memory m updated in cell (n,i) to contain (a pointer to node) k. In order to define what is an accessible node, we introduce the function `points_to`, which defines what it means for one node, n1, to point to another, n2, in the memory m.

```
Memory[NODES:posnat, SONS:posnat, ROOTS:posnat] : THEORY
BEGIN
  ASSUMING roots_within : ASSUMPTION ROOTS <= NODES ENDASSUMING
  Memory : TYPE+
  Node    : TYPE = {n : nat | n < NODES}
  Index   : TYPE = {i : nat | i < SONS}
  Root    : TYPE = {r : nat | r < ROOTS}
  m          : VAR Memory
  n,n1,n2,k : VAR Node
  i,i1,i2    : VAR Index

  null_array : Memory
  son         : [Node,Index -> [Memory -> Node]]
  set_son     : [Node,Index,Node -> [Memory -> Memory]]

  mem_ax1 : AXIOM son(n,i)(null_array) = 0

  mem_ax2 : AXIOM son(n1,i1)(set_son(n2,i2,k)(m)) =
                   IF n1=n2 AND i1=i2 THEN k ELSE son(n1,i1)(m) ENDIF

  points_to(n1,n2)(m):bool = EXISTS (i:Index): son(n1,i)(m)=n2

  accessible(n)(m): INDUCTIVE bool =
    n < ROOTS OR
    EXISTS k: accessible(k)(m) AND points_to(k,n)(m)

  append_to_free : [Node -> [Memory -> Memory]]
  append_ax: AXIOM (NOT accessible(k)(m)) IMPLIES
                     (accessible(n)(append_to_free(k)(m))
                      IFF (n = k OR accessible(n)(m)))
END Memory
```

The function `accessible` is then defined inductively, yielding the least predicate on nodes n (true on the smallest set of nodes) where either n is a root, or n is pointed to from an already reachable node k. Finally we define the operation for appending a garbage node to the list of free nodes, that can be allocated by the mutator. This operation is defined abstractly, assuming as little as possible about its behaviour. Note that, since the free list is supposed to be part of the memory, we could easily have defined this operation in terms of the functions `son` and `set_son`, but this would have required that we took some design decisions as to how the list was represented (for example where the head of the list should be and whether new elements should be added first or last). The axiom `append_ax` defining the append operation says that *in appending a garbage node, only that node becomes accessible, and the accessibility of all other nodes stays unchanged.*

A.2.2   The Mutator and the Collector

The complete PVS formalization of the top level specification presented in Sect. 5 is given below.

```
Garbage_Collector[NODES:posnat, SONS:posnat, ROOTS:posnat] : THEORY
BEGIN
  ASSUMING roots_within : ASSUMPTION ROOTS <= NODES ENDASSUMING
  IMPORTING Memory[NODES,SONS,ROOTS]
  State   : TYPE = Memory
  O_State : TYPE = Memory
  s,s1,s2 : VAR State
  n,k     : VAR Node
  i       : VAR Index

  proj(s):O_State = s

  init(s):bool = (s = null_array)

  Rule_mutate(n,i,k)(s):State =
    IF accessible(k)(s) THEN set_son(n,i,k)(s) ELSE s ENDIF

  Rule_append(n)(s):State =
    IF NOT accessible(n)(s) THEN append_to_free(n)(s) ELSE s ENDIF

  next(s1,s2):bool =
    (EXISTS n,i,k: s2 = Rule_mutate(n,i,k)(s1)) OR
    (EXISTS n: s2 = Rule_append(n)(s1)) OR
    s2 = s1
END Garbage_Collector
```

The state is simply the memory, and so is the observable state. Hence, there are no hidden variables, and the projection function `proj` is the identity. The next-state relation `next` is defined as a disjunction between three disjuncts, each representing a possible single transition of the total system. The first two disjuncts represent a move of the mutator and the collector, respectively, each move defined through a function. The third possibility just represents *stuttering*: the fact that a process does not change the state (needed for technical reasons).

Since each process (mutator, collector) only has one location we do not model these locations explicitly. The function `Rule_mutate` represents a move by the mutator, which is non-deterministic in the choice of the nodes `n,k` and index `i`. The function, when applied to an *old* state, yields a *new* state, where (if `k` is accessible) a pointer has been changed. Non-deterministic choices are modeled via existential quantifications. Each transition function is defined in terms of an IF-THEN-ELSE expression, where the condition represents the guard of the transition (the situation where the transition may meaningfully be applied), and where the ELSE part returns the unchanged state, in case the guard is false[4]. The function Rule_append represents a move by the collector. In each step, either the mutator makes a move, or the collector does. This corresponds to an interleaving semantics of concurrency. Note how the repeated execution is guaranteed by our interpretation of what is a trace in terms of the next-state relation.

A.3   The First Refinement

In this section we outline how the first refinement from Sect. 6.1 of the garbage collector is modeled in PVS. In order to keep the presentation reasonably sized, we only illustrate this first refinement. The remaining refinements follow the same pattern. First, we describe a collection of colouring functions. The theory Coloured_Memory below introduces the primitives needed for colouring memory nodes. The type Colour represents the colours *black* (true) and *white* (false). The type Colours contains possible colourings of the memory, each being a mapping from nodes to their colours. The functions colour, set_colour and blackened are formalizations of those presented in Fig. 7.

```
Coloured_Memory[NODES:posnat, SONS:posnat, ROOTS:posnat] : THEORY
BEGIN
  ASSUMING roots_within : ASSUMPTION ROOTS <= NODES ENDASSUMING
  IMPORTING Memory[NODES,SONS,ROOTS]
  Colour  : TYPE = bool
  Colours : TYPE = [Node -> Colour]
  n  : VAR Node
  i  : VAR Index
  c  : VAR Colour
  cs : VAR Colours
  m  : VAR Memory

  colour(n)(cs):Colour = cs(n)

  set_colour(n,c)(cs):Colours = cs WITH [n := c]

  blackened(cs,m):bool = FORALL n: accessible(n)(m) IMPLIES colour(n)(cs)
END Coloured_Memory
```

We now show how the first refinement is formulated in PVS. The entire theory called Garbage_Collector1 is presented below.

---

[4] This allows for *stuttering* where rules are applied without changing the state.

```
Garbage_Collector1[NODES:posnat, SONS:posnat, ROOTS:posnat] : THEORY
BEGIN ASSUMING roots_within : ASSUMPTION ROOTS <= NODES ENDASSUMING
  IMPORTING Coloured_Memory[NODES,SONS,ROOTS]
  MuPC : TYPE = {MUTATE,COLOUR} CoPC : TYPE = {COLOUR,TEST_L,APPEND}
  State   : TYPE = [# MU:MuPC,CHI:CoPC,Q:nat,L:nat,C:Colours,M:Memory #]
  O_State : TYPE = Memory
  s,s1,s2 : VAR State n,k : VAR Node i : VAR Index
  proj(s):O_State = M(s)
  init(s):bool = MU(s) = MUTATE & CHI(s) = COLOUR & M(s) = null_array

  Rule_mutate(n,i,k)(s):State =
    IF MU(s) = MUTATE AND accessible(k)(M(s)) THEN
      s WITH [M := set_son(n,i,k)(M(s)), Q := k, MU := COLOUR]
    ELSE s ENDIF
  Rule_colour_target(s):State =
    IF MU(s) = COLOUR AND Q(s) < NODES THEN
      s WITH [C := set_colour(Q(s),TRUE)(C(s)), MU := MUTATE]
    ELSE s ENDIF
  MUTATOR(s1,s2):bool =
    (EXISTS n,i,k: s2 = Rule_mutate(n,i,k)(s1)) OR
    s2 = Rule_colour_target(s1)

  Rule_stop_colouring(s):State =
    IF CHI(s) = COLOUR AND blackened(C(s),M(s)) THEN
      s WITH [L := 0, CHI := TEST_L] ELSE s ENDIF
  Rule_colour(n)(s):State =
    IF CHI(s) = COLOUR THEN
      s WITH [C := set_colour(n,TRUE)(C(s))] ELSE s ENDIF
  Rule_stop_appending(s):State =
    IF CHI(s) = TEST_L AND L(s) = NODES THEN
      s WITH [CHI := COLOUR] ELSE s ENDIF
  Rule_continue_appending(s):State =
    IF CHI(s) = TEST_L AND L(s) < NODES THEN
      s WITH [CHI := APPEND] ELSE s ENDIF
  Rule_black_to_white(s):State =
    IF CHI(s) = APPEND AND L(s) < NODES AND colour(L(s))(C(s)) THEN
      s WITH [C:=set_colour(L(s),FALSE)(C(s)),L:=L(s)+1,CHI:=TEST_L]
    ELSE s ENDIF
  Rule_append_white(s):State =
    IF CHI(s) = APPEND AND L(s) < NODES AND NOT colour(L(s))(C(s)) THEN
      s WITH [M := append_to_free(L(s))(M(s)),L:=L(s)+1,CHI:=TEST_L]
    ELSE s ENDIF
  COLLECTOR(s1,s2):bool =
      s2 = Rule_stop_colouring(s1) OR (EXISTS n:s2 = Rule_colour(n)(s1))
   OR s2 = Rule_stop_appending(s1) OR s2 = Rule_continue_appending(s1)
   OR s2 = Rule_black_to_white(s1) OR s2 = Rule_append_white(s1)

  next(s1,s2):bool = MUTATOR(s1,s2) OR COLLECTOR(s1,s2) OR s2 = s1
END Garbage_Collector1
```

First of all, the state type is a record type with a field for each program variable. In addition to the ordinary program variables, there is a program counter "variable" for each process: MU for the mutator, and CHI for the collector. Each program counter ranges over a type that contains the possible labels. The observed state is still just the memory, hence ignoring, for example, the colouring C. We see that the mutator next-state relation MUTATOR is now defined as a disjunction between a *mutate* transition and a *colour* transition. The collector next-state relation COLLECTOR is defined as the disjunction between six possible transitions.

B   The Proof in PVS

The proof of a single refinement lemma (step) is divided into three activities: discovery and proof of *function lemmas*; discovery and proof of *invariant lemmas*; and proof of the *refinement lemma*. A *function lemma* states a property of one or more auxiliary functions involved, which in our case are for example properties about the functions accessible and blackened. An invariant is a predicate on states, and an *invariant lemma* states that an invariant holds in every reachable state of the concrete implementation (Garbage_Collector1 in our case). Recall that we needed such an invariant when applying the Refinement theory (page 21). The function lemmas are used in proofs of invariant lemmas, which again are used in proofs of *refinement lemmas.*

We shall show these lemmas for the first refinement, using a bottom-up presentation for pedagogical reasons, starting with function lemmas, and ending with the refinement lemma. In, reality, however, the proof was "discovered" top down: the refinement lemma was stated (by applying the Refinement theory to proper arguments), and during the proof of the corresponding ASSUMPTIONs, the need for invariant lemmas were discovered, and during their proofs, function lemmas were discovered.

B.1   Function Lemmas

During the proof, we need a new set of auxiliary functions to "observe" (or calculate) certain values based on the current state of the memory. These *observer functions* occur in invariants. In the first refinement step, we shall need the function blackened defined in the theory Memory_Observers below.

This function is similar to the function which is part of the first refinement, page 25, except that it has an additional natural number argument. The function returns true if all nodes above (and including) that argument are black if accessible. The theory contains other functions, but these are first needed in later refinements and will not be discussed here. The lemmas about auxiliary functions that we need for the first refinement are given in the theory Memory_Properties below.

```
Memory_Observers[NODES:posnat, SONS:posnat, ROOTS:posnat] : THEORY
BEGIN
  ASSUMING
    roots_within : ASSUMPTION ROOTS <= NODES
  ENDASSUMING
  IMPORTING Coloured_Memory[NODES,SONS,ROOTS]
  cs : VAR Colours
  m  : VAR Memory
  n  : VAR Node
  N  : VAR nat

  blackened(N)(cs,m):bool =
    FORALL (n | N <= n): accessible(n)(m) IMPLIES colour(n)(cs)
  ...
END Memory_Observers
```

```
Memory_Properties[NODES:posnat, SONS:posnat, ROOTS:posnat] : THEORY
BEGIN
  ASSUMING roots_within : ASSUMPTION ROOTS <= NODES ENDASSUMING
  IMPORTING Memory_Observers[NODES,SONS,ROOTS]
  cs : VAR Colours c : VAR Colour m : VAR Memory n,n1,n2,k : VAR Node
  i,i1,i2,j : VAR Index N,N1,N2 : VAR nat

  accessible1 : LEMMA
    accessible(k)(m) AND accessible(n1)(set_son(n,i,k)(m))
      IMPLIES accessible(n1)(m)

  blackened1 : LEMMA
    blackened(n)(cs,m) AND accessible(n)(m) IMPLIES colour(n)(cs)

  blackened2 : LEMMA
    accessible(k)(m) AND blackened(N)(cs,m)
      IMPLIES blackened(N)(cs,set_son(n,i,k)(m))

  blackened3 : LEMMA
    blackened(N)(cs,m) IMPLIES blackened(N)(set_colour(n,TRUE)(cs),m)

  blackened4 : LEMMA
    blackened(n)(cs,m) IMPLIES blackened(n+1)(set_colour(n,FALSE)(cs),m)

  blackened5 : LEMMA
    NOT accessible(n)(m) AND blackened(n)(cs,m)
      IMPLIES blackened(n+1)(cs,append_to_free(n)(m))

  blackened6 : LEMMA
    blackened(cs,m) IMPLIES blackened(0)(cs,m)
END Memory_Properties
```

The theory in its entirety contains other lemmas, needed for later refinements, which we shall however not present here. The lemma `accessible1` is a key lemma, and it says that the `set_son` operator cannot turn garbage nodes into accessible nodes.

B.2   Invariant Lemmas

We can now state the invariant needed for the first refinement step. This is given in the theory `Garbage_Collector1_Inv`. The invariant really needed for the refinement proof is `inv1`, corresponding to the invariant on page 13; but during the proof of that, invariant `inv2` is needed.

```
Garbage_Collector1_Inv[NODES:posnat, SONS:posnat, ROOTS:posnat] : THEORY
BEGIN
  ASSUMING
    roots_within : ASSUMPTION ROOTS <= NODES
  ENDASSUMING
  IMPORTING Memory_Properties[NODES,SONS,ROOTS]
  IMPORTING Garbage_Collector1[NODES,SONS,ROOTS]
  IMPORTING Invariant_Predicates[State]
  s : VAR State

  inv1(s):bool =
    CHI(s)=APPEND AND L(s) < NODES AND accessible(L(s))(M(s))
      IMPLIES colour(L(s))(C(s))

  inv2(s):bool =
    CHI(s)=TEST_L OR CHI(s)=APPEND IMPLIES blackened(L(s))(C(s),M(s))

  I : pred[State] = inv1 & inv2

  inv : LEMMA invariant(init,next)(I)
END Garbage_Collector1_Inv
```

Invariant `inv1` is in fact the safety property originally formulated for the garbage collector in [19]. Its proof requires a generalization, which is `inv2`. This shows an example, where we have to strengthen an invariant (`inv1`) to a stronger invariant (`inv2`), which is then proven instead.

B.3   The Refinement Lemma

The first refinement step is formulated as an application of the `Refinement` theory which we defined on page 21. This is done in the theory `Refinement1` shown below.

```
Refinement1[NODES:posnat, SONS:posnat, ROOTS:posnat] : THEORY
BEGIN
  ASSUMING
    roots_within : ASSUMPTION ROOTS <= NODES
  ENDASSUMING
  S  : THEORY = Garbage_Collector [NODES,SONS,ROOTS]
  I1 : THEORY = Garbage_Collector1[NODES,SONS,ROOTS]
  IMPORTING Garbage_Collector1_Inv[NODES,SONS,ROOTS]
  s     : VAR I1.State
  r1,r2 : VAR (I)
  n,k   : VAR Node
  i     : VAR Index
  cs    : VAR Colours

  abs(s):S.State = M(s)


  ...


  R1 : THEORY =
    Refinement[S.O_State,
      S.State,S.init,S.next,S.proj,
      I1.State,I1.init,I1.next,I1.proj,
      abs,I]
END Refinement1
```

The theory imports the specification garbage collector Garbage_Collector, giving it the name S; the implementation Garbage_Collector1, named I1; and the implementation invariant I defined in the theory Garbage_Collector1_Inv. The theory further defines the abstraction function abs, and finally applies the Refinement theory. This application gives rise to four TCCs (Type Checking Conditions) generated by PVS, which have to be proven in order for the PVS specification to be well formed (type check). Furthermore, the proof of these TCCs yields the correctness of the refinement. The TCCs are shown below:

```
R1_TCC1: OBLIGATION FORALL s: S.proj(abs(s)) = I1.proj(s);

R1_TCC2: OBLIGATION FORALL s: I1.init(s) IMPLIES S.init(abs(s));

R1_TCC3: OBLIGATION (FORALL (r1: (I), r2: (I)):
                     I1.next(r1, r2) IMPLIES S.next(abs(r1), abs(r2)));

R1_TCC4: OBLIGATION invariant(I1.init, I1.next)(I);
```

There is a TCC for each ASSUMPTION of the Refinement theory. In particular R1_TCC3 states the simulation property, and R1_TCC4 states the invariant property. As illustrated in Subsect. 6.1.2 p. X, we show for each concrete transition which abstract transition it simulates, for example we had that APPEND.1 ≪ COLLECT.1, which in this PVS setting is formulated as the following lemma.

```
sim_append_white : LEMMA
  r2 = Rule_append_white(r1) IMPLIES
    (EXISTS n: abs(r2) = Rule_append(n)(abs(r1))) OR abs(r2) = abs(r1)
```

The technique illustrated above for the first refinement step is repeated for the next two, yielding two further theories Refinement2 and Refinement3. All 3 refinements can now be composed, and the bottom level implementation can be shown to refine the top level specification using transitivity of the refinement relation. This is expressed in the theory Composed_Refinement below, where the theorem ref is our main correctness criteria.

```
Composed_Refinement[NODES:posnat, SONS:posnat, ROOTS:posnat] : THEORY
BEGIN
  ASSUMING
    roots_within : ASSUMPTION ROOTS <= NODES
  ENDASSUMING
  IMPORTING Refinement1[NODES,SONS,ROOTS]
  IMPORTING Refinement2[NODES,SONS,ROOTS]
  IMPORTING Refinement3[NODES,SONS,ROOTS]
  IMPORTING Refine_Predicate
  IMPORTING Refine_Predicate_Transitive

  ref2 : LEMMA
    refines[S.O_State,S.State,I2.State]
      (I2.init,I2.next,I2.proj)(S.init,S.next,S.proj)

  ref : THEOREM
    refines[S.O_State,S.State,I3.State]
      (I3.init,I3.next,I3.proj)(S.init,S.next,S.proj)
END Composed_Refinement
```

References

1. PVS specification and verification system. http://pvs.csl.sri.com. Accessed 03 Mar 2019
2. Abadi, M., Lamport, L.: The existence of refinement mappings. Theor. Comput. Sci. **82**, 253–284 (1991)
3. Ben-Ari, M.: Algorithms for on-the-fly garbage collection. ACM TOPLAS **6**, 333–344 (1984)
4. Burdy, L.: B vs. Coq to prove a garbage collector. In: Boulton, R.J., Jackson, P.B. (eds.) 14th International Conference on Theorem Proving in Higher Order Logics: Supplemental Proceedings, pp. 85–97. September (2001)
5. Coupet-Grimal, S., Nouvet, C.: Formal verification of an incremental garbage collector. J. Logic Comput. **13**(6), 815–833 (2003)
6. Dijkstra, E.W., Lamport, L., Martin, A., Scholten, C.S., Steffens, E.F.M.: On-the-fly garbage collection: an exercise in cooperation. ACM **21**(11), 966–975 (1978)

7. Doligez, D., Gonthier, G.: Portable, unobtrusive garbage collection for multiprocessor systems. In: Proceedings of the 21st ACM SIGPLAN-SIGACT Symposium on Principles of Programming Languages, pp. 70–83. ACM (1994)

8. Sandberg Ericsson, A., Myreen, M.O., Åman Pohjola, J.: A verified generational garbage collector for CakeML. In: Ayala-Rincón, M., Muñoz, C.A. (eds.) ITP 2017. LNCS, vol. 10499, pp. 444–461. Springer, Cham (2017). https://doi.org/10.1007/978-3-319-66107-0_28

9. Gammie, P., Hosking, A.L., Engelhardt, K.: Relaxing safely: verified on-the-fly garbage collection for x86-tso. In: ACM SIGPLAN Notices, vol. 50, pp. 99–109. ACM (2015)

10. Gonthier, G.: Verifying the safety of a practical concurrent garbage collector. In: Alur, R., Henzinger, T.A. (eds.) CAV 1996. LNCS, vol. 1102, pp. 462–465. Springer, Heidelberg (1996). https://doi.org/10.1007/3-540-61474-5_103

11. Havelund, K.: Mechanical verification of a garbage collector. In: Rolim, J., et al. (eds.) IPPS 1999. LNCS, vol. 1586, pp. 1258–1283. Springer, Heidelberg (1999). https://doi.org/10.1007/BFb0098007

12. Havelund, K., Shankar, N.: Experiments in theorem proving and model checking for protocol verification. In: Gaudel, M.-C., Woodcock, J. (eds.) FME 1996. LNCS, vol. 1051, pp. 662–681. Springer, Heidelberg (1996). https://doi.org/10.1007/3-540-60973-3_113

13. Havelund, K., Shankar, N.: A mechanized refinement proof for a garbage collector. Technical report, October 1997. http://www.havelund.com/Publications/gc-refine-report.pdf

14. Stenzel, O.: The Physics of Thin Film Optical Spectra. SSSS, vol. 44, pp. 163–180. Springer, Cham (2016). https://doi.org/10.1007/978-3-319-21602-7

15. Jackson, P.B.: Verifying a garbage collection algorithm. In: Grundy, J., Newey, M. (eds.) TPHOLs 1998. LNCS, vol. 1479, pp. 225–244. Springer, Heidelberg (1998). https://doi.org/10.1007/BFb0055139

16. Lamport, L.: The temporal logic of actions. ACM TOPLAS 16(3), 872–923 (1994)

17. McCreight, A., Shao, Z., Lin, C., Li, L.: A general framework for certifying garbage collectors and their mutators. In: ACM SIGPLAN Notices, vol. 42, pp. 468–479. ACM (2007)

18. Pixley, C.: An incremental garbage collection algorithm for multi-mutator systems. Distrib. Comput. 3, 41–50 (1988)

19. Russinoff, D.M.: A mechanically verified incremental garbage collector. Formal Aspects Comput. 6, 359–390 (1994)

20. van de Snepscheut, J.L.A.: Algorithms for on-the-fly garbage collection revisited. Inf. Process. Lett. 24(4), 211–216 (1987)

Synthesis of Models, Parameters and Benchmarks

Model Repair Revamped
— On the Automated Synthesis of Markov Chains —

Milan Češka[1], Christian Dehnert[2], Nils Jansen[3], Sebastian Junges[2], and Joost-Pieter Katoen[2(✉)]

[1] FIT, IT4I Centre of Excellence, Brno University of Technology,
Brno, Czech Republic
[2] RWTH Aachen University, Aachen, Germany
katoen@cs.rwth-aachen.de
[3] Radboud University, Nijmegen, The Netherlands

Abstract. This paper outlines two approaches—based on counter-example-guided abstraction refinement (CEGAR) and counterexample-guided inductive synthesis (CEGIS), respectively—to the automated synthesis of finite-state probabilistic models and programs. Our CEGAR approach iteratively partitions the design space starting from an abstraction of this space and refines this by a light-weight analysis of verification results. The CEGIS technique exploits critical subsystems as counterexamples to prune all programs behaving incorrectly on that input. We show the applicability of these synthesis techniques to sketching of probabilistic programs, controller synthesis of POMDPs, and software product lines.

1 Introduction

Model Repair. In 2011, Smolka *et al.* [5] coined the following *model repair* problem [8]: given a finite Markov chain D and a probabilistic specification φ such that $D \not\models \varphi$, find a Markov chain D' that differs from D only in the transition probabilities, such that $D' \models \varphi$. Typical probabilistic specifications impose a threshold on reachability probabilities, such as "is the probability to reach a bad state at most $1/1000$?" Model repair thus amounts to tweaking (some of) the probabilities in a given Markov chain in order to obtain a chain satisfying the specification. It can be solved using parameter synthesis [5] techniques as, e.g., supported by the Prophesy tool [21]. An extension of model repair in which repairs are associated a cost and a minimal-total-cost repair is to be found can be solved by non-linear programming [5]. The scalability of model repair can be improved in several ways: by solving a series of convex programs instead of a non-linear program [19], by repairing abstractions of Markov chains [13], or by a greedy approach exploiting monotonicity [32]. Particle swarm optimisation has been used to model repair of Markov decision processes (MDPs) [14].

This work has been supported by the DFG RTG 2236 "UnRAVeL", the ERC Advanced Grant 787914 "FRAPPANT", the Czech Science Foundation grant No. AUTODEV GA19-24397S, and the IT4Innovations excellence in science project No. LQ1602.

Topology Changes. In the original setting of model repair, only transition probabilities are subject to change. Adding or removing transitions is not admitted. That is to say, every possible repair keeps the topology of the Markov chain invariant. This notion of repair is thus in fact *transition probability repair*. In this paper, we take this idea a step further, and allow for amending the Markov chain's topology. More precisely, in addition to the possibility of modifying transition probabilities, we consider the possible deletion and/or addition of transitions. Changing the topology results in varying sets of reachable states. Viewing Markov chains as operational model for (discrete) probabilistic programs, repairs may affect the control structure as well as the probabilistic choices. Traditional parameter synthesis techniques are inadequate for this problem, as these techniques restrict parameter expressions like $1/2 - \varepsilon$ to range over $(0, 1)$, i.e., excluding zero (no transition) and one (a Dirac transition). Topology changes often come at a price; e.g., for parametric Markov chains the complexity of qualitative (i.e., zero-one) reachability becomes NP-complete whereas in absence of topology changes a polynomial-time algorithm suffices [15].

Synthesis. Model (or: program) repair in the aforementioned sense is a natural instance of model (or: program) synthesis [1,22,23]. Program synthesis amounts to automatically provide an instantiated probabilistic program satisfying all quantitative properties, or returns that such design does not exist. Though the synthesis problem is undecidable in general, there are interesting sub-cases—such as our variant of model repair—that are decidable (but computationally intensive). We consider a family $\mathfrak{D}$ of Markov chains where each family member can be viewed as an admissible repaired version of Markov chain $D \in \mathfrak{D}$. Families are finite and consist of finite chains. As in syntax-guided synthesis, possible repairs are described by some grammar rules, either at the model level or in some high-level description language such as the probabilistic guarded command language [30] or the PRISM modelling language [27]. The successful approach of program sketching [35] naturally fits within this setting. Starting from a program sketch, i.e., a program with "holes", it aims to obtain a program satisfying the specification φ by filling the holes with possible repairs. Holes are the unknown parts of the program and can be replaced by one of finitely many options. All possible program sketch realisations constitute the family $\mathfrak{D}$. The synthesis problems considered in this paper can be used to answer queries like: (a) give a possible repair (if one exists)?, (b) what are all possible repairs?, and (c) which repairs are optimal in the sense of minimising the probability to reach a bad state? Each of these queries can be considered under the additional constraint of minimising the total cost of repairs, e.g., what are all possible repairs for φ that are cost minimal?

Our Synthesis Approaches. A naive enumerative solution is to analyse each individual family member, i.e., each possible amendment, or each possible hole instantiation. This is infeasible for large families. We therefore outline two approaches to the automated synthesis of finite-state probabilistic models: the first one fits within the realm of counterexample-guided abstraction refinement

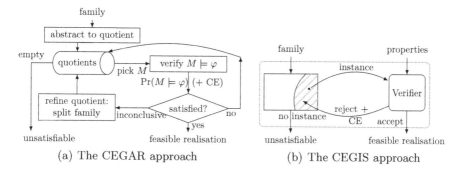

Fig. 1. CEGAR and CEGIS approaches to (feasibility) synthesis.

(CEGAR [17]) while the second approach fits within counterexample-guided inductive synthesis (CEGIS) [36]. Full details of the approaches can be found in [37,38]. We present both techniques at the level of Markov chains for threshold problems on reachability problems and illustrate their usage on simple probabilistic programs.

Using CEGAR. We represent all possible designs, thus the entire family, by a single MDP. A single, initial, non-deterministic choice determines according to which family member the MDP behaves. This technique is adopted from [16] and originated in software product lines [18]. As the MDP can be prohibitively large, we do not solve the synthesis problems directly on this model, but rather on an abstraction of it—similar in spirit as repairing abstract models [13]. Verifying the abstraction, i.e., the quotient MDP M, yields under- and over-approximations of the min and max probability of satisfying φ, respectively. A repair is impossible if e.g., the verification reveals that the min probability exceeds r for φ with threshold $\leq r$. If the model checking is inconclusive, i.e., the abstraction is too coarse, we iteratively refine the quotient MDP by splitting the family into sub-families, see Fig. 1(a). The refinement is guided using the so-called inconsistent schedulers (aka: counterexamples) that optimise the probability on the MDP.

Using CEGIS. Starting from a family, a candidate realisation D is selected and discharged to a verifier, see Fig. 1(b). Using off-the-shelf probabilistic model-checking techniques [3,26], it verifies whether $D \models \varphi$ in case a solution is found. If $D \not\models \varphi$, a counterexample (CE) is derived which in our setting is a fragment [41] of the realisation D that refutes φ. The key is that this CE is exploited in a clever way by an SMT (satisfiability modulo theory)-based synthesiser to rule out potentially many realisations (the dashed area in Fig. 1(b))—rather than the just refuted realisation D—at once. Thus, in a sense counterexamples are "extended" to a set of refuting realisations. This synthesis-verification loop is repeated until either a satisfying realisation is found or the entire family is pruned implying the non-existence of a realisation $D \models \varphi$.

Design Space Partitioning. Both the CEGAR and CEGIS approach iteratively partition the family into "good", "bad" and inconclusive realisations. Phrased in terms of model repair, they partition the family into repaired, failed, and unknown Markov chains. The two approaches use complementary partitioning strategies. Whereas the CEGAR approach starts from considering all possible realisations, and successively splits the entire family of realisations into sub-families, the CEGIS approach starts with a single candidate realisation, and rules out several realisations by effectively exploiting counterexamples.

2   Preliminaries

We start with basic foundations, for details, see [3,4]. Then, we formalise the notion of families of Markov chains, and define various synthesis problems.

2.1   Probabilistic Models and Specifications

Probabilistic Models. A *probability distribution* over countable set X is a function $\mu \colon X \to [0,1]$ with $\sum_{x \in X} \mu(x) = \mu(X) = 1$. Let $Distr(X)$ denote the set of all distributions on X.

Definition 1 (MC). *A* Markov chain *(MC)* $D = (S, s_0, \mathbf{P})$ *with finite set S of states, initial state $s_0 \in S$, and transition probability function* $\mathbf{P} \colon S \to Distr(S)$.

MCs have unique distributions over successor states at each state. A sub-Markov chain (sub-MC) is induced by a MC and a subset of its states. For $X \subseteq S$, let the set $\mathsf{Succ}(X)$ denote the successor states of X, i.e., $\mathsf{Succ}(X) = \{t \in S \mid \exists s \in X.\ \mathbf{P}(s,t) > 0\}$.

Definition 2 (sub-MC). *Let MC $D = (S, s_0, \mathbf{P})$ and $C \subseteq S$ a set of* (critical) *states with $s_0 \in C$. The* sub-MC *of D, C is the MC $D' = (S', s_0, \mathbf{P}')$ with $S' = C \cup \mathsf{Succ}(C)$, and*

$$\mathbf{P}'(s,t) = \begin{cases} \mathbf{P}(s,t) & s \in C, t \in S \\ 1 & s \in \mathsf{Succ}(C) \setminus C \wedge t = s \\ 0 & otherwise. \end{cases}$$

Adding non-determinism over distributions leads to Markov decision processes.

Definition 3 (MDP). *A* Markov decision process *(MDP) is a tuple $M = (S, s_0, Act, \mathcal{P})$ where S, s_0 as in Definition 1, Act is a finite set of actions, and $\mathcal{P} \colon S \times Act \nrightarrow Distr(S)$ is a partial transition probability function.*

The *available actions* in $s \in S$ are $Act(s) = \{a \in Act \mid \mathcal{P}(s,a) \neq \bot\}$. An MDP with $|Act(s)| = 1$ for all $s \in S$ is an MC. A *path* of an MDP M is an (in)finite sequence $\pi = s_0 \xrightarrow{a_0} s_1 \xrightarrow{a_1} \cdots$, where $s_i \in S$, $a_i \in Act(s_i)$, and $\mathcal{P}(s_i, a_i)(s_{i+1}) \neq 0$ for all $i \in \mathbb{N}$. For finite π, $last(\pi)$ denotes the last state of π. Let Paths_{fin}^M denote the set of finite paths of M. The notions of paths carry over to MCs (actions are omitted).

Definition 4 (Scheduler). *A scheduler for an MDP $M = (S, s_0, Act, \mathcal{P})$ is a function $\sigma \colon \mathsf{Paths}^M_{fin} \to Act$ such that $\sigma(\pi) \in Act(last(\pi))$ for all $\pi \in \mathsf{Paths}^M_{fin}$. Scheduler σ is memoryless if $last(\pi) = last(\pi') \implies \sigma(\pi) = \sigma(\pi')$ for all $\pi, \pi' \in \mathsf{Paths}^M_{fin}$. Let Σ^M denote the set of all schedulers of M.*

Schedulers resolve the non-determinism over actions in the MDP. Applying scheduler σ to an MDP M yields the *induced* Markov chain M_σ.

Specifications. For simplicity, we only consider reachability specifications $\varphi = \mathbb{P}_{\sim\lambda}(\Diamond G)$ where $G \subseteq S$ is a set of goal states, $\lambda \in [0,1] \subseteq \mathbb{R}$ is a threshold, and $\sim \in \{<, \leq, \geq, >\}$ is a binary comparison operator. Extensions to expected rewards, PCTL* [2], or ω-regular properties are rather straightforward.

The interpretation of φ for MC D is as follows. Let $\mathtt{Prob}(D, \phi)(s)$ denote the probability to satisfy $\phi = \Diamond G$ from state $s \in S$ in MC D. For initial state s_0, we abbreviate $\mathtt{Prob}(D, \phi)(s_0)$ by $\mathtt{Prob}(D, \phi)$. Then, $D \models \varphi$ iff $\mathtt{Prob}(D, \phi) \sim \lambda$. The specification φ holds in MDP M, denoted $M \models \varphi$, iff it holds for the induced MCs under all schedulers. The maximum probability to satisfy ϕ in MDP M is given by a maximising scheduler $\sigma^* \in \Sigma^M$, i.e., there is no scheduler $\sigma' \in \Sigma^M$ with $\mathtt{Prob}(M_{\sigma^*}, \phi) < \mathtt{Prob}(M_{\sigma'}, \phi)$. As we consider finite models, such a maximising scheduler always exists. Minimum probabilities are defined analogously.

2.2 Families of Markov Chains

We present our approaches on an explicit representation of a *family of MCs* using a parametric transition probability function. Such an explicit representation allows to reason about practically interesting synthesis problems, see Sect. 4.

Definition 5 (Family of MCs). *A family of MCs is a tuple $\mathfrak{D} = (S, s_0, K, \mathfrak{P})$ where S and s_0 are as before, K is a finite set of discrete parameters such that the domain of each parameter $k \in K$ is $T_k \subseteq S$, and $\mathfrak{P} \colon S \to Distr(K)$.*

The transition probability function of MCs maps states to distributions over successor states. For families of MCs, this function maps states to distributions over parameters. Instantiating each of these parameters with a value from its domain yields a "concrete" MC, called a *realisation*.

Definition 6 (Realisation). *A realisation of a family $\mathfrak{D} = (S, s_0, K, \mathfrak{P})$ is a function $r \colon K \to S$ where $\forall k \in K \colon r(k) \in T_k$. A realisation r yields an MC $D_r = (S, s_0, \mathfrak{P}(r))$, where $\mathfrak{P}(r)$ is the transition probability matrix in which each $k \in K$ in $\mathfrak{P}$ is replaced by $r(k)$. Let $\mathcal{R}^\mathfrak{D}$ denote the set of all realisations for $\mathfrak{D}$.*

As a family $\mathfrak{D}$ of MCs is defined over finite parameter domains, the number of family members (i.e. realisations from $\mathcal{R}^\mathfrak{D}$) of $\mathfrak{D}$ is finite, viz. $|\mathfrak{D}| := |\mathcal{R}^\mathfrak{D}| = \prod_{k \in K} |T_k|$, but exponential in $|K|$. Subsets of $\mathcal{R}^\mathfrak{D}$ induce so-called *subfamilies* of $\mathfrak{D}$. While all these MCs share the same state space, their *reachable* states may differ, as demonstrated by the following example.

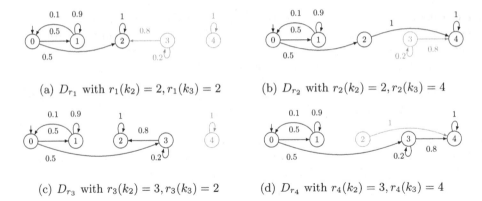

(a) D_{r_1} with $r_1(k_2) = 2, r_1(k_3) = 2$

(b) D_{r_2} with $r_2(k_2) = 2, r_2(k_3) = 4$

(c) D_{r_3} with $r_3(k_2) = 3, r_3(k_3) = 2$

(d) D_{r_4} with $r_4(k_2) = 3, r_4(k_3) = 4$

Fig. 2. The four different realisations of family $\mathfrak{D}$.

Example 1 (Family of MCs). Consider the family of MCs $\mathfrak{D} = (S, s_0, K, \mathfrak{P})$ where $S = \{0, \ldots, 4\}$, $s_0 = 0$, and $K = \{k_0, \ldots, k_5\}$ with domains $T_{k_0} = \{0\}$, $T_{k_1} = \{1\}$, $T_{k_2} = \{2, 3\}$, $T_{k_3} = \{2, 4\}$, $T_{k_4} = \{3\}$ and $T_{k_5} = \{4\}$. The parametric transition function is defined by:

$$\mathfrak{P}(0) = 0.5 \colon k_1 + 0.5 \colon k_2 \qquad \mathfrak{P}(1) = 0.1 \colon k_0 + 0.9 \colon k_1 \qquad \mathfrak{P}(2) = 1 \colon k_3$$
$$\mathfrak{P}(3) = 0.8 \colon k_3 + 0.2 \colon k_4 \qquad \mathfrak{P}(4) = 1 \colon k_5$$

We can simplify the representation by substituting the constants:

$$\mathfrak{P}(0) = 0.5 \colon 1 + 0.5 \colon k_2 \qquad \mathfrak{P}(1) = 0.1 \colon 0 + 0.9 \colon 1 \qquad \mathfrak{P}(2) = 1 \colon k_3$$
$$\mathfrak{P}(3) = 0.8 \colon k_3 + 0.2 \colon 3 \qquad \mathfrak{P}(4) = 1 \colon 4 \qquad .$$

Figure 2 shows the four MCs that result from the realisations $\{r_1, r_2, r_3, r_4\} = \mathcal{R}^{\mathfrak{D}}$ of $\mathfrak{D}$. States that are unreachable from the initial state are greyed out. The family has five states, each of which are reachable in one of the realisations. Yet, every realisation has at most four reachable states.

2.3   Synthesis Problems

Problem 1 (Synthesis). Let $\mathfrak{D}$ be a family of MCs and $\varphi = \mathbb{P}_{\sim \lambda}(\phi)$ with $\phi = \Diamond G$ for $G \subseteq S$. We consider the following synthesis problems:

1. Find a realisation $r \in \mathcal{R}^{\mathfrak{D}}$ with $D_r \models \varphi$.
2. Partition $\mathcal{R}^{\mathfrak{D}}$ into T and F with $r \in T$ iff $D_r \models \varphi$ and $r \in F$ otherwise.
3. Find a realisation $r^* \in \mathcal{R}^{\mathfrak{D}}$ with $r^* = \underset{r \in \mathcal{R}^{\mathfrak{D}}}{\mathrm{argmax}} \{\mathrm{Prob}(D_r, \phi)\}$.

The first synthesis problem (referred to as feasibility synthesis) is to determine a realisation satisfying φ, provided some exists. The second problem (referred to as threshold synthesis) is to identify the set of realisations satisfying and violating a given specification, respectively. The feasibility synthesis problem is in a sense just a simple instance of threshold synthesis to find one realisation $r \in T$. The last problem (referred to as max synthesis) is to find a realisation that maximises the reachability probability. It can be defined for minimising such probabilities in a similar way. As our families are finite, such optimal realisations r^* always exist. Phrased in terms of model repair, the first problem is concerned with the question whether a possible repair (under all admissible repairs) does exist, the second problem partitions the realisations into those that are repaired and those that cannot, while the last problem is about finding the repair that maximises (or, dually, minimises) the objective. The simplest synthesis problem, feasibility, is NP-complete [38] (for a minor extension to families).

Example 2 (Synthesis problems). Recall the family of MCs $\mathfrak{D}$ from Example 1. For the specification $\varphi = \mathbb{P}_{\geq 1/10}(\Diamond\{4\})$, the solution to the threshold synthesis problem is $T = \{r_2, r_4\}$ and $F = \{r_1, r_3\}$, as the goal state 4 is not reachable for D_{r_1} and D_{r_3}. For $\phi = \Diamond\{4\}$, the solution to the max synthesis problem on $\mathfrak{D}$ is r_2 or r_4, as D_{r_2} and D_{r_4} almost surely reach state 1.

Remark 1. It is sometimes beneficial to consider a mild variant of the max-synthesis problem in which the realisation r^* is not required to achieve the maximal reachability probability, but it suffices to be sufficiently close to it. This notion of *ε-optimal synthesis* for a given $0 < \varepsilon \leq 1$ amounts to find a realisation r^* with $\mathtt{Prob}(D_{r^*}, \phi) \geq (1-\varepsilon) \cdot \max\limits_{r \in \mathcal{R}^{\mathfrak{D}}} \{\mathtt{Prob}(D_r, \phi)\}$.

2.4 Synthesis Costs

As in model repair [5], it is quite natural to associate non-negative integer costs to the various realisation options. This enables distinguishing cheap and expensive repairs. The realisation (aka: repair) costs should not be confused with the concept of rewards in MCs; the latter impose a cost structure on the MC while realisation costs impose costs on the realisation at hand.

Definition 7 (Realisation costs). *For family $\mathfrak{D}$, the function $c : \mathcal{R}^{\mathfrak{D}} \to \mathbb{N}$ assigns to each realisation r of $\mathfrak{D}$ a realisation cost $c(r)$.*

The realisation costs are deliberately defined in a rather abstract manner. Concrete instances may depend on the probability distribution over K, the number of options, weighted combinations thereof, and so forth. By imposing an available budget on the possible realisations, we obtain the following cost-dependent variants of the earlier synthesis problems.

Problem 2 (Cost-constrained synthesis). Let $\mathfrak{D}$ be a family of MCs, φ and ϕ as before, and $B \in \mathbb{N}$ a budget. Consider the synthesis problems:

1. Find a realisation $r \in \mathcal{R}^{\mathfrak{D}}$ with $D_r \models \varphi$ and $c(r) \leq B$.
2. Partition $\mathcal{R}^{\mathfrak{D}}$ with $r \in T$ iff $(D_r \models \varphi$ and $c(r) \leq B)$, and $r \in F$ otherwise.
3. Find $r^* \in \mathcal{R}^{\mathfrak{D}}$ with $r^* = \underset{r \in \mathcal{R}_{\mathfrak{D}}}{\mathrm{argmax}} \{\mathtt{Prob}(D_r, \phi) \mid c(r) \leq B\}$.

```
hole k2 either { 2, 3 }
hole k3 either { 2, 4 }
module encode
s : [0..4] init 0;
s = 0 -> 0.5: s'=1 + 0.5: s'=k2;
s = 1 -> 0.1: s'=0 + 0.9: s'=1;
s = 2 -> 1: s'=k3
s = 3 -> 0.2: s'=3 + 0.8: s'=k3;
s = 4 -> 1: s'=s
endmodule
```

Fig. 3. Toy-encoding of the family in Example 1.

Cost-constrained maximal synthesis does not need to have a solution; therefore argmax $\varnothing$ equals undefined. Cost-optimal versions of the synthesis problems are:

Problem 3 (Cost-optimal synthesis). Let $\mathfrak{D}$ be a family of MCs, φ and ϕ as before. We consider the following cost-optimal synthesis problems:

1. Find a realisation $r^* \in T = \{r \in \mathcal{R}^{\mathfrak{D}} \mid D_r \models \varphi\}$ with $c(r^*) = \min_{r \in T}\{c(r)\}$.
2. Find a minimal-cost realisation r^* for the max/min-synthesis problem.

Example 3 (Cost-constrained and cost-optimal synthesis). Consider our running example, and let the cost of a realisation r be the sum of its number of reachable states and their outgoing transitions. That is, $c(r_1) = 8, c(r_2) = 10, c(r_3) = 11$, and $c(r_4) = 11$. For $\phi = \Diamond\{4\}$, and budget $B=10$, cost-constrained max synthesis yields r_2. Lowering the budget B to 9, yields r_1, while for B less than 8, no realisation is found.

2.5 A Program Sketching Language

Probabilistic models are typically specified by means of a high-level modelling language, such as PRISM [27], PIOA [42], JANI [9], or MODEST [7]. Let us briefly describe how the model-based concepts translate to language concepts in the PRISM guarded-command language. The aim is to describe families of MCs, possible constraints on its members, and repair costs in a succinct manner. A (basic) encoding for the family of Example 1 is given in Fig. 3.

A PRISM program consists of one or more reactive modules that may interact with each other. Consider a single module. This is not a restriction as every PRISM program can be flattened into this form. A module has a set of (bounded) variables that span its state space. The possible transitions between states of a module are described by a set of guarded commands of the form:

$$\texttt{guard} \quad \rightarrow \quad p_1 : \texttt{update}_1 \ldots \ldots + p_n : \texttt{update}_n$$

The guard is a boolean expression over the variables of the module. If the guard evaluates to true, the module can evolve into a successor state by updating its variables. An update is chosen according to the probability distribution given by expressions p_1 through p_n. In every state enabling the guard, the evaluation of these expressions must sum up to one.

A PRISM sketch is a program that may contain "holes". Holes are the unknown parts of the program and can be replaced by one of finitely many options. A hole is of the form:

$$\texttt{hole } h \texttt{ either}\{\, \texttt{expr}_1, \ldots, \texttt{expr}_k \,\}$$

where h is the hole identifier and $\texttt{expr}_i$ is an expression over the program variables. A hole h can be used in commands in a similar way as a constant, and may occur multiple times within a command. To distinguish cheap and expensive options, options within a hole can have a cost:

$$\texttt{hole } h \texttt{ either}\{\, x_1 \texttt{ is } \texttt{expr}_1 \texttt{ cost } c_1, \ldots, x_k \texttt{ is } \texttt{expr}_k \texttt{ cost } c_k \,\}$$

where option i is named x_i and has associated cost c_i. Costs can be constants or expressions that evaluate to natural numbers. The option names x_1 through x_n can be used to describe constraint on realisations. These propositional formulae over option names restrict hole instantiations, e.g.,

$$\texttt{constraint}(x_1 \vee x_2) \implies x_3$$

requires that whenever the options x_1 or x_2 are taken for some (potentially different) holes, option x_3 (for some hole) is also to be taken.

The family of realisations of a given PRISM program sketch is now obtained by all possible substitutions of holes h by their options x_1 through x_n that satisfy all specified constraints.

3   Counterexample-Guided Synthesis

Enumeration. A straightforward approach to the synthesis problems for finite families of MCs is to just enumerate all realisations and analyse each of them individually. This naive method is practically applicable to small- to medium-sized families only. For more realistic settings, alternative approaches to this baseline are needed. We present two different counterexample-guided approaches: one based on CEGAR [17] and one on CEGIS [36].

A Bird's Eye View on Our Two Approaches. Let us explain the intuition behind the CEGAR and CEGIS approaches towards synthesis. Both approaches successively partition the family $\mathfrak{D}$ into MCs satisfying φ and those refuting φ. Figure 4 illustrates this for a two-dimensional parameter space, each parameter having five possible values. Each cell thus corresponds to a realisation. CEGAR first checks if all realisations satisfy φ on a sound abstraction. Figure 4(a) shows the situation when the verification fails, i.e. it gives an inconclusive result. This can happen either due to the subfamily consisting of both satisfying and refuting realisations, or because the abstraction is too coarse. In the next step, CEGAR refines the family into two subfamilies and establishes e.g., that all members in the subfamily represented by the first two columns refute φ (indicated in

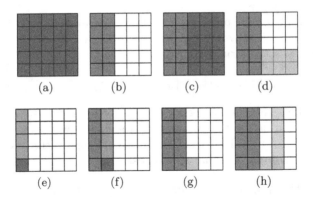

Fig. 4. CEGAR (a)–(d) vs. CEGIS (e)–(h) illustrated. The grid depicts a family with two parameters, each with 5 possible values. Thus, each cell corresponds to a realisation. Blue indicates a verification call that fails, green/red a covered region satisfying/refuting φ. The lighter shaded cells indicate realisations ruled out by counterexample analysis. (Color figure online)

red in Fig. 4(b)), while verifying the remaining subfamily is again inconclusive (Fig. 4(c)). Partitioning that subfamily reveals that the six realisations in the lower two rows fulfil φ. In contrast, CEGIS starts to select a realisation r, e.g., the one in the lower left corner. As $D_r \not\models \varphi$ (indicated dark red in Fig. 4(e)), the counterexample provided by the verifier rules out all realisations in the leftmost column (indicated in lighter shade). This scheme is repeated. In Fig. 4(f), a realisation is selected (second column, lowest row), and similar to the first case, its counterexample rules out all realisations in that column. In Fig. 4(g), a satisfying realisation for φ is selected. In contrast to Fig. 4(g), (h) shows that the analysis of counterexamples to $\neg\varphi$ gives rise to more satisfying realisations. Besides the selected candidate (lowest row), the counterexamples to $\neg\varphi$ cover the entire column.

3.1   CEGAR

We first represent the family $\mathfrak{D}$ by a single *all-in-one* MDP. Selecting action a_r in the (fresh) initial state $s_0^{\mathfrak{D}}$ of the MDP corresponds to choosing the realisation $r \in \mathcal{R}^{\mathfrak{D}}$ and entering the concrete MC D_r. Let us illustrate this with our example.

Figure 5 shows the MDP $M^{\mathfrak{D}}$ for the family $\mathfrak{D}$ from Example 1, where for the sake of readability, only the transitions and states corresponding to realisations r_1 and r_2 are included. Transitions to states (s, r_i) are labeled with action a_{r_i}; these action labels are omitted here. Unreachable states from the initial MDP state $s_0^{\mathfrak{D}}$ are marked grey. There is a one-to-one relationship between a deterministic memoryless scheduler of MDP $M^{\mathfrak{D}}$ and a realisation of $\mathfrak{D}$. Thus, model checking $M^{\mathfrak{D}}$ yields extremal probabilities for all realisations of the family $\mathfrak{D}$.

The MDP model grows linearly with the number of family members. To mitigate the complexity, we apply a simple abstraction where the realisation of a state in the MDP $M^\mathfrak{D}$ is abstracted away, i.e. the item r is ignored in state (s, r). Applying this to our running example amounts to a column-wise grouping of states in Fig. 5. This results in the quotient MDP $M^\mathfrak{D}_\sim$ in Fig. 6. By the over-approximation in the quotient MDP $M^\mathfrak{D}_\sim$, a scheduler may first choose actions a_r and then $a_{r'}$. This corresponds to switching from realisation r to r'. Such inconsistent regimes result in an MC outside the family $\mathfrak{D}$. There is one-to-one relationship between consistent schedulers—those that globally stick to a single realisation r—and the realisation of $\mathfrak{D}$.

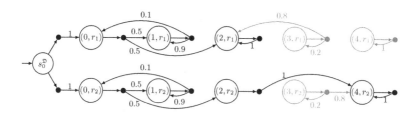

Fig. 5. Reachable fragment of the all-in-one MDP $M^\mathfrak{D}$ for realisations r_1 and r_2.

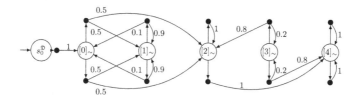

Fig. 6. The quotient MDP $M^\mathfrak{D}_\sim$ for realisations r_1 (top actions) and r_2 (bottom actions)

Example 4. Consider the quotient MDP $M^\mathfrak{D}_\sim$ in Fig. 6. Transitions from previously unreachable states, marked grey before, are reachable in the quotient. The scheduler σ on the quotient $M^\mathfrak{D}_\sim$ that picks a_{r_1} in $[2]_\sim$ and a_{r_2} in state $[3]_\sim$ is inconsistent, as it behaves according to two different realisations r_1 and r_2.

3.2   CEGIS

We follow the typical separation of concerns as in oracle-guided inductive synthesis [1,22,23]: a *synthesiser* selects single realisations that have not been considered before, and a *verifier* checks the selected realisation. Let us first focus on the *verifier*. Consider our running example with $\varphi = \mathbb{P}_{\leq 2/5}(\Diamond\{2\})$. Assume the synthesiser picks realisation r_1. The verifier then builds D_{r_1} and determines $D_{r_1} \not\models \varphi$. Observe that the verifier does not need the full realisation D_{r_1} to refute φ. In fact, the paths in the fragment of D_{r_1} in Fig. 7(a) suffice to show that the probability to reach state 2 exceeds $2/5$. Formally, the fragment in Fig. 7(b) is a sub-MC with critical states $C = \{0\}$. The essential property is [41]:

If a sub-MC of a MCD refutes the safety property φ, then D refutes φ too.

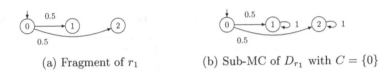

(a) Fragment of r_1 (b) Sub-MC of D_{r_1} with $C = \{0\}$

Fig. 7. Fragment and corresponding sub-MC that suffices to refute φ

Now observe that the considered sub-MC is part of realisation r_2 too. Thus, $D_{r_2} \not\models \varphi$. This can be concluded by considering r_2, $\mathfrak{D}$ and C *without constructing* D_{r_2}. First, take the parameters occurring in $\mathfrak{P}(c)$ for any $c \in C$. This yields k_1 and k_2. The values for the other parameters thus do not affect the shape of the sub-MC induced by C. Realisation r_2 only varies from r_1 in the value of k_3. Therefore, the sub-MC of D_{r_2} induced by C is isomorphic to the sub-MC of D_{r_1} induced by C. This results in concluding $D_{r_2} \not\models \varphi$.

Let us generalise our observations: The verifier gets a realisation r, builds D_r and checks whether $D_r \models \varphi$. If yes, then $\neg\varphi$ is considered to seek for other realisations satisfying φ^1. Otherwise, some sub-MC of D_r refutes φ. (These counterexamples can be constructed from MC models using techniques from [41], or as snippets of PRISM programs using [20].) The verifier constructs the conflict set C and checks which parameters K' occur on the outgoing transitions of states in C. Each r' with the same parameter values for K' can be immediately refuted, without building the realisation $D_{r'}$. Put in a nutshell, counterexamples are exploited to rule out several realisations in one shot.

The main task that remains for the *synthesiser* is to book-keep the considered and excluded realisations, and, heuristically select realisations that lead to small[2] counterexamples, as these exclude potentially many realisations.

4   Applications

This section illustrates the potential wide applicability of probabilistic model synthesis by providing examples from three different areas: program sketching, software product lines, and controller synthesis for partially observable models.

4.1   Program Sketching

Background. The idea of program sketching [35] is to start with a program sketch, a partial program in which difficult expressions, guards, and statements are left unspecified. The hypothesis of program sketching is that programmers often have an idea about the main control flow of the program but filling in all low-level details is laborious and error prone. Completing these low-level details

---

[1] Note that $\neg\varphi$ is not a safety property, but the presented idea can be extended to liveness properties too.

[2] For some suitable measure of size.

is left to an automated synthesiser. Syntax generators are used to describe a space of the possible code fragments that can be used to complete the program. The synthesised program has to satisfy the specification φ. Program sketching has been successfully applied to e.g., scientific programs and concurrent data structures [1]. We show how our approaches can be applied to sketching of probabilistic programs.

Concrete Challenge. Our program sketch is describing a *dynamic power manager (DPM)*, a key component in dynamically optimising energy consumption [6]. A DPM controls changing the system's power states at run time. Depending on workload and performance constraints, it issues commands (e.g., go into sleep mode, wake up) to the system. We consider a DPM system with two request priorities, low and high; these priorities typically depend on the time-criticality. Requests are placed in finite buffers (based on their priority), provided the buffers are not full. Otherwise, the requests are lost. A similar DPM has been analysed by probabilistic model checking [34].

Problem Statement. Our goal is to *synthesise a DPM program* that decides to switch power state based on the current workload expressed in terms of the occupancy of the low-priority and high-priority request buffers.

Approach. The starting point is a program sketch that includes partially specified commands of the form:

$$g_H \ \& \ g_L \ \longrightarrow \ 1 : state' = X$$

where g_H and g_L are partially specified guards concerning the low-priority and high-priority request buffer, respectively, and hole X represents an unknown update of the DPM state. Possible code fragments to complete the commands are e.g., in $state = 1$, the DPM sends a control signal to switch to an active state, while g_H (and similarly g_L) indicates that the occupancy is within a given interval, e.g., at most 50%. We synthesise the guards and updates such that the resulting DPM control program meets a conjunction of objectives (inspired by [22]) that constrain the expected number of lost low- and high-priority requests and the expected energy consumption, for different thresholds λ imposed on these expected values.

Results. The MC family has over $3 \cdot 10^5$ realisations, i.e., control programs. The average realisation has more than 5000 states. We consider an unsatisfiable conjunction of 3 properties describing a possible DPM specification. Within 20 min, the conjunction is shown to be unsatisfiable (although each property alone is satisfiable). An enumerative approach takes more than 20 h to show this. For a satisfiable conjunction, we find a realisation within minutes.

4.2 Software Product Lines

Background. A software product line is (according to wikipedia) "a set of software-intensive systems that share a common, managed set of features

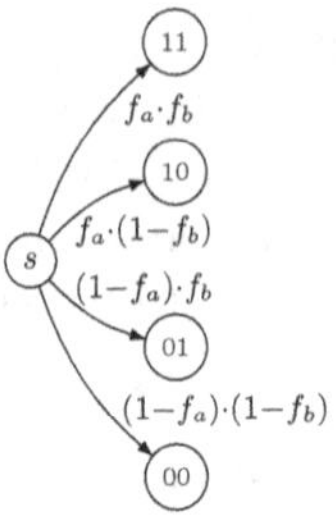


```
hole fa either { 0, 1 }
hole fb either { 0, 1 }
module encode
s : [0..1] init 0;
FA : [0..1] init 0;
FB : [0..1] init 0;
s = 0 -> 1: s'=1 & FA'=fa & FB'=fb;
..
endmodule
```

(a) Parametric MC (b) The PRISM encoding for the family

Fig. 8. Translating a parametric MC formulation to an encoding of a family of MCs.

satisfying the specific needs of a particular market segment or mission and that are developed from a common set of core assets in a prescribed way". Products in a software product line have different features which can be understood as functionalities changing the behaviours of a core software system. They thus provide an elegant way to specify families of systems: every member of the family comprises the core system and a combination of features. Randomness appears when modelling energy consumption or failure probabilities.

Concrete Challenge. We consider the BSN (Body Sensor Network) software product line benchmark from [33], the largest benchmark analysed by probabilistic model checking with the ProFeat tool [16]. BSN describes a network of connected sensors that send measurements to a unit identifying health-critical situations. The family contains the various configurations of 10 binary features, that is, whether a sensor is available or not. We are interested in the reliability of the system, that is, in the probability that the system behaves as described. The system is described as a parametric Markov chain:

Example 5. We consider a variation point (a state whose future behaviour depends on the features) where depending on the availability of features F_a, F_b the model behaves differently. For each feature, a Boolean parameter f is 1 if the feature is active and 0 otherwise. At a variation point, the probability of every transition is scaled by factor p, which equals f if the feature enables the transition and $1-f$ otherwise. This results in parametric MC in Fig. 8(a).

Problem Statement. Find all features combinations where the induced system does not meet a certain reliability.

Approach. The formulation in [33] is a parametric MC, and therefore seems amenable to standard parameter synthesis in which probabilities have to be synthesised. However, in absence of certain features, transitions are taken with probability zero. Traditional parameter synthesis techniques do not allow for such assignments. We translate the parametric MC into a PRISM-description of a family, as illustrated in the following example:

Example 6. We adapt the encoding in Fig. 8(a) to an encoding in Fig. 8(b).

Results. Though this is the largest product line example used in [16], verifying a family with just 1024 family members, with an average size of the realisation of roughly 100 states is mostly trivial. Within seconds, we can categorise the different realisations based on their reliability, either by our approaches or by enumeration.

4.3 Controller Synthesis in Partially Observable Systems

Background. As a next application, we consider controller synthesis (aka: scheduler synthesis) in partially-observable MDPs (POMDPs, for short). A POMDP [25] is an MDP in which an observation $o(s)$ is associated with every state s. POMDP controllers do not have access to the current state of the POMDP; instead, they can only use the observations of the visited states. Thus, whereas an MDP scheduler bases its decisions on finite paths of the form $\pi = s_0 \xrightarrow{a_0} \cdots \xrightarrow{a_{n-1}} s_n$, a POMDP controller does so using the observation sequence $o(\pi) = o(s_0) \xrightarrow{a_0} \cdots \xrightarrow{a_{n-1}} o(s_n)$. Several paths in the underlying MDP M may give rise to the same observation sequence. Controllers have to take this restricted observability into account: They cannot distinguish paths with the same observation sequence. Controller synthesis for POMDPs is notoriously hard: Finding an optimal strategy is undecidable [12] and finding an optimal memoryless strategy is already NP- and SQRT-SUM hard [39]. The complexity of the problem makes the possibility to guide the search for a strategy by means of synthesis very interesting.

Concrete Challenge. We consider Maze, a classical motion planning problem considered as POMDP, see e.g., [29]. A robot is put in a maze with paths surrounded by walls, and its aim is to go to a goal position in the maze. The problem is partially observable because the robot cannot perceive its true location, but only the presence or the absence of a wall on either side of its current position. There is a non-zero probability of slipping, so that the robot does not always know if its last attempt to make a move had any consequence on its actual position in the maze.

Problem Statement. The objective is to *synthesise a deterministic finite-state controller* [11,29] for a Maze (of different size) with a bounded number of states that minimises the expected time for the robot to reach the goal.

Approach. To cast this POMDP problem in our framework of families of MCs, we adapt a recent result [24] that established a one-to-one correspondence between finding finite memory randomised controllers in POMDPs and satisfying parameter valuations in parametric MCs. We sketch a controller by restricting the memory to a fixed bound. Costs are used to penalise the complexity of the controllers such that simple, i.e., easy implementable, finite-memory controllers result. The family describes all MCs induced by small-memory observation-based deterministic strategies with a fixed upper bound on their amount of memory. We are interested in the expected time to the goal. (This problem can be formalised by adding rewards to MDPs in the usual way.)

Results. The MC family has a bit more than 10^6 realisations, i.e., observation-based strategies. The average realisation has 134 states. Among other results, within seconds, we find the 4 strategies that were at most 2% off the maximum. In comparison, an enumeration-based approach takes several hours, and enumerating all consistent strategies of the quotient (see Sect. 3.1) takes more than an hour.

5 Epilogue

Summary. This paper outlined two techniques for the automated synthesis of finite-state probabilistic models or programs. The CEGAR approach takes as a starting point an abstract representation of a family of Markov chains and exploits inconsistent policies—policies that switch between different realisations—to iteratively refine the design space. The CEGIS approach exploits critical subsystems as counterexamples and uses SMT techniques to prune the design space by analysing the counterexamples. We foresee a wide applicability of these kind of synthesis techniques; we illustrated this by examples from program sketching, controller synthesis, and software product lines. Both techniques significantly outperform a naive enumerative approach and differ substantially from the few existing approaches to synthesising probabilistic programs [10,31]. CEGAR works particularly well if the quotient MDP is succinct while CEGIS excels the "more unsatisfiable" the synthesis problem is. CEGAR has difficulties treating constraints on family members (which are straightforward with CEGIS), whereas the performance of CEGIS significantly drops for synthesis problems for which the threshold is close to the true reachability probability.

Future Work. The approaches in this paper are first stepping stones towards the automated synthesis of probabilistic models. This topic has plenty of interesting directions for future work. This includes synthesising infinite-state probabilistic programs, integrating efficient parameter synthesis and model synthesis, developing adequate modeling formalisms for families of probabilistic models, and learning algorithms for probabilistic models [28,40].

Acknowledgement. This chapter is a birthday salute to Scott Smolka on the occasion of his 65th birthday. Scott's research is extremely novel—he is always "ahead of the pack". He pioneered probabilistic aspects in formal modeling and verification with his seminal works on probabilistic processes, testing pre-orders, and approximate bisimulation. His work with Grosu on Monte Carlo model checking emerged into (what others misnamed) statistical model checking. Scott was the first to combine logical programming with model checking and applied formal methods to new applications such as cardiac devices and, more recently, bird flocking. His work has been (and still is) an enormous source of inspiration. This paper celebrates his (and his co-authors') work on model repair for probabilistic models and illustrates how tweaking probabilities (as in model repair) can be generalised towards synthesising model structures. Happy birthday, Scott!

References

1. Alur, R., Singh, R., Fisman, D., Solar-Lezama, A.: Search-based program synthesis. Commun. ACM **61**(12), 84–93 (2018)
2. Aziz, A., Singhal, V., Balarin, F., Brayton, R.K., Sangiovanni-Vincentelli, A.L.: It usually works: the temporal logic of stochastic systems. In: Wolper, P. (ed.) CAV 1995. LNCS, vol. 939, pp. 155–165. Springer, Heidelberg (1995). https://doi.org/10.1007/3-540-60045-0_48
3. Baier, C., de Alfaro, L., Forejt, V., Kwiatkowska, M.: Model checking probabilistic systems. Handbook of Model Checking, pp. 963–999. Springer, Cham (2018). https://doi.org/10.1007/978-3-319-10575-8_28
4. Baier, C., Katoen, J.P.: Principles of Model Checking. MIT Press, Cambridge (2008)
5. Bartocci, E., Grosu, R., Katsaros, P., Ramakrishnan, C.R., Smolka, S.A.: Model repair for probabilistic systems. In: Abdulla, P.A., Leino, K.R.M. (eds.) TACAS 2011. LNCS, vol. 6605, pp. 326–340. Springer, Heidelberg (2011). https://doi.org/10.1007/978-3-642-19835-9_30
6. Benini, L., Bogliolo, A., Paleologo, G.A., Micheli, G.D.: Policy optimization for dynamic power management. IEEE Trans. CAD Integr. Circuits Syst. **18**(6), 813–833 (1999)
7. Bohnenkamp, H.C., D'Argenio, P.R., Hermanns, H., Katoen, J.P.: MODEST: a compositional modeling formalism for hard and softly timed systems. IEEE Trans. Softw. Eng. **32**(10), 812–830 (2006)
8. Buccafurri, F., Eiter, T., Gottlob, G., Leone, N.: Enhancing model checking in verification by AI techniques. Artif. Intell. **112**(1–2), 57–104 (1999)
9. Budde, C.E., Dehnert, C., Hahn, E.M., Hartmanns, A., Junges, S., Turrini, A.: JANI: quantitative model and tool interaction. In: Legay, A., Margaria, T. (eds.) TACAS 2017. LNCS, vol. 10206, pp. 151–168. Springer, Heidelberg (2017). https://doi.org/10.1007/978-3-662-54580-5_9
10. Chasins, S., Phothilimthana, P.M.: Data-driven synthesis of full probabilistic programs. In: Majumdar, R., Kunčak, V. (eds.) CAV 2017, Part I. LNCS, vol. 10426, pp. 279–304. Springer, Cham (2017). https://doi.org/10.1007/978-3-319-63387-9_14
11. Chatterjee, K., Chmelik, M., Davies, J.: A symbolic SAT-based algorithm for almost-sure reachability with small strategies in POMDPs. In: AAAI, pp. 3225–3232. AAAI Press (2016)
12. Chatterjee, K., Chmelik, M., Tracol, M.: What is decidable about partially observable Markov decision processes with ω-regular objectives. J. Comput. Syst. Sci. **82**(5), 878–911 (2016)
13. Chatzieleftheriou, G., Bonakdarpour, B., Katsaros, P., Smolka, S.A.: Abstract model repair. Log. Methods Comput. Sci. **11**(3) (2015)
14. Chen, T., Hahn, E.M., Han, T., Kwiatkowska, M.Z., Qu, H., Zhang, L.: Model repair for Markov decision processes. In: TASE, pp. 85–92. IEEE (2013)

15. Chonev, V.: Reachability in augmented interval Markov chains. CoRR arXiv:1701.02996 (2017)
16. Chrszon, P., Dubslaff, C., Klüppelholz, S., Baier, C.: ProFeat: feature-oriented engineering for family-based probabilistic model checking. Formal Asp. Comput. **30**(1), 45–75 (2018)
17. Clarke, E., Grumberg, O., Jha, S., Lu, Y., Veith, H.: Counterexample-guided abstraction refinement. In: Emerson, E.A., Sistla, A.P. (eds.) CAV 2000. LNCS, vol. 1855, pp. 154–169. Springer, Heidelberg (2000). https://doi.org/10.1007/10722167_15
18. Classen, A., Cordy, M., Heymans, P., Legay, A., Schobbens, P.: Model checking software product lines with SNIP. STTT **14**(5), 589–612 (2012)
19. Cubuktepe, M., Jansen, N., Junges, S., Katoen, J.-P., Topcu, U.: Synthesis in pMDPs: a tale of 1001 parameters. In: Lahiri, S.K., Wang, C. (eds.) ATVA 2018. LNCS, vol. 11138, pp. 160–176. Springer, Cham (2018). https://doi.org/10.1007/978-3-030-01090-4_10
20. Dehnert, C., Jansen, N., Wimmer, R., Ábrahám, E., Katoen, J.-P.: Fast debugging of PRISM models. In: Cassez, F., Raskin, J.-F. (eds.) ATVA 2014. LNCS, vol. 8837, pp. 146–162. Springer, Cham (2014). https://doi.org/10.1007/978-3-319-11936-6_11
21. Dehnert, C., Junges, S., Jansen, N., Corzilius, F., Volk, M., Bruintjes, H., Katoen, J.-P., Ábrahám, E.: PROPhESY: a PRObabilistic ParamEter SYnthesis tool. In: Kroening, D., Păsăreanu, C.S. (eds.) CAV 2015. LNCS, vol. 9206, pp. 214–231. Springer, Cham (2015). https://doi.org/10.1007/978-3-319-21690-4_13
22. Gerasimou, S., Tamburrelli, G., Calinescu, R.: Search-based synthesis of probabilistic models for quality-of-service software engineering (T). In: ASE, pp. 319–330. IEEE Computer Society (2015)
23. Gulwani, S., Polozov, O., Singh, R.: Program synthesis. Found. Trends Program. Lang. **4**(1–2), 1–119 (2017)
24. Junges, S., et al.: Finite-state controllers of POMDPs using parameter synthesis. In: UAI, pp. 519–529. AUAI Press (2018)
25. Kaelbling, L.P., Littman, M.L., Cassandra, A.R.: Planning and acting in partially observable stochastic domains. Artif. Intell. **101**(1–2), 99–134 (1998)
26. Katoen, J.P.: The probabilistic model checking landscape. In: LICS, pp. 31–45. ACM (2016)
27. Kwiatkowska, M., Norman, G., Parker, D.: PRISM 4.0: verification of probabilistic real-time systems. In: Gopalakrishnan, G., Qadeer, S. (eds.) CAV 2011. LNCS, vol. 6806, pp. 585–591. Springer, Heidelberg (2011). https://doi.org/10.1007/978-3-642-22110-1_47
28. Mao, H., Chen, Y., Jaeger, M., Nielsen, T.D., Larsen, K.G., Nielsen, B.: Learning deterministic probabilistic automata from a model checking perspective. Mach. Learn. **105**(2), 255–299 (2016)
29. Meuleau, N., Kim, K., Kaelbling, L.P., Cassandra, A.R.: Solving POMDPs by searching the space of finite policies. In: UAI, pp. 417–426. Morgan Kaufmann (1999)
30. Morgan, C., McIver, A., Seidel, K.: Probabilistic predicate transformers. ACM Trans. Program. Lang. Syst. **18**(3), 325–353 (1996)
31. Nori, A.V., Ozair, S., Rajamani, S.K., Vijaykeerthy, D.: Efficient synthesis of probabilistic programs. In: PLDI, pp. 208–217. ACM (2015)

32. Pathak, S., Ábrahám, E., Jansen, N., Tacchella, A., Katoen, J.-P.: A greedy approach for the efficient repair of stochastic models. In: Havelund, K., Holzmann, G., Joshi, R. (eds.) NFM 2015. LNCS, vol. 9058, pp. 295–309. Springer, Cham (2015). https://doi.org/10.1007/978-3-319-17524-9_21
33. Rodrigues, G.N., et al.: Modeling and verification for probabilistic properties in software product lines. In: HASE, pp. 173–180. IEEE (2015)
34. Sesic, A., Dautovic, S., Malbasa, V.: Dynamic power management of a system with a two-priority request queue using probabilistic-model checking. IEEE Trans. CAD Integr. Circuits Syst. 27(2), 403–407 (2008)
35. Solar-Lezama, A.: Program sketching. STTT 15(5–6), 475–495 (2013)
36. Solar-Lezama, A., Rabbah, R.M., Bodík, R., Ebcioglu, K.: Programming by sketching for bit-streaming programs. In: PLDI, pp. 281–294. ACM (2005)
37. Češka, M., Hensel, C., Junges, S., Katoen, J.P.: Counterexample-driven synthesis for probabilistic program sketches. CoRR abs/1904.12371 (2019)
38. Češka, M., Jansen, N., Junges, S., Katoen, J.-P.: Shepherding hordes of Markov chains. In: Vojnar, T., Zhang, L. (eds.) TACAS 2019. LNCS, vol. 11428, pp. 172–190. Springer, Cham (2019). https://doi.org/10.1007/978-3-030-17465-1_10
39. Vlassis, N., Littman, M.L., Barber, D.: On the computational complexity of stochastic controller optimization in POMDPs. TOCT 4(4), 12:1–12:8 (2012)
40. Wang, J., Sun, J., Yuan, Q., Pang, J.: Learning probabilistic models for model checking: an evolutionary approach and an empirical study. STTT 20(6), 689–704 (2018)
41. Wimmer, R., Jansen, N., Ábrahám, E., Katoen, J., Becker, B.: Minimal counterexamples for linear-time probabilistic verification. Theor. Comput. Sci. 549, 61–100 (2014)
42. Wu, S., Smolka, S.A., Stark, E.W.: Composition and behaviors of probabilistic I/O automata. Theor. Comput. Sci. 176(1–2), 1–38 (1997)

Generating Hard Benchmark Problems
for Weak Bisimulation

Bernhard Steffen and Marc Jasper[✉]

TU Dortmund University, Dortmund, Germany
{steffen,marc.jasper}@cs.tu-dortmund.de

Abstract. In this paper, we propose a method to automatically generate arbitrarily complex benchmark problems for bisimulation checking. Technically, this method is a variant of an incremental generation approach for model checking benchmarks where given benchmark scenarios of controllable size are expanded to arbitrarily complex benchmark problems. This expansion concerns both the number of parallel components and the component sizes. Whereas our property-preserving parallel decomposition is maintained in this variant, the alphabet extension is flexibilized as, in contrast to temporal logics, weak bisimulation is not sensitive to liveness properties.

Keywords: (Verification) Benchmark (Generation) ·
(Weak) Bisimulation · Modal transition system · Modal refinement ·
Modal contract · (Observable) Alphabet · Model checking ·
Parallel decomposition · Alphabet extension

1 Introduction

In July 1987, my (Bernhard's) first official meeting with Robin Milner's team in Edinburgh and the starting point of my involvement in the Concurrency Workbench project: Almost everything was strange to me, the coffee, the subject, and the entire way of thinking, which was so different from what I was used to in Kiel. The only concrete technological aspect I remember from this meeting is that there was a nice algorithm by Kanellakis and Smolka for checking bisimulation, and that its implementation would be part of my future project work. Without bisimulation [31], its beautiful checking algorithm [25], and the Concurrency Workbench project [8], my career would have developed quite differently. A year later, Scott Smolka came to Edinburgh for his sabbatical and we became close friends. We had endless discussions and were among the first who published about probabilistic processes [40], a topic that later on developed with a pace that I would have never expected. It was Scott who believed in it, in the same way that he later on believed in his Monte Carlo Model Checking [16], today subsumed by the popular statistical model checking [28].

Checking (weak) bisimulation of realistic concurrent systems is hard because of the state explosion problem: The state spaces grow exponentially with the

© Springer Nature Switzerland AG 2019
E. Bartocci et al. (Eds.): From Reactive Systems to Cyber-Physical Systems, LNCS 11500, pp. 126–145, 2019.
https://doi.org/10.1007/978-3-030-31514-6_8

number of parallel components [39]. People therefore developed technologies and heuristics to fight state explosion [6,7,13,36]. Still, there does not exist a silver bullet, a method/tool that is superior in all cases. Thus, choosing the best tool for a given application scenario is very difficult.

Competitions for verification tools [1,4,20,22,26] have turned out to be a good means to (i) better profile their strengths and weaknesses, (ii) improve their capabilities and performance, and (iii) develop ideas for new algorithms and heuristics. In fact, machine learning has even been applied to make predictions concerning the performance of verification tools [10]. However, their prediction very much depends on the availability of sufficiently many and expressive test scenarios. In order to provide scalable and intricate test scenarios, we developed automatic generation approaches based on formal property preservation [24,37,38] for the international Rigorous Examination of Reactive Systems (RERS) Challenge [19,22,23].

Today, the number of tools for (weak) bisimulation checking (cf. e.g. [5,8,11]) is rather small. It is our intention to push the development of (weak) bisimulation checkers by introducing a corresponding competition.

In this paper, we propose a method to automatically generate arbitrarily complex benchmark problems for bisimulation checking. Technically, this method is a variant of the incremental generation approach for model checking benchmarks presented in [23,34,38], where given benchmark scenarios $B(M,\Phi)$ consisting of a modal transition system (MTS) [27] specification M for some concurrent implementation of controllable size[1] together with a set of proven properties Φ are expanded to arbitrarily complex benchmark scenarios.

As we are dealing with weak bisimulation in this paper, we consider benchmark problems $B = (L_1, L_2, \Sigma)$ essentially consisting of two systems L_1 and L_2 in standard concurrent form [30], i.e. parallel compositions of labeled transitions systems [32], and Σ, the observable alphabet relative to which weak bisimulation has to be checked. Similar to the model checking case, our automated benchmark generation algorithm for weak bisimulation starts with an initial benchmark of controllable size and allows us to arbitrarily scale the

1. number of parallel components in L_1 and L_2,
2. size of the expanded parallel compositions of L_1 and L_2,
3. size of an individual parallel component in L_1 and L_2, and
4. size of the alphabets $\Sigma(L_1)$ and $\Sigma(L_2)$

in a light-weight assumption commitment style. Bisimilarity is maintained on the basis of *modal contracts* that keep track of the dependencies between transitions required to guarantee that the decompositions into system and context components preserves (weak) modal refinement. Important here is that weak modal refinement reduces to weak bisimulation for systems that are totally defined, i.e., where the set of may and must transitions coincide. Therefore, whenever we start

---

[1] What we mean here is that M can be conveniently model checked with state-of-the-art technology.

with an initial benchmark that is totally defined, the result of our expansion is guaranteed to be weakly bisimilar [21]. In fact, the modalities can be considered here as a means to elegantly 'juggle' with unreachable states.

The main technical difference between the generation of benchmarks for model checking and for weak bisimulation concerns alphabet extensions (see Sect. 5.2). Whereas model checking benchmarks must preserve liveness properties, we do not have to care about liveness here as weak bisimulation is insensitive to it. This eases the alphabet extension process because we do not have to prohibit the introduction of divergence, i.e. infinite unobservable behavior. The entire development is accompanied by an illustrative example.

After introducing relevant preliminaries in Sect. 2, Sect. 3 presents our notion of parallel composition that requires synchronization whenever the alphabets of components overlap. Section 4 introduces our notion of a benchmark problem for weak bisimulation checking along with its hardness. Subsequently, Sect. 5 elaborates on our iterative expansion that allows to generate hard benchmark problems, before Sect. 6 concludes this paper.

2 Preliminaries

This section introduces formal foundations that are relevant throughout this paper. Section 2.1 covers (modal) transition systems and defines their languages. Afterwards, Sect. 2.2 is concerned with (weak) modal refinement and (weak) bisimulation. During this section, we focus on modalities as they are a fundamental aspect of our approach. Because concepts such as modal transition systems and the corresponding refinement relation extend common notions of labeled transition systems and bisimulation, we introduce the latter as special instances of the former.

2.1 MTS, LTS, and Their Languages

Modal transition systems (MTSs) [27] can be seen as the formal backbone of all approaches presented in this paper. An MTS is defined as follows (see [38]):

Definition 1 (Modal Transition System). *Let S be a set of states and Σ an alphabet of action symbols. $M = (S, s_0, \Sigma, \diamond, \Box)$ is called a **(rooted) modal transition system (MTS)** with root $s_0 \in S$ if the following condition holds:*

$$\Box \subseteq \diamond \subseteq (S \times \Sigma \times S)$$

Elements of $\diamond$ are called may transitions, those of $\Box$ must transitions, and those of $(\diamond \setminus \Box)$ may-only transitions. This paper sometimes uses the notations $p \xrightarrow{\sigma}_T q$ or $(p \xrightarrow{\sigma} q) \in T$ to denote a transition $(p, \sigma, q) \in T$. Throughout this paper, the domain of all possible MTSs is referred to as $\mathcal{M}$.

We define the operator $\Sigma(M) =_{def} \Sigma$ to access the alphabet of M. For any $t = (p \xrightarrow{\sigma} q) \in \diamond$, $\Sigma(t) =_{def} \sigma$ is called the symbol or label of t. Operator $\Sigma(\cdot)$ extends naturally to transition relations, $\Sigma(T) =_{def} \bigcup_{t \in T}(\{\Sigma(t)\})$ for any $T \subseteq (S \times \Sigma \times S)$.

For all illustrated MTSs M within this paper, it holds that $\Sigma(M) = \Sigma(\diamond(M))$, meaning that M's alphabet is exactly the union of all transition labels that occur in M. An MTS can be seen as an extension of a traditional (rooted) labeled transition system (LTS), which allows the following definition [38]:

Definition 2 (Labeled Transition System). *A **labeled transition system** (**LTS**) is an MTS $M = (S, s_0, \Sigma, \diamond, \Box)$ with*

$$\diamond = \Box.$$

*The **language** $\mathcal{L}(M)$ of an LTS M is defined as the language of the related prefix-closed non-deterministic finite automaton (NFA) that results from marking all states in S as accepting.*

For the property-preserving parallel decomposition explained in a later section, the maximal language defined by an MTS is important (see [38]):

Definition 3 (Maximal Language of an MTS). *Let $M = (S, s_0, \Sigma, \diamond, \Box)$ be an MTS. The languages $\mathcal{L}_\top(M) =_{def} \mathcal{L}((S, s_0, \Sigma, \diamond, \diamond))$ is called the **maximal language of** M.*

2.2 (Weak) Refinement and (Weak) Bisimulation

Intuitively speaking, a may transition in an MTS stands for an underspecification and indicates a transition that may or may not be present in an actual implementation. An MTS therefore specifies a set of LTSs. These LTSs can be retrieved by MTS refinement [27] according to the following definition [38]:

Definition 4 (MTS Refinement). *Let $M_p = (S_p, s_0^p, \Sigma_p, \diamond_p, \Box_p)$, $M_q = (S_q, s_0^q, \Sigma_q, \diamond_q, \Box_q) \in \mathcal{M}$ be two MTSs. A relation $\precsim \subseteq (S_p \times S_q)$ is called a **refinement** if the following hold for all $(p, q) \in \precsim$:*

$$1.) \ \forall (p \xrightarrow{\sigma} p') \in \diamond_p, \exists (q \xrightarrow{\sigma} q') \in \diamond_q : (p', q') \in \precsim$$
$$2.) \ \forall (q \xrightarrow{\sigma} q') \in \Box_q, \exists (p \xrightarrow{\sigma} p') \in \Box_p : (p', q') \in \precsim$$

*M_p **refines** M_q, written as $M_p \precsim M_q$, if there exists a refinement $\precsim$ with $(s_0^p, s_0^q) \in \precsim$.*

Given the above, it makes sense to introduce a conjunction operator between MTSs that, semantically, serves as set intersection (see [38]):

Definition 5 (MTS Conjunction). *Let $M_p = (S_p, s_0^p, \Sigma, \diamond_p, \Box_p)$, $M_q = (S_q, s_0^q, \Sigma, \diamond_q, \Box_q) \in \mathcal{M}$ be two MTSs. The **conjunction***

$$(M_p \wedge M_q) =_{def} (S_p \times S_q, (s_0^p, s_0^q), \Sigma, \diamond, \Box)$$

of M_p and M_q is then defined as a commutative and associative operation satisfying the following operational rules with $p, p' \in S_p$ and $q, q' \in S_q$: [2]

$$\frac{p \xrightarrow{\sigma}_{\square_p} p' \quad q \xrightarrow{\sigma}_{\diamond_q} q'}{(p,q) \xrightarrow{\sigma}_{\square} (p',q')} \qquad \frac{p \xrightarrow{\sigma}_{\diamond_p} p' \quad q \xrightarrow{\sigma}_{\diamond_q} q'}{(p,q) \xrightarrow{\sigma}_{\diamond} (p',q')} \qquad \frac{p \xrightarrow{\sigma}_{\square_p} p' \quad q \xrightarrow{\sigma}_{\diamond_q}}{(p,q) \xrightarrow{\sigma} error}$$

Whenever an error occurs, the conjunction of M_p and M_q is undefined.

The MTS conjunction of Definition 5 guarantees that a refining MTS refines both components [38]:

Proposition 1 (Conjunction of Refinement Constraints). *Let $M, M_p, M_q \in \mathcal{M}$ be three MTSs. If $(M_p \wedge M_q)$ is defined, then the following holds:*

$$(M \precsim (M_p \wedge M_q)) \Longleftrightarrow (M \precsim M_p \text{ and } M \precsim M_q)$$

As a result, refinements of a conjunction inherit all the properties of the component MTSs. Our MTS decomposition methods strongly depend on this fact.

With the goal to define weak modal refinement, we introduce the common notion of hiding (see [38]):

Definition 6 (Label Hiding). *Let $M = (S, s_0, \Sigma, \diamond, \square) \in \mathcal{M}$ be an MTS. Let $\Gamma \subseteq \Sigma$ be a sub-alphabet. The Γ-hiding*

$$hide_\Gamma(M) =_{def} (S, s_0, ((\Sigma \setminus \Gamma) \cup \{\tau\}), hide_\Gamma(\diamond), hide_\Gamma(\square))$$

of M relabels all transitions t of M such that $\Sigma(t) \in \Gamma$ with the (unobservable) special symbol τ and therefore features the following transition relations for all $T \in \{\diamond, \square\}$:

$$hide_\Gamma(T) = \{(p, \tau, q) \mid \exists \gamma \in \Gamma : (p, \gamma, q) \in T\} \cup \{(p, \sigma, q) \in T \mid \sigma \in (\Sigma \setminus \Gamma)\}$$

In order to compare two MTSs based on a certain alphabet Γ, it helps to express that all of their symbols are hidden which are not in Γ:

Definition 7 (Label View). *Let $M = (S, s_0, \Sigma, \diamond, \square) \in \mathcal{M}$ be an MTS. Let $\Gamma \subseteq \Sigma$ be a sub-alphabet. Then we define the Γ view $[M]_\Gamma$ of M as follows:*

$$[M]_\Gamma =_{def} hide_{\Sigma(M) \setminus \Gamma}(M)$$

We prepare the (standard) definition of weak MTS refinement by defining the usual observational relation of a transition relation as in [38]:

Definition 8 (Observational Relation). *Let $(\Sigma \cup \{\tau\})$ be an alphabet with τ and let $T \subseteq (S \times (\Sigma \cup \{\tau\}) \times S)$ be a transition relation between states in S.*

---

[2] This definition depends on the fact that each must transition is also a may transition.

Let $p, p', q, q' \in S$. The **observational relation** $\mathbf{obs(T)}$ of T is then recursively defined as follows:

$$p \stackrel{\epsilon}{\Longrightarrow} p \qquad \frac{p \stackrel{\tau}{\to} p' \quad p' \stackrel{\epsilon}{\Longrightarrow} q}{p \stackrel{\epsilon}{\Longrightarrow} q} \qquad \frac{p \stackrel{\epsilon}{\Longrightarrow} p' \quad p' \stackrel{\sigma}{\to} q' \quad q' \stackrel{\epsilon}{\Longrightarrow} q}{p \stackrel{\sigma}{\Longrightarrow} q}$$

where $\sigma \in \Sigma$, $p \stackrel{\sigma}{\to} p'$ denotes a feasible transition $(p, \sigma, p') \in T$ and $p \stackrel{\sigma}{\Longrightarrow} p'$ a feasible transition $(p, \sigma, p') \in obs(T)$.

The observational MTS is now simply defined by replacing the original transition relations with their observable counterparts (see [38]):

Definition 9 (Observational MTS). *Let* $M = (S, s_0, \Sigma, \diamond, \square) \in \mathcal{M}$ *be an MTS. The* **observational MTS** $\omega(M)$ *of* M *is based on the observational expansion of its transition relations (Definition 8):*

$$\omega(M) =_{def} (S, s_0, ((\Sigma \setminus \{\tau\}) \cup \{\epsilon\}), obs(\diamond), obs(\square))$$

This is sufficient to introduce weak MTS refinement [21, 38]:

Definition 10 (Weak MTS Refinement). *Let* $M, M' \in MTS$ *be two MTSs. Then* **Weak refinement** $\lesssim\!\!\!\!\sim$ *is defined as follows:*

$$(M \lesssim\!\!\!\!\sim M') \iff (\omega(M) \lesssim \omega(M'))$$

The frequently used concept of (weak) bisimulation can now be derived from the notion of (weak) refinement:

Definition 11 ((Weak) Bisimulation). *Let* L, L' *be two LTSs. Then* L *is* **bisimilar** *to* L', *denoted as* $\mathbf{L \sim L'}$, *iff* $L \lesssim L'$. *Furthermore,* L *is* **weakly bisimilar** *to* L', *denoted as* $\mathbf{L \approx L'}$, *iff* $L \lesssim\!\!\!\!\sim L'$.

This correspondence is based on the fact that according to Definition 2, may and must transition relations are identical within an LTS.

3 Parallel MTS Composition

Our parallel composition operator for MTSs as introduced in [38] is reminiscent of CSP [18] with synchronization of components on their common alphabets:

Definition 12 (Parallel MTS Composition). *Let* $M_1 = (S_1, s_0^1, \Sigma_1, \diamond_1, \square_1)$, $M_2 = (S_2, s_0^2, \Sigma_2, \diamond_2, \square_2) \in \mathcal{M}$ *be two MTSs, and let* $T \in \{\diamond, \square\}$ *identify the type of transition. The* **parallel composition**

$$(M_1 \parallel M_2) =_{def} (S_1 \times S_2, (s_0^1, s_0^2), \Sigma_1 \cup \Sigma_2, \diamond, \square)$$

is then defined as a commutative and associative operation satisfying the following operational rules with $p, p' \in S_1$ *and* $q, q' \in S_2$:[3]

$$\frac{p \stackrel{\sigma}{\to}_T p' \quad q \stackrel{\sigma}{\to}_T q'}{(p, q) \stackrel{\sigma}{\to}_T (p', q')} \qquad \frac{p \stackrel{\sigma}{\to}_T p' \quad \sigma \notin \Sigma_2}{(p, q) \stackrel{\sigma}{\to}_T (p', q)}$$

---

[3] This definition again depends on the fact that each must transition is also a may transition.

Throughout this paper, all components within a parallel composition $M = (M_1 \parallel \ldots \parallel M_n)$ are different. This allows us to abbreviate $M' = M_i$ for some $i \in \mathbb{N}_{\leq n}$ with $M' \in M$ in a set notation-like fashion. Moreover, similar to a product over multiple operands, the term $\parallel_{M_i \in M} M_i =_{def} (M_1 \parallel \ldots \parallel M_n)$ abbreviates the regular notation of parallel composition.

In the following, we begin with a running example based on an initial parallel composition of two LTSs. Because every LTS is also an MTS according to Definition 2, we can use Definition 12 for the composition. More involved examples including modalities can be found in [38] and in later sections of this paper.

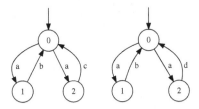

Fig. 1. A parallel composition $(L_1 \parallel L_2)$ of two LTSs. Transitions with the same label have to synchronize (see Definition 12).

Example 1 (Parallel LTS Composition). Figure 1 illustrates two LTSs that are components in a parallel composition $L = (L_1 \parallel L_2)$. The expanded LTS that represents the semantics of this parallel composition is depicted in Fig. 2.

It has been established that $\parallel$ preserves refinement for both operands [38]:

Proposition 2 (Refinement Monotonicity). *Let $M, M', M'' \in \mathcal{M}$ be three arbitrary MTSs. Refining a component of a parallel composition also refines the composition:*

$$(M \lesssim M') \implies ((M \parallel M'') \lesssim (M' \parallel M''))$$

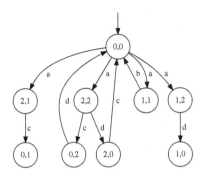

Fig. 2. Expanded LTS $L = (L_1 \parallel L_2)$ that represents the semantics of the parallel composition illustrated in Fig. 1.

Note that due to the commutativity of operator $||$, this monotonicity holds for both components of a composition.

4   Benchmark Scenario and Hardness

Within this paper, we focus on the generation of intricate benchmark problems that challenge state-of-the-art approaches to weak bisimulation checking. This section introduces our notion of such a benchmark problem and states why we can generate problems that are hard to solve. We define a benchmark problem (for weak bisimulation checking) as follows:

Definition 13 (Benchmark Problem). Let $L_1 = (L_{11} \, || \, ... \, || \, L_{1n})$ and $L_2 = (L_{21} \, || \, ... \, || \, L_{2n})$ be two parallel compositions of LTSs. Let $\Sigma \subseteq (\Sigma(L_1) \cap \Sigma(L_2))$. Then the triple $B = (L_1, L_2, \Sigma)$ is called a **benchmark problem** for weak bisimulation checking.

The **correct answer** to B is 'equivalent' iff $[L_1]_\Sigma \approx [L_2]_\Sigma$ holds and 'non-equivalent' otherwise (see Definitions 7 and 11).

Characteristic for these benchmark problems is their focus on a sub-alphabet Σ: Alphabet symbols that are not in Σ are considered invisible, introducing a notion of abstraction/projection reminiscent of temporal logic specifications, which are, on the other hand, powerful enough to characterize systems up to bisimulation [35].

Example 2 (Benchmark Problem). Consider the (unexpanded) parallel LTS composition $L = (L_1 \, || \, L_2)$ depicted in Fig. 1. A trivial example of a benchmark problem is $B = (L, L, \{a, c, d\})$. The correct answer to B is 'equivalent'.

As an alternative, consider the LTSs L_1' and L_2' that are identical to L_1 and L_2, respectively, except for the fact that the transitions labeled with b have been removed. As a consequence, the expanded parallel composition $L' = (L_1' \, || \, L_2')$ is identical to the LTS depicted in Fig. 2, except that the single transition labeled with b is missing. The correct answer to the benchmark problem $B' = (L, L', \{a, c, d\})$ (with L, L' again being represented by their individual parallel components) is 'nonequivalent': The root of $[L']_{\{a,c,d\}}$ features a self loop labeled with a whereas $[L]_{\{a,c,d\}}$ does not.

Within this paper, we present an approach to generate hard benchmark problems $B = (L_1, L_2, \Sigma)$ that (not necessarily independently) scales the

1. number of parallel components in L_1 and L_2,
2. size of the expanded parallel compositions of L_1 and L_2,
3. size of an individual parallel component in L_1 and L_2, and
4. size of the alphabets $\Sigma(L_1)$ and $\Sigma(L_2)$.

In addition, it is guaranteed that generated benchmark problem $B = (L_1, L_2, \Sigma)$ cannot simply be decomposed, as we guarantee:

$$\mathop{||}_{L_i \in L} [L_i]_\Sigma \not\approx [\, \mathop{||}_{L_i \in L} L_i \,]_\Sigma$$

In fact, we believe that it is hard to exploit the knowledge of the generation process for solving these benchmark problems.

5   Iterative Expansion of a Benchmark Problem

This section presents our iterative generation process of hard benchmark problems (see Sect. 4). It starts with an easy-to-solve initial benchmark problem $B = (L_1, L_2, \Sigma)$ according to Definition 13 which it then expands by iterating the following three steps:

1. Split every $L_{ij} \in (L_{i1} \parallel \ldots \parallel L_{in}) = L_i$, $i \in \{1, 2\}$, into two MTSs using property-preserving parallel decomposition (Sect. 5.1)
2. Extend the alphabet of every parallel MTS that results from the first step using alphabet extensions (Sect. 5.2)
3. Modally refine each MTS that results from the second step (Sect. 5.3).

The degree of parallelism of the resulting parallel compositions L_i' doubles with each iteration, and their alphabets as well as the sizes of the individual components grow, while weak bisimulation is preserved: $[L_i]_\Sigma \approx [L_i']_\Sigma$. In particular we have that $[L_1]_\Sigma \approx [L_2]_\Sigma$ holds if and only if $[L_1']_\Sigma \approx [L_2']_\Sigma$ holds.

As the iteration treats each of the parallel components individually, it is sufficient to describe how an individual parallel component is transformed.

5.1   Property-Preserving Parallel Decomposition

Although the initial components of the L_i, $i \in \{1, 2\}$, are guaranteed to be LTSs, this may change in the course of iteration. In this section, we therefore describe how an MTS M is split into two MTSs M_s and M_c^* such that they together refine M, i.e., $(M_s \parallel M_c^*) \lesssim M$.

In fact, it is sufficient to require that the initial components are LTSs to guarantee that each modal refinement of the component expansions (cf. step 3) still guarantees that the expanded parallel systems L_i', $i \in \{1, 2\}$ are weakly bisimilar to their sources L_i.

In [38], *modal contracts* were introduced as a means of property-preserving parallel decomposition. This notion depends on label projection as defined below:

Definition 14 (Label Projection). *Let T be a transition relation with $\Sigma(T) = \Sigma$. Let $\Gamma \subseteq \Sigma$ be a subset of Σ. We call the transition relation*

$$\alpha_\Gamma(T) =_{def} \{(p \xrightarrow{\gamma} q) \in T \mid \gamma \in \Gamma\}$$

the (label) projection of T onto Γ.

A Modal contract can now be defined as follows:

Definition 15 (Modal Contract (MC)). *Let $M = (S, s_0, \Sigma, \diamond, \Box)$ be an MTS and $\Gamma \subseteq \Sigma$. A modal contract (MC) of M with communication alphabet $\Gamma(I) =_{def} \Gamma$ is a tuple*

$$I = (S, s_0, \Sigma, \diamond, \Box, G, R)$$

where

- $G =_{def} \alpha_\Gamma(\square)$, *and*
- R *is a set of transitions over the alphabet* Γ *that do not exist in* $\diamond$ *and such that they are not in conflict with* G, *meaning there do not exist two paths of may transitions in* M *with the same label sequence such that one ends with a transition in* G *and the other with one in* R.[4]

Moreover $G(I) =_{def} G$ *and* $R(I) =_{def} R$, *and we color transitions of* $G(I)$ *green and transitions of* $R(I)$ *red.*

A modal contract allows to decompose an MTS as follows:

Definition 16 (Meaning of an MC). *Let* $I = (S, s_0, \Sigma, \diamond, \square, G, R)$ *be an MC,*

$$R' =_{def} \{(p \xrightarrow{\sigma} r) \mid q \in S : (p \xrightarrow{\sigma} q) \in R\}$$

be a redirection of transitions in R *to a new (sink) state* $r \notin S$ *and*

$$R^* =_{def} R' \cup \{(r \xrightarrow{\sigma} r) \mid \sigma \in \Sigma\}$$

denote the extension of R *with arbitrary subsequent behavior. Then we can define the* **system MTS** *for* I *as*

$$M_s(I) =_{def} ((S \uplus \{r\}), s_0, \Sigma, (\diamond \cup R^*), \square)$$

and the set of corresponding **context MTSs** *for* I *as*

$$\mathcal{M}_C(I) =_{def} \{M' \mid (M_s(I) \parallel M_c(I)) \precsim M\}.$$

The elements of $\mathcal{M}_C(I)$ *are called* **admissible contexts** *of* I.

Example 3 (Modal Contract and System Component). Figure 3 illustrates two MCs based on the LTSs in Fig. 1 with corresponding system components. An admissible context for each of these MCs will be generated in the following example.

By definition, any admissible context can be composed with the system MTS for I to construct a modally refining parallel decomposition.[5] As the system MTS for I can be constructed straightforwardly, the challenge remains how to generate adequate admissible contexts for I.

---

[4] Such a conflict can easily be detected via the determinization of the may automaton of I.

[5] Intuitively, an MC specifies an assume-guarantee contract [2,3,17,33] based on an MTS M such that the parallel composition of the system MTS and a corresponding context MTS is guaranteed to refine M. The system component makes assumptions about the (non-)availability of transitions to synchronize with, and the context guarantees these assumptions.

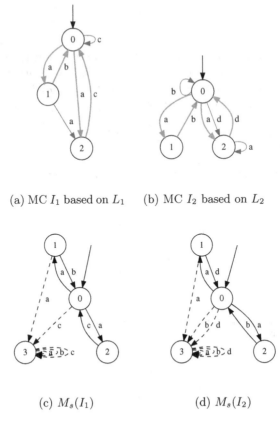

(a) MC I_1 based on L_1 (b) MC I_2 based on L_2

(c) $M_s(I_1)$ (d) $M_s(I_2)$

Fig. 3. (a) and (b): Two MCs I_1 (The transitions $1 \xrightarrow{a} 2$ and $0 \xrightarrow{c} 0$ are colored red. All others are colored green.) and I_2 (The transitions $0 \xrightarrow{b} 0$, $0 \xrightarrow{d} 2$, and $2 \xrightarrow{a} 2$ are colored red. All others are green.) based on L_1 and L_2 from Fig. 1, respectively. (c) and (d): System components $M_s(I_1)$ and $M_s(I_2)$, respectively. (Color figure online)

Automatic Generation of Admissible Contexts

Admissible contexts play a dual role:

- As enabler: They may never prohibit a required action.
- As prohibiter: They may never allow an unwanted action.

These roles are dual, and they can be enforced separately. In fact, we can construct so-called green contexts that guarantee the enabling power, and so-called red contexts that serve for prohibition. Moreover, given red and green contexts, admissible contexts, so-called green/red contexts, can easily be constructed via conjunction (see Definition 5).

The construction of green and red contexts that we present in the following tries to avoid unnecessary constraints on the structure of generated admissible contexts. Prerequisite is the following definition:

Definition 17 (Language Projection). *Let Σ, Γ be two alphabets with $\Gamma \subseteq \Sigma$. For any word $w = (\sigma_1, ..., \sigma_n) \in \Sigma^*$, the **projection** $\alpha_\Gamma(w)$ of w onto Γ results from skipping symbols $\sigma_i \notin \Gamma$. This projection extends naturally to languages.*

Using this projection, we can now define the green-only context [38]:

Definition 18 (Green-Only Context $M_c^g(I)$). *Let $M \in \mathcal{M}$ be an MTS and let I be an MC of M (Definition 15), and F_d be the minimal DFA that describes the prefix-closed language $\alpha_{\Gamma(I)}(\mathcal{L}_\top(M))$. The **green-only context** $M_c^g(I)$ can then be constructed as follows on the basis of F_d:*

1.) *Consider all incoming and outgoing transitions of the unique non-accepting sink state as may-only transitions.*
2.) *Consider all other transitions as must transitions.*
3.) *Disregard the property of accepting/non-accepting states.*

The following lemma states the admissibility of the green-only context in the case where $R(I^g) = \emptyset$ [38]:

Lemma 1 (Admissibility of Green-Only Context). *Let $M \in \mathcal{M}$ be an MTS. Let I^g be an MC of M (Definition 15) with $R(I^g) = \emptyset$ and $M_c^g(I^g)$ be the corresponding green-only context according to Definition 18. Then the following holds:*

$$(M_s(I^g) \parallel M_c^g(I^g)) \precsim M$$

Red-only contexts can now be constructed in a similar fashion:

Definition 19 (Red-Only Context $M_c^r(I)$). *Let I (Definition 15) be an MC, $\mathcal{L}_R$ be the language of words for which a path in I exists that contains a red transition $t \in R$, and F_d be the minimal DFA that describes the prefix-closed language $(\Gamma(I)^* \setminus \alpha_{\Gamma(I)}(\mathcal{L}_R))$ (see also Definition 17). The **red-only context** $M_c^r(I)$ can then be constructed as follows on the basis of F_d:*

1.) *Remove all incoming and outgoing transitions of the unique non-accepting sink state together with this sink state itself.*
2.) *Consider all remaining transitions as may-only transitions.*
3.) *Disregard the property of accepting/non-accepting states.*

The following lemma states the admissibility of a red-only context [38] in case of $G(I^r) = \emptyset$:

Lemma 2 (Admissibility of Red-Only Context). *Let $M \in \mathcal{M}$ be an MTS, I^r be an MC of M (Definition 15) with $G(I^r) = \emptyset$, and $M_c^r(I^r)$ be the red-only context according to Definition 19. Then the following holds:*

$$(M_s(I^r) \parallel M_c^r(I^r)) \precsim M$$

Green/red contexts $M_c^*(I)$ can now simply be defined via conjunction (see [38]):

Definition 20 (Green/Red Context $M_c^*(I)$).
*Let I be an MC with green-only context $M_c^g(I)$ (Definition 18) and red-only context $M_c^r(I)$ (Definition 19). Then the corresponding **green/red context** $M_c^*(I)$ is defined as follows:*

$$M_c^*(I) =_{def} (M_c^r(I) \wedge M_c^g(I))$$

As green and red transitions are guaranteed to be non-conflicting (see Definition 15), the following theorem follows straightforwardly from Proposition 1 and Lemmas 1 and 2 [38]:

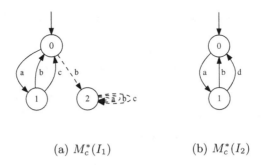

(a) $M_c^*(I_1)$ (b) $M_c^*(I_2)$

Fig. 4. Two green/red contexts for the MCs from Example 3 (see Fig. 3). (Color figure online)

Theorem 1 (Admissibility of Green/Red Context). *Let $M \in \mathcal{M}$ be an MTS, and I be an MC of M (Definition 15) with its green/red context $M_c^*(I)$ according to Definition 20. Then $M_c^*(I)$ is well-defined and the following holds:*

$$(M_s(I) \parallel M_c^*(I)) \lesssim M$$

Note that this means that may-only transitions in the generated system and context components can never trigger in the expanded parallel composition whenever the initial system is an LTS. This suffices to guarantee that bisimulation is preserved in this case:

Theorem 2 (Preservation of Bisimulation). *Let L be an LTS, and I be an MC of L (Definition 15) with its green/red context $M_c^*(I)$ according to Definition 20. Then $M_c^*(I)$ is well-defined and the following holds:*

$$(M_s(I) \parallel M_c^*(I)) \sim L$$

Example 4 (Green/Red Context). Figure 4 illustrates the green/red context MTSs $M_c^*(I_1)$ and $M_c^*(I_2)$ based on the MCs of Example 3 (see Fig. 3). Due to Theorem 2, it follows that

$$(M_s(I_1) \parallel M_c^*(I_1) \parallel M_s(I_2) \parallel M_c^*(I_2)) \sim (L_1 \parallel L_2).$$

5.2   Alphabet Extension

The parallel decomposition in Sect. 5.1 enables one to increase the number of parallel components in a composition, however it does neither increase the size of the expanded parallel composition nor the size of that composition's alphabet. In order to generate hard benchmark scenarios as described in Sect. 4, we overcome these limitations by applying alphabet extensions:

Definition 21 (Alphabet Extension (AE)). *Let $M \in \mathcal{M}$ be an MTS, Σ_E be a new alphabet, i.e. $(\Sigma_E \cap \Sigma(M)) = \emptyset$, and $\Sigma \subseteq \Sigma(M)$. An MTS $M' = (S, s_0, \Sigma \uplus \Sigma_E, \diamond, \Box)$ is called Σ_E alphabet extension (AE) of M if it adheres to the following two constraints:*

1. *The directed graph $(S, \{(s, s') \mid (\exists (s \xrightarrow{\sigma} s') \in \Box) \wedge \sigma \in \Sigma_E\})$ is strongly connected*
2. *$\forall \sigma \in \Sigma. \exists s, s' \in S : (s \xrightarrow{\sigma} s') \in \Box$*

The definition of an AE is comparably unconstrained and allows for a variety of possible choices as illustrated in Example 5.[6] Important is only that an alphabet extension M' of M can never 'block' transitions in M if composed with it because of the following: (i) The alphabet Σ_E only occurs in M' and (ii) within M', we can always reach every state by traversing transitions with labels from Σ_E. Thus it is straightforward to show:

Theorem 3 (Correctness of Alphabet Extension). *Let $M \in \mathcal{M}$ be an MTS, $\Sigma \subseteq \Sigma(M)$ a sub-alphabet of M, and M_E any Σ_E alphabet extension of M (Definition 21). Then we have:*

$$hide_{\Sigma_E}(M \parallel M_E) \approx M$$

Example 5 (Alphabet Extension). Figure 5 illustrates four different AEs, one for each of the components of Example 4. Because of Theorem 3, it follows that the parallel composition of $(M_s(I_1) \parallel M_c^*(I_1) \parallel M_s(I_2) \parallel M_c^*(I_2))$ with their AEs depicted in Fig. 5 is weakly bisimilar to $(L_1 \parallel L_2)$ (Fig. 1) when only considering the alphabet of the latter. In order to further intertwine the alphabet extensions with the MTSs that they extend, we choose to replace them pairwise with their expanded parallel compositions. Figure 6 depicts the expanded parallel composition of $M_c^*(I_1)$ with its AE that was chosen for this example.

5.3   Modal Refinement

As a last step during one iteration of our expansion, we may randomly refine each component of the parallel composition based on modal refinement as illustrated in Example 6. This step also allows for significant enlargement via node splitting and loop unrolling.

---

[6] Note that this definition of alphabet extension differs from the context extension introduced for model checking benchmarks in [38]: Because we do not need to guarantee liveness properties for weak bisimulation, Floyd-like cut points that guarantee an eventual synchronization are no longer required here.

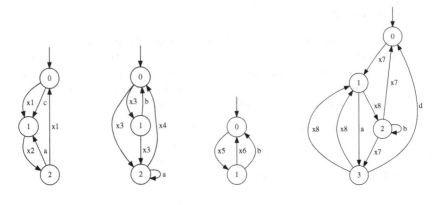

(a) AE of $M_s(I_1)$ (b) AE of $M_c^*(I_1)$ (c) AE of $M_s(I_2)$ (d) AE of $M_c^*(I_2)$

Fig. 5. Four different alphabet extensions based on the MTSs of Example 4.

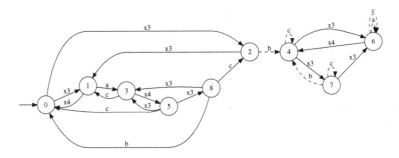

Fig. 6. Expanded composition of $M_c^*(I_1)$ (Fig. 4a) and its AE from Fig. 5b.

Example 6 (Modal Refinement). Consider the composition $(M_s(I_1) \parallel M_c^*(I_1) \parallel M_s(I_2) \parallel M_c^*(I_2))$ (Example 4) together with their AEs from Example 5. As shown in Example 5, we choose to group the AEs with their respective components and partially evaluate those compositions. In general, this does not result in LTSs. We therefore randomly refine the four resulting MTSs by eliminating may-only transitions or implementing them as must behavior.[7] The resulting composition of LTSs is illustrated in Fig. 7.

---

[7] Further refinement choices akin to bisimulation-preserving transformations would be possible too.

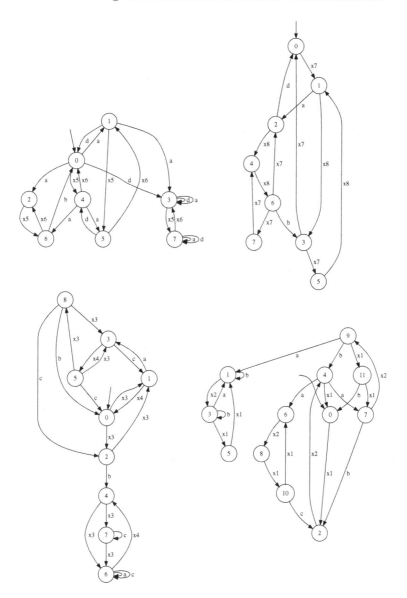

Fig. 7. Final four LTSs that result from one iteration of our expansion. Composed in parallel, they are weakly bisimilar to the two LTSs of Fig. 1 when only viewing the alphabet of the latter.

Finally, the origin of alphabet symbols may be obfuscated at the end using relabeling.

6   Conclusion

In this paper, we proposed a method to automatically generate arbitrarily complex benchmark problems for bisimulation checking. Technically, this method is a variant of an incremental generation approach for model checking benchmarks. Using this approach, a given benchmark scenario of controllable size is expanded to an arbitrarily complex benchmark problem, concerning both the number of parallel components and the component sizes, in an assumption commitment style. Whereas the property-preserving parallel decomposition is maintained in this variant, the alphabet extension is flexibilized as, in contrast to temporal logics, weak bisimulation is not sensitive to liveness properties.

In contrast to classical assumption commitment [2,17,33] and approaches like the ones presented in [14,15], the iterative decomposition based on MCs scales very well. However, admittedly, to achieve a different kind of goal because we do not require completeness and can therefore focus on a simplistic approach [29]. This scalability, which intuitively exists due to the difference between a-posteriori verification and correctness by construction, can be regarded as the essence of our benchmark generation approach [12,19,37].

Our MC, an extension of MTSs following and generalizing the ideas of [9], is specifically designed to manage the system/context relationship in a way so that the system can be iteratively decomposed into arbitrarily many parallel components while propagating dependencies throughout the entire system. Accordingly, generated benchmark problems are dominated by deterministic components as non-deterministic behavior in parallel components easily introduces unwanted behavior. We are currently investigation how to overcome this limitation based on a notion of context-dependent semantic determinism.

Acknowledgment. We are very grateful to Maximilian Schlüter for his implementation of the automatic context generation that was used to create the illustrations in this paper.

References

1. Bartocci, E., et al.: First international competition on runtime verification: rules, benchmarks, tools, and final results of CRV 2014. STTT, pp. 1–40, April 2017
2. Bauer, S.S., et al.: Moving from specifications to contracts in component-based design. In: de Lara, J., Zisman, A. (eds.) FASE 2012. LNCS, vol. 7212, pp. 43–58. Springer, Heidelberg (2012). https://doi.org/10.1007/978-3-642-28872-2_3
3. Benveniste, A., Caillaud, B.: Synchronous interfaces and assume/guarantee contracts. In: Aceto, L., Bacci, G., Bacci, G., Ingólfsdóttir, A., Legay, A., Mardare, R. (eds.) Models, Algorithms, Logics and Tools. LNCS, vol. 10460, pp. 233–248. Springer, Cham (2017). https://doi.org/10.1007/978-3-319-63121-9_12
4. Beyer, D.: Competition on software verification. In: Flanagan, C., König, B. (eds.) TACAS 2012. LNCS, vol. 7214, pp. 504–524. Springer, Heidelberg (2012). https://doi.org/10.1007/978-3-642-28756-5_38

5. Bunte, O., et al.: The mCRL2 toolset for analysing concurrent systems. In: Vojnar, T., Zhang, L. (eds.) TACAS 2019. LNCS, vol. 11428, pp. 21–39. Springer, Cham (2019). https://doi.org/10.1007/978-3-030-17465-1_2

6. Clarke, E., Grumberg, O., Jha, S., Lu, Y., Veith, H.: Counterexample-guided abstraction refinement. In: Emerson, E.A., Sistla, A.P. (eds.) CAV 2000. LNCS, vol. 1855, pp. 154–169. Springer, Heidelberg (2000). https://doi.org/10.1007/10722167_15

7. Clarke, E., Grumberg, O., Jha, S., Lu, Y., Veith, H.: Progress on the state explosion problem in model checking. In: Wilhelm, R. (ed.) Informatics. LNCS, vol. 2000, pp. 176–194. Springer, Heidelberg (2001). https://doi.org/10.1007/3-540-44577-3_12

8. Cleaveland, R., Parrow, J., Steffen, B.: The concurrency workbench: a semantics-based tool for the verification of concurrent systems. ACM Trans. Program. Lang. Syst. 15(1), 36–72 (1993)

9. Cleaveland, R., Steffen, B.: A preorder for partial process specifications. In: Baeten, J.C.M., Klop, J.W. (eds.) CONCUR 1990. LNCS, vol. 458, pp. 141–151. Springer, Heidelberg (1990). https://doi.org/10.1007/BFb0039057

10. Czech, M., Hüllermeier, E., Jakobs, M.C., Wehrheim, H.: Predicting rankings of software verification tools. In: Proceedings of the 3rd ACM SIGSOFT International Workshop on Software Analytics. SWAN 2017, pp. 23–26. ACM (2017)

11. Garavel, H., Lang, F., Mateescu, R., Serwe, W.: CADP 2011: a toolbox for the construction and analysis of distributed processes. Int. J. Softw. Tools Technol. Transfer 15(2), 89–107 (2013)

12. Geske, M., Jasper, M., Steffen, B., Howar, F., Schordan, M., van de Pol, J.: RERS 2016: parallel and sequential benchmarks with focus on LTL verification. In: Margaria, T., Steffen, B. (eds.) ISoLA 2016. LNCS, vol. 9953, pp. 787–803. Springer, Cham (2016). https://doi.org/10.1007/978-3-319-47169-3_59

13. Godefroid, P. (ed.): Partial-Order Methods for the Verification of Concurrent Systems. LNCS, vol. 1032. Springer, Heidelberg (1996). https://doi.org/10.1007/3-540-60761-7

14. Graf, S., Steffen, B.: Compositional minimization of finite state systems. In: Clarke, E.M., Kurshan, R.P. (eds.) CAV 1990. LNCS, vol. 531, pp. 186–196. Springer, Heidelberg (1991). https://doi.org/10.1007/BFb0023732

15. Graf, S., Steffen, B., Lüttgen, G.: Compositional minimisation of finite state systems using interface specifications. Formal Aspects Comput. 8(5), 607–616 (1996)

16. Grosu, R., Smolka, S.A.: Monte carlo model checking. In: Halbwachs, N., Zuck, L.D. (eds.) TACAS 2005. LNCS, vol. 3440, pp. 271–286. Springer, Heidelberg (2005). https://doi.org/10.1007/978-3-540-31980-1_18

17. Grumberg, O., Long, D.E.: Model checking and modular verification. ACM Trans. Program. Lang. Syst. (TOPLAS) 16(3), 843–871 (1994)

18. Hoare, C.A.R.: Communicating sequential processes. In: Hansen, P.B. (ed.) The Origin of Concurrent Programming, pp. 413–443. Springer, New York (1978). https://doi.org/10.1007/978-1-4757-3472-0_16

19. Howar, F., Isberner, M., Merten, M., Steffen, B., Beyer, D., Păsăreanu, C.: Rigorous examination of reactive systems. The RERS challenges 2012 and 2013. STTT 16(5), 457–464 (2014)

20. Huisman, M., Klebanov, V., Monahan, R.: VerifyThis 2012. STTT 17(6), 647–657 (2015)

21. Hüttel, H., Larsen, K.G.: The use of static constructs in a model process logic. In: Meyer, A.R., Taitslin, M.A. (eds.) Logic at Botik 1989. LNCS, vol. 363, pp. 163–180. Springer, Heidelberg (1989). https://doi.org/10.1007/3-540-51237-3_14

22. Jasper, M., et al.: RERS 2019: combining synthesis with real-world models. In: Beyer, D., Huisman, M., Kordon, F., Steffen, B. (eds.) TACAS 2019. LNCS, vol. 11429, pp. 101–115. Springer, Cham (2019). https://doi.org/10.1007/978-3-030-17502-3_7

23. Jasper, M., Mues, M., Schlüter, M., Steffen, B., Howar, F.: RERS 2018: CTL, LTL, and reachability. In: Margaria, T., Steffen, B. (eds.) ISoLA 2018. LNCS, vol. 11245, pp. 433–447. Springer, Cham (2018). https://doi.org/10.1007/978-3-030-03421-4_27

24. Jasper, M., Steffen, B.: Synthesizing subtle bugs with known witnesses. In: Margaria, T., Steffen, B. (eds.) ISoLA 2018. LNCS, vol. 11245, pp. 235–257. Springer, Cham (2018). https://doi.org/10.1007/978-3-030-03421-4_16

25. Kanellakis, P.C., Smolka, S.A.: CCS expressions, finite state processes, and three problems of equivalence. Inf. Comput. **86**(1), 43–68 (1990)

26. Kordon, F., et al.: Report on the model checking contest at petri nets 2011. In: Jensen, K., van der Aalst, W.M., Ajmone Marsan, M., Franceschinis, G., Kleijn, J., Kristensen, L.M. (eds.) Transactions on Petri Nets and Other Models of Concurrency VI. LNCS, vol. 7400, pp. 169–196. Springer, Heidelberg (2012). https://doi.org/10.1007/978-3-642-35179-2_8

27. Larsen, K.G.: Modal specifications. In: Sifakis, J. (ed.) CAV 1989. LNCS, vol. 407, pp. 232–246. Springer, Heidelberg (1990). https://doi.org/10.1007/3-540-52148-8_19

28. Legay, A., Delahaye, B., Bensalem, S.: Statistical model checking: an overview. In: Barringer, H., et al. (eds.) RV 2010. LNCS, vol. 6418, pp. 122–135. Springer, Heidelberg (2010). https://doi.org/10.1007/978-3-642-16612-9_11

29. Margaria, T., Steffen, B.: Simplicity as a driver for agile innovation. Computer **43**(6), 90–92 (2010)

30. Milner, R.: Communication and Concurrency. Prentice-Hall Inc., Upper Saddle River (1989)

31. Park, D.: Concurrency and automata on infinite sequences. In: Deussen, P. (ed.) GI-TCS 1981. LNCS, vol. 104, pp. 167–183. Springer, Heidelberg (1981). https://doi.org/10.1007/BFb0017309

32. Pnueli, A., Rosner, R.: On the synthesis of a reactive module. In: Proceedings of the 16th ACM SIGPLAN-SIGACT Symposium on Principles of Programming Languages. POPL 1989, pp. 179–190. ACM (1989)

33. Raclet, J.B., Badouel, E., Benveniste, A., Caillaud, B., Legay, A., Passerone, R.: A modal interface theory for component-based design. Fundamenta Informaticae **108**(1–2), 119–149 (2011)

34. Steffen, B., Jasper, M., Meijer, J., van de Pol, J.: Property-preserving generation of tailored benchmark petri nets. In: 17th International Conference on Application of Concurrency to System Design (ACSD), pp. 1–8, June 2017

35. Steffen, B.: Characteristic formulae. In: Ausiello, G., Dezani-Ciancaglini, M., Della Rocca, S.R. (eds.) ICALP 1989. LNCS, vol. 372, pp. 723–732. Springer, Heidelberg (1989). https://doi.org/10.1007/BFb0035794

36. Steffen, B., Howar, F., Merten, M.: Introduction to active automata learning from a practical perspective. In: Bernardo, M., Issarny, V. (eds.) SFM 2011. LNCS, vol. 6659, pp. 256–296. Springer, Heidelberg (2011). https://doi.org/10.1007/978-3-642-21455-4_8

37. Steffen, B., Isberner, M., Naujokat, S., Margaria, T., Geske, M.: Property-driven benchmark generation: synthesizing programs of realistic structure. Int. J. Softw. Tools Technol. Transfer **16**(5), 465–479 (2014)

38. Steffen, B., Jasper, M.: Property-preserving parallel decomposition. In: Aceto, L., Bacci, G., Bacci, G., Ingólfsdóttir, A., Legay, A., Mardare, R. (eds.) Models, Algorithms, Logics and Tools. LNCS, vol. 10460, pp. 125–145. Springer, Cham (2017). https://doi.org/10.1007/978-3-319-63121-9_7
39. Valmari, A.: The state explosion problem. In: Reisig, W., Rozenberg, G. (eds.) ACPN 1996. LNCS, vol. 1491, pp. 429–528. Springer, Heidelberg (1998). https://doi.org/10.1007/3-540-65306-6_21
40. Vanglabbeek, R., Smolka, S., Steffen, B.: Reactive, generative, and stratified models of probabilistic processes. Inf. Comput. **121**(1), 59–80 (1995)

Robustness of Neural Networks to Parameter Quantization

Abhishek Murthy[1](✉), Himel Das[2], and Md. Ariful Islam[2]

[1] Signify Research North Americas, Cambridge, MA, USA
amurthy.sunysb@gmail.com
[2] Texas Tech University, Lubbock, TX, USA
{himel.das,ariful.islam}@ttu.edu

Abstract. Quantization, a commonly used technique to reduce the memory footprint of a neural network for edge computing, entails reducing the precision of the floating-point representation used for the parameters of the network. The impact of such rounding-off errors on the overall performance of the neural network is estimated using testing, which is not exhaustive and thus cannot be used to guarantee the safety of the model. We present a framework based on Satisfiability Modulo Theory (SMT) solvers to quantify the robustness of neural networks to parameter perturbation. To this end, we introduce notions of local and global robustness that capture the deviation in the confidence of class assignments due to parameter quantization. The robustness notions are then cast as instances of SMT problems and solved automatically using solvers, such as dReal. We demonstrate our framework on two simple Multi-Layer Perceptrons (MLP) that perform binary classification on a two-dimensional input. In addition to quantifying the robustness, we also show that Rectified Linear Unit activation results in higher robustness than linear activations for our MLPs.

Keywords: Neural networks · Edge computing ·
Parameter quantization · Robustness · Satisfiability modulo theories

1 Introduction

Neural networks entail interconnected computational nodes that transform weighted combinations of their inputs using nonlinear functions. The interconnections lead to compositional behavior at the network-level, which enables neural networks to approximate highly nonlinear functions as their responses. The advent of the Backpropagation algorithm [28], the availability of large datasets [10], and optimized hardware [9] has led to widespread success in supervised and unsupervised learning.

Supervised learning of a neural network is the process of optimizing the network's parameters using reference data. Supervised learning can be used to

---

Research was performed with other authors at Texas Tech University.

© Springer Nature Switzerland AG 2019
E. Bartocci et al. (Eds.): From Reactive Systems to Cyber-Physical Systems, LNCS 11500, pp. 146–161, 2019.
https://doi.org/10.1007/978-3-030-31514-6_9

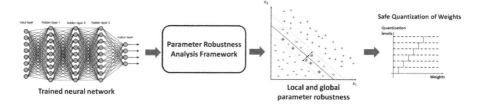

Fig. 1. Robustness analysis of neural network enables safe parameter quantization.

(i) learn classifiers, which can label an input into one of finitely many classes and (ii) learn the more general class of regressors, which capture relationships across continuous domains. Learning a model, also known as training, involves formulating a loss function that quantifies the performance of the model as a function of the parameters, and then minimizing the function using numerical techniques over the reference data, also known as training data. Backpropagation is the most popular class of numerical techniques used to optimize the parameters of the modern neural networks. Unsupervised learning, on the other hand, entails learning patterns and underlying distributions in unlabelled data.

Large networks contain millions of parameters and are trained using Graphics Processing Units (GPUs). Deploying trained neural networks in real-world production systems entails fetching the input from the user/client-device and then passing it through the neural network, also known as the forward pass, and obtaining the output, which could be a class-label or a regressed value, *in real time*. Web services, which perform the forward pass on the cloud can utilize the power of GPUs for time-sensitive calculations. The downside is that such applications suffer from (i) the latency of sending the input to the remote server and waiting for the output of the neural network and (ii) privacy concerns of exposing potentially sensitive inputs on the network.

An alternative design involves performing the forward pass on the client device (edge) by running the neural networks on it. This eliminates the network latencies and also avoids exposing the user's inputs to the network. Running neural networks on edge devices, such as mobile phones, tablets and low-power devices like wearables and Raspberry Pis present unique challenges. Storing the millions of parameters in floating-point representations incurs significant memory costs and the computational power needed for the forward pass may be prohobitive. Executing complex neural networks on the low computational power and memory available on edge devices is a well-known challenge in the industry and thus is an active area of interest.

In addition to dedicated hardware for low-power devices, the community has evolved three main approaches to the problem of running neural networks on resource-constrained edge devices.

1. *Quantization of Parameters*: The precision of the floating-point representation used to store the network parameters is reduced to lower the memory footprint of storing the network in the memory [15].

2. *Pruning*: The edges, represented by the weights, between nodes that do not significantly influence the network's output are made 0 and thus removed from the network, resulting in a reduction in the memory footprint [25].
3. *Optimized Neural-Network Architectures*: The network architecture is designed to reduce the floating-point operations, thereby reducing the running time of the forward pass, see [18] for an example.

These techniques have emerged using empirical benchmarking and have found limited success in the community. Today, there are a handful of applications that deploy neural networks on edge devices. The main reason behind this lack of widespread success is the unpredictability of the aforementioned techniques in preserving the performance of the network after training. Specifically, the state of the art on estimating the impact of pruning and quantization on the network's accuracy is limited to testing on a finite number of test cases.

In this paper, we introduce a framework to quantify the robustness of neural networks to parameter quantization, thereby automating the process of bounding the change in performance of the neural network. We introduce notions of local and global robustness of networks to parameter changes. Given a bounded perturbation in the parameter vector, local robustness measures the maximal change in the confidence of class assignment for an input. Global robustness extends this notion to the entire input-space. We cast these notions into instances of SMT problems and solve them automatically using solvers, such as dReal [14]. See Fig. 1 for an overview.

Robustness of neural networks has been an active area of research, but most of the authors have focused on input perturbations, rather than parameter changes. Our framework is focused on parameter perturbations. In summary, the main contributions of our paper are as follows.

- An automated framework is presented for bounding the deviation in the performance of neural networks due to parameter quantization. The framework enables the implementation of deep-learning-based applications on edge devices, like mobile phones, tablets and other embedded environments.
- We present two use-cases to demonstrate our framework: the parameters of two small MLPs that perform binary classification are perturbed and the robustness is analyzed using our approach.
- In addition to estimating parameter robustness, we also show that ReLU activations are more robust than linear activations for our MLPs.

The rest of the paper is organized as follows. Section 2 presents background on neural networks and SMT solvers. Section 3 introduces the theory of local and global robustness to parameter perturbations and Sect. 4 details the corresponding SMT problem formulations. Section 5 presents the case studies and their corresponding trained neural networks. Section 6 presents robustness analysis on the neural networks. Section 7 reviews related work and Sect. 8 presents our conclusions and the directions for future work.

2   Background

Every node of an NN performs two operations: weighted averaging of the inputs, and a nonlinear transformation of the weighted sum using a so-called *activation function*, see Fig. 2. Some of the commonly used activation functions are depicted in Fig. 3.

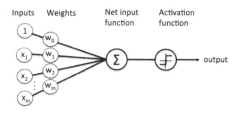

Fig. 2. Weighted averaging, followed by nonlinear activation.

A neural network is formed by interconnecting several such nodes using different architectures. Each connection from node i to node j is characterized by the weight that is used for the output of node i for the weighted average performed at node j. Typical architectures consists of layers of nodes connected to the nodes of the subsequent layer. The output of the neural network is vector with each entry representing the output of the corresponding node in the final layer. It is common to construct the network to have k output nodes if the goal is to assign one (or more) of k possible class assignments. Moreover, all the k values lie in $[0, 1]$ and sum to 1. The input is assigned the class label $0 \leq l \leq k - 1$ if the value of the lth node is the highest among the k outputs.

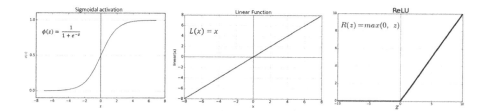

Fig. 3. Commonly used activation functions in neural networks.

We introduce notations for the parameter vector of a neural network as follows. NN_p denotes an instance of the neural network with p being the vector of parameter assignments. Given an input x, and the instance if the neural network NN_p, the vector of k outputs is returned by the function $f_{NN_p}(x)$. $NN_p(x)$ is the index of the highest output and thus corresponds to the class label l assigned to the input.

The dReal Solver

The dReal [14] tool is an SMT solver [11] for nonlinear theories over the reals. The tool can handle first order formula defined by nonlinear real functions such as polynomials, trigonometric functions, exponential functions, etc. It implements the framework of δ-complete decision procedure [13], which has two possible outputs:

- unsat: no variable assignment satisfying the formula.
- δ-sat: exists a variable assignment ξ satisfying the formula if we consider a user-specified numerical perturbation $\delta \in \mathcal{Q}^+$.

We note that the satisfiability of first-order formula over the real is in general undecidable [3]. The tool is implemented in the framework of delta-complete analysis, which provides an algorithm for the originally undecidable problem by using approximation (the use of δ in the analysis).

The latest version of dReal [21] now implements Optimization Modulo Theory (OMT) [5,29]. OMT is an extension of SMT which allows for finding models that optimize given objectives.

3 Parameter Robustness

In this section, we present various definitions of parameter robustness analysis for neural networks.

We begin with a definition of parameter robustness locally to an input similar to local input robustness as presented in [4,17,20]. Note that, we consider $\mathcal{L}_2$ norm for distance in both parameter vector space and NN confidence space in our definitions, but it is to possible to generalize them for other norms.

Definition 1. *An NN with parameter vector p_0 is (δ, ε)-parameter robust locally at an input x_0 if and only if:*

$$\forall p.|p - p_0| \leq \delta \implies |f_{NN_{p_0}}(x) - f_{NN_p}(x)| \leq \varepsilon \tag{1}$$

Definition 1 gives a quantitative measure on the change in confidence of labeling a certain input. This definition, however, does not cover all inputs in the input domain. The following definition address this:

Definition 2. *An NN with parameter vector p_0 is (δ, ε)-parameter robust globally for a input domain $\mathcal{D}$ if and only if:*

$$\forall x \in \mathcal{D}, \forall p.|p - p_0| \leq \delta \implies |f_{NN_{p_0}}(x) - f_{NN_p}(x)| \leq \varepsilon \tag{2}$$

Though the definitions of parameter robustness described above give a quantitative measure on the change of confidence, it does not say whether the decision label will actually be changed. For example, if the confidence value changes positively for a given label, the decision label might remain the same, even though ε could be higher. As a result, the above robustness measures gives only an idea on relative change in confidence value, but not how the actual label might get changed.

Now, we define the parameter robustness that specifies whether an actual label of an input changes. Both local and global versions are defined as follows:

Definition 3. *An NN with parameter vector p_0 is locally δ-parameter robust locally at an input x_0 if and only if:*

$$\forall p.|p - p_0| \leq \delta \implies NN_{p_0}(x_0) = NN_p(x_0) \tag{3}$$

Definition 4. *An NN with parameter vector p_0 is locally δ-parameter robust globally for an input domain $\mathcal{D}$ if and only if:*

$$\forall x \in \mathcal{D}, \forall p. |p - p_0| \leq \delta \implies NN_{p_0}(x) = NN_p(x) \qquad (4)$$

Definition 4 states that for an NN to be δ-parameter robust globally for all input in the domain, no input cannot be mislabeled. This is rather a very strict definition of robustness. In particular, when a quantization technique is applied to NN, it is expected that the labels for some inputs will be changed, at least the inputs close to the decision boundary. To incorporate this, we slightly modify the Definition 4 as follows:

Definition 5. *An NN with parameter vector p_0 is locally δ_σ-parameter robust globally for an input domain $\mathcal{D}$ if and only if:*

$$\forall x \in \mathcal{D}, \forall p. |p - p_0| \wedge |f_{NN_{p_0}}(x) - l| \geq \sigma \leq \delta \implies NN_{p_0}(x) = NN_p(x) \quad (5)$$

where l denotes the level set of the confidence function, which is used to label the input, i.e, $f_{NN_{p_0}}(x) = l$ represents a decision boundary.

The δ_σ-parameter robustness of NN is illustrated in Fig. 4. The red line represents the decision boundary and '$-$' and '$+$' represent the decision labels. The yellow lines are σ distance away from the decision boundary. Definition 5 states that all the inputs that are σ or more distance away from the decision boundary (i.e., all the points either above the top yellow line or below the bottom yellow line) will be labeled as same in both NN_{p_0} and NN_p. The inputs between the yellow lines, however, may be be mislabeled, as illustrated by the points inside the yellow circles in the figure.

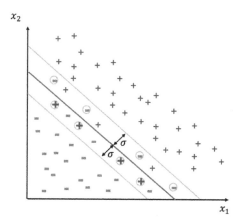

Fig. 4. Illustration of δ_σ-parameter robustness on a two-class classifier. (Color figure online)

4   Verification and Estimation of Parameter Robustness

In this section we will present how to verify and estimate parameter robustness using SMT solver.

4.1   Verifying Parameter Robustness

We apply SMT solver to verify all the parameter robustness defined in Sect. 3. The key idea is to construct a formula for each of them by the negating their definition. The robustness property will then be verified if the SMT solver returns unsat. The formula for all the parameter robustness given to SMT solver are as follows (for simplicity we encode them considering a binary classification problem):

– To verify Eq. 1, we use the following formula:

$$\exists p.(p \geq p_0 - \delta) \wedge (p \leq p_0 + \delta) \wedge abs(f_{NN_{p_0}}(x_0) - f_{NN_p}(x_0)) > \varepsilon \qquad (6)$$

– To verify Eq. 2, we use the following formula:

$$\exists p, x, (p \geq p_0 - \delta) \wedge (p \leq p_0 + \delta) \wedge (x \geq \underline{x}) \wedge (x \leq \bar{x}) \wedge abs(f_{NN_{p_0}}(x_0)$$
$$- f_{NN_p}(x_0)) > \varepsilon \qquad (7)$$

where we define the input domain $\mathcal{D}$ as a bounding box, i.e., $\mathcal{D} = [\underline{x}, \bar{x}]$
– To verify Eq. 3, we use the following formula:

$$\exists p.(p \geq p_0 - \delta) \wedge (p \leq p_0 + \delta) \wedge ((f_{NN_{p_0}}(x_0) \leq l) \wedge (f_{NN_p}(x_0) > l)$$
$$\vee (f_{NN_{p_0}}(x_0) < l) \wedge (f_{NN_p}(x_0) \geq l)) \qquad (8)$$

Here we encode $NN_{p_0}(x_0) = NN_p(x_0)$ as follows:

$$((f_{NN_{p_0}}(x_0) \leq l) \wedge (f_{NN_p}(x_0) \leq l)) \vee ((f_{NN_{p_0}}(x_0) > l) \wedge (f_{NN_p}(x_0) > l))$$

That is x_0 falls in the same side of the decision boundary both in NN_{p_0} and NN_p. For the verification purpose, we consider its negation.
– To verify Eq. 4, we use the following formula:

$$\exists p, x.(p \geq p_0 - \delta) \wedge (p \leq p_0 + \delta) \wedge (x \geq \underline{x}) \wedge (x \leq \bar{x}) \wedge ((f_{NN_{p_0}}(x_0) \leq l)$$
$$\wedge (f_{NN_p}(x_0) > l) \vee (f_{NN_{p_0}}(x_0) < l) \wedge (f_{NN_p}(x_0) \geq l)) \qquad (9)$$

– To verify Eq. 5, we use the following formula:

$$\exists p, x.(p \geq p_0 - \delta) \wedge (p \leq p_0 + \delta) \wedge (x \geq \underline{x}) \wedge (x \leq \bar{x}) \wedge (abs(f_{NN_{p_0}}(x) - l) \geq \sigma)$$
$$\wedge ((f_{NN_{p_0}}(x_0) \leq l) \wedge (f_{NN_p}(x_0) > l)) \vee ((f_{NN_{p_0}}(x_0) < l) \wedge (f_{NN_p}(x_0) \geq l)) \qquad (10)$$

We verify all the robustness properties on dReal solver [21].

4.2   Estimating Maximum Parameter Robustness

For (δ, ε)-parameter robustness, we allow δ-perturbation on the parameter space and check whether the confidence value is bounded by ε. The estimation problem is defined as computing maximum possible value of ε for a given value of δ. We are interested in this estimation problem, as the maximum value of ε represents the least robustness measure for a given δ value. The estimation problem can be formulated as an optimization problem as follows:

- ε-Estimation for (δ, ϵ)-parameter robustness locally at x_0:

$$\underset{\varepsilon \in [0, \bar{\varepsilon}]}{\text{minimize}} \ - \varepsilon$$

subject to:

$$(p \geq p_0 - \delta)$$
$$(p \leq p_0 + \delta) \tag{11}$$
$$abs(f_{NN_{p_0}}(x_0) - f_{NN_p}(x_0)) = \varepsilon$$

where, $\bar{\varepsilon}$ is the maximum value of ε. Note that, instead of maximizing, ε, we minimize its negation, as the SMT solver we used implements only the minimization problem.

- ε-Estimation for (δ, ϵ)-parameter robustness globally for $\mathcal{D} = [\underline{x}, \bar{x}]$:

$$\underset{\varepsilon \in [0, \bar{\varepsilon}]}{\text{minimize}} \ - \varepsilon$$

subject to:

$$(p \geq p_0 - \delta)$$
$$(p \leq p_0 + \delta)$$
$$(x \geq \underline{x}) \tag{12}$$
$$(x \leq \bar{x})$$
$$abs(f_{NN_{p_0}}(x_0) - f_{NN_p}(x_0)) = \varepsilon$$

Similarly, for δ_σ-parameter robustness, we consider estimation problem for σ. For a given value δ, we want to maximize σ, which tells us how far away the boundary needs to be shifted so that no input beyond it cannot be mislabeled. We formulate this estimation problem as follows:

$$\underset{\sigma \in [0, \bar{\sigma}]}{\text{minimize}} \ - \sigma$$

subject to

$$(p \geq p_0 - \delta)$$
$$(p \leq p_0 + \delta)$$
$$(x \geq \underline{x}) \tag{13}$$
$$(x \leq \bar{x})$$
$$abs(f_{NN_{p_0}}(x) - l)) = \sigma$$
$$(f_{NN_{p_0}}(x) \leq l) \wedge ((f_{NN_p}(x) \leq l)) \vee ((f_{NN_{p_0}}(x) > l) \wedge (f_{NN_p}(x) > l))$$

where maximum value of $\bar{\sigma}$ is the maximum value of σ.

5   Case Studies

We describe two datasets and the corresponding neural networks as case studies for our robustness analysis framework.

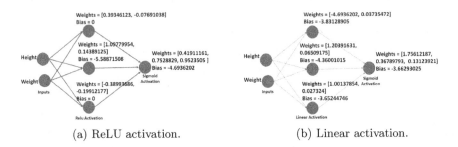

(a) ReLU activation.   (b) Linear activation.

Fig. 5. Two MLPs trained on the Athletes dataset.

The first dataset, known as *cats*, contains the height, weight, and gender of 144 domesticated cats (47 female and 97 male) [2]. The gender identification problem entails learning a classifier to estimate if a cat is Male or Female based on its height and weight. We present a simple one-node model that implements logistic regression and examine its robustness.

Given the height (H) and the weight (W) of a cat, the classifier, learned using Python Scikit-Learn 0.20.3, is given by $y = sig(x)$, where $x = c_0 + c_1 H + c_2 W$. We assign the class label "Male" if the $y \geq 0.5$ and "Female" otherwise. The parameters of the model that were learned on 78% of the data were $c_0 = -3.51518067, c_1 = 0.07577862$, and $c_2 = 1.18118408$. The multinomial loss function was optimized using the *lbgfs* algorithm [27]. The testing accuracy on the remaining 22% was 87.5%.

A second dataset contains the official statistics on the 11, 538 athletes (6,333 men and 5,205 women) that participated in the 2016 Olympic games at Rio de Janeiro [1]. Each row contains an id, the name, nationality, gender, date birth, height, weight, sport of the athletes and the medals tally. The gender identification problem entails learning an MLP to guess the gender of the athlete based on their height and weight. We present two MLPs for this problem and examine their robustness in the next section.

Given the height and weight of an athlete as the input, the MLPs is constructed using two layers: a hidden layer and an output node. Three nodes that make up the hidden layer perform weighted averaging of the inputs and transform them using a nonlinear activation. Their outputs are then fed to the output node, which again takes a weighted average and uses the Sigmoid activation to obtain a number between 0 and 1. If the output is greater than 0.5, the input is assigned "Male", otherwise it is assigned "Female". We implemented two variations of the model. We used ReLU and linear activations in the three nodes of the hidden layer. The two models and their parameters are illustrated in Fig. 5.

Both the Cats and the Athletes examples entail linear decision boundaries that separate the two classes. Thus, linear activation functions can be used to learn these boundaries. In the subsequent sections, we compare the robustness of the two activation functions.

The models were implemented in Keras and trained on a GPU-based instance of Amazon Web Services. The training accuracy was 77.19% and 77.36% for the ReLU and Linear versions respectively after 200 epochs.

In the next section, we apply our robustness analysis framework to examine the effect of quantizing the parameters of the logistic regression model for the Cats dataset and the two MLPs for the athletes dataset. Exploring the scalability of our framework to larger models is part of our future work.

6   Results

In this section we discuss our results. For all three NNs (one for first case study and two for second case study), we present results for (δ, ε)- and δ_σ-parameter robustness both locally at an input and globally at input domain.

Table 1. Estimated values for ε and σ for (δ, ε)- and δ_σ-parameter robustness, respectively, globally for input domains.

δ	ε		
	CAT	ATH-ReLU	ATH-Linear
0.005	0.00691	0.166	0.545
0.01	0.05054	0.0825	0.219
δ	σ		
	CAT	ATH-ReLU	ATH-Linear
0.005	(0.024, 0.021)	(0.082, 0.076)	(0.268, 0.218)
0.01	(0.052, 0.04)	(0.165, 0.144)	(0.44, 0.34)

Table 1 shows the estimated value of ε of (δ, ε)-parameter robustness, computed using Eq. (12), and σ of δ_σ-parameter robustness, computed using Eq. (13), for entire input domains. We compute them for two different δ values. The column CAT, ATH-ReLU and ATH-Linear represent the results for cat classifier, athletic classifier with ReLU activation and athletic classifier with Linear activation, respectively. The tuple in the table for σ represents values for *male* and *female* class, respectively. If we compare the results of ATH-ReLU and ATH-Linear, it is clear that the former classifier is much more robust than the latter for δ pertubation of the parameter values.

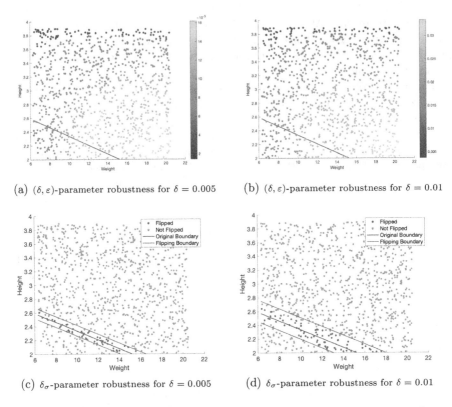

(a) (δ, ε)-parameter robustness for $\delta = 0.005$

(b) (δ, ε)-parameter robustness for $\delta = 0.01$

(c) δ_σ-parameter robustness for $\delta = 0.005$

(d) δ_σ-parameter robustness for $\delta = 0.01$

Fig. 6. Parameter robustness analysis of Cat classifier. (Color figure online)

Figure 6 illustrates parameter robustness of the Cat classifier presented. For (δ, ε)-parameter robustness, we choose two different δ values (0.005 and 0.01). For both cases, we randomly chose 1000 points from the input domain. We then computed ε for all inputs using Eq. (11). Figure 6(a,b) shows (δ, ε)-parameter robustness locally at each randomly selected points. The blue line represents the decision boundary of NN, whereas the colorbar represents the range of ε. It is clear from the figures that ε value is higher in the bottom right region, which means the region is more susceptible to be mislabeled in the perturbed network. Note that does not mean that the input would actually be mislabeled (see explanation in Sect. 3).

Figure 6(c,d) illustrates both δ- and δ_σ-parameter robustness for two different δ values. For δ-parameter robustness, we selected 1000 random inputs from the domain. We then checked whether the input labeled will be flipped in the perturbed network using Eq. (8). In the figures, green and red points represent *non-flippable* and *flippable* inputs, respectively. The top (bottom) red line is generated by adding (subtracting) σ to the decision boundary, where σ is computed using Eq. (13).

Figures 7 and 8 illustrate the parameter robustness analysis of the athletics classifier with ReLU and Linear activation, respectively. Comparing these figures, we can conclude that the athletics classifier with ReLU activation is much more robust as compared to the classifier with linear activation.

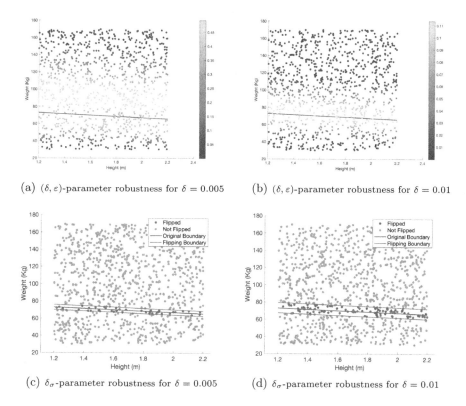

(a) (δ, ε)-parameter robustness for $\delta = 0.005$ (b) (δ, ε)-parameter robustness for $\delta = 0.01$

(c) δ_σ-parameter robustness for $\delta = 0.005$ (d) δ_σ-parameter robustness for $\delta = 0.01$

Fig. 7. Parameter robustness analysis of Athletics classifier with ReLU activation.

7   Related Work

Robustness analysis of neural networks is an active area of research. In this section, we compare and contrast some of the recent papers with our framework. Robustness typically refers to an NN's ability to handle perturbations in the input data. The efforts to characterize robustness can be broadly classified into two types: model-centric approaches and data-centric approaches.

Model-centric approaches focus on improving the problem formulation to construct robust networks. Distillation training, one of the earliest attempts, entails training one model to predict the output probabilities of another model that was trained on an earlier, baseline standard to emphasize accuracy [16,26]. In [8], the authors proposed a new set of attacks for the L_0, L_2, and L_∞ distance metrics to construct upper bounds on the robustness of neural networks and thereby demonstrate that defensive distillation is limited in handling adversarial examples. Adversarial perturbations, random noise; and geometric transformations were studied in [12] and the authors highlight close connections between the robustness to additive perturbations and geometric properties of the classifier's decision boundary, such as the curvature. Spatial Transform Networks, which entail geometrical transformation of the a network's filter maps were proposed in [19] to improve the robustness to geometric perturbations. Recently, a generic analysis framework CROWN was proposed to certify NNs using linear or quadratic upper and lower bounds for general activation functions [31]. The authors extended their work to overcome the limitation of simple fully-connected

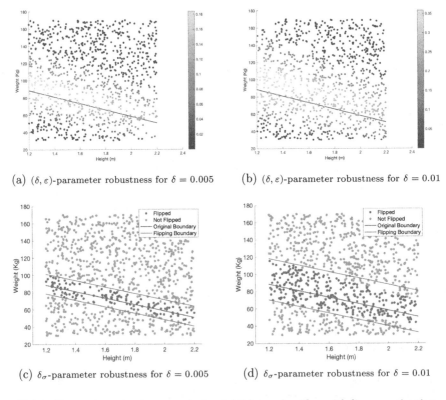

(a) (δ, ε)-parameter robustness for $\delta = 0.005$

(b) (δ, ε)-parameter robustness for $\delta = 0.01$

(c) δ_σ-parameter robustness for $\delta = 0.005$

(d) δ_σ-parameter robustness for $\delta = 0.01$

Fig. 8. Parameter robustness analysis of Athletes classifier with linear activation

layers and ReLU activations to propose CNN-Cert. The new framework can handle various architectures including convolutional layers, max-pooling layers, batch normalization layer, residual blocks, as well as general activation functions and capable of certifying robustness on general convolutional neural networks [6].

Data-centric approaches entail identifying and rejecting perturbed samples, or increasing the training data to handle perturbations appropriately. Binary detector networks that can spot adversarial samples [22,24], and augmenting data to reflect different lighting conditions [30] are typical examples. Additionally, robust optimization using saddle point(min-max) formulation [23] and region-based classification by assembling information in a hypercube centered [7] have also shown promising results. The above-mentioned approaches focus on perturbations to data, but our framework focuses on perturbations to the parameters with the end goal of safely implementing the neural networks on resource-constrined platforms.

8 Conclusions and Directions for Future Work

We presented a framework to automatically estimate the impact of rounding-off errors in the parameters of a neural network. The framework uses SMT solvers to estimate the local and global robustness of a given network. We applied our framework on a single-node logistic regression model and two small MLPs. We will consider larger convolutional neural networks in the future and investigate the scalability of our framework to larger parameter vectors. Compositionality will be critical to analyzing real-world neural networks and we will explore extending the theory of approximate bisimulation and the related Lyapunov-like functions to our problem.

References

1. Athletes dataset. https://github.com/flother/rio2016. Accessed 19 Mar 2019
2. Cats dataset. https://stat.ethz.ch/R-manual/R-devel/library/boot/html/catsM.html. Accessed 19 Mar 2019
3. Alur, R., Courcoubetis, C., Henzinger, T.A., Ho, P.-H.: Hybrid automata: an algorithmic approach to the specification and verification of hybrid systems. In: Grossman, R.L., Nerode, A., Ravn, A.P., Rischel, H. (eds.) HS 1991-1992. LNCS, vol. 736, pp. 209–229. Springer, Heidelberg (1993). https://doi.org/10.1007/3-540-57318-6_30
4. Bastani, O., Ioannou, Y., Lampropoulos, L., Vytiniotis, D., Nori, A., Criminisi, A.: Measuring neural net robustness with constraints. In: Advances in Neural Information Processing Systems, pp. 2613–2621 (2016)
5. Bjørner, N., Phan, A.-D., Fleckenstein, L.: νZ - an optimizing SMT solver. In: Baier, C., Tinelli, C. (eds.) TACAS 2015. LNCS, vol. 9035, pp. 194–199. Springer, Heidelberg (2015). https://doi.org/10.1007/978-3-662-46681-0_14
6. Boopathy, A., Weng, T.W., Chen, P.Y., Liu, S., Daniel, L.: CNN-Cert: an efficient framework for certifying robustness of convolutional neural networks (2018). http://arxiv.org/abs/1811.12395

7. Cao, X., Gong, N.Z.: Mitigating evasion attacks to deep neural networks via region-based classification (2017). http://arxiv.org/abs/1709.05583
8. Carlini, N., Wagner, D.A.: Towards evaluating the robustness of neural networks (2016). http://arxiv.org/abs/1608.04644
9. Chetlur, S., et al.: cuDNN: efficient primitives for deep learning (2014). http://arxiv.org/abs/1410.0759
10. Deng, J., Dong, W., Socher, R., Li, L.J., Li, K., Fei-Fei, L.: ImageNet: a large-scale hierarchical image database. In: CVPR09 (2009)
11. D'silva, V., Kroening, D., Weissenbacher, G.: A survey of automated techniques for formal software verification. IEEE Trans. Comput. Aided Des. Integr. Circuits Syst. **27**(7), 1165–1178 (2008)
12. Fawzi, A., Moosavi-Dezfooli, S.M., Frossard, P.: The robustness of deep networks - a geometric perspective. IEEE Signal Process. Mag. **34**(6), 13.50–62 (2017)
13. Gao, S., Avigad, J., Clarke, E.M.: δ-complete decision procedures for satisfiability over the reals. In: Gramlich, B., Miller, D., Sattler, U. (eds.) IJCAR 2012. LNCS (LNAI), vol. 7364, pp. 286–300. Springer, Heidelberg (2012). https://doi.org/10.1007/978-3-642-31365-3_23
14. Gao, S., Kong, S., Clarke, E.M.: dReal: an SMT solver for nonlinear theories over the reals. In: Bonacina, M.P. (ed.) CADE 2013. LNCS (LNAI), vol. 7898, pp. 208–214. Springer, Heidelberg (2013). https://doi.org/10.1007/978-3-642-38574-2_14
15. Guo, Y.: A survey on methods and theories of quantized neural networks (2018). http://arxiv.org/abs/1808.04752
16. Hinton, G., Vinyals, O., Dean, J.: Distilling the knowledge in a neural network. In: NIPS Deep Learning and Representation Learning Workshop (2015). http://arxiv.org/abs/1503.02531
17. Huang, X., Kwiatkowska, M., Wang, S., Wu, M.: Safety verification of deep neural networks. In: Majumdar, R., Kunčak, V. (eds.) CAV 2017. LNCS, vol. 10426, pp. 3–29. Springer, Cham (2017). https://doi.org/10.1007/978-3-319-63387-9_1
18. Iandola, F.N., Moskewicz, M.W., Ashraf, K., Han, S., Dally, W.J., Keutzer, K.: SqueezeNet: AlexNet-level accuracy with 50x fewer parameters and <1mb model size (2016). http://arxiv.org/abs/1602.07360
19. Jaderberg, M., Simonyan, K., Zisserman, A., Kavukcuoglu, K.: Spatial transformer networks (2015). http://arxiv.org/abs/1506.02025
20. Katz, G., Barrett, C.W., Dill, D.L., Julian, K.D., Kochenderfer, M.J.: Towards proving the adversarial robustness of deep neural networks. In: FVAV@iFM (2017)
21. Kong, S.: The dreal4 tool (2019). https://github.com/dreal/dreal4
22. Lu, J., Issaranon, T., Forsyth, D.A.: SafetyNet: detecting and rejecting adversarial examples robustly. CoRR abs/1704.00103 (2017). http://arxiv.org/abs/1704.00103
23. Madry, A., Makelov, A., Schmidt, L., Tsipras, D., Vladu, A.: Towards deep learning models resistant to adversarial attacks. In: International Conference on Learning Representations (2018). https://openreview.net/forum?id=rJzIBfZAb
24. Metzen, J.H., Genewein, T., Fischer, V., Bischoff, B.: On detecting adversarial perturbations. In: Proceedings of 5th International Conference on Learning Representations (ICLR) (2017). http://arxiv.org/abs/1702.04267
25. Molchanov, P., Tyree, S., Karras, T., Aila, T., Kautz, J.: Pruning convolutional neural networks for resource efficient transfer learning (2016). http://arxiv.org/abs/1611.06440
26. Papernot, N., McDaniel, P.D., Wu, X., Jha, S., Swami, A.: Distillation as a defense to adversarial perturbations against deep neural networks (2015). http://arxiv.org/abs/1511.04508

27. Pedregosa, F., et al.: Scikit-learn: machine learning in python. J. Mach. Learn. Res. **12**, 2825–2830 (2011)
28. Rumelhart, D.E., Hinton, G.E., Williams, R.J.: Learning representations by back-propagating errors. Nature **323**, 533–536 (1986). https://doi.org/10.1038/323533a0
29. Sebastiani, R., Trentin, P.: OptiMathSAT: a tool for optimization modulo theories. In: Kroening, D., Păsăreanu, C.S. (eds.) CAV 2015. LNCS, vol. 9206, pp. 447–454. Springer, Cham (2015). https://doi.org/10.1007/978-3-319-21690-4_27
30. Sivaraman, K., Murthy, A.: Object recognition under lighting variations using pretrained networks. IEEE Appl. Imag. Pattern Recognit. Work. (AIPR) **2018**, 1–7 (2018)
31. Zhang, H., Weng, T.W., Che, P.Y., Hsieh, C.J., Daniel, L.: Efficient neural network robustness certification with general activation functions (2018). http://arxiv.org/abs/1811.00866

Model-Based Design

Model-Based Energy Characterization
of IoT System Design Aspects

Alexios Lekidis$^{(\boxtimes)}$ and Panagiotis Katsaros

Department of Informatics, Aristotle University of Thessaloniki,
54124 Thessaloniki, Greece
{alekidis,katsaros}@csd.auth.gr

Abstract. The advances towards IoT systems with increased autonomy support improvements to existing applications and open new perspectives for other application domains. However, the design of IoT systems is challenging, due to the multiple design aspects that need to be considered. Connectivity and storage aspects are amongst the most significant ones, as IoT devices are resource-constrained and in many cases battery-powered. On top of them, it is also essential to consider privacy and security aspects that are linked to the protection of the IoT system, as well as of the data exchanged through its connectivity interfaces. Ensuring security in an IoT system, though, is an evident need and a complex challenge, due to its impact in the battery lifetime. In this paper, we propose a methodology to manage energy consumption through a model-based approach for the energy characterization of IoT design aspects using the BIP (Behavior, Interaction, Priority) component framework. Our approach is exemplified based on an Intelligent Transport System (ITS) that uses Zolertia Zoul devices placed in traffic lights and road signs to broadcast environmental and road hazard information to crossing vehicles. The results allow to find a feasible design solution that respects battery lifetime and security requirements.

Keywords: Internet of Things (IoT) · Energy characterization ·
Security · Model-based design

1 Introduction

The combination of connected intelligence in systems of the Internet of Things (IoT) with energy-constrained devices featuring limited computational resources poses new challenges in application design. To better control the consumption of battery lifetime, application developers have to consider a number of design aspects not only at the application level, but also at the system level. These aspects include the system's connectivity, the data processing and the data storage. Furthermore, security and data privacy aspects should be also taken into account, since the IoT has attracted the interest of malicious actors, who may

© Springer Nature Switzerland AG 2019
E. Bartocci et al. (Eds.): From Reactive Systems to Cyber-Physical Systems, LNCS 11500, pp. 165–180, 2019.
https://doi.org/10.1007/978-3-030-31514-6_10

attempt to tamper with the provided functionality of an IoT system. Widely known attacks as the Distributed Denial of Service (DDoS) Mirai botnet [3] on OVH[1] have recently demonstrated the feasibility of opening system ports with default authentication credentials through remote TELNET or SSH connections.

Important risks emerge due to: (i) the available connectivity interfaces and IoT protocol implementations and (ii) the exposed web services that allow continuous service delivery but usually are not designed with security in mind. The former refer to the absence of security measures in IoT protocols (e.g. MQTT [7]), which opens possibilities to eavesdrop or tamper with the exchanged data. For the latter, the absence of security protection is due to the additive computational power and storage memory required for the implementation of security mechanisms (e.g. encryption). This may lead to memory overflow, as well as to considerably reduced battery lifetime.

In overall, the design of IoT systems is characterized by a high complexity due to the multiple overlapping design aspects, which have to be taken into account and the initial system requirements that often are not directly feasible within the IoT system architecture. As a consequence, the system requirements are usually refined multiple times until they converge to those that can be eventually implemented. The overall gap in system design could be bridged by a method for the estimation and characterization of the system's energy life-span, with respect to the design aspects considered in the initial system requirements.

To this end, we propose a systematic model-based approach that leverages the Behavior, Interaction, Priority (BIP) component framework [5] towards an energy profiling scheme for the overlapping system design aspects. Our scheme enables the prediction of tight bounds for the various design aspects by utilzing a software-based solution of the Contiki IoT operating system, called powertrace [8], which are then used to include energy constraints in the BIP models [11]. Such scheme allows to overcome challenges related to energy monitoring, as it currently requires direct hardware interactions, which in most devices are not supported [8]. Furthermore, it provides an automated energy cost analysis for IoT design aspects compared to manual energy consumption calculations, which rely on the manufacturer characteristics that might also be inaccurate according to actual system measurements [17].

The method is illustrated through an Intelligent Transport System (ITS), i.e. an application scenario selected from one of the main IoT system domains[2]. In the ITS system, road hazard and environment information are broadcasted by infrastructure components, as traffic lights and road signs. To facilitate such communication the infrastructure components include Zolertia Zoul modules[3]. In this context, we use the system requirements defined by the European Transportation Committee (ETSI)[4] to evaluate the feasibility of ITS system design

---

[1] French cloud computing company - https://ovhcloud.com.

[2] https://www.technavio.com/blog/intelligent-transport-system-iot-promote-smart-safe-urban-mobility.

[3] https://zolertia.io/zoul-module/.

[4] https://www.etsi.org/.

aspects that are linked to IoT connectivity protocols for data processing and storage schemes, as well as to security protocols such as lightweight implementations of TLS and DTLS. In overall, this paper has the following contributions:

- an energy profiling technique for estimating the energy impact of various design aspects in an IoT application;
- an energy-aware model allowing a feasible design solution for IoT applications given the energy cost for each design aspect;
- a use case of our energy profiling technique on an ITS system deployed on Zolertia Zoul motes.

The rest of the paper is organized as follows. Section 2 provides a brief introduction to the powertrace IoT energy measuring module, as well as our previous work on energy-aware models using the BIP framework. Section 3 illustrates the proposed energy profiling technique for deriving estimates for the IoT system design aspects, which are later used in Sect. 4 to evaluate the use of communication, data storage and security aspects in the ITS case study. Finally, Sect. 5 provides conclusions and perspectives for future work.

2   Background

2.1   Measuring Energy Consumption with Powetrace

Powertrace [8] is a Contiki library that allows the annotation of Contiki programs with primitives, for monitoring the energy flow in IoT devices. It identifies four individual operating modes that contribute to a device's energy consumption:

- Low Power (LPM): the device is idle waiting for an event
- CPU: the device microcontroller is used for calculations/data processing
- Radio transmission (Tx): indicating data transmission
- Radio reception (Rx): indicating data reception

The energy consumption depends on the time that a device remains in each of the above modes. To measure this time, the library provides code primitives that can be used for every IoT device type. A data logger supporting energy analytics is utilized to store the data. Examples of such analytics are the duty cycle or the device lifetime. The former refers to the percentage of time that a device remains in one operating mode, whereas the latter refers to the total time duration that a device operates autonomously. The period that powertrace uses to measure and log the data is user-configurable and has an impact on the performance and accuracy of the mechanism. Finally, the energy calculation in powertrace also supports hardware-specific parameters, such as the real-time timer (RTIMER[5]) that is used to measure the hardware clock cycles of the device per second.

---

[5] http://anrg.usc.edu/contiki/index.php/Timers#Step_5_-_Introduction_to_rtimer.

2.2 Energy-Aware Modeling of IoT Systems

In a related article [11] we have presented a systematic methodology to characterize the impact of various application design parameters to the total energy consumption of IoT devices. This methodology allows the estimation of tight energy bounds for the energy consumption of an IoT application through the use of Statistical Model Checking (SMC) [14].

Since energy consumption is closely related to connectivity design aspects, the parameters found to have a high impact are related to IoT connectivity. Nevertheless, energy consumption is also impacted by additional equally important aspects and hence we focus here on revisiting the initial energy model and associated design parameters. The identified parameters in [11] were classified into (i) the application, (ii) the MAC and (iii) the physical network layers.

Our methodology is driven by a model for the system design that is based on the BIP (Behavior-Interaction-Priority) [5] executable modeling language. BIP is a particularly expressive, component-based framework with rigorous semantics. It allows the construction of complex, hierarchically structured models from atomic components, which are characterized by their behavior and interfaces. The components are transition systems enriched with data. Transitions represent state changes from a source to a destination control location. Each time a transition is taken, component data (variables) may be assigned new values, which are computed by user-defined functions (in C/C++). Atomic components are composed by layered application of interactions and priorities. Interactions express synchronization constraints and define the transfer of data between interacting components. Priorities are used to filter amongst possible interactions and to steer system evolution so as to meet performance requirements, e.g. to express scheduling policies. A set of atomic components can be composed into a generic compound component by the successive application of connectors, representing sets of interactions, and priorities.

3 Characterization of IoT System Design Aspects

In this section, we present a method (Fig. 1) to bridge the gap between IoT system requirements and the energy impact that they have in the context of the IoT architecture. Our method allows (1) the energy characterization of all aspects contributing to the energy consumption and (2) the design of the application with respect to those aspects.

Given as input a set of requirement specifications for the relevant design aspects, and the high-level design of the application expressed in a Domain Specific Language (DSL) [12], our method proceeds as follows:

1. **Transformation for the System Model**: The actions comprising this step are two-fold. First, the Contiki code behaviour of the application modules is specified in the DSL-based description, which is used to generate an Application Model in BIP. This model is later enhanced with the OS/kernel model

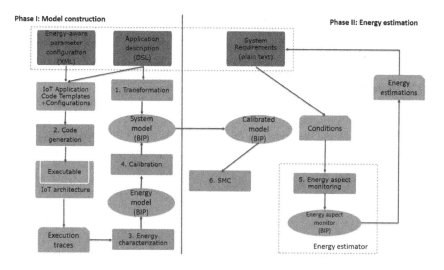

Fig. 1. Design phases of the proposed method

that is formed from a library of BIP components. The two models are composed by incorporating information specified in the DSL description for how the application modules are deployed to the IoT system's devices.

2. **Code generation from IoT application templates**: This step leverages the DSL description and an XML-based configuration file with the parameters that are presented in Sect. 3.1 that affect the energy consumption. Both are used as inputs to instantiate Contiki code templates for the IoT application and form an executable program for the devices.

3. **Energy characterization**: The analysis of powertrace execution traces is provided to a distribution fitting technique (Sect. 3.2). This technique allows to associate a probabilistic distribution to the data, in order to prepare them for being injected to a BIP energy model for IoT systems. This model is presented in [11] and includes the influential hardware/software energy constraints from the execution of the IoT application.

4. **Calibration for the construction of an energy-aware System Model**: This step concerns with the addition of parameters to the BIP model for the runtime characterization of the IoT application, as well as the generation of glue code for the composition of the BIP System Model with the energy model.

5. **Energy aspect monitoring:** The Calibrated BIP Model is also connected to energy monitors (Sect. 3.3) for the design aspects of interest. This allows the simulation-based analysis of energy consumption such that the designer can check the feasibility of the various (combinations of) design aspects with respect to the available resources.

6. **Statistical model checking (SMC):** At the end the designer can verify if the Calibrated BIP Model satisfies the system requirements through SMC.

3.1   Energy-Relevant Parameters for IoT Design Aspects

Given that the connectivity aspects were covered in our previous work [11], this section focuses on the data processing and security aspects.

Data Processing Aspects
The amount of available memory in IoT devices, allows for the implementation of a limited number of IoT application features, with respect to those envisioned in system requirements. The selection of which features are necessary and should be implemented requires a characterization of their energy constraints. Given these constraints, the main parameters that influence data processing are:

Resource Processing: Resources provide important information in IoT applications through the interaction with hardware sensors. Sensors are or are not built-in, in which case they are mounted in the device as peripherals (e.g. Phidgets[6] sensors for Zolertia Z1). Resource communication depends on their processing time, which when lengthy, can lead to timeout and retransmissions on the requester side. This increases substantially the energy consumed in processing and transmission mode. CoAP provides a mechanism to optimize the energy consumed in such scenario by acknowledging the resource request and then sending the response when it becomes available [16]. Overall, peripheral communication is unpredictable and thus can influence strongly IoT device energy consumption.

Routing Protocol: Many IoT applications configure edge entities to route all data that require processing in remote cloud servers. This emerged a new type of IoT applications, called Software-Defined Networks (SDN) [13], where control and logic is placed on the sensors and data processing on remote cloud servers. To allow energy-efficient data routing to cloud servers, a number of protocols were developed with RPL [18] being the one widely used in IoT. RPL builds an Destination Oriented Directed Acyclic Graph (DODAG) that provides the best route from each leaf node to the edge to direct all data encapsulated in network packets. Other routing protocols, include the cognitive RPL (CORPL) [2], a variation of RPL for cognitive radio networks [1], as well as the Channel-Aware Routing Protocol (CARP) [4], a non-standardized protocol that is used for underwater communication due to its link quality considerations.

Memory Block Management: The limited memory available in IoT devices requires new techniques to allocate memory dynamically. Apart from the commonly used heap memory allocation using the *malloc* library[7], IoT systems also employ dynamic block allocation through the *mmem* library[8]. The latter defragments the managed memory area, which in turn allows the IoT application designer to manage the features to be implemented by estimating their block size. Additionally, by avoiding device operations when in a low memory state, a balanced energy consumption can be achieved.

---

[6] http://wiki.zolertia.com/wiki/index.php/Phidgets.

[7] https://en.cppreference.com/w/c/memory/malloc.

[8] http://www.eistec.se/docs/contiki/a02115.html.

Security Aspects

Security is receiving substantial attention in IoT application development, due to the underlying risks especially for safety-critical systems as connected vehicles or avionics. Mechanisms as encryption or authentication offer protection against imminent threats, though they should also have a lightweight energy footprint to respect the constraints of IoT systems.

Security Level: The protection of IoT devices is managed by the security level that they offer. Security levels are categorized according to the system requirements for security aspects. The currently available levels are:

[**SL-0**] No security
[**SL-1**] Encryption only
[**SL-2**] Authentication and encryption

A higher security level results in better protected schemes, but leads to higher energy consumption. The security level is based on the system requirements.

Security Protocol: The protocols allowing secure data exchange are implemented in different layers of the IoT protocol stack. Each of these protocols contributes to a security level, but it also uses a specific communication mechanism between the IoT devices. As an example, TLS uses a handshake mechanism to establish a connection by agreeing on the connection parameters and by the exchange of a secret cipher key. A similar procedure is applied for protocols of other layers such as the IPsec in the IP layer. Overall, even though these protocols offer solid encryption/authentication mechanisms they introduce a substantial overhead on the energy consumption. This is due to the time that a device remains on the processing (i.e. CPU) mode for encrypting/decrypting the packets, as well as the additive transmissions for establishing a connection.

Session Key Size: In traditional Internet systems, security is handled through sufficiently large key sizes through the commonly used AES encryption. Instead, in IoT a large key size (i) would increase the processing demand for encryption/decryption of messages and (ii) would prolong the time the IoT device remains in transmission mode, since the key should be distributed to the other IoT devices upon connection establishment. These considerations along with the dynamicity of the IoT environment lead to the conclusion that the key size should be considered as an important aspect when providing security for IoT devices.

3.2   Energy Characterization

Energy characterization (step 3 in Fig. 1) is performed through distribution fitting, a technique to derive models that characterize input data. In our scope, distribution fitting considers that the target model is a probability distribution. This technique allows to characterize the energy evolution over a certain period, to reflect the actual energy consumption in the IoT system under study.

The technique itself is based on the randomness of input data and thus cannot be applied to deterministic or statistically correlated data. Instead of this, the data should be independent, such that one outcome of a random sample does not affect the outcome of another. This holds for energy data as IoT devices have asynchronous and not correlated changes, which is a consequence of relying in event-driven operating systems as the Contiki OS [8].

The fitting process is using well-known methods, such as moments matching and maximum likelihood. The moments matching method estimates the model parameters by using as many moments as the number of missing parameters of the candidate distribution. These moments depend on the probability law that the chosen candidate distribution follows. On the other hand, maximum likelihood finds the parameters that maximize the likelihood function. Then, the fitted distributions are validated against the input energy data using goodness-of-fit tests, such as the Kolmogorov-Smirnov (K-S).

An example fitted distribution characterizing the energy consumed while a device is in Tx mode is illustrated in Fig. 2. Horizontal axis reflects the range in which energy values can vary, whereas the vertical illustrates the Probability Density Function (PDF). In this example, the distribution that is selected as a best fit is Generalized Pareto with $\kappa = 0.40227, \sigma = 1.6739, \mu = 35.105$ moments. For energy samples given by: $X = [x_1, x_2, ..., x_n]$, the distribution parameters θ_1 and θ_2 that maximize the likelihood function are computed as follows:

$$L(\theta_1, \theta_2; x_1, \ldots, x_n) = \prod_{i=1}^{n} \theta_1 * \frac{\theta_2^{\theta_1}}{x_i^{\theta_1+1}} = \theta_1{}^n * \theta_2^{n*\theta_1} \prod_{i=1}^{n} \frac{1}{x_i^{\theta_1+1}} \quad (1)$$

During the validation phase, the goodness-of-fit tests have given 0.09415 error for Kolmogorov-Smirnov (K-S).

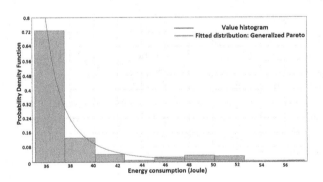

Fig. 2. Fitted energy distribution for the transmission (Tx) mode

The fitted distributions are calibrating the energy model in the form of probabilistic variables. These variables take values based on a non-deterministic selection that is following the probability law of the fitted distribution.

3.3   Energy Aspect Monitoring

An energy aspect monitor is instantiated according to the number of aspects that influence the IoT system. Following Sect. 3.1, these parameters lead to three instances of the component, namely the connectivity, data processing and security monitors. Each instance interacts with the energy model using a dedicated BIP connector as illustrated in Fig. 3. The monitor component has two main characteristics: (i) acting as an interaction advisor, such that when present it can consider the energy cost of each design aspect (ii) implementing all the required equations for evaluating if the conditions that are derived by the system requirements are met.

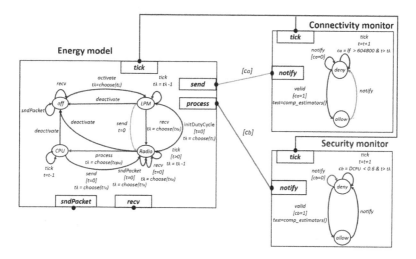

Fig. 3. Energy aspect monitor interactions with energy model

The aspect monitor is initially informed when the device switches operating mode by receiving the time value of the probabilistic distribution that was selected through the *tick* transition. With this value it can estimate if the condition can be met or not. In the example of Fig. 3 there are two monitors (i.e. connectivity and security) and each one evaluates a different condition:

1. Condition A (associated with connector value c_a): The device is sustained for full working day on battery power
2. Condition B (associated with connector value c_b): The processing time of security operations should not be higher than 60% of the overall duty cycle

Each condition is computed by the monitor during its own *tick* transition. When the condition is met, the boolean value is set and the monitor can proceed through the *valid* internal transition (connectivity monitor of Fig. 3). Otherwise, it will remain on the *deny* state until satisfying the condition. On the other hand, when the allocated time on the energy model has elapsed, it has first to interact with the monitor (through the *notify* transition) prior of interacting with the Contiki system model [11]. During this interaction (depicted in red in Fig. 3) the monitor uploads the condition value, which either allows the energy model to proceed (c_a or $c_b = true$), or notifies the energy model that the condition is invalidated and thus the system violates the requirements. When the condition is met as with condition A in Fig. 3, the time value counted by the *tick* transition of the energy model (t_{est}) is send to the monitor through the condition connector, which calculates the estimated energy consumption (in Joule) using the following equation:

$$E_{est_y} = I_y * V_y * t_{est} \tag{2}$$

where in every tuple $\{Iy, Vy\}$, y indicates the device's operating mode and I, V indicate respectively the current (in Ampere) and voltage (in Volts).

Energy Estimation
After simulating the Calibrated BIP Model, the monitor provides analytics regarding the estimated values for energy characteristics, which differ from the actual ones that are logged in the execution traces of Fig. 1 using the power-trace module (Sect. 2). These characteristics cover all the IoT design aspects of Sect. 3.1 and are given by the following equations:

$$E_{est_{total}} = E_{est_{conn}} + E_{est_{proc}} + E_{est_{sec}} + \sum_{i=1}^{N_{LPM}} I_{LPM} * V_{LPM} * \Delta t_{LPM_i} \tag{3}$$

Except from the last parameter (energy in LPM mode), each of the remaining equation parameters reflects the aspects presented in Sect. 3.1, defining their contribution to the energy consumption. Δt_y indicates the time intervals in which the device remains in an operating mode and D_y indicates the duty cycle for each mode ($y = LPM$ for LPM mode).

$$D_y = \frac{\sum_{i=1}^{N_y} I_y * V_y * \Delta t_{y_i}}{E_{est_{total}}} \tag{4}$$

where N_y the relative number of occurrences that the device has visited the operating mode y. The rest of the equation parameters are computed as:

$$E_{est_{conn}} = \sum_{j=1}^{N_{Tx}} I_{Tx} * V_{Tx} * \Delta t_{Tx_j} + \sum_{k=1}^{N_{Rx}} I_{Rx} * V_{Rx} * \Delta t_{Rx_k} \tag{5}$$

$$E_{est_{proc}} = \sum_{z=1}^{N_{CPU}} I_{CPU} * V_{CPU} * \Delta t_{CPU_z} + \sum_{w=1}^{N_{PER}} I_{PER} * V_{PER} * \Delta t_{PER_w} \tag{6}$$

Energy consumption for security aspects is linked to both connectivity and data processing aspects, however the contribution percentage for each one varies and depends on the energy parameters of the IoT application. Hence:

$$E_{est_{sec}} = \Delta E_{conn} + \Delta E_{proc} \tag{7}$$

where ΔE_{conn} and ΔE_{proc} indicate the additional overhead that is added by security aspects. Finally, the device lifetime is computed by the following equation:

$$lf_{est} = \frac{C_{batt} * Vcc}{E_{est_{total}}} \tag{8}$$

where C_{batt} indicates the overall capacity of the battery for autonomous operation (in Ampere hours) and Vcc the operating voltage (in Volts).

The designer can then update the system requirements iteratively according to the difference between the estimated model parameters and the actual ones.

4 Case-Study: Energy Characterization of ITS Design Aspects

In this section, we illustrate our method through a case study in the smart mobility IoT domain by presenting an Intelligent Transport System (ITS). This case study provides environmental condition awareness to different parts of a city through the ITS data exchange scheme defined by the ETSI EN 302 637-2 [10] and ETSI EN 302 637-3 [9] standards. The case study (Fig. 4) aims to measuring and characterizing energy design aspects in a real ITS system that was deployed as a prototype within our premises. Since ITS architectures handle sensitive user-data, they require the existence of security mechanisms to prevent attacks from malicious actors. Characteristic ITS attack examples aim to take control of the network, such as DDoS [15], spoofing or frame replay [6]. Hence, to protect the system against such attacks we have implemented a lightweight security library that includes the TLS, DTLS and IPSec protocols.

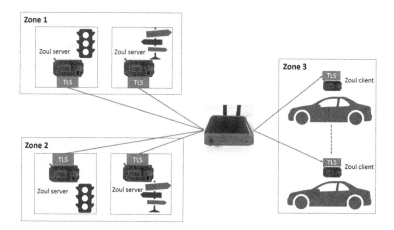

Fig. 4. Topology of the ITS prototype

The deployed architecture of Fig. 4 allows Zolertia Zoul devices that are located in certain zones to send environmental data (i.e. temperature, humidity) to an Orion border router[9], which is configured as data forwarder for supporting awareness of vehicles that are about to enter these areas. Specifically, in Fig. 4 vehicles from Zone 3 are about to enter Zone 1 and 2, hence after establishing a secure connection with the border router they ask for real-time data analytics about the environmental conditions. The border router also runs a web-server, where vehicles have access and can get live updates. Furthermore, the Zoul modules run the Contiki OS and are placed into ITS devices, as traffic lights and road signs that we have configured in our prototype (Fig. 5).

Fig. 5. Deployment of the ITS prototype

4.1   Application of the Proposed Method

Step 1: Transformation for the System Model
We used the described energy-relevant parameter XML configuration along with the DSL description to generate the BIP System Model.

Step 2: Code generation from IoT application templates
In this step, we have considered the parameters of Sect. 3 combined with the connectivity parameters presented in [11]. The value range of all parameters that influence energy consumption is shown in Table 1. The default value for each parameter is specified by the ITS system requirements.

Step 3: Energy characterization
We have used the technique of Sect. 3 to derive probabilistic dsitributions, aiding in the calibration of the Energy Model with energy constrains for the ITS case study. The derived probabilistic distributions were found to follow the Generalized Pareto or the Cauchy distributions. These distributions were used in *Step 4* to calibrate the energy model (presented in Fig. 3).

Step 5: Energy aspect monitoring
We identified two conditions for the ITS system, that are presented in Sect. 3. The system requirements for the ITS[10] lie on the usage of security level SL-2,

---

[9] https://zolertia.io/product/orion-router/.
[10] https://www.etsi.org/e-brochure/Work-Programme/2017-2018/files/basic-html/ page17.html.

Table 1. Parameters of the energy-aware configuration

Energy model parameter	Associated aspect	Default value	Variation range
RDC protocol	Connectivity	X-MAC	[Contiki-MAC, X-MAC, LPP, nullRDC]
RDC frequency	Connectivity	8 Hz	[2–32] Hz (even number)
Packet retransmissions	Connectivity	4	[0–5] $\in \mathbb{Z}$
Service protocol	Connectivity	CoAP	[CoAP, MQTT, HTTP]
Header size	Connectivity	48 bytes	[32–64] bytes (even number)
Interference	Connectivity	0	[0–1] $\in \mathbb{R}$
Resource processing	Data processing	Application resources: Temperature, Humidity	Available resources: Temperature, Humidity, Motion, Light, Accelerometer
Routing protocol	Data processing	RPL	[RPL, CORPL, CARP, none]
Memory block management	Data processing	Mmem	[Malloc, mmem]
Security level	Security	SL-2	[SL-0, SL-1, SL-2, SL-3]
Security protocol	Security	TLS	[TLS, DTLS, IPSec]
Session key size	Security	256	[128, 192, 256] bits

meaning strong encryption (256-bit key size) and authentication mechanisms for the communication (Default value in Table 1). Hence, the energy monitors for all aspects are enabled to ensure that conditions A and B in Sect. 3 hold. As an additional step, the estimations for possible changes in the IoT architecture can be validated through the use of *SMC* in *Step 6*.

4.2 Experiments

In this section, we demonstrate the experiments for evaluating the aforementioned requirements. To automate these experiments we developed a tool that given the parameter configuration XML, executes the system model for all combinations of parameters and saves the energy estimations that satisfy at least one of the conditions in dedicated files. The current and voltage values that were used for the calculation of the total energy, duty cycle and device lifetime for Sect. 3 equations, were obtained from the IoT devices' datasheet. The experiments were conducted by leaving the Zoul devices on battery power for an entire working day and then charging them to reach their full battery capacity.

Condition A. By experimenting with multiple variations for the parameters of Table 1 we concluded that the largest contribution to the energy consumption is given by the connectivity and security aspects. Specifically, the use of TLS increases substantially the device energy consumption (Actual Energy in Fig. 6) in the processing mode. This invalidates condition A, since the security monitor allows energy consumption up to 60 Joules for sustaining the device for an entire day of continuous operation. Hence, this scenario is excluded from the feasible ones in the energy estimation feedback report that is returned to the user. Instead, the experiments with 128 key size and no authentication scheme allowed condition A to be satisfied (Estimated Energy in Fig. 6), as the duty cycle in processing mode is significantly reduced.

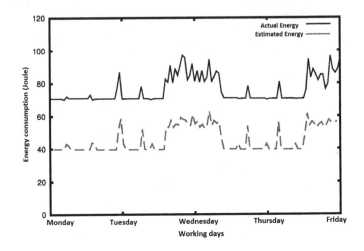

Fig. 6. Actual energy consumption compared to the estimated

Condition B. As with condition A, B was also not met for the Zoul devices. Additionally, the scenario that led condition A to be met i.e. 128 key size and no authentication scheme did not satisfy condition B, since it led to a duty cycle: $D_{CPU} = 67\%$. However, the combination of this scenario with an increased RDC frequency to 32 Hz resulted in meeting condition B, as $D_{CPU} = 58\%$.

5   Conclusion

We presented a novel method for estimating the energy consumption for various design aspects of IoT applications. The method is based on the principles of rigorous system design by using the BIP component framework. It takes as input the application design description in a DSL and an XML-based set of energy parameters, and generates a system model in BIP calibrated with energy constraints. These constraints are obtained by energy characterization mechanisms applied to the execution traces of the deployed IoT application. The calibrated model is then monitored through model conditions that allow to verify if the system requirements are met and also to estimate scenarios where they can be met. The estimations are given as feedback to the IoT system designer.

As a proof of concept, the described method has been applied to an Intelligent Transport System. The system consists of road signs and traffic lights that are informing vehicles for climate conditions upon entering their area. This system requires the presence of strong security mechanisms to respect the privacy of exchanged data and to avoid security threats. We have verified conditions related to the IoT device lifetime and the CPU duty-cycle for security mechanisms. The results allow to provide a feasible design solution for the ITS application by considering the energy cost of each IoT design aspect.

Currently, the energy aspect monitoring technique requires extensive tests for all the combinations of energy parameters in each IoT application. We plan to improve this by testing only the relevant scenarios according to the system requirements. This will allow faster estimations for the IoT application designer.

References

1. Aijaz, A., Aghvami, A.H.: Cognitive machine-to-machine communications for Internet-of-Things: a protocol stack perspective. IEEE Internet Things J. **2**(2), 103–112 (2015)
2. Aijaz, A., Su, H., Aghvami, A.H.: CORPL: a routing protocol for cognitive radio enabled ami networks. IEEE Trans. Smart Grid **6**(1), 477–485 (2015)
3. Antonakakis, M., et al.: Understanding the mirai botnet. In: USENIX Security Symposium, pp. 1092–1110 (2017)
4. Basagni, S., Petrioli, C., Petroccia, R., Spaccini, D.: CARP: a channel-aware routing protocol for underwater acoustic wireless networks. Ad Hoc Netw. **34**, 92–104 (2015)
5. Basu, A., Bensalem, B., Bozga, M., Combaz, J., Jaber, M., Nguyen, T.H., Sifakis, J.: Rigorous component-based system design using the BIP framework. IEEE Softw. **28**(3), 41–48 (2011). https://doi.org/10.1109/MS.2011.27
6. Chim, T.W., Yiu, S., Hui, L.C., Li, V.O.: Security and privacy issues for inter-vehicle communications in VANETs. In: 6th Annual IEEE Communications Society Conference on Sensor, Mesh and Ad Hoc Communications and Networks Workshops, 2009. SECON Workshops 2009, pp. 1–3. IEEE (2009)
7. Collina, M., Corazza, G.E., Vanelli-Coralli, A.: Introducing the QEST broker: scaling the IoT by bridging MQTT and REST. In: 2012 IEEE 23rd International Symposium on Personal Indoor and Mobile Radio Communications (PIMRC), pp. 36–41. IEEE (2012)
8. Dunkels, A., Osterlind, F., Tsiftes, N., He, Z.: Software-based on-line energy estimation for sensor nodes. In: Proceedings of the 4th Workshop on Embedded Networked Sensors, pp. 28–32. ACM (2007). https://doi.org/10.1145/1278972.1278979
9. ETSI, E.: 302 637–3 V1. 2.2 (2014–11) Intelligent Transport Systems (ITS). Vehicular Communications
10. ETSI, T.: Intelligent transport systems (its); vehicular communications; basic set of applications; part 2: specification of cooperative awareness basic service. Draft ETSI TS **20**, 448–451 (2011)
11. Lekidis, A., Katsaros, P.: Model-based design of energy-efficient applications for IoT systems. In: Proceedings of the 1st International Workshop on Methods and Tools for Rigorous System Design, MeTRiD@ETAPS 2018, pp. 24–38 (2018). https://doi.org/10.4204/EPTCS.272.3
12. Lekidis, A., Stachtiari, E., Katsaros, P., Bozga, M., Georgiadis, C.K.: Model-based design of IoT systems with the BIP component framework. Software - Practice and Experience (2018). https://doi.org/10.1002/spe.2568
13. Nastic, S., Sehic, S., Le, D.H., Truong, H.L., Dustdar, S.: Provisioning software-defined IoT cloud systems. In: 2014 2nd International Conference on Future Internet of Things and Cloud (FiCloud), pp. 288–295. IEEE (2014)

14. Nouri, A., Bensalem, S., Bozga, M., Delahaye, B., Jegourel, C., Legay, A.: Statistical model checking QoS properties of systems with SBIP. Int. J. Software Tools Technol. Transfer **17**(2), 171–185 (2015). https://doi.org/10.1007/s10009-014-0313-6
15. Parno, B., Perrig, A.: Challenges in securing vehicular networks. In: Workshop on hot topics in networks (HotNets-IV), pp. 1–6. Maryland, USA (2005)
16. Shelby, Z., Hartke, K., Bormann, C.: The constrained application protocol (CoAP). Technical reports (2014)
17. Vilajosana, X., Wang, Q., Chraim, F., Watteyne, T., Chang, T., Pister, K.S.: A realistic energy consumption model for TSCH networks. IEEE Sens. J. **14**(2), 482–489 (2014). https://doi.org/10.1109/JSEN.2013.2285411
18. Winter, T., et al.: RPL: IPv6 routing protocol for low-power and lossy networks. Technical report (2012)

A Logic-Inspired Approach to Reconfigurable System Modelling

Alessandro Maggi[1](✉), Rocco De Nicola[1](✉), and Joseph Sifakis[2](✉)

[1] IMT School for Advanced Studies Lucca, Lucca, Italy
{alessandro.maggi,rocco.denicola}@imtlucca.it
[2] Université Grenoble Alpes, Saint-Martin-d'Hres, France
joseph.sifakis@univ-grenoble-alpes.fr

Abstract. Software systems have reached a level of complexity that demands new approaches to software design in order to support continuous adaptation to the changes in their internal and external environment. This implies the capability of capturing at design-time the dynamic features of systems that are composed of large numbers of interacting components in order to reduce the risks of undesirable interferences and unpredictable outcomes. The L-DReAM framework ("Light Dynamic Reconfigurable Architecture Modelling") relies on a logic-based modelling language that is expressive enough to capture different approaches to systems coordination, reconfiguration and dynamicity. L-DReAM components have a "loose" structure that, combined with the flexibility of the adopted coordination language, results in a framework that can be used to model many different computational paradigms while offering a readable syntax easy to understand.

1 Introduction

Software systems have reached a level of complexity that calls for new approaches to software design taking advantage of decomposition and indirection. When applied to classes of systems that globally consist of large numbers of interacting components and feature complex interaction mechanisms, the lack of rigorous methodologies and formally grounded frameworks for modelling them increases the risks of undesirable interferences and unpredictable outcomes. These risks are amplified by the fact that these systems are usually distributed, heterogeneous, interdependent, and are operating in unpredictable environments. To cope with these issues, software needs to be developed in such a way that systems can continuously adapt to internal changes and to changes in their operating environment.

The notion of reconfigurability implies the capability of capturing the dynamic aspects of modern software already at design-time. This is even more challenging for frameworks that aim at modelling architectures that not only support parametric system instantiation, but also dynamic reconfiguration of their inner structure and of their coordination patterns. Architecture modelling

© Springer Nature Switzerland AG 2019
E. Bartocci et al. (Eds.): From Reactive Systems to Cyber-Physical Systems, LNCS 11500, pp. 181–201, 2019.
https://doi.org/10.1007/978-3-030-31514-6_11

languages should be expressive enough to support these features while offering an intuitive syntax and clear design methodologies in order to foster their practical use.

This paper introduces the L-DReAM framework, a light variant of the DReAM framework introduced in [1] for modelling Dynamic Reconfigurable Architectures. Both frameworks rely on a logic-based modelling language that is expressive and powerful enough to support different approaches to coordination and all the key features required to capture dynamicity. In L-DReAM a system is a hierarchical structure of components. Each non-atomic component hosts a "pool" of components and defines the coordination rules that regulate the way they interact and evolve. The overall structure of systems can also change as components can leave and join different pools. Components will thus be subject to different coordination rules as they change their position in the hierarchy. L-DReAM rules include an interaction constraint, modelled as a formula of the Propositional Interaction Logic (PIL) [2], and some operations allowing data transfer as well as more complex reconfigurations of the component's state. Parametric coordination between classes of components is achieved through the introduction of the concepts of *component types* - blueprints for actual components - and *component instances* created from specific types. Their coordination is characterized by rules in a first order extension to PIL with quantification over instance variables of a given type.

Differently from DReAM, in L-DReAM there is no separation between behaviour and coordination of components. The two frameworks share a common structure characterized by an *interface* of *ports*, a *store* of *local variables*, and a *rule*, but L-DReAM components are not transition systems so they do not have control locations or transitions between them. In fact, L-DReAM rules are used both to coordinate sub-components in a compound's pool and to characterize the behaviour and capabilities of components in general. Furthermore, the possibility of having compounds hosting other compounds in their pool allows to treat every element in the hierarchy uniformly, to the point where the overall system itself is a component.

All this allows L-DReAM to be more expressive than DReAM while boasting a more streamlined and uniform operational semantics, making it better suited for theoretical analysis and comparison with other formalisms. Indeed, rules can even be characterized just by predicates over local variables without the need to define looping transitions over dummy ports and control states. This allows using L-DReAM to model, with a minimal overhead, also data-driven systems like, e.g., systems adopting *attribute-based communication* for messaging, coordination and adaptation [3].

The rest of the paper is organized as follows. Section 2 presents the non-parametric version of the framework that relies on the Propositional Interaction Logic (PIL) that is used to model static architectures. Section 3 provides a formal definition of the full L-DReAM framework where a first order extension that allows quantification over component variables can be used to express coordination constraints. Section 4 compares the presented framework with a number of other representatives of the category. By giving hints on how some of their defining features can be translated into L-DReAM implementations, we further explore the expressive power and specification flexibility of our language. The conclusion recaps the main results of this early analysis and discusses avenues for further development of both L-DReAM and its parent framework DReAM.

2 Non-parametric Systems

In this Section we introduce the syntax and semantics of L-DReAM in the simple scenario of static systems with non-parametric initial configurations. This will enable us to lay the foundation for the dynamic and parametric extension of the framework described in Sect. 3.

The building blocks of a L-DReAM system are *components*, which are characterized by an *interface* (i.e. a set of port names), a *store* (i.e. a set of local variables), a *pool* (i.e. a set of constituent sub-components) and a behaviour *rule*. We refer to components with an empty pool as *atomic*, whereas we call a non-atomic component a *compound* (see Fig. 1).

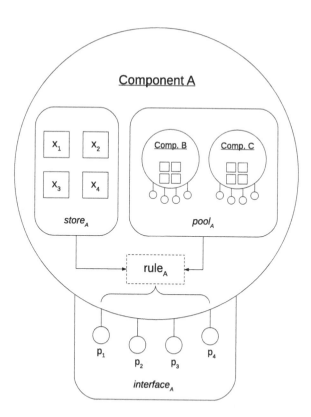

Fig. 1. A schematic representation of a L-DReAM compound (i.e. non-atomic component)

Definition 1 (Component). *Let $\mathcal{C}$, $\mathcal{P}$ and $\mathcal{X}$ respectively be the domain of components, ports and local variable names. A component is a tuple $c = (P, X, C, r)$ with*

- interface $P \subseteq \mathcal{P}$: *finite set of ports;*
- store $X \subseteq \mathcal{X}$: *finite set of local variables;*
- pool $C \subseteq \mathcal{C}$: *finite set of constituent components;*
- rule r: *constraint built according to the syntax in (1) characterizing the behaviour of the component and the coordination between constituents of its pool.*

The state *of component c is the tuple $s = \big(\sigma, C, \{s_i\}_{c_i \in C}\big)$, where σ is the valuation function for the set of local variables X, $\sigma : \mathcal{X} \mapsto V$, and $\{s_i\}_{c_i \in C}$ is the set of states of the components in the pool of c. We will use S to denote the set of all states. It is assumed that the sets of ports and local variables of different components are disjoint. Furthermore, we do not allow any component to belong to its own pool or to the pools of two different compounds.*

In the rest of the paper we will adopt a "dot" notation to highlight elements associated to specific components, e.g. $c.p$ will refer to a port p in the interface of c, $c.X$ the set of local variables of c, and $c.s$ the state of c.

Behaviour and coordination of components are realized only through L-DReAM *rules*, which are expressed in PILOps [1]. PILOps formulas are constructed by combining terms with either the *conjunction operator* & or the *disjunction operator* ∥. Each term is essentially a *guarded command* composed of a PIL formula, which encodes a constraint on ports involved in interactions and on states of the associated components, and a set of operations to be performed when the formula is satisfied. The syntax for non-parametric L-DReAM rules is thus defined as follows:

$$
\begin{aligned}
\text{(L-DReAM rule)} \quad & r ::= \Psi \to \Delta \mid r_1 \;\&\; r_2 \mid r_1 \parallel r_2 \\
\text{(PIL formula)} \quad & \Psi ::= \textbf{true} \mid p \mid \pi \mid \neg\Psi \mid \Psi_1 \wedge \Psi_2 \\
\text{(set of operations)} \quad & \Delta ::= \emptyset \mid \{\delta\} \mid \Delta_1 \cup \Delta_2
\end{aligned}
\tag{1}
$$

where:

- operators & and ∥ are *associative* and *commutative*, and & has higher precedence than ∥;
- $\pi : S \mapsto \{\textbf{true}, \textbf{false}\}$ is a state predicate;
- $\delta : S \mapsto S$ is an operation that transforms the state s of a component.

The models of the logic are *interactions* A, i.e. finite subsets of the universe of port names $\mathcal{P}$ such that no two ports belong to the same component. To determine whether an interaction is *admissible* for a given L-DReAM rule, we define a *satisfaction relation* parametrized by the state s of the component "owning" the rule. This relation ignores operations and essentially translates the L-DReAM rule to a PIL formula by substituting terms $\Psi \to \Delta$ with Ψ and changing operators $\&, \|$ with the logical $\wedge, \vee$. The resulting formula will be a conjunction/disjunction of port names and state predicates that can be checked against A and s.

Formally, the satisfaction relation is defined by the following set of rules:

$$
\begin{aligned}
A &\models_s \Psi \to \Delta & &\text{if } A \models_s \Psi \\
A &\models_s r_1 \,\&\, r_2 & &\text{if } A \models_s r_1 \text{ and } A \models_s r_2 \\
A &\models_s r_1 \,\|\, r_2 & &\text{if } A \models_s r_1 \text{ or } A \models_s r_2 \\
A &\models_s \textbf{true} & &\text{for any } A \\
A &\models_s p & &\text{if } p \in A \\
A &\models_s \pi & &\text{if } \pi(s) = \textbf{true} \\
A &\models_s \Psi_1 \wedge \Psi_2 & &\text{if } A \models_s \Psi_1 \text{ and } A \models_s \Psi_2 \\
A &\models_s \neg\Psi & &\text{if } A \nvDash_s \Psi
\end{aligned}
\tag{2}
$$

Given an admissible interaction A for a component c in state s, the operations to be performed under A, s are either:

- for rules combined with "$\&$": all the associated operations if the relevant PIL formulas hold for (A, s) or none at all if at least one formula does not;
- for rules combined with "$\|$": a maximal union of operations having the relevant PIL formulas satisfied by (A, s).

Formally, the set of operations $[\![r]\!]_{A,s}$ to be performed for r under (A, s) is defined according to the following rules:

$$
[\![\Psi \to \Delta]\!]_{A,s} = \begin{cases} \Delta & \text{if } A \models_s \Psi \\ \emptyset & \text{otherwise} \end{cases}
$$

$$
[\![r_1 \,\&\, r_2]\!]_{A,s} = \begin{cases} [\![r_1]\!]_{A,s} \cup [\![r_2]\!]_{A,s} & \text{if } A \models_s r_1 \text{ and } A \models_s r_2 \\ \emptyset & \text{otherwise} \end{cases}
$$

$$
[\![r_1 \,\|\, r_2]\!]_{A,s} = [\![r_1]\!]_{A,s} \cup [\![r_2]\!]_{A,s}
\tag{3}
$$

Two rules r_1, r_2 are *equivalent* if, for any interaction A and component state s, $[\![r_1]\!]_{A,s} = [\![r_2]\!]_{A,s}$.

At this stage we are considering operations δ to be only *assignments* on local variables of components involved in an interaction, allowing transfer of data between them. The syntax is of the form $x := f$, where x is the local variable subject to the assignment and $f : V^k \mapsto V$ is a function on local variables $y_1, \ldots, y_k$ ($y_i \in \mathcal{X}$) on which the assigned value depends.

We can define the evolution of a L-DReAM component c with the following operational semantics rule:

$$
\frac{\forall c_i \in c.C : c_i.s \xrightarrow{A} c_i.s' \qquad c.s' = \left(c.\sigma, c.C, \{c_i.s'\}_{c_i \in c.C}\right)}{A \models_{c.s'} c.r \qquad c.s'' = [\![c.r]\!]_{A,c.s'} (c.s')}{c.s \xrightarrow{A} c.s''}
\tag{4}
$$

that can be intuitively understood as follows: component c changes state from $c.s$ to $c.s''$ through interaction A provided that every component c_i in its pool changes state to $c_i.s'$ through A, and that $c.s''$ is the state of c reached from $c.s'$ (i.e. the initial state $c.s$ of c with the updated states of components in its pool) by applying the operations to be performed for $A, c.s'$ when A is a model of the rule $c.r$ under state $c.s'$. Rule (4) applies to any component. For atomic components with empty pools, the intermediate state will be equal to the initial state, i.e. $s \equiv s'$. For compounds, it is worth pointing out that A must be an admissible interaction both for the component c, and recursively for every sub-component in the pool of c (and every sub-component in the pool of each sub-component of c, etc.).

A system model can be seen as a hierarchical tree structure where the leaves are atomic components and the rest of the nodes are compounds that aggregate child components in their pools. As such, the system itself is the root compound of this structure, and by applying rule (4) to it we can characterize the evolution of the whole system. Note that we did not explicitly define a notion of "scope" on port names and local variables, but we shall assume that the rule of a component will only mention ports/variables belonging to itself or to those components downward in the hierarchy.

The *configuration* Γ of a system coincides with the state of the root compound c_0:

$$\Gamma = c_0.s \equiv (c_0.\sigma, c_0.C, c_0.C.s) \tag{5}$$

where $c_0.C.s = \{c.s \mid c \in c_0.C\}$ is the set of states of the pool of c_0 and $\nexists c \in C$ s.t. $c_0 \in c.C$.

Axioms for L-DReAM rules. The following axioms hold for L-DReAM rules:

$$\& \text{ is associative, commutative and idempotent} \tag{6}$$

$$\Psi_1 \to \Delta_1 \ \& \ \Psi_2 \to \Delta_2 = \Psi_1 \wedge \Psi_2 \to \Delta_1 \cup \Delta_2 \tag{7}$$

$$r \ \& \ \mathbf{true} \to \emptyset = r \tag{8}$$

$$\| \text{ is associative, commutative and idempotent} \tag{9}$$

$$\Psi_1 \to \Delta \ \| \ \Psi_2 \to \Delta = \Psi_1 \vee \Psi_2 \to \Delta \tag{10}$$

$$\Psi \to \Delta_1 \ \| \ \Psi \to \Delta_2 = \Psi \to \Delta_1 \cup \Delta_2 \tag{11}$$

$$\mathbf{false} \to \Delta \ \| \ r = r \tag{12}$$

$$\text{Absorption: } r_1 \ \| \ r_2 = r_1 \ \| \ r_2 \ \| \ r_1 \ \& \ r_2 \tag{13}$$

$$\text{Distributivity: } r \ \& \ (r_1 \ \| \ r_2) = r \ \& \ r_1 \ \| \ r \ \& \ r_2 \tag{14}$$

$$\text{Normal disjunctive form (DNF):} \tag{15}$$

$$\Psi_1 \to \Delta_1 \ \| \ \Psi_2 \to \Delta_2 = \Psi_1 \wedge \neg\Psi_2 \to \Delta_1 \ \| \ \Psi_2 \wedge \neg\Psi_1 \to \Delta_2 \ \| \ \Psi_1 \wedge \Psi_2 \to \Delta_1 \cup \Delta_2$$

The operator $\&$ is the extension of conjunction with neutral element $\mathbf{true} \to \emptyset$ and $\|$ is the extension of the disjunction with an absorption (13) and distributivity axiom (14). The DNF is obtained by application of the axioms, and there is no conjunctive normal form.

Example 1 (Server with two Nodes). Let us model a simple portion of a system where we have a *Server* component that, given some input data, accepts requests to process it and returns a result. Furthermore, we assume that the requested computation can be easily parallelized, therefore our *Server* component will use two distinct computational *Nodes* to perform the operations.

Since the *Nodes* are effectively an integral part of the *Server* from an external point of view, we will model them as atomic components belonging to the *Server*'s pool. Their specification will be:

$$Node_k = (\{receive_k, return_k\}, \{data_k, result_k\}, \emptyset, r_k)$$

meaning that:

- the interface consists of two ports: $receive_k$ (to signal that $Node_k$ can receive new data from the *Server*) and $return_k$ (to send back the result of the computation to the *Server*);
- the store has two local variables: $data_k$ (storing the data to be processed) and $result_k$ (storing the results of the computation);
- the pool of the *Nodes* is empty (i.e., they are atomic components).

Let $f(x)$ be the function representing the computation that each *Node* has to perform on input x. Rules r_k can be defined as follows:

$$r_k = data_k = \mathbf{null} \wedge receive_k \rightarrow result_k := \mathbf{null}$$
$$\|$$
$$data_k \neq \mathbf{null} \wedge return_k \rightarrow result_k := f(data_k); data_k := \mathbf{null}$$
$$\|$$
$$\neg receive_k \wedge \neg return_k \rightarrow \emptyset$$

This means that the *Nodes* can:

- *receive* new input data when the variable used to store it is empty (**null**), resetting the variable that will store the result;
- *return* the results when some input data is present, assigning it to the appropriate local variable and resetting the input data;
- avoid participating in an interaction (negation of all their ports with no associated operation).

Note that a transfer of values between components is achieved by accessing their respective stores through *assignment* operations. In this particular instance r_k does not involve any transfer of data, as the specification of the *Nodes* simply assumes that someone can assign values to the $data_k$ variables and read values from $result_k$.

The component that will actually perform such operations is the *Server*:

$$Server = (\{acceptReq, returnRes\}, \{input, output\}, \{Node_1, Node_2\}, r_s)$$

meaning that:

- the interface of the *Server* consists of two ports: *acceptReq* (to accept new requests) and *returnRes* (to notify that the response to the request is ready);

– the store of the *Server* has two local variables: *input* (storing all the data to be processed) and *output* (storing the complete results of the computation);
– the pool of the *Server* contains $Node_1$ and $Node_2$.

Let $split(x, k)$ be a functions that given an input value x splits it into two chunks and returns the k-th, and $merge(x, y)$ one that does the opposite returning a value by merging x and y. Rule r_s can be specified as follows:

$$r_s = input = \textbf{null} \wedge acceptReq \rightarrow output := \textbf{null}$$

$$\|$$

$$input \neq \textbf{null} \wedge output = \textbf{null} \wedge receive_1 \wedge receive_2$$
$$\rightarrow data_1 := split\,(input, 1)\,;\,data_2 := split\,(input, 2)$$

$$\|$$

$$input \neq \textbf{null} \wedge output = \textbf{null} \wedge return_1 \wedge return_2$$
$$\rightarrow output := merge\,(result_1, result_2)$$

$$\|$$

$$input \neq \textbf{null} \wedge output \neq \textbf{null} \wedge returnRes \rightarrow input := \textbf{null}$$

$$\|$$

$$\neg acceptReq \wedge \neg returnRes \wedge \bigwedge_{k=1,2} \neg receive_k \wedge \neg return_k \rightarrow \emptyset$$

We can describe the behaviour of the *Server* induced by the rule r_s as follows:

– it can accept a request ($acceptReq$) when its variable storing the input is not initialized ($input = \textbf{null}$), resetting at the same time the *output* variable;
– when its *input* variable has a value ($input \neq \textbf{null}$) and *output* is empty ($output = \textbf{null}$), it can have both $Node_1$ and $Node_2$ synchronize through their $receive_k$ ports, initializing their $data_k$ local variables, or through $return_k$ ports, assigning to *output* the value obtained by merging the individual results of the *Nodes*;
– it can signal that the response to the original request is ready ($returnRes$) when both *input* and *output* variables are initialized, resetting the *input* variable in the process;
– it can skip participating in an interaction (negation of all ports with no operation).

Let us consider a concrete case where the $f(x)$ that the *Nodes* compute is a simple "character count" function (returning the number of characters in x excluding spaces), and the $merge(x, y)$ is the sum $x + y$. To represent the evolution of a system where its root component is the *Server*, we will start from a configuration where its *input* variable is already initialized:

$$Server.s_0 = \big(\,\{input \mapsto \text{"hello DReAM!"}, output \mapsto \textbf{null}\}, \{Node_1, Node_2\},$$
$$\{Node_1.s_0, Node_2.s_0\}\,\big)$$
$$Node_k.s_0 = (\{data_k \mapsto \textbf{null}, result_k \mapsto \textbf{null}\}, \emptyset, \emptyset)$$

From here we evaluate which valid interaction A can transform the current state of the system according to (4). Since the premise requires that A can transform the state of the $Nodes$ first, we check for interactions satisfying r_1, r_2 over the interfaces of $Node_1, Node_2$. Given that $data_k = $ **null** for $k = [1, 2]$, the results are $\{receive_1\}$, $\{receive_2\}$, and $\{receive_1, receive_2\}$. Of these three interactions, only one can model the $Server$'s rule r_s, that is $\{receive_1, receive_2\}$. There are no other admissible interactions in the current state, so this is the one that is performed.

The operations that will be carried out are first the ones derived from $Nodes$' rules r_k:

$$\llbracket r_k \rrbracket_{A, Node_k.s_0} = \{result_k := \textbf{null}\}$$

Given the choice for the initial state $Node_k.s_0$ having already $result_k = $ **null**, the intermediate state of the system $Server.s_0'$ produced by the execution of the operations $\llbracket r_k \rrbracket_{A, Node_k.s_0}$ will be identical to $Server.s_0$.

Finally we evaluate the operations that will be carried out according to the $Server$'s rule r_s:

$$\llbracket r_s \rrbracket_{A, Server.s_0'} = \{data_1 := split(input, 1); data_2 := split(input, 2)\}$$

By applying the operations to $Server.s_0'$ we obtain the new state $Server.s_1$:

$$Server.s_1 = \big(\{input \mapsto \text{``hello DReAM!''}, output \mapsto \textbf{null}\}, \{Node_1, Node_2\},$$
$$\{Node_1.s_1, Node_2.s_1\} \big)$$
$$Node_1.s_1 = (\{data_1 \mapsto \text{``hello''}, result_1 \mapsto \textbf{null}\}, \emptyset, \emptyset)$$
$$Node_2.s_1 = (\{data_2 \mapsto \text{``DReAM!''}, result_2 \mapsto \textbf{null}\}, \emptyset, \emptyset)$$

In the new state, the only admissible interaction is now $\{return_1, return_2\}$. At $Node$ level, each one will perform:

$$result_k := f(data_k); data_k := \textbf{null} \tag{16}$$

given that $f(\text{``hello''}) = 5$ and $f(\text{``DReAM!''}) = 6$. The intermediate state $Server.s_1'$ will be:

$$Server.s_1' = \big(\{input \mapsto \text{``hello DReAM!''}, output \mapsto \textbf{null}\}, \{Node_1, Node_2\},$$
$$\{Node_1.s_1', Node_2.s_1'\} \big)$$
$$Node_1.s_1' = (\{data_1 \mapsto \textbf{null}, result_1 \mapsto 5\}, \emptyset, \emptyset)$$
$$Node_2.s_1' = (\{data_2 \mapsto \textbf{null}, result_2 \mapsto 6\}, \emptyset, \emptyset)$$

Finally the $Server$ will perform $output := 11$ given that $merge(result_1, result_2) = 5 + 6 = 11$, producing the new state $Server.s_2$:

$$Server.s_2 = \big(\{input \mapsto \text{``hello DReAM!''}, output \mapsto 11\}, \{Node_1, Node_2\},$$
$$\{Node_1.s_1', Node_2.s_1'\} \big)$$

Now the $Server$ can synchronize with an external "client" component through the $returnRes$ port and start over.　□

2.1 Disjunctive and Conjunctive Styles

The problem of designing a system that has to evolve through a set of given interactions in L-DReAM can be approached in many ways, as there are multiple - possibly infinite - ways of writing rules that, for a given initial configuration, produce equivalent systems. In [1] we described two very distinct styles that can be adopted when defining the rules describing interactions which we call *disjunctive* and *conjunctive*.

The *disjunctive style* approach is to start from an initial rule which does not allow any interaction for the component. From this "false" rule, the capabilities of the component are incrementally *extended* by using the disjunction operator ∥ to combine rules that model individual interaction patterns. In other words, each sub-rule can describe an interaction in its entirety. Example 1 uses this style.

The *conjunctive style* approach starts from the opposite premise, i.e., considering that any interaction is allowed. From this "true" rule, the capabilities of the component are incrementally *restricted* by using the conjunction operator & to combine rules that model individual contributions to interaction patterns and the relevant requirements that must hold. A minimal contribution to a rule written in conjunctive style needs to combine two L-DReAM rules: one expresses which ports of the component are offered for participation in the interaction, the other under which conditions they will participate and which operations will be performed as a result. More concretely, the two rules will be:

- $\neg\Psi \to \emptyset$: if the component is not involved in terms of its offering (Ψ), do not perform any operation;
- $\Psi \wedge \Psi_r \to \Delta$: when the interaction and the current state of the component satisfy both the offer (Ψ) and the requirements (Ψ_r), perform Δ.

To express this structure in a more concise way, we introduce the *conjunctive term* as follows:

$$\Psi \triangleright \Psi_r \to \Delta = (\neg\Psi \to \emptyset \parallel \Psi \wedge \Psi_r \to \Delta) \tag{17}$$

A L-DReAM rule can be written in conjunctive style by using conjunctive terms as sub-rules, joined via the & operator.

Example 2 (Server with two Nodes - conjunctive style). We will now revisit Example 1 and define coordination rules adopting the conjunctive style.

Rules r_k of *Nodes* can be redefined as follows:

$$r_k' = receive_k \triangleright data_k = \mathbf{null} \to result_k := \mathbf{null}$$
$$\&$$
$$return_k \triangleright data_k \neq \mathbf{null} \to result_k := f(data_k); data_k := \mathbf{null}$$

The *Server* rule r_s can be rewritten in the conjunctive form r_s':

$$r_s' = acceptReq \rhd input = \mathbf{null} \to output := \mathbf{null}$$

&

$$receive_1 \rhd receive_2 \land input \neq \mathbf{null} \land output = \mathbf{null}$$
$$\to data_1 := split\,(input, 1)$$

&

$$receive_2 \rhd receive_1 \land input \neq \mathbf{null} \land output = \mathbf{null}$$
$$\to data_2 := split\,(input, 2)$$

&

$$return_1 \land return_2 \rhd input \neq \mathbf{null} \land output = \mathbf{null}$$
$$\to merge\,(result_1, result_2)$$

&

$$return_1 \rhd return_2 \to \emptyset$$
&
$$return_2 \rhd return_1 \to \emptyset$$

&

$$returnRes \rhd input \neq \mathbf{null} \land output \neq \mathbf{null} \to input := \mathbf{null}$$

Notice that each sub-rule in the disjunctive rule r_s coordinating $Node_1$ and $Node_2$ has been decomposed in the two highlighted conjunctive sub-rules in r_s'. For instance, $receive_k \rhd receive_k' \land input \neq \mathbf{null} \land output = \mathbf{null} \to data_k := split\,(input, k)$ models the constraint from the perspective of $Node_k$, whose $receive_k$ port is being offered for interaction. Accordingly, the assignment $data_k := split\,(input, k)$ modifies only the store of $Node_k$ as it is - in principle - related to the offering port. The conjunctive term having as offer $return_1 \land return_2$ characterizes instead an internal behaviour of the *Server* that needs to merge the individual results of the $Nodes$ to produce the output, and as such it is isolated in a separate sub-rule.   □

3   Parametric Architectures and Dynamic Systems

Now we expand the language introduced in Sect. 2 allowing L-DReAM to describe dynamic system architectures with an arbitrary (finite) number of components.

To have a modelling language with sufficient expressive power to describe classes of systems with an arbitrary number of components while supporting dynamic reconfiguration of their structure, L-DReAM is enriched on three fronts:

1. The concepts of *component type* and *component instance* are introduced in order to decouple the architecture specification from the instanced system;

2. A first-order extension, with quantifiers over component instances, of the logic
   used in (1) is considered;
3. Appropriate operations to *create* and *delete* component instances, and to
   migrate them from one pool to another are introduced.

Definition 2 (Component type). *Let* $\mathcal{C}$, $\mathcal{P}$ *and* $\mathcal{X}$ *respectively be the domain
of components, ports and local variable names. A component type is a tuple*
$t = (P, X, r)$ *where:*

- interface $P \subseteq \mathcal{P}$ *is a finite set of ports;*
- store $X \subseteq \mathcal{X}$ *is a finite set of local variables;*
- rule r *is a constraint built according to the syntax in (1) that characterizes
  the behaviour of the component instances of this type and the coordination
  between constituents of their pools.*

A component type can be considered as the blueprint for actual components of
a L-DReAM system, which we refer to as *component instances*.

Definition 3 (Component instance). *Let* lid *be the domain of instance identifiers and* $t = (P, X, r)$ *be a component type. A* component instance c *of type* t,
identified by $i \in$ lid, *is a component as defined in (Definition 1) with set of ports
P, local variables X whose corresponding references in the rule r are indexed
with* i:

$$c = t[i] = (P[i], X[i], C, r[P[i]/P][X[i]/X]) \tag{18}$$

*It is assumed that each instance is characterized by a unique identifier, regardless
of its type.*

Notice that even though we do not require interfaces and stores of different
component types to be disjoint sets, the assumption of uniqueness of instance
identifiers ensures that interfaces and stores of actual component instances are
always disjoint.

In order to have rules sufficiently expressive to model the interactions between
arbitrary component instances without any prior knowledge of their identifiers,
we equip the language for specifying L-DReAM rules with first-order logic quantifiers in the form of *component instance variable declarations*. The syntax in (1)
then becomes:

$$
\begin{aligned}
\text{(L-DReAM rule)} \quad & r ::= \Psi \rightarrow \Delta \mid D\{r\} \mid r_1 \,\&\, r_2 \mid r_1 \parallel r_2 \\
\text{(declaration)} \quad & D ::= \forall c : c^*.t \mid \exists c : c^*.t \quad \text{where } c \in c^*.C \\
\text{(PIL formula)} \quad & \Psi ::= \mathbf{true} \mid p \mid \pi \mid \neg\Psi \mid \Psi_1 \wedge \Psi_2 \\
\text{(set of operations)} \quad & \Delta ::= \emptyset \mid \{\delta\} \mid \Delta_1 \cup \Delta_2
\end{aligned} \tag{19}
$$

A declaration of the form $\forall c : c^*.t$ can be understood as the definition of a
variable name c representing component instances of type t in the pool of the
component instance c^*. If the scope of a declaration in a rule of a component
instance is its own pool, then we simply omit the reference to it and write

$\forall c : t$ instead. Similarly, if we do not want to restrict the type of the component instance in the declaration, we simply omit it and write $\forall c : c^*$ (or $\forall c$ if the scope of the variable c is the pool of the same component). $\exists c : c^*.t$ can be interpreted similarly.

Note that ports p and predicates π in PIL formulas can now be parametric with respect to the instance variables defined in the enclosed declaration (e.g. a rule with a declaration $\forall c : t$ can refer to a port p of all component instances c that match the declaration, using the dot notation $c.p$).

Under the assumption that L-DReAM systems have a finite number of component instances, each declaration in the rule of a component instance can be removed by transforming the rule itself into a combination of rules (via the $\&$ and $\parallel$ operators for the universal and existential quantifiers, respectively) where the instance variable is replaced with the actual component instances of the given type in the given pool. We refer to this transformation as the *declaration expansion* $\langle r \rangle_s$ of rule r of a component instance with state $s = (\sigma, C, C.s)$, which is formally defined by the following rules:

$$\langle \Psi \to \Delta \rangle_s = \Psi \to \Delta$$
$$\langle \forall c : c^*.t\{r\} \rangle_s = \underset{t[i] \in c^*.C}{\&} r\,[t\,[i]\,/c]$$
$$\langle \forall c : c^*\{r\} \rangle_s = \underset{\forall t}{\&} \langle \forall c : c^*.t\{r\} \rangle_s$$
$$\langle \exists c : c^*.t\{r\} \rangle_s = \underset{t[i] \in c^*.C}{\parallel} r\,[t\,[i]\,/c] \qquad (20)$$
$$\langle \exists c : c^*\{r\} \rangle_s = \underset{\forall t}{\parallel} \langle \exists c : c^*.t\{r\} \rangle_s$$
$$\langle r_1 \,\&\, r_2 \rangle_s = \langle r_1 \rangle_s \,\&\, \langle r_2 \rangle_s$$
$$\langle r_1 \parallel r_2 \rangle_s = \langle r_1 \rangle_s \parallel \langle r_2 \rangle_s$$

where $r\,[t\,[i]\,/c]$ is the rule r after applying the substitution of the instance variable c with the actual instance $t\,[i]$.

Example 3 (Server with n Nodes - declaration expansion). Let us expand Examples 1 and 2 by considering a scenario where we have a variable pool of *Nodes* that the *Server* can use to handle the computation.

We will define the component types *Server* and *Node* as follows:

$$Server = (\{acceptReq, returnRes\}, \{input, output, nodesReady\}, r_s)$$
$$Node = (\{receive, return\}, \{id, data, result\}, r_n)$$

where we introduced the local variables *nodesReady* and *id* to keep track of the number and identifier of *Node* instances ready to process their *Server*'s input.

Consider now a system with the same initial configuration described in Example 1, where we have one *Server* instance - $Server[0]$ - and two *Node* instances - $Node[1], Node[2]$. The initial state s_0 of $Server[0]$ will be:

$$Server[0].s_0 = (\{input \mapsto \text{"hello DReAM!"}, output \mapsto \textbf{null}, nodesReady \mapsto 2\},$$
$$\{Node[1], Node[2]\}, \{Node[1].s_0, Node[2].s_0\})$$

Let us define a fragment r of rule r_s of the *Server* component type modelling how *Nodes* are fed input data to be processed using the conjunctive style:

$$r = \forall c : Node\{c.receive \rhd input \neq \textbf{null} \wedge output = \textbf{null} \wedge nodesReady > 0$$
$$\rightarrow c.data := split\,(input, nodesReady, c.id)\,\}$$

where we extended the *split* function in order to parametrize the splitting degree with $nodesReady$. The declaration expansion of rule r under state $Server[0].s_0$ is performed by generating a new rule for each *Node* instance in the pool of *Server* and substituting it in place of the instance variable c:

$$\langle r \rangle_{s_0} \equiv Node[1].receive \rhd input \neq \textbf{null} \wedge output = \textbf{null} \wedge nodesReady > 0$$
$$\rightarrow Node[1].data := split\,(input, nodesReady, Node[1].id)$$
$$\&$$
$$Node[2].receive \rhd input \neq \textbf{null} \wedge output = \textbf{null} \wedge nodesReady > 0$$
$$\rightarrow Node[2].data := split\,(input, nodesReady, Node[2].id)$$

$\square$

To encompass this additional step of declaration expansion in the description of the behaviour of a L-DReAM component, the inference rule (4) used to describe the operational semantics of the non-parametric version of the language needs to be modified accordingly:

$$\frac{\forall c_i \in c.C : \; c_i.s \xrightarrow{A} c_i.s' \qquad c.s' = (c.\sigma, c.C, \{c_i.s'\}_{c_i \in c.C})}{c.s \xrightarrow{A} c.s''} \; (21)$$

with middle line: $A \models_{c.s'} \langle c.r \rangle_{c.s'} \qquad c.s'' = [\![\langle c.r \rangle_{c.s'}]\!]_{A,c.s'}\,(c.s')$

Rule (21) now requires that, at each state of a component instance, the problem of finding an interaction that satisfies its coordination rule is solved after it is reduced to the static, non-parametric case by expanding the declarations.

Since the higher-order language now allows to express constraints without prior knowledge of the individual component instances in a system, reconfiguration operations are extended in order to allow dynamic variations in the population of component instances. We thus have three new operations:

- $c' = create\,(t, c)$: to create a new component instance of type t, add it to the pool of component instance c, and bind it to the instance variable c' (which can be omitted if no further manipulation of the created instance is required);

- *delete* (c): to delete the component instance c;
- *migrate* (c, c'): to migrate component instance c to the pool of c' (removing it from the pool where it previously belonged).

Example 4 (Server with dynamic instantiation of Nodes). Recall the extended scenario presented by Example 3. We will now integrate the definition of the *Server* and *Node* component types with their L-DReAM rules using the conjunctive style. Rule r_n of the type *Node* will be essentially the same as r_k in Example 2:

$$r_n = receive \rhd data = \mathbf{null} \rightarrow result := \mathbf{null}$$
$$\&$$
$$return \rhd data \neq \mathbf{null} \rightarrow result := f(data); data := \mathbf{null}$$

Since all the ports and local variables mentioned in r_n will be local to each *Node* instance, no scoping or quantification is needed.

On the other hand r_s will now have to deal with an arbitrary number of nodes. Recall that the service that we want our *Server* to provide is the "character count" function. Let us define r_s as the conjunction of the following six subrules $r_1 \& \ldots \& r_6$:

$$r_1 = \forall c : Node \{ acceptReq \rhd input = \mathbf{null}$$
$$\rightarrow output := \mathbf{null}; delete\,(c)\,; nodesReady := nodesReady - 1 \}$$

Rule r_1 implements the *output* reset of the *Server* as in the non-parametric case of Example 2, but it also deletes every *Node* instance updating the *nodesReady* local variable.

$$r_2 = input \neq \mathbf{null} \wedge nodesReady = 0 \rhd \mathbf{true}$$
$$\rightarrow nodesReady := input/5;$$
$$\mathsf{FOR}\,\big(i = 1..length(input)/5\big)\,\mathsf{DO}\,\big(c = create\,(Node, \mathtt{self})\,; c.id := i\big)$$

Rule r_2 is completely new to the parametric variant, and it is used to create as many *Node* instances as needed (e.g. in this case one every five characters in *input*). The "FOR $(\ldots)$ DO $(\ldots)$" statement used here has the usual semantics of iterative loops over an integer index, where we are also using the latter to initialize the local variable *id* of the newly created instance.

$$r_3 = \forall c : Node \{ c.receive \rhd input \neq \mathbf{null} \wedge output = \mathbf{null} \wedge nodesReady > 0$$
$$\rightarrow c.data := split\,(input, nodesReady, c.id)\,\}$$

Rule r_3 is exactly the same rule as r discussed in Example 3 describing how *Nodes* receive input data from the *Server*.

$$r_4 = \forall c : Node \{ c.return \rhd input \neq \mathbf{null} \wedge output = \mathbf{null}$$
$$\rightarrow output := output + c.result \}$$

Rule r_4 characterizes how processed data is collected by the *Server* by accumulating the results in its *output* local variable.

$$r_5 = returnRes \triangleright input \neq \mathbf{null} \wedge output \neq \mathbf{null} \rightarrow input := \mathbf{null}$$

Rule r_5 is left unchanged from the non-parametric case.

$$r_6 = \forall c : Node\{\forall c' : Node\{c.receive \triangleright c'.receive \rightarrow \emptyset\}\}$$
$$\&$$
$$\forall c : Node\{\forall c' : Node\{c.return \triangleright c'.return \rightarrow \emptyset\}\}$$

Lastly, r_6 enforces strong synchronization between all *Node* instances when interacting through the *receive* and *return* ports.   □

4   L-DReAM Encoding of Other Coordination Languages

The "loose" characterization of individual components and the freedom to hierarchically compose them makes L-DReAM extremely flexible and capable of describing a variety of systems and programming paradigms.

Consider for example a labelled transition system (S, L, T) defined over the states S, labels L and transitions $T \subset S \times L \times S$. One of the possible modelling of an LTS as a L-DReAM atomic component $c = (P, X, \emptyset, r)$ is the following:

- every label $l \in L$ has a corresponding port $p_l \in P$;
- every state $s \in S$ has a corresponding (boolean) local variable $x_s \in X$;
- for every transition $(s_i, l_i, s_i') \in T$ there is a rule $r = \|_i \left(x_{s_i} \wedge p_{l_i} \rightarrow x_{s_i} := \mathbf{false}; x_{s_i'} := \mathbf{true}; \right)$.

L-DReAM can also be used in an imperative, sequential fashion. To do so, one possibility is to simply add a "program counter" local variable pc in the store of each component type and conjunct the appropriate predicate over it in the requirements of each conjunctive term describing its behaviour:

$$r_{seq} = \underset{i}{\&} \Psi_i \triangleright \Psi_i' \wedge pc = i \rightarrow \Delta_i \cup \{pc := pc + 1\} \tag{22}$$

More generally, by using the conjunctive style L-DReAM can be used as an endogenous coordination language comparable to process calculi relying on a single associative parallel composition operator. Consider for instance the CCS [4] process P_0 defined as the parallel composition of two processes P_1 and P_2 that can synchronize over the actions q and u:

$$P_0 = P_1 \mid P_2$$
$$P_1 = q.\bar{u}.0 \qquad P_2 = \bar{q}.u.0$$

where 0 is the inaction. To translate this simple system in L-DReAM we define three components c_i, each one modelling the process P_i:

$$c_0 = (\{\tau\}, \emptyset, \{c_1, c_2\}, r_0)$$
$$c_1 = (\{q, \bar{u}\}, \{pc_1\}, \emptyset, r_1)$$
$$c_2 = (\{\bar{q}, u\}, \{pc_2\}, \emptyset, r_2)$$

Rules r_1, r_2 will model a simple sequential process according to (22):

$$r_1 = q \triangleright pc_1 = 1 \rightarrow pc_1 := 2$$
$$\&$$
$$\bar{u} \triangleright pc_1 = 2 \rightarrow pc_1 := 3$$
$$r_2 = \bar{q} \triangleright pc_2 = 1 \rightarrow pc_2 := 2$$
$$\&$$
$$u \triangleright pc_2 = 2 \rightarrow pc_2 := 3$$

The rule r_0 of the root component c_0 will instead characterize the semantics of the CCS parallel composition, which provides that two parallel processes can synchronize over the matching actions (in this case represented by the interactions $\{q, \bar{q}\}$ and $\{u, \bar{u}\}$) causing the system to perform an internal action τ:

$$r_0 = \tau \triangleright (q \wedge \bar{q}) \vee (u \wedge \bar{u}) \rightarrow \emptyset$$

Notice that r_0 still allows interleaving between c_1 and c_2 just like for P_0.

Another way of modelling communicating sequential processes in L-DReAM is to equip every component with two ports in, out and characterize the communication channel (or the action label in CCS) with a specific local variable $chan$. This allows to model even more complex calculi like π-calculus [5] and one of its main features: *channel mobility*. Let us consider a simple process that we will call again P_0, representing the parallel composition of three processes P_1, P_2 and P_3:

$$P_0 = P_1 \mid P_2 \mid P_3$$
$$P_1 = q(x).\bar{x}\langle v\rangle.0 \qquad P_2 = \bar{q}\langle u\rangle.0 \qquad P_3 = u(y).0$$

The idea is that P_1 wants to communicate with P_3, but initially can only communicate with P_2. Through the output/input pair of actions $\bar{q}\langle u\rangle$ and $q(x)$, P_2 can send the channel u to P_1 which then allows it to send a message to P_3 by binding u to x.

To represent this system in L-DReAM, we will first define the root component type t_0 as before:

$$t_0 = (\{\tau\}, \emptyset, r_0)$$

To model the other processes, we will instead define three component types t_1, t_2 and t_3:

$$t_1 = (\{in, out\}, \{pc, chan, val, x\}, r_1)$$
$$t_2 = (\{in, out\}, \{pc, chan, val\}, r_2)$$
$$t_3 = (\{in, out\}, \{pc, chan, y\}, r_3)$$

Rules r_1, r_2 and r_3 will again model sequential processes, but will now also handle channel names and value output:

$$r_1 = in \triangleright pc = 1 \rightarrow chan := \text{``}q\text{''};\ pc := 2$$
$$\&$$
$$out \triangleright pc = 2 \rightarrow x := val;\ chan := x;\ val := \text{``}v\text{''};\ pc := 3$$
$$r_2 = out \triangleright pc = 1 \rightarrow chan := \text{``}q\text{''};\ val := \text{``}u\text{''};\ pc := 2$$
$$r_3 = in \triangleright pc = 1 \rightarrow chan := \text{``}u\text{''};\ pc := 2$$

The assignments on the *chan* variable here are used to indicate the channel name associated with the preceding interaction constraint, while the *val* variable is used to store the channels being passed.

Synchronization and actual value passing is instead implemented by rule r_0 of the root component c_0:

$$r_0 = \exists c \{\exists c' \{c.in \wedge c'.out \triangleright \tau \rightarrow \emptyset\}\}$$
$$\&$$
$$\forall c \{\exists c' \{c.in \triangleright c'.out \wedge c.chan = c'.chan \rightarrow c.val := c'.val\}\}$$

This rule characterizes both the behaviour of the root component type t_0 - which performs τ if two instances of any type interact via ports *in* and *out* - and the coordination between components in its pool - i.e., for one to interact with port *in* there must be another one participating with port *out* and also having the same values for their local variables *chan*. For the sake of simplicity, we are omitting further parts of rule r_0 to enforce only binary synchronization between component instances.

L-DReAM can be also used to encode many other process algebras relying on more complex and flexible strategies to realize communication and coordination between components than simple channels matching. For instance, specifications written with the AbC calculus [3,6] can be translated to L-DReAM preserving most of the features of the source language.

In AbC, a system is a set of parallel components equipped with a set of *attributes*. Communication happens in a broadcast fashion with the caveat that only components that satisfy some predicates over specific attributes do receive the message given that also the sender satisfies other predicates. The core actions of the language that characterize its communication paradigm are the *input* and *output* actions:

$$(input)\quad \Pi_1(\tilde{x})$$
$$(output)\quad (\tilde{E})@\Pi_2$$

where $\tilde{x}$ is a sequence of "placeholders" for the received values and $\tilde{E}$ is a sequence of expressions representing the values being sent. Π are predicates, which can be defined over attributes only (i.e. for output actions) or also over received values (i.e. for input actions). A simple example of matching input/output actions in AbC could be:

- $(x > 1 \land color = blue)(x, y)$: bind two values to variables x, y from messages having $x > 1$ and coming from components with attribute $color$ equal to $blue$;
- $(2, 0)@(color = red)$: send values $2, 0$ to all components with attribute $color$ equal to red.

Broadcast communication can be easily implemented in L-DReAM. To maintain uniformity with AbC where actions are defined at component level, we can adopt the conjunctive style and define two rules that implement its input/output actions:

$$(input) \quad \forall c\{\exists c'\{c.in \triangleright c'.out \land \Pi_1(c'.\tilde{E}) \to c.\tilde{x} := c'.\tilde{E}\}\}$$
$$(output) \quad \forall c\{\exists c'\{c.out \triangleright c'.in \land \Pi_2 \to \emptyset\}\}$$

where we assume that:

- the interface of all component types includes two ports in, out;
- the store of all component types contains local variables describing attributes, values being passed through messages, and the variables that are bound to values being passed;
- the predicates Π_1, Π_2 are equivalent to the respective AbC counterparts, with the appropriate references to local variables modelling attributes and values being passed.

Going back to the simple example mentioned above, we could translate the given pair of input/output actions as:

$$(x > 1 \land color = blue)(x, y)$$
$$\downarrow$$
$$\forall c\{\exists c'\{c.in \triangleright c'.out \land c'.x > 1 \land c'.color = blue \to c.x := c'.x; c.y := c'.y\}\}$$
$$(2, 0)@(color = red)$$
$$\downarrow$$
$$\forall c\{\exists c'\{c.out \triangleright c'.in \land c'.color = red \to \emptyset\}\}$$

There are many more nuances to AbC that we are not representing here, such as the fact that the in action is blocking while the out action is not. To model this, we need to combine the previously mentioned encoding of the in and out actions with the approach described earlier to simulate sequential processes in L-DReAM.

Obviously, since L-DReAM is based on DReAM [1], specifications written using the latter can be seamlessly translated to the former. Component types and instances in DReAM correspond to atomic component types and instances of L-DReAM. DReAM's motifs - which represent *dynamic architectures* with their own coordination rules and are parametrized with a *map* data structure - are translated to L-DReAM in the form of composite components with only atomic component instances in their pools and an appropriate local variable to implement their map. The L-DReAM rules of compounds implementing motifs will be exactly the same as their DReAM counterparts, except for operations and predicates involving the maps, which will have an implementation that depends on the way the map is represented in L-DReAM. Finally the overall DReAM system will be a L-DReAM root component having all the other compounds in its pool. The rule of the root component has also to appropriately implement the *migration term* of the DReAM system - a coordination rule that defines how component instances are transferred from one motif to another.

5   Conclusion and Related Work

The L-DReAM framework we have presented allows to describe dynamic reconfigurable systems by focusing on the interaction patterns between constituent components from an abstracted point of view. It supports different styles of interaction constraint definition, including conjunctive and disjunctive styles. Complex architectures can be incrementally constructed from atomic components to higher-degrees of compounds. These characteristics make L-DReAM very flexible and expressive, as it is capable of encoding many languages and frameworks based on very different coordination paradigms.

As its name suggests, L-DReAM draws heavily from its parent framework DReAM, sharing the entirety of its theoretical foundation but offering a simpler, more abstract structure. These characteristics make it more suitable for an in-depth study on the relationship between conjunctive and disjunctive styles that will be the subject of future work. On the other hand some features currently exclusive to L-DReAM - such as the unbounded hierarchical structure of compounds - will be backported to DReAM and integrated in its Java executable environment under development.

L-DReAM, and DReAM before it, draws inspiration from two very different coordination languages: BIP [2] and Dy-BIP [7].

BIP is a mature framework that leverages *connectors* to model interactions among components and define the computation flow between them. System definitions can be parametric, but connectors remain essentially "static" and defined from a somewhat "global" perspective by matching ports from different components. This restriction allows BIP to synthesize very efficient executable runtimes from system specifications, but prevents it from modelling dynamic systems effectively.

Dy-BIP was introduced with the intent of addressing the efficient specification of dynamic systems sharing some ground theory and terminology with BIP. It uses previous work on the encoding of BIP connectors with PIL, but instead of specifying them from a global perspective it adopts a more "compositional" approach by attaching *interaction constraints* to the ports of components. From these, a *global interaction constraint* is built at each system state as the conjunction of individual constraints, and the interaction that is performed is a solution to it.

L-DReAM adopts a coordination language that, just like Dy-BIP, is built on the foundation of PIL, but gives the user more freedom on how to use it. In fact, the disjunctive style described in Sect. 2.1 relates closely to the exogenous approach used by BIP for connectors definition. On the other hand, it is easy to show that coordination rules written as the conjunction of conjunctive terms of the form $p \triangleright \Psi \rightarrow \Delta_p$ can be easily mapped to transitions of individual components having p in their interface. This matches closely the Dy-BIP approach, where Ψ is the interaction constraint associated with port p.

A similar "hybrid" approach inspired by the BIP framework and aimed at aiding the design of dynamic systems is DR-BIP [8]. It combines a PIL-based constraint language to define interactions that is fully compositional with another layer that handles reconfiguration with semantics inspired by guarded commands. While DR-BIP shares the same conceptual framework with L-DReAM, its structured approach based on motifs and maps makes it more comparable to DReAM.

References

1. De Nicola, R., Maggi, A., Sifakis, J.: DReAM: dynamic reconfigurable architecture modeling. In: Margaria, T., Steffen, B. (eds.) ISoLA 2018. LNCS, vol. 11246, pp. 13–31. Springer, Cham (2018). https://doi.org/10.1007/978-3-030-03424-5_2
2. Bliudze, S., Sifakis, J.: The algebra of connectors - structuring interaction in BIP. IEEE Trans. Comput. **57**(10), 1315–1330 (2008)
3. Alrahman, Y.A., De Nicola, R., Loreti, M.: On the power of attribute-based communication. In: Proceedings of the Formal Techniques for Distributed Objects, Components, and Systems - FORTE 2016 - 36th IFIP WG 6.1 International Conference, pp. 1–18 (2016)
4. Milner, R. (ed.): A Calculus of Communicating Systems. LNCS, vol. 92. Springer, Heidelberg (1980). https://doi.org/10.1007/3-540-10235-3
5. Milner, R., Parrow, J., Walker, D.: A calculus of mobile processes, I. Inf. Comput. **100**(1), 1–40 (1992)
6. Alrahman, Y.A., De Nicola, R., Loreti, M., Tiezzi, F., Vigo, R.: A calculus for attribute-based communication. In: Proceedings of the 30th Annual ACM Symposium on Applied Computing, SAC 2015, pp. 1840–1845. ACM, New York (2015)
7. Bozga, M., Jaber, M., Maris, N., Sifakis, J.: Modeling dynamic architectures using Dy-BIP. In: Gschwind, T., De Paoli, F., Gruhn, V., Book, M. (eds.) SC 2012. LNCS, vol. 7306, pp. 1–16. Springer, Heidelberg (2012). https://doi.org/10.1007/978-3-642-30564-1_1
8. El Ballouli, R., Bensalem, S., Bozga, M., Sifakis, J.: Four exercises in programming dynamic reconfigurable systems: methodology and solution in DR-BIP. In: Margaria, T., Steffen, B. (eds.) ISoLA 2018. LNCS, vol. 11246, pp. 304–320. Springer, Cham (2018). https://doi.org/10.1007/978-3-030-03424-5_20

Data-Driven Design

Topological Interpretation of Interactive Computation

Emanuela Merelli[1(✉)] and Anita Wasilewska[2]

[1] Department of Computer Science, University of Camerino, Camerino, Italy
emanuela.merelli@unicam.it
[2] Department of Computer Science, Stony Brook University, Stony Brook, NY, USA
anita@cs.stonybrook.edu

Abstract. It is a great pleasure to write this tribute in honor of Scott A. Smolka on his 65th birthday. We revisit Goldin, Smolka hypothesis that *persistent Turing machine* (PTM) can capture the intuitive notion of *sequential interaction computation*. We propose a topological setting to model the abstract concept of *environment*. We use it to define a notion of a *topological Turing machine* (TTM) as a universal model for interactive computation and possible model for concurrent computation.

Keywords: Persistent Turing machine · Topological environment · Topological Turing machine

1 Introduction

In 2004, Scott A. Smolka worked with Dina Goldin[1] and colleagues on a formal framework for interactive computing; the *persistent Turing machine (PTM)* was at the heart of their formalization [1–3]. A *PTM* is a *Turing machine (TM)* dealing with *persistent sequential interactive computation* a class of computations that are sequences (possibly infinite) of non-deterministic *3-tape TMs*. A computation is called sequential interactive computation because it continuously interacts with its *environment* by alternately accepting an input string on the *input-tape* and computing on the *work-tape* a corresponding output string to be delivered on the *output-tape*. The computation is *persistent*, meaning that the content of the work-tape *persists* from one computation step to the next by ensuring a *memory* function.

The definition of *PTM* was based on Peter Wegner's *interaction theory* developed to embody distributed network programming.

> *Interaction is more powerful than rule-based algorithms for computer problem solving, overturning the prevailing view that all computing is expressible as algorithms [4, 5].*

---

[1] The work was developed in connection of the celebration of Paris Kanellakis for his 50th birthday. They were his first and last Ph.D student.

© Springer Nature Switzerland AG 2019
E. Bartocci et al. (Eds.): From Reactive Systems to Cyber-Physical Systems, LNCS 11500, pp. 205–224, 2019.
https://doi.org/10.1007/978-3-030-31514-6_12

Since in this framework interactions are more powerful than rules-based algorithms they are not expressible by an initial state described in a *finite terms*. Therefore, one of the four Robin Gandy's principles (or constraints) for computability is violated, as stated in [6]. The need to relax such constraints allows one to think that interactive systems might have a richer behavior than algorithms, or that algorithms should be seen from a different perspective. Although *PTM* makes the first effort to build a *TM* that accepts *infinite input*, we strongly support the idea that the interaction model should also include the formal characterization of the notion of *environment*.

In this paper, we focus on Smolka et al. original point of view on *persistent* and *interactive computation*. We revisit and formalize a concept of *computational environment* for *PTM* following Avi Wigderson's machine learning paradigm in [7].

Many new algorithms simply 'create themselves' with relatively little intervention from humans, mainly through interaction with massive data[2].

We use the notion of *computational environment* to define class of abstract computable functions as sets of relations between inputs and outputs of *PTM*. The computational environment depends on *time* and *space*. It can evolve and so the effectiveness of these functions depends on a given moment and a given context.

Computational environment is defined in terms of *ambient space*. The ambient space is a generalization of a notion of ambient manifold introduced in [8] to describe the topological quantum computation model.

We do it in such a way that the infinite computation can be reduced to a set of *relations*, constrained within its ambient space by loops of *non-linear interactions*. The ambient space is not necessarily a vector space, hence there is a problem of linearity and non-linearity of computation. The non-linearity originated from the *shape* that can be associated to the ambient space, which can be obtained by the topological analysis of the set of *data* provided by the *real* environment. Figure 1 shows the synthesis of this concept. The ambient space and *PTM* can be thought as mathematical representation of complex systems, merely defined as systems composed of many non-identical elements, constituent agents living in an environment and entangled in loops of non-linear interactions.

We built a topological *PTM* to model both the behavior of an interactive machine and its computational environment. The main idea of the generalization is that output-tape is forced to be connected to the input-tape through a *feedback loop*. The latter can be modeled in a way that the input string can be affected by the last output strings, and by the current *state* of the computational environment. A state of a topological *PTM* becomes a set of input and output relations constrained to an environment whose geometric representation formally defines the *context* of the computation. If many topological *PTM*s share the same computational environment, the computation becomes a stream of interactions of *concurrent processes*, which at higher dimension can be seen

---

[2] https://www.ias.edu/ideas/mathematics-and-computation.

as a collection of streams, such as an n-string braid as examined in topological quantum information [8]. In this scenario, the computational environment, envisaged as a *discrete* geometric space, may even *evolve* while computations take place.

The informal description given above depicts the environment. We define it as follows. Given a *PTM*, let X be a set of its input and output strings. Since the computational environment depends on *time* and *space*. In this case the time is represented by collection of steps. For each step i in time, we define an equivalence relation $\sim_i$ on X such that $input_i$ in X there exists an operator f_i such that $f_i(input_i) = output_i$.

In classical Turing machine the set of operators f_i is given, called rules or transformations. Our goal is to build an environment where this set of functions f_i can be discovered. Each element of X represents a transition from one state of the machine to a next guided by the operator f_i (unknown for the model) constrained over the computational environment. The mathematical objects we are looking for should reflect the collective properties of the set X in a natural way to support the discovery of the set of operators f_i. These operators allow us to represent X as a union of quotient spaces of the set of equivalence classes $X/\sim_i$ of all the *feasible* relations hidden in X. The resulting functional matrix of f_i, also called *interaction matrix*, represents the computational model or what we called the learnt algorithm [9].

In order to characterize the set of operators $\{f_i\}$, we decided to analyze the set X of environmental data by a *persistent homology*, a procedure used in topological data analysis (TDA). TDA is a subarea of the computational topology that filters the optimal space among *simplicial complexes* [10]. A simplicial complex can be seen as a generalization of the notion of graph, where the relations are not binary between vertices, but n-ary among simplices. A simplex expresses any relation among points. For example, a 0-dimensional simplex is a unary relation of a single point, a 1-dimensional simplex is a binary relation of two points (a line), a 2-dimensional simplex is a three points relation (a full triangle), and so on. For the interested reader, Appendix 1 gives some useful definitions for algebraic and computational topology. Although a simplicial complex allows us to shape the environment as a discrete topological space, the new model of *PTM* also requires to express the feedback loop between the output at step i with the input at the next step $i+1$ of the computation. To this end, we follow a recent approach proposed in the context of big data and complex systems for embedding a set of correlation functions (e.g. the encoding of a given data set) into a *field theory of data* which is relied on a topological space naturally identified with a simplicial complex [11]. The resulting mathematical structure is a *fiber bundle* [12], whose components are summarized in Fig. 1.

The framework consists of three topological spaces $\mathbf{B}, \mathbf{H}, \mathbf{G}$, and one projection map π. The *base space* $\mathbf{B}$, the set of input/output strings embedded in a simplicial complex; the *fiber* $\mathbf{H}$, the set of all possible computations (the set of f_i) constrained by the 'gauged' transformations over the base point $\mathbf{P_B}$ of the fiber; the *total space* $\mathbf{G}$ of the fiber bundle obtained by the product of the other

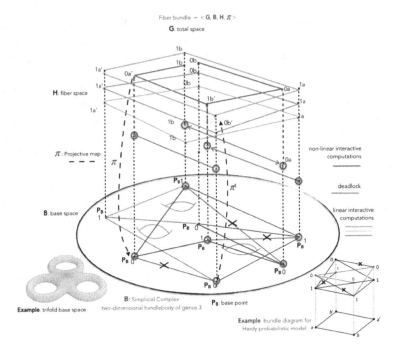

Fig. 1. Example of topological interpretation of computation. The *base space* **B** is a two-dimensional handlebody of genus 3, such as a trifold. The small *red* circles around some points of the *fiber space* **H** indicate the presence of states that make the computation inconsistent. The *violet* lines over the *base space* **B** show the corresponding unfeasible paths to be avoided due to the topological constraints imposed by the base space. The non-linear transformations of the fibers states, induced by the *projection map* π over the simplicial complex, guarantees the choice of the admissible paths with respect to the topology of the base space. The lines marked with a black cross correspond to inconsistent states of the system, which do not exist in the topological interpretation. The picture at the bottom right corner is an example of computation, it refers to the notion of contextuality [18], informally a family of data – a piece of information – which is locally consistent and globally inconsistent. (Color figure online)

two spaces (**G** = **B** × **H**), and *the projection map* π : **G** → **G/H** that allows us to go from the total space **G** to the base space **B** obtained as a quotient space of the fiber **H**. In Fig. 1, the π projection map is represented by dashed lines and used to discover if the geometry of the base space can constrain the ongoing computation in order to predict and avoid unfeasible transformations, the red lines in the figure. In our model, the obstructions that characterize the ambient space and constraint the computation are represented by the presence of n-dimensional holes ($n > 1$) in the geometry of the topological space. In our framework the holes represent the lack of specific relations among input and output of topological Turing machine. It means that the topological space, in our representation as simplicial complex, has a non trivial topology. As an example, in Fig. 1, the base space **B** is two-dimensional handlebody of *genus* 3. The formal description of the proposed approach rests on three pillars: (i) *algebraic and computational topology* for modeling the environment as a simplicial space **B**; (ii) *field theory* to represent the total space **G** of the machine as a system of global coordinates that changes according to the position $\mathbf{P_B}$ of the observer respect to the reference space **H**, and (iii) *formal languages* to enforce the semantic interpretation of the system behaviour into a logical space of geometric forms, in terms of operators f_i that here we call correlation functions in the space of the fiber **H**.

Consequently, an *effective PTM* is nothing but a change of coordinates, consistently performed at each location according to the 'field action' representing the *language* recognized by the machine.

While the algorithmic aspect of a computation expresses the effectiveness of the computation, the topological field theory constraints the effectiveness of a computation to a specific environment where the computation might take place at a certain time in space.

It is right here to recall Landin's metaphor of the ball and the plane, introduced to describe the existence of a double link between a program and machine [13]:

> One can think of the ball as a program and the plane as the machine on which it runs. ... the situation is really quite symmetric; each constrains the other [14].

Alan Turing himself, in his address to the London Mathematical Society in 1947, said

> ... if a machine is expected to be infallible, it cannot also be intelligent [15].

It is becoming general thinking that intelligence benefits from *interaction* and evolves with something similar to *adaptability checking* [9]. Accordingly, the *PTM*, and its topological interpretation seem to be a good starting point for modeling *concurrent processes* as interactive TMs [19]. Also considering that the set of *PTMs* reveals to be isomorphic to a general class of effective transition systems as proved in Smolka et al. in [1]. This result allows to make the hypothesis that the *PTM* captures the intuitive notion of sequential interactive computation [2], in analogy to the Church-Turing hypothesis that relates Turing machines to algorithmic computation.

Computation. Turing, Church, and Kleene independently formalized the notion of computability with the notion of Turing machine, λ-calculus, partial recursive functions. Turing machine manipulates strings over a finite alphabet, λ-calculus manipulate λ-terms, and μ-recursive functions manipulate natural numbers. The Church-Turing thesis states that

> every effective computation can be carried out by a Turing machine or equivalently a certain informal concept (algorithm) corresponds to a certain mathematical object (Turing machine) [16].

The demonstration lies on the fact that the three notions of computability are formally equivalent. In particular, the Turing machine is a model of computation like a finite states control unit with an unbounded tape used to memorize strings of symbols. A deterministic sequence of computational steps transforms a finite input string in the output string. For each step of the computation, a Turing machine contains all the *information* for processing input in output, an algorithmic way to computing a function, those functions that are *effectively computable*. The *Universal TM* is the basic model of all effectively computable functions, formally defined by a mathematical description.

Definition 1 (Turing machine). *A Turing machine (TM) is* $\mathcal{M} = \langle Q, \Sigma, \mathcal{P} \rangle$,

- Q *is a finite set of* states;
- Σ *is a finite* alphabet *containing* the blank symbol $\#$; L *and* R *are special symbols*.
- $\mathcal{P} \subseteq Q \times \Sigma \times \Sigma \times Q \times \{L, R\}$, *the set of configurations of* $\mathcal{M}$.

A computation is a chain of elements of $\mathcal{P}$ such that the last one cannot be linked to any possible configuration of $\mathcal{P}$.

The *multi-tape Turing machine* is a *TM* equipped with an arbitrary number k of tapes and corresponding heads.

Definition 2 (k-tape Turing machine). *A non-deterministic k-tape TM is a quadruple* $\langle Q, \Sigma, \mathcal{P}, s_0 \rangle$, *where*

- Q *is a finite set of* states; $s_0 \in Q$ *is the* initial state *and* $h \notin Q$ *is the* halting state.
- Σ *is a finite* alphabet *containing* the blank symbol $\#$. L *and* R *are special symbols*.
- $\mathcal{P} \subseteq Q \times \Sigma^k \times (Q \cup \{h\}) \times (\Sigma \cup \{L, R\})^k$ *is the set of configurations*.

The machine makes a transition from its current configuration (state) to a new one (possibly the halt state h). For each of the k tapes, either a new symbol is written at the current head position or the position of the head is shifted by one location to the left (L) or right (R).

The above definitions of *TMs* do not take into account the notion of *environment*; the input is implicitly represented in the configurations $\mathcal{P}$ of $\mathcal{M}$ machine modulo *feasible relations*. The objective of this contribution is to represent the *environment* explicitly in a way such that the *admissible relations* are naturally determined. Our view is supported by a recent, even though not formal, definition of computation.

Computation is the evolution process of some environment via a sequence of simple and local steps [7].

A Computational Environment is the base space over which the process of transformation of an input string happens. For the *TM*, an *environment* is any configuration of $\mathcal{P}$ of a machine $\mathcal{M}$, from the initial one to the final one. It is a closed set – represented by the functional matrix, – whose feasible relations should be known a priori to assure the algorithmic aspect of the computation. Indeed, in *TM* the *environment* does not evolve, it remains unchanged during the computation.

If we consider the *environment* as an open set - the set of configurations may changes along the way due to computation - accordingly, the set of feasible relations may change. As Sect. 3 describes, one way to capture this variation is to associate a topology to the space of all possible configurations and use the global invariants of the space to classify the relations in categories whose elements are isomorphic to those of some model of computation, such as the *TM*. In this setting, the local steps (feasible relations) – the functional matrix – are affected by global topology. As a consequence, the evolution of an *environment* corresponds to a change of the topological invariants. Then the classical *TM* is equivalent to working with a space of states whose topology is trivial, which allows the process of transformation to run linearly.

While an *interactive computation* takes into account the *non-linearity* of the computation due to the structure of the transformations characterizing it. The non-linearity is implied by the topology of the base space **B**, and induced by the semi-direct product factorization of the transformation group, the simplicial analog of the mapping class group, denoted by $\mathcal{G}_{\mathcal{MC}}$.

In the viewpoint of computation as a process, the global context induces *non-linear interactions* among the processes affecting the semantic domain of the computation. The semantic object associated to *TM*, that is the function that *TM* computes, or the formal language that it accepts, becomes an *interactive transition system* for a *PTM*. In the topological setting it changed into the pair of ⟨function, structure⟩, entangled as a unique object. The function represents the behavior and the structure the context. Formally represented by the fiber subgroup in the semi-direct product form of the group of computations (connected to process algebra), denoted by $\mathcal{G}_{\mathcal{AC}}$, and $\mathcal{G}_{\mathcal{MC}}$ the group of self-mapping of the topological spaces (the environmentself-transformations algebra, i.e. automorphisms which leave the topology invariant), quotient by the set of feasible relations. The new semantic object, a *gauge group* $G = \mathcal{G}_{\mathcal{AC}} \wedge \mathcal{G}_{\mathcal{MC}}$, provides another way to understand the meaning of *contextuality* [17], as a tool to distinguish effective computation from interactive computations. That is to identify configurations that are 'locally consistent, but globally inconsistent', as shown in Fig. 1 and informally summarised in the following sentence

Contextuality arises where we have a family of data which is locally consistent but globally inconsistent.

Section 3 introduces the new interpretation. We leave the formal definition and full formalization of the theory corresponding to the group of computations for an evolving *environment* as future work.

2   Interactive Computation

In this section, we recall the definition of the persistent Turing Machine, *PTM* as defined by Smolka et al. in [1] and the related notion of *environment* introduced in their earlier work [2]. We introduce the definitions needed to support the construction of a new topological model that is a generalization of the *PTM*. The new model allows one to re-interpret the classic scheme of computability, which envisages a unique and complete space of problems.

The *PTM* provides a new way of interpreting *TM* computation, based on dynamic stream semantics (comparable to behavior as a linear system). A *PTM* is a non-deterministic 3-tape *TM* (N3TM) that performs an infinite sequence of classical *TM* computations. Each such computation starts when the *PTM* reads input from its *input-tape* and ends when the *PTM* produces an output on its *output-tape*. The additional *work-tape* retains its content from one computational step to the next to carry out the persistence.

Definition 3 (Smolka, Goldin Persistent Turing machine). *A persistent Turing machine (PTM) is a N3TM having a read-only* input-tape, *a read/write* work-tape, *and a write-only* output-tape.

Let w_i and w_0 denote the content of the input and output tapes, respectively, while w and w' the content of work-tape, and $\#$ empty content, then

- an *interaction stream* is an infinite sequence of pairs of (w_i, w_o) representing a computation that transforms w_i in w_o;
- a *macrostep* of *PTM* is a computation step denoted by $w \xrightarrow{w_i/w_o} w'$, that starts with w and ends with w' on the work-tape and transforms w_i in w_o;
- a *PTM computation* is a sequence of *macrosteps*.

$w \xrightarrow{w_i/\mu} s_{div}$ denotes a macrostep of a computation that diverges (that is a non-terminating computation); s_{div} is a particular state where each divergent computations falls, and μ is special output symbol signifying divergence; $\mu \notin \Sigma$.

Moreover, the definition of the *interactive transition system* (*ITS*) equipped with three notions of behavioral equivalence – *ITS* isomorphism, interactive bisimulation, and interaction stream equivalence – allows them to determine the *PTMs* equivalence.

Definition 4 (Interactive transition system). *Given a finite alphabet Σ not containing μ, an ITS over Σ is a triple $\langle S, m, r \rangle$ where*

- $S \subseteq \Sigma^* \cup \{s_{div}\}$ *is the set of states;*
- $m \subseteq S \times \Sigma^* \times S \times (\Sigma^* \cup \{\mu\})$ *is the transition relation;*
- r *denotes the initial state.*

It is assumed that all the states in S are reachable from r. Intuitively, a transition $\langle s, w_i, s', w_o \rangle$ of an ITS states that while the machine is in the state s and having received the input string w_i from the environment, the ITS transits to state s' and output w_o.

Unfortunately, the sake of space economy forced to omit most of the results; we only recall Theorem 24, Theorem 32 and Thesis 50 (in the sequel renumbered Theorem 1, Theorem 2 and Thesis 1, respectively) and address the reader eager for more information to the original article [1].

Theorem 1. *The structures* $\langle \mathbb{M}, =_{ms} \rangle$ *and* $\langle \mathbb{T}, =_{iso} \rangle$ *are isomorphic.*

Theorem 1 states that there exists a one-to-one correspondence between the class of *PTMs*, denoted by $\mathbb{M}$ up to macrostep equivalence, denoted by $=_{ms}$, and the class of *ITSs*, denoted by $\mathbb{T}$ up to isomorphism, denoted by $=_{iso}$.

Theorem 2. *If a PTM $\mathcal{M}$ has unbounded nondeterminism, then $\mathcal{M}$ diverges.*

Theorem 2 states that a *PTM* $\mathcal{M}$ diverges if there exists some $w \in \text{reach}(\mathcal{M})$, $w_i \in \Sigma^*$ such that there is an infinite number of $w_o \in \Sigma^* \cup \{\mu\}$, $w' \in \Sigma^* \cup \{s_{div}\}$, such that $w \xrightarrow{w_i/w_o} w'$.

Thesis 1. *Any sequential interactive computation can be performed by a PTM.*

Like the Church-Turing Thesis, Thesis 1 cannot be proved. Informally, each step of a sequential interactive computation, corresponding to a single input/output-pair transition, is algorithmic. Therefore, by the Church-Turing Thesis, each step is computable by a *TM*. A sequential interactive computation may be history-dependent, so state information must be maintained between steps. A *PTM* is just a *TM* that maintains state information on its work-tape between two steps. Thus, any sequential interaction machine can be simulated by a *PTM* with possibly infinite input.

The *PTM* Environment. In her earlier work [2], D. Goldin proposed a notion of *environment* to highlight that the class of behaviors captured by the *TM*, the class of algorithmic behaviors, is different from that represented by the *PTM* model, the *sequential interactive behaviors*. The conceptualization of the *environment* provides the observational characterization of *PTM* behaviors given by the input-output streams. In fact, given two different environments $\mathcal{O}_1$ and $\mathcal{O}_2$ and a *PTM* $\mathcal{M}$, the behavior of $\mathcal{M}$ observed by interacting with an environment $\mathcal{O}_1$ can be different if observed by interacting with $\mathcal{O}_2$. Also, given two machines $\mathcal{M}_1$ and $\mathcal{M}_2$ and one environment $\mathcal{O}$, if the behaviors of the two machines are equal (one can be reduced to the other), they must be equivalent in $\mathcal{O}$. This claim gives the go-ahead to Theorem 3. Any environment $\mathcal{O}$ induces a partitioning of $\mathbb{M}$ into equivalence classes whose members appear behaviorally equivalent in $\mathcal{O}$; the set of equivalence classes is denoted by β_o. Indeed, the equivalences of the behaviors of two *PTMs* can be expressed by the language represented in the set of all interaction streams.

Let $\mathcal{B}(\mathcal{M})$ denote the operator that extracts the behavior of a given machine $\mathcal{M}$, and $\mathcal{O}(\mathcal{M})$ a mapping that associates any machine $\mathcal{M}$ to the class of the behaviors feasible for the environment $\mathcal{O}$. Therefore, each machine can be classified by analyzing its interaction streams with the two operators, $\mathcal{B}$ and $\mathcal{O}$.

Definition 5 (Environment). *Given a class* $\mathbb{M}$ *of PTMs and a set of suitable domains* $\beta_{\mathcal{O}}$*, that is the set of equivalence classes of feasible behaviours. An environment* $\mathcal{O}$ *is a mapping from machines to some domains* $\mathcal{O} : \mathbb{M} \to \beta_{\mathcal{O}}$ *and the following property holds:*

$$\forall \mathcal{M}_1, \mathcal{M}_2 \in \mathbb{M}, \ \ if \ \mathcal{B}(\mathcal{M}_1) = \mathcal{B}(\mathcal{M}_2) \ then \ \mathcal{O}(\mathcal{M}_1) = \mathcal{O}(\mathcal{M}_2)$$

When $\mathcal{O}(\mathcal{M}_1) \neq \mathcal{O}(\mathcal{M}_2)$*, we say that* $\mathcal{M}_1$ *and* $\mathcal{M}_2$ *are* distinguishable *in* $\mathcal{O}$*; otherwise, we say that* $\mathcal{M}_1$ *and* $\mathcal{M}_2$ appear *equivalent in* $\mathcal{O}$*.*

Theorem 3. *Let* Θ *denote the set of all possible environments. The environments in* Θ *induce an infinite expressiveness hierarchy of PTM behaviors, with TM behaviors at the bottom of the hierarchy.*

So far, we have assumed that all the input streams are all feasible. However, this is not a reasonable assumption for the context in which interactive machines normally run. Typically an environment can be constrained and limited by some obstructions when generating the output streams. In our view, this is the case where the space of all possible configurations lies on a topological space with not trivial topology. In order to contribute to this theory, in the following we will tackle the issue of specifying these constraints, and relating them to the *PTM* model.

3   Topological Interpretation of Interactive Computation

Topological Environment. This section deals with the notion of *topological environment* as an integral part of the model of topological computation. In a classical *TM* the environment is not represented (Definition 1), whereas in a *PTM* the environment is a mapping between the class of *PTMs* and their feasible domains. As described above the two functions $\mathcal{B}$ and $\mathcal{O}$ permit to identified the behavior of a *PTM* machine by observing its stream of interactions. In this case the environment $\mathcal{O}$ is a static mapping that associates machines with an equivalent behavior $\mathcal{B}(\mathcal{M})$ to the same equivalence class. In this case the environment plays the role of an observer. In our approach the environment is part of the system that evolves together with the behavior of the machine over time step i. The environment constrains the behavior of a machine *PTM* so as the output generated by the machine affects the evolution of the environment.

To detect dynamic changes in the environment, we propose to define a dynamic analysis of the set of all the interactions streams available at any single *PTM* computation step i. Since interaction streams are infinite sequences of pairs of the form (w_i, w_o) representing the input and output strings of *PTMs* computation step i, we use the set $\mathcal{P}$ of *PTM* configurations to represent them.

The resulting model of computation consists of two components entangled and coexisting during the interactive computation, a functional unit of computation and a *self-organizing memory*.

In our model, the infinite input of the *PTM* should be seen as a feedback loop of a dynamic system. Its functional behavior is represented by a class $\mathbb{T}$

of *ITS* constrained by the information contained in the self-organizing memory associated with the notion of topological environment. The data structure used to store information is the simplicial complex $\mathcal{S}_\mathcal{P}$, that is a topological space $\mathcal{S}$ constructed over the set of *PTM* configuration $\mathcal{P}$. The $\mathcal{S}_\mathcal{P}$ is equipped with a finite presentation in terms of homology groups whose relations are fully representable. In this view the *PTM* functional behavior can be determined by $\mathcal{S}_\mathcal{P}$ modulo *ITS* isomorphism. We operate in a discrete setting where full information about topological space is inherent in their simplicial representation. Appendix 1 provides some useful definitions for algebraic and computational topology.

Definition 6 (Topological environment). *Given the set of PTM configurations $\mathcal{P}_i$ available at a given time i, the* topological environment *is the simplicial complex $\mathcal{S}_{\mathcal{P}_i}$ constructed over $\mathcal{P}_i$.*

The topological environment $\mathcal{S}_\mathcal{P}$, as any topological space is equipped with a set of invariants that are important to understand the characteristics of the space. For the sake of simplicity we will refer to topological space as a continuous space. The n-dimensional holes, the language of paths, the homology and the genus are topological invariants. The n-dimensional holes are determined during the process of filtration, called persistent homology, that is used to construct a topological space starting from a set of points. The numbers of holes and their associated dimensions are determined by the *homology* structure fully represented by the homology groups associated with a *topological space*. Also the homology is a topological invariant of the space, it is always preserved by homeomorphisms of the space.

A *path* $\mathcal{S}$ is a continuous function $f : [0,1] \to \mathcal{S}$ from the unit interval to $\mathcal{S}$. Paths are oriented, thus $f(0)$ is the starting point and $f(1)$ is the end-point, if we label the starting point v and the end-point v', we call f a path from v to v' as shown in Fig. 2-(a). Two paths a and b, that is two continuous functions, from a topological space $\mathcal{S}$ to a topological space $\mathcal{S}'$ are homotopic if one can be continuously deformed into the other. Being homotopic is an equivalence relation on the set of all continuous functions from $\mathcal{S}$ to $\mathcal{S}'$. The homotopy relation is compatible with function composition.

Therefore, it is interesting to study the effect of the existence of holes (at any dimension) in a topological space $\mathcal{S}$ (for simplicity the discussion is made thinking of $\mathcal{S}$ as a 2D surface) built from the space of configurations $\mathcal{P}$ where a sequential interactive computation takes place as a *sequential composition of paths*. Figures 2-(b) and -(c) show the composition of two paths a and b, and the proof that they are not homotopic, respectively. Given two-cycle paths, a and b, with a point in common in x, if the composition of the two paths ab or ba is not commutative, the two composed paths are not equivalent. In this case, the two cycle paths, a and b can be considered the generators of a topological space with one 2-dimensional hole, as shown in Fig. 3. Each generator represents a distinct class of paths, $[a]$ those going around the neck, and $[b]$ those around the belt of the torus, respectively.

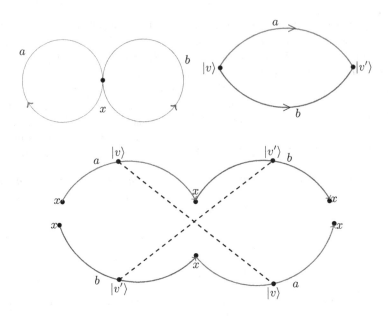

Fig. 2. (a) homotopic paths $a \sim b$; (b) composition of paths ab; (c) not homotopic paths $ab \nsim ba$

Computable Functions and Topological Space. We start taking into account those classes of problems whose computable functions are defined over a space $\mathcal{S}$ endowed with a trivial topology, and it is a Vector Space. Figure 4 shows how an algorithmic computation A associated with the function $f_A : \mathcal{S} \to \mathcal{S}$, evolves over $\mathcal{S}$, representing the space of the states. Each state v is defined by a vector that moves over $\mathcal{S}$ driven by the configurations of the TM. In Fig. 4, from left to right, the first two pictures represent a successful computation and a computation with an infinite loop, respectively. When the algorithm moves the vector towards a *boundary*, see the last picture, the computation is deadlocked. This happens because $\mathcal{S}$ has not been defined globally. In fact, the boundary breaks the translational symmetry. If we allow the boundary to disappear by adding an extra-relation, global in nature, we obtain a global topology that is not trivial – the space is characterized by a not empty set of n-dimensional holes ($n \geq 2$). Figure 5 shows how the computation with a deadlock on the plane could have succeeded if the manifold of the space is a torus.

Figure 6 shows how we can transform a rectangle, 2-dimensional space $\mathcal{S}$ homomorphic to 2-manifold with boundary, into a cylinder and then into a torus by adding two relations among the generators of the manifold $\mathcal{P}$ that will be proved to be *without boundary*.

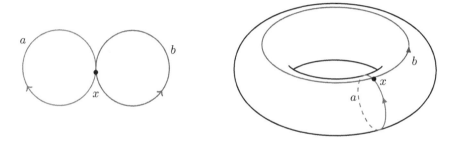

Fig. 3. From cycling paths to generators of a space $\mathcal{S}$

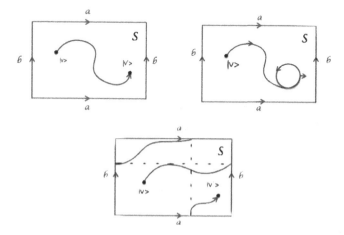

Fig. 4. (a) successful computation, (b) computation with an infinite loop, (c) computation with a deadlock.

Hence, we proceed to analyze those classes of problems whose computable functions are defined over a space $\mathcal{S}$ endowed with non-trivial topology. The class of functions $F_{\mathcal{S}}$ effectively computable over a space $\mathcal{S}$, and for each single function $f_A \in F_{\mathcal{S}}$ and a couple of points $v, v' \in \mathcal{S}$, we associate a computation $f_A(v) = v'$, as a path that connects the two points v and v' in the space $\mathcal{S}$. The path can be semantically interpreted as an interaction stream.

In Fig. 7, the first two pictures from left to right, show that a close path π in a surface that starts and ends to a fixed point P_B is homotopic to 0; it means that any π can be reduced to the point P_B. The class of behavioral equivalence to τ denoted by $[\pi]$ belongs to space or subspace space with trivial topology $g = 0$ (g is the *genus*). The other pictures show irreducible paths belonging to space with a topological genus $g \neq 0$. E.g. if $g = 1$, i.e. is a torus there are three different classes of behaviors: (i) the set of closed paths homotopic to 0. In this case, we are given a local interpretation and we are not aware that at the global level the *genus* can be different from 0; (ii) the set of closed paths homotopic to the first generator a of the homology group of the topological space $\mathcal{S}$. The cycle

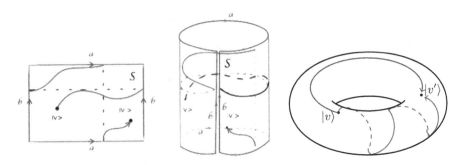

Fig. 5. A deadlocked computation on the plane may successes over a space with non-trivial topology.

fixed on the base point P_B can be used to reduce any path going around the belt of the torus to a by a continuous deformation; (iii) similar to the previous set, but the paths are homotopic to the second generator b of S. The cycle fixed on the base point P_B goes around the belt of the torus. The last picture shows the composition of paths.

The interpretation of interaction streams over a S_P is indeed nothing but its identification with an element of the path algebra corresponding to a quiver representation of the transformation group G of S, say Q (or, more generally, a set of quivers, over some arbitrary ring). The different ways to reach any point $p \in P$ from P_B generate a path algebra A whose elements are describable words in a language L. Any point of P can be related to any other point by a group element. By selecting a point p_0 of P as a unique base point, every point of P is in one-to-one correspondence with an element of such group $G_{MC} \approx \mathfrak{MCG}$, the simplicial analog of the mapping class group. G_{MC} is a group of transformations which do not change the information hidden in the data, such as the group of diffeomorfisms that do not change the topology of the base space. $\mathfrak{MCG}$ is an algebraic invariant of a topological space, that is a discrete group of symmetries. Since the algebras manipulate the data, the transformations applied to space are 'processes' carried on through the fiber, which is the representation space of the process algebra. Whenever Q can give the representation of the algebra, the algebra can be exponentiated to a group G_{AP} and t a gauge group. We have now all the ingredients for defining a fiber bundle enriched with a group $G = G_{AP} \wedge G_{MC}$, called *gauge group*, (see Fig. 1). Summarizing, fiber bundle is the mathematical structure that allows us to represent computation and its context (the environment) as a unique model. In terms of TM, the context represents the *transition function*, also called the *functional matrix*.

While the algorithmic aspect of a computation expresses the effectiveness of the computation, the topology provides a global characterization of the environment.

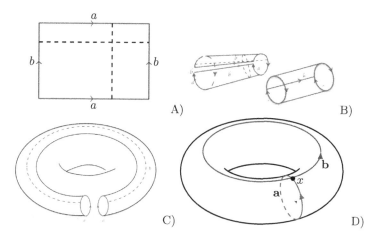

Fig. 6. The pictures (A–D) summarize the main steps to transform a space $\mathcal{S}$ of *PTM* into a topological space $\mathcal{S_P}$. The construction is obtained by gluing together – put in relation – the two boundaries of the space $\mathcal{S}$, a and b respectively, which become the generators **a** and **b** of the new space $\mathcal{S_P}$. The topological space $\mathcal{S_P}$, finite but not limited, naturally supports the notion of the environment of *PTM*.

Both the computation and the environment can be represented as groups (algebras), and their *interaction* is captured as the set of accessible transformations of the semi-direct product of the two groups, carrying constrained by the restrictions imposed by topology. Incidentally, it is this set of constraints together with the semidirect product structure that implies the non-linearity of the process.

Definition 7 (Topological Turing machine). *A Topological Turing machine (TTM) is a group $\mathcal{G}$ consisting of all interaction streams generated by the group of PTMs entangled with the group of all transformations of the topological space $\mathcal{S_P}$ preserving the topology. Formally $\mathcal{G} = \mathcal{G}_{AP} \wedge \mathcal{G}_{MC}$, where $\mathcal{G}_{AP}$ is the group of PTMs and $\mathcal{G}_{MC}$ the simplicial analog of the mapping class group.*

Proposition 1. *If $\mathcal{G}$ is automatic, the associated language $\mathcal{L}$ is regular. Since the representations of $\mathcal{G}$ can then be constructed in terms of quivers $\mathcal{Q}$ with relations induced by the corresponding path algebra induced by PTMs, the syntax of $\mathcal{L}$ is fully contained in $\mathbb{T}$ and its semantics in $\mathbb{M}$.*

Definition 8 (Constrained interactive computation). *An interactive computation is constrained if it is defined over a topological space $\mathcal{S_P}$ and it is an element of the language of paths of $\mathcal{S_P}$.*

Theorem 4. *Any constrained interactive computation is an effective computation for a TTM.*

Thesis 2. *Any concurrent computation can be performed by a TTM.*

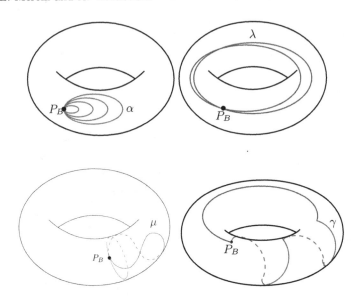

Fig. 7. A class of behaviors over a torus α close paths, λ path around the neck, μ path around the belt, γ complex path

4   Final Remarks

In 2013, Terry Tao in his blog [20] posted this question: if there is any computable group G which is "Turing complete" in the sense that the halting problem for any Turing machine can be converted into a question of the above form. In other words, there would be **an algorithm** which, when given a Turing machine T, would return (in a finite time) a pair x_T, y_T of elements of G with the property that x_T, y_T generate a free group in G if and only if T does not halt in finite time. Or more informally: *can a 'group' be a universal Turing machine?*

Acknowledgements. E. M. thanks Mario Rasetti for bringing her to conceive a new way of thinking about computer science and for numerous and lively discussions on topics related to this article; and Samson Abramsky with his group for insightful conversations on the topological interpretation of contextuality and contextual semantics. E. M. and A. W. thank the anonymous referees for suggesting many significant improvements.

Funding statements. We acknowledge the financial support of the Future and Emerging Technologies (FET) programme within the Seventh Framework Programme (FP7) for Research of the European Commission, under the FP7 FET-Proactive Call 8 - DyMCS, Grant Agreement TOPDRIM, number FP7-ICT-318121.

Appendix 1: Definitions of Algebraic and Computational Topology

Definition 9. *Topology*
A topology on a set X is a family $T \subseteq 2^X$ such that

- *If $S_1, S_2 \in T$, then $S_1 \cap S_2 \in T$ (equivalent to: If $S_1, S_2, \ldots, S_n \in T$ then $\cap_{i=1}^n S_i \in T$)*
- *If $\{S_j | j \in J\} \subseteq T$, then $\cup_{j \in J} S_j \in T$.*
- *$\emptyset, X \in T$.*

Definition 10. *Topological spaces*
The pair (X, T) of a set X and a topology T is a topological space. We will often use the notation $\mathbb{X}$ for a topological space X, with T being understood.

Definition 11. *Simplices*
Let $u_0, u_1, \ldots, u_k$ be points in $\mathbb{R}^d$. A point $x = \sum_{i=0}^k \lambda_i u_i$ is an affine combination of the u_i if the λ_i sum to 1. The affine hull is the set of affine combinations. It is a k-plane if the k+1 points are affinely independent by which we mean that any two affine combinations, $x = \sum_{i=0}^k \lambda_i u_i$ and $y = \sum_{i=0}^k \mu_i u_i$ are the same iff $\lambda_i = \mu_i$ for all i. The k+1 points are affinely independent iff the k vectors $u_i \ldots u_0$, for $1 \leq i \leq k$, are linearly independent. In $\mathbb{R}^d$ we can have at most d linearly independent vectors and therefore at most d+1 affinely independent points.
k-simplex is the convex hull of k+1 affinely independent points, $\sigma = \{u_0, u_1, u_2, \ldots u_k\}$. We sometimes say the u_i span σ. Its dimension is $\dim \sigma = k$. Any subset of affinely independent points is again independent and therefore also defines a simplex of lower dimension.

Definition 12. *Face*
A face of σ is the convex hull of a non-empty subset of the u_i and it is proper if the subset is not the entire set. We sometimes write $\tau \leq \sigma$ if τ is a face and $\tau < \sigma$ if it is a proper face of σ. Since a set of k+1 has 2^{k+1} subsets, including empty set, σ has $2^{k+1} - 1$ faces, all of which are proper except for σ itself. The boundary of σ, is the union of all proper faces.

Definition 13. *Simplicial complexes*
A simplical complex is a finite collection of simplices K such that $\sigma \in K$ and $\tau \in K$, and $\sigma, \sigma_0 \in K$ implies $\sigma \cap \sigma_0$ is either empty or a face of both.

Definition 14. *Filtration*
A filtration of a complex K is a nested sequence of subcomplex, $\emptyset = K^0 \subseteq K^1 \subseteq K^2 \subseteq \ldots \subseteq K^m = K$. We call a complex K with a filtration a filtered complex.

Definition 15. *Chain group*
The k-th chain group of a simplicial complex K is $\langle C_k(K), + \rangle$, let $\mathbb{F}$ be a field.
The $\mathbb{F}-$linear space on the oriented k-simplices, where $[\sigma] = -[\tau]$ if $\sigma = \tau$
and σ and τ have different orientations. An element of $C_k(K)$ is a k-chain,
$\sum_q n_q[\sigma_q], n_q \in \mathbb{Z}, \sigma_q \in K.$

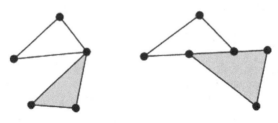

A simplicial complex (left) and not valid simplicial complex (right).

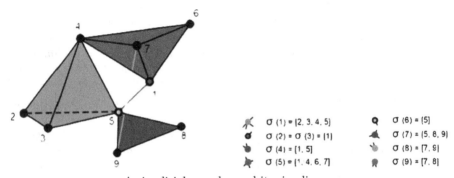

σ (1) = [2, 3, 4, 5] σ (6) = [5]

σ (2) = σ (3) = [1] σ (7) = [5, 8, 9]

σ (4) = [1, 5] σ (8) = [7, 9]

σ (5) = [1, 4, 6, 7] σ (9) = [7, 8]

A simplicial complex and its simplices.

Definition 16. *Boundary homomorphism*
Let K be a simplicial complex and $\sigma \in K, \sigma = [v_0, v_1, ..., v_k]$. The boundary
homomorphism $\partial_k : C_k(K) \to C_{k-1}(K)$ is $\quad \partial_k \sigma = \sum_i (-1)^i [v_0, v_1, ..., \widehat{v_i}, ..., v_n]$
where $\widehat{v_i}$ indicates that v_i is deleted from the sequence.

Definition 17. *Cycle and boundary*
The k-th cycle group is $Z_k = \ker \partial_k$. A chain that is an element of Z_k is a k-
cycle. The k-th boundary group is $B_k = \operatorname{im} \partial_{k+1}$. A chain that is an element of
B_k is a k-boundary. We also call boundaries bounding cycles and cycles not in
B_k nonbounding cycles.

Definition 18. *Homology group*
The k-th homology group is $\quad H_k = Z_k/B_k = \ker \partial_k / \operatorname{im} \partial_{k+1}$

If $z_1 = z_2 + B_k, z_1, z_2 \in Z_k$, we say z_1 and z_2 are homologous and denote it with
$z_1 \sim z_2$

Definition 19. *k-th Betti number*
The *k*-th Betti number B_k *of a simplicial complex K is the dimension of the k-th homology group of K. Informally,* β_0 *is the number of connected components,* β_1 *is the number of two-dimensional holes or "handles" and* β_2 *is the number of three-dimensional holes or "voids" etc. . . .*

Definition 20. *Invariant*
A topological invariant is a property of a topological space which is invariant under homeomorphisms. Betti numbers are topological invariants.

Definition 21. *Genus*
The genus is a topological invariant of a close (oriented) surface. The connected sum of g tori is called a surface with genus g. genus refers to how many 'holes' the donut surface has.

As an example, a torus is homeomorphic to a sphere with a handle. Both of them have just one hole (handle). The sphere has g = 0 and the torus has g = 1.

References

1. Goldin, D.Q., Smolka, S.A., Attie, P.C., Sondereggera, E.L.: Turing machines, transition systems, and interaction. In: Information and Computation 194, 2004. - ENTCS Vol. 52, No. 1, Elsevier (2001)
2. Goldin, D.Q.: Persistent turing machines as a model of interactive computation. In: Schewe, K.-D., Thalheim, B. (eds.) FoIKS 2000. LNCS, vol. 1762, pp. 116–135. Springer, Heidelberg (2000). https://doi.org/10.1007/3-540-46564-2_8
3. Goldin, D.Q., Smolka, S.A., Wegner, P.: Interacting Computation: The New Paradigm. Springer, Heidelberg (2006). https://doi.org/10.1007/3-540-34874-3
4. Wegner, P.: Why Intera is More P Than Algorit. CACM, vol. 40, No. 5. ACM (1997)
5. Wegner, P.: Interactive foundations of computing. TCS, vol. 192. Elsevier (1998)
6. Gandy, R.O.: Church's thesis and principles for mechanisms. In: Barwise, J., Keisler, H.J., Kunen, K. (eds.) The Kleene Symposium. North-Holland Publishing Company (1980)
7. Wigderson, A.: Mathematics and Computation. IAS, Draft (March 2018)
8. Garrone, S., Marzuoli, A., Rasetti, M.: Spin networks, quantum automata and link invariants. J. Phys. Conf. Ser. **33**, 95 (2006)
9. Merelli, E., Pettini, M., Rasetti, M.: Topology driven modeling: the IS metaphor. Nat. Comput. **14**(3), 421–430 (2015)
10. Carlsson, G.: Topology and data. Bull. Am. Math. Soc. **46**(2), 255–308 (2009)
11. Rasetti, M., Merelli, E.: Topological field theory of data: mining data beyond complex networks. In: Contucci, P. (ed.) Advances in Disordered Systems. Random Processes and Some Applications. Cambridge University Press, Cambridge (2016)
12. Steenrod, N.: The topology of Fiber Bundles. Princeton Mathematical Series. Princeton University Press, Princeton (1951)
13. Landin, P.J.: A Program Machine Symmetric Automata Theory. In: Meltzer and Michie (ed.) Machine Intelligence, Vol. 5. Edinburgh University Press (1969)
14. Abramsky, S.: An algebraic characterisation of concurrent composition. ArXiv:1406.1965v1 (2014)

15. Turing, A.M.: Lecture to the London Mathematical Society, 20 February 1947. Quoted in Carpenter, B.E., Doran, R.W. (eds.), A. M. Turing's Ace Report of 1946 (1946)
16. Lewis, H., Papadimitriou, C.H.: Elements of the Theory of Computation, 2nd edn. Prentice Hall, Upper Saddle River (1998)
17. Abramsky, S.: Contextuality: at the borders of paradox. In: Landry, E. (ed.) Categories for the Working Philosophers (2017)
18. Abramsky, S.: Contextual semantics: from quantum mechanics to logic, databases, constraints, and complexity. ArXiv:1406.7386v1 (2014)
19. Abramsky, S.: What are the Fundamental Structures of Concurrency? We still don't know! Electronic Notes in Theoretical Computer Science vol. 162 (2006)
20. Mathoverflow.   https://mathoverflow.net/questions/88368/can-a-group-be-a-universal-turing-machine

Conformal Predictions for Hybrid System State Classification

Luca Bortolussi[1,4], Francesca Cairoli[1], Nicola Paoletti[2(✉)],
and Scott D. Stoller[3]

[1] Department of Mathematics and Geosciences, Università di Trieste, Trieste, Italy
[2] Department of Computer Science, Royal Holloway, University of London,
Egham, UK
nclpltt@gmail.com
[3] Department of Computer Science, Stony Brook University, Stony Brook, USA
[4] Modelling and Simulation Group, Saarland University, Saarbrücken, Germany

Abstract. Neural State Classification (NSC) [19] is a scalable method
for the analysis of hybrid systems, which consists in learning a neural
network-based classifier able to detect whether or not an unsafe state
can be reached from a certain configuration of a hybrid system. NSC has
very high accuracy, yet it is prone to prediction errors that can affect system safety. To overcome this limitation, we present a method, based on
the theory of conformal prediction, that complements NSC predictions
with statistically sound estimates of prediction uncertainty. This results
in a principled criterion to reject potentially erroneous predictions *a priori*, i.e., without knowing the true reachability values. Our approach is
highly efficient (with runtimes in the order of milliseconds) and effective,
managing in our experiments to successfully reject almost all the wrong
NSC predictions.

1 Introduction

Hybrid systems, i.e., systems characterized by the interaction between discrete
(digital) and continuous (physical) components, are a central model for many
cyber-physical system applications, from avionics to biomedical devices [1]. Formal verification of hybrid systems typically boils down to solving a hybrid
automata (HA) reachability checking problem [13]: given a model $\mathcal{M}$ of the
system expressed as an HA and a set of unsafe states U of $\mathcal{M}$, check whether U
is reached in any (time-bounded) path from a set of initial states. HA reachability
checking is undecidable in general [13], a difficulty that current HA reachability
checking algorithms address by over-approximating the set of reachable states.
These algorithms are computationally very expensive, and thus, usually limited
to design-time (offline) analysis.

This material is based on work supported in part by NSF Grants CNS-1421893 and
CCF-1414078 and ONR Grant N00014-15-1-2208.

© Springer Nature Switzerland AG 2019
E. Bartocci et al. (Eds.): From Reactive Systems to Cyber-Physical Systems, LNCS 11500, pp. 225–241, 2019.
https://doi.org/10.1007/978-3-030-31514-6_13

Motivated by the need to make HA reachability checking more efficient and suitable for online analysis, Phan et al. [19] recently proposed *Neural State Classification (NSC)*, an approach for approximating reachability checking using deep neural networks (DNNs). Their work shows that it is possible to train, using examples computed via suitable HA model checkers, DNN-based state classifiers that approximate the result of reachability checking with very high accuracy. For any state s of the HA, such a classifier labels s as *positive* if an unsafe state is reachable from s within a given time bound; otherwise, s is labeled as *negative*.

The key advantage of this approach is its efficiency. Neural state classifiers indeed run in constant time and space, because the computation is not directly affected by the size and complexity of the HA model or specification, but only by the complexity of the chosen DNN architecture.

The main drawback is that DNNs for NSC (like any other machine learning model) are subject to *classification errors*, the most important being false negatives, i.e., when the DNN classifies a state as negative while it is actually positive. While Phan et al.'s work allows estimation of the classification accuracy for a region of states (i.e., the probability that a state in the region is wrongly classified), it does not provide any indication about the reliability of single-point predictions, i.e., DNN predictions on individual HA states whose true reachability value is unknown. This limits the applicability of NSC for online analysis, where state classification errors can compromise the safety of the system. This is in contrast with methods like smoothed model checking [4], which leverages Gaussian Processes and Bayesian statistics to quantify uncertainty, but on the other side faces severe scalability issues as the dimension of the system increases.

The aim of this work is to equip NSC with rigorous methods for quantifying the reliability of single-point predictions. For this purpose, we investigate *Conformal Prediction (CP)* [22], a method that provides statistical guarantees on the predictions of machine learning models. Importantly, CP requires only very mild assumptions on the data (i.e., exchangeability, a weaker version of the independent and identically distributed assumption).

By applying CP, we estimate two statistically sound measures of NSC prediction uncertainty, *confidence* and *credibility*. Informally, the confidence of a prediction is the probability that a reachability prediction for an HA state s corresponds to the true reachability value of s. Credibility quantifies how a given state is likely to belong to the same distribution as the training data.

Using confidence and credibility, we show how to derive criteria for anomaly detection, that is, for rejecting NSC predictions that are likely to be erroneous. The key advantage of such an approach is that predictions are rejected on rigorous statistical grounds, and we show experimentally its superiority with respect to discrimination based on the DNN's class likelihood. Furthermore, computation of CP-based confidence and credibility is very efficient (approximately 3 ms in our experiments), which makes our method suitable for online analysis.

In summary, the main contributions of this paper are the following:

- We extend the framework of neural state classification with conformal prediction to quantify the reliability of NSC predictions.
- We derive criteria for anomaly detection based on CP to reject unreliable NSC predictions.
- We evaluate our method on three hybrid automata models showing that, with adequate choices of confidence and credibility thresholds, our method successfully rejects almost all prediction errors: over a total of 30,000 test samples, our method successfully rejected 43 out of 44 errors.

The paper is structured as follows. Sections 2 and 3 provide background on neural state classification and conformal prediction, respectively. In Sect. 4, we introduce our CP-based measures of prediction reliability. Results of the experimental evaluation are given in Sect. 5. Related work is discussed in Sect. 6. Section 7 offers concluding remarks.

2 Neural State Classification for Hybrid System Reachability

Neural state classification seeks to solve the *State Classification Problem* (SCP) [19], a generalization of the reachability checking problem for hybrid systems. Let $\mathbb{B} = \{0, 1\}$ be the set of Boolean values. Given an HA $\mathcal{M}$ with state space $S(\mathcal{M})$, time bound T, and set of unsafe states $U \subset S(\mathcal{M})$, the SCP problem is to find a *state classifier*, i.e., a function $F^* : S(\mathcal{M}) \to \mathbb{B}$ such that for all $s \in S(\mathcal{M})$, $F^*(s) = 1$ if $\mathcal{M} \models \mathsf{Reach}(U, s, T)$, i.e., if it is possible for $\mathcal{M}$, starting in s, to reach a state in U within time T; $F^*(s) = 0$ otherwise. A state $s \in S(\mathcal{M})$ is called *positive* if $F^*(s) = 1$. Otherwise, s is *negative*.

Neural State Classification [19] offers an approximate solution to the SCP based on machine learning models, deep neural networks (DNNs) in particular. The NSC method is summarized in Fig. 1. The state classifier is trained using supervised learning, where the training examples are derived by sampling the state space according to some distribution and labelling the sampled states with the corresponding reachability values. The latter are computed by invoking an oracle, e.g., an hybrid system model checker [11]. The approach can handle parametric HA, by encoding parameters as additional inputs to the classifier.

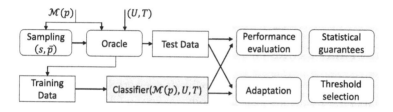

Fig. 1. Overview of the NSC approach (diagram from [19]).

NSC supports arbitrary state distributions. In [19], the following distributions and corresponding sampling methods are considered:

- Uniform sampling, where every state is equi-probable.
- Dynamics-aware sampling, which is based on the probability that a state is visited in any time-bounded evolution of the system, where such probabilities are estimated by performing isotropic random walks of the HA (i.e., by uniformly sampling the non-deterministic choices during the HA simulation).
- Balanced sampling, which seeks to draw a balanced number of positive and negative states. This is useful when U is a small portion of $S(\mathcal{M})$, in which case uniform sampling would produce imbalanced datasets with an insufficient number of positive samples, leading to classifiers with poor accuracy. For this purpose, in [19] the authors introduce a new method for the construction and simulation of reverse hybrid automata. Indeed, arbitrary numbers of positive samples can be generated by simulating the reverse HA starting from an unsafe state [19].

The performance of a trained classifier is evaluated by computing the empirical accuracy, rate of false positives (FPs), and rate of false negatives (FNs) using, as commonly done in supervised learning, test datasets of samples unseen during training. Inspired by statistical model checking [14], NSC also applies sequential hypothesis testing [23] to certify that a classifier meets prescribed accuracy, FN, or FP levels on unseen data, up to some given confidence level. Albeit useful, these kinds of statistical guarantees are, however, only applicable to regions of the HA state space, and as such, cannot be used to quantify the reliability of single-point predictions. The present paper aims to solve this very problem.

NSC includes two methods to reduce FNs: *threshold selection*, which adjusts the DNN's classification threshold to favor FPs over FNs, and a more advanced technique called *falsification-guided adaptation* that iteratively re-trains the classifier with false negatives found through adversarial sampling, i.e., by solving a non-linear optimization problem that maximizes the disagreement between DNN-predicted and true reachability values.

In [19], the authors applied NSC to six nonlinear hybrid system benchmarks, achieving an accuracy of 99.25% to 99.98%, and a false-negative rate of 0.0033 to 0, which was further reduced to 0.0015 to 0 by applying falsification-guided adaptation. While, with such performance, NSC can derive nearly perfect approximations of the HA reachability function, it does not provide a recipe for rejecting uncertain predictions *a priori*, i.e., without knowing the true reachability value. Our work extends NSC in this direction.

3   Conformal Prediction for Neural Networks

Conformal Prediction (CP) [22] is a flexible framework built on top of any traditional supervised machine learning model, called in CP the *underlying model*.

In this section, we describe CP in relation to a generic classification problem (of which NSC is an instance), where we denote with X the set of inputs and with $Y = \{y^1, \dots, y^c\}$ the set of classification labels (or classes). The underlying classification model is a function $h : X \rightarrow [0,1]^c$ mapping inputs into a vector of class likelihoods, such that the class predicted by h corresponds to the class with the highest likelihood. For a generic input x_i, we will denote with y_i the true label of x_i and with $\hat{y}_i$ the label predicted by h (i.e., the label with highest likelihood). Further, we will often use the notation x_* to indicate test points whose true label is unknown.

The interpretation of CP is two-fold. On one hand, conformal predictors output *prediction regions*, instead of single point predictions. In the case of classification, given a test point x_i and a significance level $\epsilon \in (0,1)$, the prediction region of x_i, $\Gamma_i^\epsilon \subseteq Y$, is a set of labels guaranteed to contain the true label y_i with probability $1 - \epsilon$. We call this the *global* interpretation of CP.

On the other hand, given a prediction $\hat{y}_i \in Y$ for x_i, we can compute the minimum value of ϵ such that the prediction region Γ_i^ϵ contains only $\hat{y}_i$. The corresponding probability $1 - \epsilon$ is called the *confidence* of the predicted label $\hat{y}_i$. Along with the confidence, CP allows computing another measure, called *credibility*, which indicates how suitable the training data are for the current prediction. Therefore, CP complements each prediction, on a new input, with a measure of confidence and a measure of credibility. We call this the *point-wise* interpretation of CP.

Importantly, CP does not require prior probabilities, unlike Bayesian methods, but only that data is exchangeable (a weaker version of the classic i.i.d. assumption). We now provide a brief description of the method, but we refer to [22] for a detailed introduction.

Let $Z = X \times Y$. The main ingredients of CP are: a *nonconformity function* $f : Z \rightarrow \mathbb{R}$, a set of labelled examples $Z' \subseteq Z$, an underlying model h trained on (a subset of) Z', and a statistical test. The nonconformity function $f(z)$ measures the "strangeness" of an example $z = (x_i, y_i)$, i.e., the deviation between the label y_i and the corresponding prediction $h(x_i)$. A natural choice for f is $f(z) = \Delta(h(x_i), y_i)$, where Δ is a suitable distance[1]. As explained below, $f(z)$ is used to construct prediction regions in CP. In general, any function $f : Z \rightarrow \mathbb{R}$ will result in valid regions. However, a good nonconformity function, i.e. one that produces tight prediction regions, should give low scores to correctly predicted inputs, and large scores to misclassified inputs. See Sect. 3.2 for details about the nonconformity function definition.

3.1 CP Algorithm

Given a set of examples $Z' \subseteq Z$, a test input $x_* \in X$, and a significance level $\epsilon \in (0,1)$, a conformal predictor computes a prediction region Γ_*^ϵ for x_* as follows.

1. Divide Z' into a training set Z_t, and calibration set Z_c. Let $q = |Z_c|$ be the size of the calibration set.
2. Train a model h using Z_t.

---

[1] The choice of Δ is not very important, as long as it is symmetric.

3. Define a nonconformity function $f((x_i, y_i)) = \Delta(h(x_i), y_i)$, i.e., choose a metric Δ to measure the distance between $h(x_i)$ and y_i (see Sect. 3.2).
4. Apply $f(z)$ to each example z in Z_c and sort the resulting nonconformity scores $\{\alpha = f(z) \mid z \in Z_c\}$ in descending order: $\alpha_1 \geq \cdots \geq \alpha_q$.
5. Compute the nonconformity scores $\alpha_*^j = f((x_*, y^j))$ for the test input x_* and each possible label $j \in \{1, \ldots, c\}$. Then, compute the smoothed p-value

$$p_*^j = \frac{|\{z_i \in Z_c : \alpha_i > \alpha_*^j\}|}{q+1} + \theta \frac{|\{z_i \in Z_c : \alpha_i = \alpha_*^j\}| + 1}{q+1}, \quad (1)$$

where $\theta \in \mathcal{U}[0, 1]$ is a tie-breaking random variable. Note that p_*^j represents the portion of calibration examples that are at least as nonconforming as the tentatively labelled test example (x_*, y^j).
6. Return the prediction region

$$\Gamma_*^\epsilon = \{y^j \in Y : p_*^j > \epsilon\}. \quad (2)$$

Note that steps 1–4 have to be performed only once, while 5–6 for every test point $x_*{}^2$.

The idea behind the above procedure is use a statistical test to check if (x_*, y^j) is particularly nonconforming compared to the calibration examples. The rationale is to estimate Q, the unknown distribution of $f(z)$, by applying $f(z)$ to calibration examples, then to compute α_*^j for every possible label y^j and test for the null hypothesis $\alpha_*^j \sim Q$. We reject the null hypothesis when the p-value associated to α_*^j is smaller than the significance level ϵ. That is, we do not include y^j in Γ_*^ϵ if it appears unlikely that $f((x_*, y^j)) \sim Q$. The prediction region therefore contains all the labels for which we could not reject the null hypothesis. This is an application of the Neyman-Pearson theory for hypothesis testing and confidence intervals [15].

Note that in Eq. 1 by setting θ to a random value between 0 and 1, we compute a so-called smoothed p-value. The main difference between a standard p-value (where $\theta = 1$) and a smoothed p-value is that in the latter situation, we treat the borderline cases where $\alpha_i = \alpha^j$ more carefully. Instead of increasing the p-value by $\frac{1}{q}$ for each $\alpha_i = \alpha^j$, we increase it by a random amount between 0 and $\frac{1}{q}$. It has been proven that any smoothed conformal predictor is exactly valid, whereas a general conformal predictor is only conservative; see [22] for a complete treatment.

3.2   Nonconformity Function

In general, the nonconformity function is a measurable function with type $f : Z \to \mathbb{R}$. A nonconformity function is well-defined if it assigns low scores to

---

^{2} The approach we use is known in literature as inductive CP. The original CP approach, also called transductive CP, requires retraining the model for each new test sample and does not use a calibration set. See [18].

correctly predicted inputs and high scores to wrong predictions. It is typically based on the underlying machine learning model h, and defined by

$$f((x_i, y_i)) = \Delta(h(x_i), y_i),$$

where Δ is some function that measures the prediction error of h. Recall that, for an input $x \in X$, the output of h is a vector of class likelihoods, which we denote by $h(x) = [P_h(y_1|x), \ldots, P_h(y_c|x)]$. For classification problems, a common choice for Δ is

$$\Delta(h(x_i), y_i) = 1 - P_h(y_i|x_i), \tag{3}$$

where $P_h(y_i|x_i)$ is the likelihood of class y_i when the model h is applied on x_i. Note that such defined Δ induces a well-defined nonconformity function. Indeed if h correctly predicts y_i for input x_i, then the corresponding likelihood $P_h(y_i|x_i)$ is high (the highest among all classes) and the resulting nonconformity score is low. The opposite holds when h does not predict y_i.

Using (3) also guarantees that the resulting p-values (see Eq. 1) preserve the ordering of the class likelihoods predicted by model h. This means that, for example, the class with the lowest likelihood will also be the class with the smallest p-value, and the class with the highest likelihood will result in the largest p-value. This property ensures that the prediction regions are consistent with the classification predicted by h.

In our experiments we use (3) as nonconformity function. Other functions designed specifically for neural networks have been proposed in [18]. However, our results showed no significant differences between the latter and (3).

3.3   Confidence and Credibility

We now describe the measures of confidence and credibility, which are point-wise measures, i.e., derived from individual predictions.

Let us first notice that the regions Γ^ϵ for different ϵ values are nested: when $\epsilon_1 \geq \epsilon_2$, we have that $\Gamma^{\epsilon_1} \subseteq \Gamma^{\epsilon_2}$. Indeed, for an input x_*, if we choose an ϵ lower than the p-values of all the classes ($\epsilon < \min_{j=1,\ldots,c} p_*^j$), then the region Γ^ϵ will necessarily contain all the class labels. On the opposite, as ϵ increases, fewer and fewer classes will have their p-value higher than ϵ, until the region becomes empty (when $\epsilon \geq \max_{j=1,\ldots,c} p_*^j$).

The *confidence* of a point $x_* \in X$, $1 - \gamma_*$, is a measure of how likely our prediction for x_* is compared to all other possible classifications (according to the calibration set). It is computed as one minus the smallest value of ϵ for which the conformal region is a single label, i.e. the second largest p-value γ_*:

$$1 - \gamma_* = \sup\{1 - \epsilon : |\Gamma_*^\epsilon| = 1\}.$$

The *credibility*, c, is an indicator of how suitable the training data are to classify that example. In practice, it is the smallest ϵ for which the prediction region is empty, i.e. the highest p-value according to the calibration set.

$$c_* = \inf\{\epsilon : |\Gamma_*^\epsilon| = 0\}.$$

A high confidence, $1 - \gamma_*$, means that there is no likely alternative to the point prediction, whereas a low credibility means that even the point prediction is unlikely. Therefore, if c_* is close to zero, the test example x_* is not representative of the data set.

If we consider γ_*, i.e., one minus the confidence, and c_*, the credibility, we obtain the range I_* of ϵ values for which we are sure that the corresponding prediction region contains a single label: $I_* = [\gamma_*, c_*) \subseteq [0, 1]$. We stress that the class contained in the singleton prediction region corresponds to the model prediction $\hat{y}_*$. This is a consequence of the chosen nonconformity function (3), by which the ordering of class likelihoods is preserved in the corresponding p-values (as discussed in Sect. 3.2).

Confidence and Credibility in Binary Classification. When $Y = \{0, 1\}$, as in NSC, the conformal classifier outputs, for each input point x_*, two probabilities: p_*^0 and p_*^1. Suppose $p_*^1 > p_*^0$ (the same reasoning applies if $p_*^0 > p_*^1$), which implies that the predicted class is 1. We define confidence as $1 - p_*^0$, and credibility as p_*^1. We call the interval $I_* = [p_*^0, p_*^1)$ the *confidence-credibility interval*. It contains all values of ϵ for which we are sure that the prediction region contains a single label (in this case, $\Gamma^\epsilon = \{1\}$, $\forall \epsilon \in I_*$).

4   Measures of Prediction Reliability

Confidence and credibility can be used as uncertainty metrics. They measure how much a prediction $h(x)$, made by the underlying model, can be trusted. We will leverage both the global and the point-wise interpretations of CP in order to generate a statistically valid acceptance criterion. The following measures and acceptance criterion are described in relation to a test set $X_* \subseteq X$ of unseen input points, i.e., whose true label is unknown. Let $K = |X_*|$ be the size of the test set. Moreover, we will assume the case of binary classification, which is the one relevant for NSC.

4.1   Global Interpretation

Recall the global interpretation of CP: given a significance level ϵ, constant along X_*, the conformal classifier produces regions Γ^ϵ for each test input $x_* \in X_*$ that guarantee a global error probability of ϵ across the entire test set X_*. We say that the CP algorithm makes an error, at point x_*, if the prediction set at this point does not contain the true label. The most interesting prediction regions are those containing only a single class label, referred to as singleton regions, since empty and double ($\Gamma^\epsilon = \{0, 1\}$) regions have little actionable information. A singleton region containing the output prediction of h makes an error, i.e., Γ^ϵ contains the wrong label, if that point is misclassified by h. An empty prediction region for x at significance level ϵ is equivalent to the case that x has credibility less than ϵ (low credibility) in the point-wise interpretation of CP, whereas a double region for x corresponds to having confidence smaller than $1 - \epsilon$ (low confidence) in the point-wise interpretation.

4.2 Acceptance Criterion

The p-values returned by the CP algorithm can be interpreted as anomaly measures. In binary classification, the two p-values of a test point x_*, p_*^0 and p_*^1 (see Eq. 1), coincide with γ_* and c_*, respectively. The rationale behind our acceptance criterion is that every unseen point x_* is required to have both values of confidence, $1 - \gamma$, and credibility, c, sufficiently high in order to accept the classification made by h with a particular certainty level α. The derivation of α is shown later in this section.

Our acceptance criterion works as follows. First, a value for the significance level ϵ, fixed along the entire test set, has to be chosen. As discussed in the previous section, ϵ represents the global error probability that we are willing to accept. The next step is to apply the conformal algorithm and obtain a confidence-credibility interval, I_*, for each test point $x_* \in X_*$. We accept the prediction of model h for x_* if and only if $\epsilon \in I_*$, i.e., if $\gamma_* \leq \epsilon < c_*$. Note that the latter condition implies that we only accept singleton prediction regions, i.e., such that $|\Gamma_*^\epsilon| = 1$ (see Sect. 3.3). Otherwise, if credibility is smaller than ϵ or confidence is smaller than $1 - \epsilon$, we reject the prediction of h for x_*. In other words, these uncertainty measures indicate if a prediction is trustworthy or not. As explained below, the certainty level α is determined by the chosen ϵ and the ratio of rejected points.

We now discuss how to derive α. With the acceptance criterion introduced above, we are sure to accept only singleton prediction regions, rejecting points with non-informative regions (empty and double regions). Since ϵ gives the error probability in relation to any test point (which might or might not be accepted), it gives no guarantees on the error of accepted predictions alone. For this purpose, we provide a revised error probability estimate, $\hat{\epsilon}$, for accepted predictions only, i.e., that does not consider the rejected points. The certainty level α that we seek to obtain is defined as $1 - \hat{\epsilon}$.

To compute $\hat{\epsilon}$, we follow the approach of [16]. Given a significance level ϵ, let $P^\epsilon(e)$, $P^\epsilon(s)$ and $P^\epsilon(d)$ be respectively the fraction of empty, single and double prediction regions observed on a test set with K examples ($P^\epsilon(e) + P^\epsilon(s) + P^\epsilon(d) = 1$). Overall, the expected number of errors is $E = \epsilon K$. Since double predictions are never erroneous (they always contain the true label) and empty predictions are always erroneous (they never do), we can rewrite the expected number of errors as:

$$\epsilon K = \hat{\epsilon} \cdot K P_\epsilon(s) + K P_\epsilon(e) \Rightarrow \hat{\epsilon} = \frac{\epsilon - P_\epsilon(e)}{P_\epsilon(s)}. \tag{4}$$

Thus, $\hat{\epsilon}$ represents the expected error rate over the $K \cdot P_\epsilon(s)$ singleton predictions. In other words, $\hat{\epsilon}$ is the error probability on accepted predictions.

5 Experimental Evaluation

To evaluate the proposed method for NSC with CP-based anomaly detection, an experimental evaluation was conducted on a selection of the hybrid-system

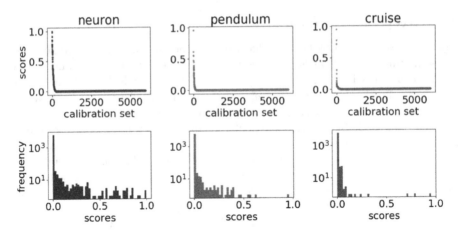

Fig. 2. Calibration scores $\alpha_1 \geq \cdots \geq \alpha_q$ for the neuron (left), pendulum (center) and cruise (right) models for a calibration set size of $q = |Z_c| = 6,000$. Histograms in the second row show the distributions of the calibration scores on a log-scale.

case studies considered in NSC (see [19] for details): a model of the spiking neuron action potential [9], the classic inverted pendulum on a cart, and a cruise controller [9].

Experimental Settings. We consider the same settings used in NSC for training sigmoid DNNs [19]. NSC neural networks were learned using MATLAB's `train` function, with the Levenberg-Marquardt backpropagation algorithm optimizing the mean square error loss function, and the Nguyen-Widrow initialization method for the NN layers. The classifier is a DNN with 3 hidden layers, each consisting of 10 neurons with the Tan-Sigmoid activation function, and an output layer with 1 neuron with the Log-Sigmoid activation function. With such DNN architecture, the only output of the underlying model is the likelihood of class 1, which we denote with o^1, that is, the likelihood that a hybrid automaton state is positive, i.e., leads to a safety violation. The likelihood of class 0 is given by $o^0 = 1 - o^1$.

We consider training datasets of 14,000 samples and calibration sets of $q = |Z_c| = 6,000$ samples. Training of the DNNs is very fast, taking 2 to 7 s. The test set contains 10,000 points. The CP algorithm was implemented in Python. Computation of confidence and credibility is very efficient, and takes around 30 s for the entire test set, approximately 3 ms per point.

5.1   Calibration Scores

We conduct a detailed analysis of the distribution of calibration scores, which depends both on the case study at hand and on the underlying model. The DNNs trained for NSC approximate the output of reachability checking with very high accuracy. Therefore, the scores $\alpha_1, \ldots, \alpha_q$ are close to zero for most

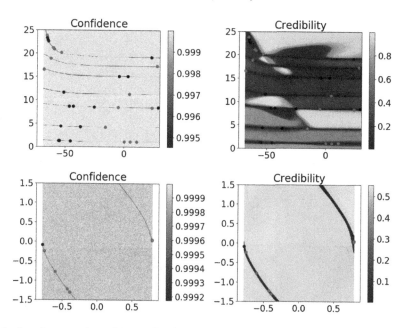

Fig. 3. Landscape of confidence (left) and credibility (right) values along the entire state space of the two-dimensional case-studies: spiking neuron (top) and inverted pendulum (bottom). Red dots indicate false-negatives, black dots false-positives. (Color figure online)

of the points in Z_c (see Fig. 2). Recall that the p-values of an unseen test point x_* count the number of calibration scores greater than that of x_*. Credibility is the p-value associated with the class predicted by h, for which we expect a small score and therefore a high p-value. On the contrary, γ is the p-value associated to the other (non-predicted) class, for which we expect a larger score. However, given the high accuracy of h, the number of large calibration scores, i.e., scores significantly greater than zero, is very small. Therefore, the fraction of calibration scores determining γ is not very sensitive to changes in the value of the nonconformity score of x_*, α_*. On the contrary, credibility is extremely sensitive to small changes in α_*. In general, the sensitivity of confidence w.r.t. α_* increases as the accuracy of h decreases, and vice versa for credibility.

5.2   Performance Evaluation

Figures 3 and 4 show the landscapes of confidence and credibility for the three case studies. Notice that both measures are able to detect the input regions with higher uncertainty, i.e., regions where misclassification occurs. However, given the high accuracy of our DNNs, credibility results in an extremely sensitive measure, as previously discussed. Indeed, we observe drastic drops in credibility values even for regions that return correct predictions. In these areas the DNN is classifying properly but with lower accuracy with respect to areas with higher

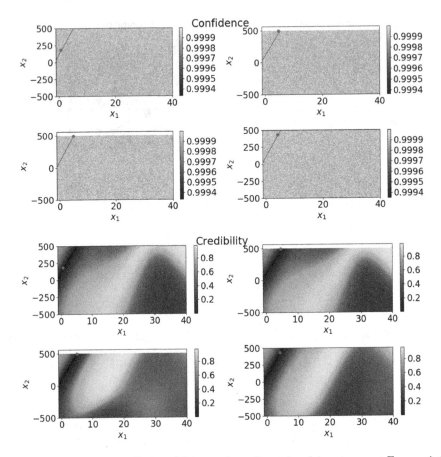

Fig. 4. The cruise controller model has a four-dimensional input space. Four points were misclassified by the DNN, and they all have coordinate $x_4 = 5.0$. The figure shows two dimensional sections ((x_1, x_2)-plane) at the x_3 coordinates of the four misclassified points and with $x_4 = 5.0$. The confidence landscapes are on top; the credibility landscapes are below them. Red dots indicate false-negatives, black dots false-positives. (Color figure online)

credibility. Confidence values, on the other hand, span in an extremely narrow interval close to 100%.

5.3 Benefit of Conformal Predictions

The key advantage of our approach is that predictions are rejected on rigorous statistical grounds. We experimentally compare it with a naive approach based on the DNN output.

We define the naive uncertainty metric as the difference between the likelihoods of the two classes, that is, $|o^0 - o^1|$. Intuitively, small differences should indicate uncertain predictions. Although this simple approach does not provide

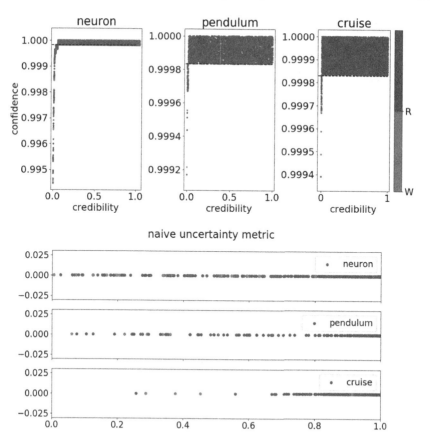

Fig. 5. Experimental superiority of conformal predictions over naive discrimination based on the DNN class likelihood. **Top:** Confidence-credibility pairs for the test datasets. The horizontal dashed line indicates the empirical and qualitative choice of ϵ. **Bottom:** Values of the naive uncertainty metric for the test datasets. In both cases (top and bottom) the true test labels were used to check the performances of the uncertainty metrics a posteriori. Green dots indicate properly classified points, red dots misclassified points. (Color figure online)

any statistical guarantee, we may still look for a rejection threshold that allows us to reject the misclassified examples and keep the overall rejection rate low. However, Fig. 5 (bottom) shows that this naive metric is not sufficiently discriminative, especially for the spiking neuron model. This supports our claim that a more principled method to measure uncertainty and define rejection criteria is needed. On the contrary, Fig. 5 (top) shows that the values of confidence-credibility pairs for misclassified points are easily separated from the majority of properly classified points. Furthermore, the distribution of points in the confidence-credibility plane helps us choose the proper value for ϵ, which leads to a statistically significant measure of uncertainty.

Table 1. For each case study, a significance level ϵ was chosen qualitatively from Fig. 5 (top), ignoring the colors, as we should not know the true labels of test points. We computed the fractions of empty, single and double prediction regions occurring along the entire test set. The sum $P_\epsilon(e) + P_\epsilon(d)$ gives the ratio of points rejected. $\alpha = 1 - \hat{\epsilon}$ is the statistical certainty level for accepted points/predictions. The last column counts how many errors, among all the errors made by the classifier in the test set, were not rejected by our criterion.

Model	ϵ	$P_\epsilon(e) + P_\epsilon(d)$	α	# accepted errors
Neuron	0.000175	4.78%	0.9998	0/31
Pendulum	0.000167	0.84%	0.9983	0/7
Cruise	0.000170	0.55%	0.9998	1/6

Table 1 summarizes the experimental performance of our rejection criterion on the three hybrid automata models. Setting an adequate threshold is very important. We choose the value of $1 - \epsilon$ that better distinguishes between points with low confidence and points with high confidence, shown with horizontal lines in Fig. 5 (top). We successfully reject almost all prediction errors, with an overall rejection rate between 0.5% and 5%. The certainty value α is always greater than 99.83%, which demonstrates that our approach only accepts predictions that have very small probability of being incorrect.

6   Related Work

Even though research on reachability checking of hybrid systems [1,13] has produced effective verification algorithms and tools [7,10,11], comparably little has been done to make these algorithms efficient for online analysis. Existing approaches are limited to restricted classes of models [8], or require handcrafted optimization of the HA's derivatives [2], or are efficient only for low-dimensional systems and simple dynamics [21]. NSC [19] (introduced in Sect. 2) overcomes these limitations because, by employing machine learning models, it is fully automated and its performance is not affected by the model size or complexity.

Applications of machine learning in verification include parameter synthesis of stochastic systems [5], techniques for inferring temporal logic specifications from examples [3], synthesis of invariants for program verification [12], and reachability checking of Markov decision processes [6].

A related approach to NSC is smoothed model checking [4], where Gaussian processes [20] are used to approximate the satisfaction function of stochastic models, i.e., mapping model parameters into the satisfaction probability of some specification. Smoothed model checking leverages Bayesian statistics to quantify prediction uncertainty, but faces scalability issues as the dimension of the system increases. On the contrary, our method for quantifying the reliability of NSC predictions is very efficient, because its performance is nearly equivalent to that of the underlying machine learning model[3].

In Bayesian approaches to uncertainty/confidence estimation, one has to assume a prior distribution, which is often chosen arbitrarily. However, in order to guarantee accurate confidence values, the correct priors must be known. In fact, if the prior is incorrect, the confidence values have no theoretical base. The CP framework instead provides confidence information based only on the standard i.i.d. or exchangeability assumption. Avoiding Bayesian assumptions makes CP conclusions more robust to different underlying data distributions. In [17] the authors show empirically that the performance of CP is close to Bayes when the prior is known to be correct. Unlike Bayes, the CP method still gives accurate confidence values even when different data distributions are considered.

7   Conclusion

We applied the theory of conformal predictions to endow the neural state classification approach with a criterion to reject unreliable predictions, predictions that can lead safety-critical state classification errors. Our criterion leverages two statistically sound measures of uncertainty, i.e., confidence and credibility. By accepting only predictions that satisfy specific confidence and credibility thresholds, our criterion is conservative and allows making safe choices with respect to any state classifier, independently of the classifier's accuracy. In the experiments, our criterion successfully rejected almost all classification errors, and doing so very efficiently, with an average runtime of 3 ms per sample.

In future work, we will investigate automated methods to derive the rejection thresholds for confidence and credibility, and how to use this approach in an active learning framework to improve accuracy, reduce false negatives, and reduce the rejection rate.

References

1. Alur, R.: Formal verification of hybrid systems. In: 2011 Proceedings of the Ninth ACM International Conference on Embedded Software (EMSOFT), pp. 273–278. IEEE (2011)
2. Bak, S., Johnson, T.T., Caccamo, M., Sha, L.: Real-time reachability for verified simplex design. In: 2014 IEEE Real-Time Systems Symposium (RTSS), pp. 138–148. IEEE (2014)
3. Bartocci, E., Bortolussi, L., Sanguinetti, G.: Data-driven statistical learning of temporal logic properties. In: Legay, A., Bozga, M. (eds.) FORMATS 2014. LNCS, vol. 8711, pp. 23–37. Springer, Cham (2014). https://doi.org/10.1007/978-3-319-10512-3_3

---

[3] Our approach reduces to computing two p-values. Each p-value is derived by computing a nonconformity score, which requires one execution of the underlying model, and one search over the array of calibration scores.

4. Bortolussi, L., Milios, D., Sanguinetti, G.: Smoothed model checking for uncertain continuous-time Markov chains. Inf. Comput. **247**, 235–253 (2016)

5. Bortolussi, L., Silvetti, S.: Bayesian statistical parameter synthesis for linear temporal properties of stochastic models. In: TACAS, pp. 396–413 (2018)

6. Brázdil, T., et al.: Verification of Markov decision processes using learning algorithms. In: Cassez, F., Raskin, J.-F. (eds.) ATVA 2014. LNCS, vol. 8837, pp. 98–114. Springer, Cham (2014). https://doi.org/10.1007/978-3-319-11936-6_8

7. Chen, X., Ábrahám, E., Sankaranarayanan, S.: Flow*: an analyzer for non-linear hybrid systems. In: Sharygina, N., Veith, H. (eds.) CAV 2013. LNCS, vol. 8044, pp. 258–263. Springer, Heidelberg (2013). https://doi.org/10.1007/978-3-642-39799-8_18

8. Chen, X., Sankaranarayanan, S.: Model predictive real-time monitoring of linear systems. In: 2017 IEEE Real-Time Systems Symposium (RTSS), pp. 297–306. IEEE (2017)

9. Chen, X., Schupp, S., Makhlouf, I.B., Ábrahám, E., Frehse, G., Kowalewski, S.: A benchmark suite for hybrid systems reachability analysis. In: Havelund, K., Holzmann, G., Joshi, R. (eds.) NFM 2015. LNCS, vol. 9058, pp. 408–414. Springer, Cham (2015). https://doi.org/10.1007/978-3-319-17524-9_29

10. Frehse, G., et al.: SpaceEx: scalable verification of hybrid systems. In: Gopalakrishnan, G., Qadeer, S. (eds.) CAV 2011. LNCS, vol. 6806, pp. 379–395. Springer, Heidelberg (2011). https://doi.org/10.1007/978-3-642-22110-1_30

11. Gao, S., Kong, S., Clarke, E.M.: dReal: an SMT solver for nonlinear theories over the reals. In: Bonacina, M.P. (ed.) CADE 2013. LNCS (LNAI), vol. 7898, pp. 208–214. Springer, Heidelberg (2013). https://doi.org/10.1007/978-3-642-38574-2_14

12. Garg, P., Neider, D., Madhusudan, P., Roth, D.: Learning invariants using decision trees and implication counterexamples. ACM SIGPLAN Not. **51**(1), 499–512 (2016)

13. Henzinger, T.A., Kopke, P.W., Puri, A., Varaiya, P.: What's decidable about hybrid automata? J. Comput. Syst. Sci. **57**(1), 94–124 (1998)

14. Legay, A., Delahaye, B., Bensalem, S.: Statistical model checking: an overview. In: RV 2010. LNCS, vol. 6418, pp. 122–135. Springer (2010)

15. Lehmann, E.L., Romano, J.P.: Testing Statistical Hypotheses. Springer, New York (2006). https://doi.org/10.1007/0-387-27605-X

16. Linusson, H., Johansson, U., Boström, H., Löfström, T.: Reliable confidence predictions using conformal prediction. In: Bailey, J., Khan, L., Washio, T., Dobbie, G., Huang, J.Z., Wang, R. (eds.) PAKDD 2016. LNCS (LNAI), vol. 9651, pp. 77–88. Springer, Cham (2016). https://doi.org/10.1007/978-3-319-31753-3_7

17. Melluish, T., Saunders, C., Nouretdinov, I., Vovk, V.: The typicalness framework: a comparison with the Bayesian approach. Royal Holloway, University of London (2001)

18. Papadopoulos, H.: Inductive conformal prediction: theory and application to neural networks. In: Tools in Artificial Intelligence. InTech (2008)

19. Phan, D., Paoletti, N., Zhang, T., Grosu, R., Smolka, S.A., Stoller, S.D.: Neural state classification for hybrid systems. In: Lahiri, S.K., Wang, C. (eds.) ATVA 2018. LNCS, vol. 11138, pp. 422–440. Springer, Cham (2018). https://doi.org/10.1007/978-3-030-01090-4_25

20. Rasmussen, C.E., Williams, C.K.: Gaussian Processes for Machine Learning, vol. 1. MIT Press, Cambridge (2006)

21. Sauter, G., Dierks, H., Fränzle, M., Hansen, M.R.: Lightweight hybrid model checking facilitating online prediction of temporal properties. In: Proceedings of the 21st Nordic Workshop on Programming Theory, pp. 20–22 (2009)
22. Vovk, V., Gammerman, A., Shafer, G.: Algorithmic learning in a random world (2005)
23. Wald, A.: Sequential tests of statistical hypotheses. Ann. Math. Stat. **16**(2), 117–186 (1945)

Control Synthesis Through Deep Learning

Doron Peled[1(✉)], Simon Iosti[2], and Saddek Bensalem[2]

[1] Department of Computer Science, Bar Ilan University, 52900 Ramat Gan, Israel
doron.peled@gmail.com
[2] University Grenoble Alpes VERIMAG, 38410 Saint Martin d'Hères, France

Abstract. Deep learning has gained unprecedented rapid popularity in computer science in recent years. It is used in tasks that were previously considered highly challenging for computers, such as speech and image recognition and natural language processing. While deep learning is often associated with complicated tasks, we look at the much more mundane task of refining a system behavior through control that is constructed with the use of learning techniques. We compare the use of deep learning for this task with other techniques such as automata learning and genetic programming.

1 Introduction

The use of machine learning (ML), and in particular, deep learning (DL), facilitated a huge leap in the capabilities of computers. DL is often used for speech recognition, natural language processing, image recognition, playing games like Chess [19] and Go [18] and more. We are interested in obtaining intuition about the suitability and effectiveness of different machine learning approaches to improve systems performance.

We look at reactive systems that interact with black box environments, both representable as finite state machines. In order to enforce some constraint that improves the combined system/environment performance, we want to construct a controller that limits the allowed behaviors of the system. We consider different learning mechanisms for the task of constructing such a controller: automata learning (AL), deep learning (DL) and genetic programming (GP).

The problem studied here is related to reinforcement learning [14], where a software agent needs to operate efficiently with respect to its environment. In this case, the agent, which is often modeled as a probabilistic structure (a Markov Decision Process) needs to be synthesized. Because the executions of the system are not bounded, reinforcement learning is often aiming to minimize the sum of rewards (discounted according to their distance from the start of the execution) obtained during the execution.

D. Peled–The research performed by this author was partially funded by Israeli Science Foundation grant 1464/18: "Efficient Runtime Verification for Systems with Lots of Data and its Applications".

© Springer Nature Switzerland AG 2019
E. Bartocci et al. (Eds.): From Reactive Systems to Cyber-Physical Systems, LNCS 11500, pp. 242–255, 2019.
https://doi.org/10.1007/978-3-030-31514-6_14

We compare three different types of learning for generating controllers. *Automata learning* [1] uses experiments to learn the structure of a black box automaton, in our case, the environment. Using AL allows separating the learning of a model for the environment from constructing a controller. Based on the provided model of the system and the learned model of the environment, a goal-dependent algorithm can be used to check the possibility of controlling the system to achieve its goal, and if so, to construct the controller. Exact automata learning can be achieved under some strong assumptions, e.g., a bound on the number of states that are required to model it. It incurs a very high complexity (exponential in the size of the environment). Alternatively, one can perform the learning in a stepwise manner, in the style of *black box checking* [16]: at some point, a learned model of the environment is assumed for constructing the controller. The executions of the controlled system with the environment are monitored for checking whether they satisfy the control goal; violating executions may be used in further learning a more accurate model.

Deep learning [6] can be used to train a neural network to control the system based on experiments. The controller is represented using a (recursive) neural network. It is constructed directly, without learning the environment first: gradually refining the controller using experiments performed on the combination of the controlled system and the environment. Deep learning uses a *loss function* that drives the gradient descent-based training process. Because the environment is not explicitly learned, the constructed controller is not guaranteed to achieve the control goal in every possible situation. On the other hand, the learning process can be resumed when the control goal is (observed to be) violated or due to a change in the behavior of the environment.

Genetic programming [13] uses evolutionary process that involves generating, combining and mutating candidate solutions. A *fitness* value, typically returning a value between 0 and 100, estimates the quality of the solution. For synthesizing a controller, the fitness can be calculated based on multiple experiments performed on the controlled system that interacts with the environment. Here too, we do not learn first a model for the environment, and there is no guarantee that the control goal is uniformly achieved (hence re-learning may be required).

The structures of the loss functions used in DL, and the fitness function used in GP, are dramatically different. But in both cases, there is no direct correspondence between the imposed control goal and the used functions. They are selected based on experience and trial-and-error experiments. For the control problem described here, we will present a set of small examples consisting of system/environment pairs. Each such pair demonstrates some aspect or difficulty that is expected in the synthesis of a controller. This allows us to test the suitability of the selected loss or fitness function for the learning task.

The qualitative comparison presented here is based on our experience with automata learning of finite systems and applying model checking to it [7,16] and with genetic programming for program synthesis [3,12]. In addition, we have been conducting experiments consisting of using DL for training a controller for the system/environment interaction using the DyNet system [15]. We are still short of presenting conclusive experimental results, but instead concentrate on comparing the merits and pitfalls of different learning techniques for achieving control in a qualitative way.

2   Preliminaries

We use a simple model that still demonstrates some strengths and weaknesses of the different learning techniques. A finite state system dynamically offers one of its currently available *actions* to the environment; if the environment can currently perform this action, the system and the environment progress synchronously making a successful *interaction*. Otherwise, the interaction fails and only the environment progresses. The system is not a-priori aware of the actions that are allowed at a particular moment by the environment, but is informed of the *success* or *failure* status of an attempted interaction.

System and Environment

We study systems that can be modeled as finite state automata:

Let $\mathcal{A} = (G, \iota, T, \delta)$ be an automaton, where

- G is a finite set of *states* with $\iota \in G$ its *initial state*.
- T is a finite set of *actions* (often called the *alphabet*).
- $\delta : (G \times T) \to T \cup \{\bot\}$ is a *transition function*, where $\bot$ stands for *undefined*. We denote $en(g) = \{t | t \in T \wedge \delta(g, t) \neq \bot\}$ i.e., $en(g)$ is the set of actions *enabled* at the state g.

For simplicity of the discussion, we assume that $en(g) \neq \emptyset$.

We consider the asymmetric combination of automata, $\mathcal{A}^s | \mathcal{A}^e$, where $\mathcal{A}^s = (G^s, \iota^s, T, \delta^s)$ is the *system* automaton, and $\mathcal{A}^e = (G^e, \iota^e, T, \delta^e)$ is the *environment* automaton, with a joint set of actions T. These automata operate synchronously starting with their initial state. The system automaton offers an action that is enabled from its current state. If this action is enabled also from the current state of the environment automaton, then the system and the environment synchronize and change their respective states, making a *successful* interaction. If this action is not enabled by the environment, the system remains at its current state, and the environment chooses some enabled action and moves according to it. This is a *failed* interaction. After a failed attempt, the system may offer the same or a different action. Note the asymmetry here: the system offers a single enabled action, whereas the environment concurs with this choice, if this is *one* of its currently enabled options (but the system may not be aware of what is currently enabled by the environment). An *execution* is an alternating sequence

$$\langle g_1^s, g_1^e \rangle \langle t_1^s, t_1^e \rangle \langle g_2^s, g_2^e \rangle \langle t_2^s, t_2^e \rangle \cdots$$

satisfying the following conditions:

- $g_1^s = \iota^s$ and $g_1^e = \iota^e$ [Initialization.]

- $t_i^s \in en(g_i^s)$ and $t_i^e \in en(g_i^e)$ [The selected actions are enabled.]
- $g_{i+1}^e = \delta^e(g_i^e, t_i^e)$ [The environment follows its transition function.]
- $t_i^s \in en(g_i^e)$ iff $t_i^s = t_i^e$ [If the system selects an action enabled by the environment, synchronize.]
- If $t_i^s = t_i^e$ [When synchronizing,]
  - then $g_{i+1}^s = \delta^s(g_i^s, t_i^s)$ [the system follows its transition function.]
  - else $g_{i+1}^s = g_i^s$ [Otherwise, the environment progresses, the system does not move.]

Supervisory Control

Supervisory control theory studies the superimposition of a system with a controller that restricts its behavior so that the combination guarantees additional properties [20]. A system, represented by a finite automaton $\mathcal{A}$, guarantees that all its behaviors $L(\mathcal{A})$ satisfy a specification property φ. When both $L(\mathcal{A})$ and φ are represented as languages over the same alphabet as $\mathcal{A}$, the requirement is that $L(\mathcal{A}) \subseteq \varphi$.

A controller $\mathcal{C}$, a finite automaton itself, is superimposed with $\mathcal{A}$: it reads the state of $\mathcal{A}$ and restricts the possible transitions that $\mathcal{A}$ can take from the current state, see Fig. 1. The combined system $\mathcal{C}/\mathcal{A}$ satisfies

$$L(\mathcal{C}/\mathcal{A}) \subseteq L(\mathcal{A}). \tag{1}$$

Consequently $\mathcal{C}/\mathcal{A}$ satisfies the property φ. Moreover, the controller is designed such that the composition is constructed in a way that would satisfy an additional goal ψ, i.e.,

$$L(\mathcal{C}/\mathcal{A}) \subseteq \psi. \tag{2}$$

Formally, a *controller* is an automaton $\mathcal{C} = (S, i, G, \rho, D, \Gamma)$, where

- S is a finite set of states, with $i \in S$ the *initial state*.
- G is the input to this automaton. Note that G coincides with the states of the controlled automaton $\mathcal{A}$.
- $\rho : S \times G \to S$ is the partial transition function.
- D is a set of output values.
- $\Gamma : S \to D$ is the output function.

The output values are used to restrict the behavior of a system automaton $\mathcal{A}$ at the current state. There are several possibilities, including the following:

Probabilistic. D is a set of probability distributions over T, where for each $d \in D$, $d : T \to [0, 1]$, where $\Sigma_{t \in T} d(t) = 1$. In this case, d represents the probability for choosing the currently enabled actions of $\mathcal{A}$. The composition $\mathcal{C}/\mathcal{A}$ is a Markov Chain, and the enabled actions $en(g)$ in the current state g of $\mathcal{A}$ are selected with probabilities according to $\Gamma(g)$, where $\Gamma(g)(t) = 0$ for $t \notin en(g)$.

Deterministic. $D \subseteq T$. Each element of D is an action. In this case, the control allows exactly one action to be taken.

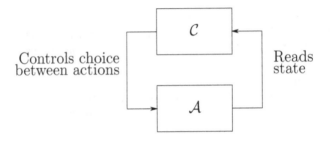

Fig. 1. A controller $\mathcal{C}$ superimposed with a system $\mathcal{A}$

Multiple Choice. $D \subseteq 2^T$. The controller allows multiple choices from the current state (this can be used to minimize the size of the controller, in particular when each state of the system only enables one of these possibilities).

We are interested in constructing a controller for the system, imposing some further goal (property) on the interaction of the controlled system and the environment. The definition of $\mathcal{C}/\mathcal{A}$ guarantees that

$$L((\mathcal{C}/\mathcal{A}^s)|\mathcal{A}^e) \subseteq L(\mathcal{A}^s|\mathcal{A}^e) \tag{3}$$

corresponding to Formula (1). Thus, the interaction of the controlled system and the environment preserves the specification φ of the uncontrolled interaction. On top of that, we want to achieve an additional goal, e.g.,

$$L((\mathcal{C}/\mathcal{A}^s)|\mathcal{A}^e) \subseteq \psi \tag{4}$$

corresponding to Formula (2).

Control Objectives. There are different types of goals that can be desired from the interaction between the controlled system and the environment. The goal can be imposed on *all the possible behaviors*, e.g., that there are no more than three failed interactions in any execution, or based on a probabilistic *expected value* of failures. It can be given using different formalisms, e.g., *linear temporal logic*, based on the states or the actions of the system. Alternatively, it can be given as a sum, or discounted sum of *penalties* (e.g., due to failed interactions) or *rewards* on various events during the execution.

3   Control and Machine Learning

We are interested here in providing control to a system that interacts with an unknown environment. Pnueli and Rosner [17] studied a related problem, where *all* the executions of a system need to guarantee some temporal specification goal, regardless of the behavior of the environment. Their model is somewhat different from ours (the system and the environment progress in turns). They provided a synthesis algorithm that is based on converting the specification into an automaton over infinite words, determinizing it, and finding a game strategy (when one exists) that enforces the given specification. A deterministic strategy may not be sufficient in case the goal is defined in terms of a probabilistic *expected value*; consider for example the (somewhat non-intuitive) goal that the expected number of failures is greater than 1 and smaller than 2.

We will restrict ourselves to goals related to the number of failed interactions allowed. The goals will be described as restrictions on the number of failures over all the executions rather than dealing with the probabilistic expected values. To avoid issues related to infinite number of failures (e.g., the use of *restricted sums* of rewards/penalties related to failures), we assume that the goal provides a given finite limit to the number of failures allowed. Moreover, we can use designated states where the number of permitted failures is counted between their subsequent occurrences (i.e., the failure counter is reset each time one of these states occurs).

Control and Automata Learning of the Environment

Automata learning methods, e.g., based on Angluin's algorithm [1,10], or a probabilistic extension of it [5], can be used to learn the structure of a finite state environment through experiments that interact with it. The conditions for achieving exact learning are quite demanding, e.g., knowing an upper bound on the size of the representation of the environment, and being able to reset the environment to its initial state for multiple experiments. The complexity of the learning process is exponential in the size of the learned automaton.

After learning a model for the environment automaton $\mathcal{A}^e$, we need to decide whether a controller $\mathcal{C}$ can be constructed such that $(\mathcal{C}/\mathcal{A}^s)|\mathcal{A}^e$ satisfies the additional goal that we want to impose. When possible, an algorithm, which is goal dependent [4], is used to construct a controller based on $\mathcal{A}^s$ and $\mathcal{A}^e$. Changes to the structure of the environment may require the re-learning of $\mathcal{A}^e$. However, the re-learning process does not necessarily have to start from scratch, and some infrastructure that was prepared for the previous model (in particular, the distinguishing and the accessing sequences used in the algorithm [1]) can be used to speed up the new automata learning phase [7].

Consider now several cases of systems and learned environment automaton. In Example **permitted** in Fig. 2, the system allows both actions a and b. If it decides to offer the action a (b, respectively), whereas the environment offers b ($a, respectively$), it waits for the next step of the environment, while the environment progresses. A controller, which would guarantee that the system never makes an attempt to interact that will fail, has the same structure as the environment, as in Fig. 2. I.e., it has three states, restricting the system to the single sequence $(abb)^*$. The set of actions denoted adjacent to states in the figure represent the ones allowed from that state.

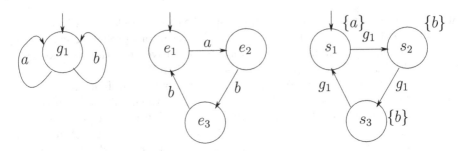

Fig. 2. permitted: System (left), Environment (middle) and Controller (right)

In Example `schedule` in Fig. 3, the controller must make sure that the system will never choose an a. Otherwise, after interacting on a, the environment will progress to e_3, and no successful interaction with b will be available further. A controller with one state that always allows $\{b, c\}$, i.e., never allows a, is sufficient to guarantee that no failure ever occurs.

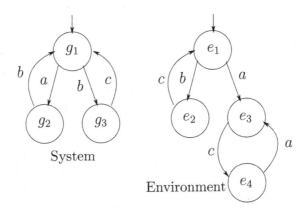

Fig. 3. schedule: The control needs to avoid the initial choice of interaction a

In Example `cases` in Fig. 4, we want to restrict the number of failures to at most two. The system is obliged to try an a from its initial state. The environment allows initially only b or c. Hence, the interaction will fail, the system will stay at the same state and the environment will progress to e_2 or to e_3, according to its choice. The choice is not visible to the system (the system is only aware that the interaction failed). After the failed first a, a is again the only action that is offered by the system. The controller knows whether a failed again. If this is not the case, the environment is in its left branch, and it will further offer $(ba)^*$. Otherwise, it knows that the environment is in its right branch and will offer ac^*.

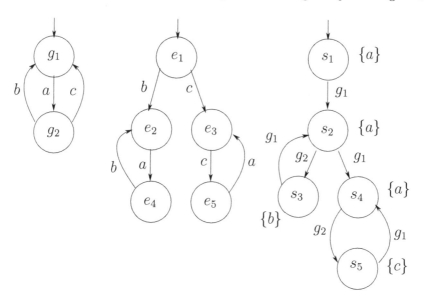

Fig. 4. cases: Needs to check if a succeeded

In Example strategy in Fig. 5, the system offers initially only the interaction a, which necessarily fails, and the environment will make a choice that is invisible to the system. After that, the system and the environment will synchronize on an a. At this point, if the system chooses, by chance, an action that immediately succeeds (b or c, respectively), it will necessarily lead to ending up in self loops that are incompatible (at g_3 and s_7, or at g_4 and s_6, respectively), and no further interaction will be available. On the other hand, if the system chooses an interaction that fails, it must subsequently repeat the same choice of action, which will lead to compatible loops (g_3 and s_6, or g_4 and s_7), and there will be no further failures; flipping to the other choice after a failure will lead again to the incompatible loops.

Unfortunately, no controller can guarantee to restrict the number of failures to two (or any finite number) in every execution. However, a weaker goal, restricting the number of failures with some probability, which depends on the probability p of the environment to choose b over c from its initial state, can be achieved. If we can learn the probability p, we could guarantee restricting the number of failures to two in at least $max(p, 1 - p) \geq 0.5$ of the cases.

4   Control and Deep Learning

When the requirements for automata learning are not met, one can try to apply reward-driven learning techniques such as deep learning or genetic programming. These methods can be used to train a controller to improve (increase the reward involved in) the interactions between the system and the environment based on the feedback of experiments.

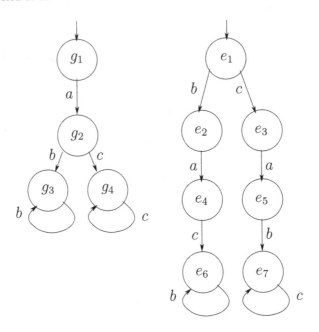

Fig. 5. strategy: Fail next, or succeed and fail forever

In our examples, the goal is to limit the failed interactions that occur between designated system states. For a gentle introduction to deep learning (with an emphasis on natural language processing applications), see e.g., [6].

Unlike automata learning, the learning is not performed by obtaining first a model for the environment (an automaton, a Markov Chain or a Markov Decision Process). Instead, it directly trains a neural network (using standard deep learning algorithms and packages) to act as the controller $\mathcal{C}$.

We use a neural network for representing a controller that changes its state based on its observed system state. The output of the controller is based both on the new input, and on a summary of the rest of the input so far. Recursive Neural Networks (RNN) are a more sensible choice of network structure than feed-forward neural networks, since they allow efficient treatments of sequential information. An RNN combines the previous outputs with the new inputs in order to provide the next output. Then, $\mathcal{C}$ is based on an RNN representation. The training is done based on a *loss function* that reflects a distance of the tested behavior from the goal. This can be, in our examples, the number of failed interactions, or a discounted sum of the interactions.

One challenge, in using deep learning for the task of constructing a controller, is that the controller needs, in some way, to encode the structure of an automaton. In principle, the controller needs to provide improved behavior that is not limited to the finite lengths of the sequences used for training. Consider Example `permitted` in Fig. 2. The learned RNN needs to represent a simple repetitive behavior. The learned controller will still behave in a cyclic way, even for executions that are longer than the training examples. In Example `scheduler` in Fig. 3, the learned RNN needs simply to constantly block the action a.

The Example `cases` in Fig. 4 is more complicated and requires learning an RNN that represents the behavior of an automaton with two different loops.

A main obstacle in training the RNNs in our setup is that the correspondence between the property that they need to enforce, and the loss function that is used for the training, is far from being clear. Experience with training neural networks is of course of great importance here. However, finding a direct relationship between the control goals and the loss functions seems rather implausible. We use a set of pre-constructed system/environment pairs. In our experimentation, as part of the process for modifying and refining the used loss function, we try to train RNNs to achieve the desired goals for these examples before dealing with more general systems and environments. Indeed, the examples shown in this section are part of a larger set of examples that we use for experiments. We are currently conducting further experiments on different examples with DyNet [15].

5   Control and Genetic Programming

During the 1970s, Holland [9] established the field known as *Genetic Algorithms* (GA). Individual candidate solutions are represented as fixed length strings of bits, corresponding to chromosomes in biological systems. Candidates are evaluated using a *fitness* function; fitness approximates the distance of the candidate from a desired solution. Genetic algorithms evolve a *set of candidates* into a successor set. Each such set forms a *generation*, and there is no backtracking. Candidates are usually represented as fixed length strings. The progress from one generation to the next one is done according to one of the following three cases:

Reproduction. Part of the candidates are selected to propagate from one generation to the subsequent one. The reproduction is done at random, with probability relative to the relation between the fitness of the individual candidate and the average of fitness values in the current generation.

Crossover. Some pairs of the candidates, selected at random for reproduction, are combined using the crossover operation. This operation takes bits from two parent solutions and combines them into a new solution, which potentially inherits useful attributes from their parents.

Mutation. This operation randomly alters the content of a small number of bits from candidates, selected for reproduction (this can also be done after performing crossover). One can decide on mutating each bit separately with some probability.

The different candidates in a single generation have a combined effect on the search; progress tends to promote, improve and combine candidates that are better than others in the same generation. The process of selecting candidates from the previous generation and deciding whether to apply crossover or mutation continues until we complete a new generation. All generations are of some predefined fixed size N. This can be, typically, a number between 50 and 500. Genetic algorithms perform the following steps:

1. Randomly generate N initial candidates.
2. Evaluate the fitness of the candidates.
3. If a satisfactory solution is found, or the number of generations created exceeds a predefined limit (say hundreds or a few thousands), terminate.
4. Select candidates for reproduction using randomization, proportional to the fitness values and apply crossover or mutation on some of them, again using randomization, until N candidates are obtained.
5. Go to step 2.

If the algorithm does not terminate with a satisfying solution after a predefined limit on the number of generations, we can restart it with a new random seed, or change the way in which we calculate the fitness function.

Genetic programming, suggested by Koza [13], is a direct successor of genetic algorithms. Each individual organism represents a computer program. Programs are represented by variable length structures, such as syntax trees or a sequences of instructions. Each node is classified as *code, Boolean, condition* or *expression*. Leaf nodes are variables or constants, and other nodes have successors according to their type. The genetic operations need to respect typing restrictions, e.g., *integer expressions* cannot be exchanged with *Boolean expressions*.

Crossover is performed on a pair of syntax trees by selecting a subtree rooted with the same node type in each tree, and then swapping between them. This results in two new programs, each having parts from both of its parents. There are several kinds of mutation transformations on syntax trees. First, a node that roots a subtree is selected at random. In *replacement* mutation, the selected subtree is discarded and replaced with a randomly generated subtree of the same type. Similarly *insertion, reduction* and *deletion* mutations can be applied.

Genetic programming can be applied for generating a controller $\mathcal{C}$ for the system $\mathcal{A}^s$. As in the case of DL, we are constructing $\mathcal{C}$ directly, rather than first learning $\mathcal{A}^e$ and then designing an appropriate control, as in the case of automata learning. Each generation of the genetic process consists of a population of candidate controllers. The first generation is constructed based on randomness. The progress from generation to generation is made through reproduction and mutations, guided by the fitness. The fitness reflects, in our examples, the number of failed synchronizations.

The fitness value for a candidate controller is determined by testing multiple randomly generated sequences of the combination $(\mathcal{C}/\mathcal{A}^s)|\mathcal{A}^e$ of the controlled system and the environment. There are different ways of combining the results of these tests into a single fitness value. A somewhat naive, but simple to implement solution, is to average a fitness calculated separately for each such sequence. There is a clear trade-off between the number of tests made and the accuracy of the fitness. One can use statistical model checking [21] to calculate probabilities of different outcomes of the controlled system. For example, one can estimate the probability of having no failures, one to three failures, and more than three failures, with a given statistical error. Then these results are combined to form a single fitness value. A common problem in statistical model checking is called *rare events* [11], where some set of behaviors can appear with a very small probability. In the case of learning a controller, this means that we may not obtain a perfect controller that guarantees to enforce the required goal on *all* of the executions. However, we can monitor the executions, and if a violation occurs, can resume the learning process. The violating executions can be accumulated and used in repeated learning phases to test the candidate controllers.

For the control automata, we define the following types of mutations:

Change a Transition. Choose randomly a state to mutate and redirect one of its outgoing edges.

Change Probabilities. In case of a controller that provides probabilistic recommendation for the next action, choose a state and assign new distribution on choosing the actions from it.

Add a State. Generate a new state and connect it to the other states in the automaton graph.

Delete a State. Choose randomly a state, delete it from the automaton and assign a random target state for each edge that previously led to it.

Sub-automaton. Create new sub-automaton. Choose one of the states and delete all states with index larger than it. Grow a new automaton with some number of states and merge it to the remaining states of the original automaton.

As in the case of using deep learning, because we do not know the structure of the system, there is no strong indication on where to stop the genetic process. Example `strategy` in Fig. 5 cannot have a controller that guarantees that the number of successful interactions will be no more than 2. Thus, the genetic process should stop when the improvement between the different generations diminishes. One can repeat the genetic process several times with different random seeds to try to alleviate local maxima of the fitness function.

6   Discussion

We discussed three learning approaches that can be used to construct a controller that will restrict interaction offered by a finite state system to its environment. Automata learning provides the tightest control results. When the structure of the environment is learned, one can apply algorithms to check whether the control goal is achievable, and in that case construct an optimal controller. However, the conditions to apply automata learning are quite demanding and the complexity is high.

Deep learning can be used under considerably weaker conditions; e.g., we do not even need to know a bound on the number of states required to represent the environment. On the other hand, we do not expect to construct an optimal controller. In fact, we may not even know whether we have finished the learning process or came close to finishing it. The training is based on test sequences. Training can resume at a later point if the possibility of better performance or a small change in the environment is suspected. The use of genetic programming also allows constructing a controller directly. Here again, we may not know whether we reached a near optimal controller or a local maxima in our search.

Compared to the impressive use cases of deep learning, such as image recognition, translating natural languages, autonomous driving or playing games, the learning-based control synthesis problem that we considered here seems much simpler. However, it allows studying the principles and effect of different learning techniques. Our long term goal is to use deep learning for constructing distributed schedulers for systems with concurrent processes that will lower the number of failed interactions between the participating processes. In this case, the environment of each concurrent thread is the collection of all other threads, interacting with it. This can then be compared with an alternative approach [2] for constructing schedulers that is based on distributed knowledge [8].

Acknowledgement. The authors would like to thank Yoav Goldberg, for useful discussions on deep learning and comments on an early draft of the paper.

References

1. Angluin, D.: Learning regular sets from queries and counter examples. Inf. Comput. **75**(2), 87–106 (1987)
2. Basu, A., Bensalem, S., Peled, D.A., Sifakis, J.: Priority scheduling of distributed systems based on model checking. Formal Meth. Syst. Des. **39**(3), 229–245 (2011)
3. Bu, L., Peled, D., Shen, D., Zhuang, Y.: Genetic synthesis of concurrent code using model checking and statistical model checking. In: Gallardo, M.M., Merino, P. (eds.) SPIN 2018. LNCS, vol. 10869, pp. 275–291. Springer, Cham (2018). https://doi.org/10.1007/978-3-319-94111-0_16
4. Cassandras, C.G., Lafortune, S.: Introduction to Discrete Event Systems, 2nd edn. Springer, Berlin (2008). https://doi.org/10.1007/978-0-387-68612-7
5. Dean, T.L., et al.: Inferring finite automata with stochastic output functions and an application to map learning. In: Proceedings of the 10th National Conference on Artificial Intelligence, San Jose, CA, USA, 12–16 July 1992, pp. 208–214 (1992)
6. Goldberg, Y.: Synthesis lectures on human language technologies. Neural Network Methods for Natural Language Processing. Morgan & Claypool Publishers, San Rafael (2017)
7. Groce, A., Peled, D.A., Yannakakis, M.: Adaptive model checking. Logic J. IGPL **14**(5), 729–744 (2006)
8. Halpern, J.Y., Moses, Y.: Knowledge and common knowledge in a distributed environment. In: Proceedings of the Third Annual ACM Symposium on Principles of Distributed Computing, Vancouver, B.C., Canada, 27–29 August 1984, pp. 50–61 (1984)
9. Holland, J.H.: Adaptation in Natural and Artificial Systems: An Introductory Analysis with Applications to Biology, Control and Artificial Intelligence. MIT Press, Cambridge (1992)

10. Isberner, M., Howar, F., Steffen, B.: The TTT algorithm: a redundancy-free approach to active automata learning. In: Bonakdarpour, B., Smolka, S.A. (eds.) RV 2014. LNCS, vol. 8734, pp. 307–322. Springer, Cham (2014). https://doi.org/10.1007/978-3-319-11164-3_26

11. Jegourel, C., Legay, A., Sedwards, S.: An effective heuristic for adaptive importance splitting in statistical model checking. In: Margaria, T., Steffen, B. (eds.) ISoLA 2014. LNCS, vol. 8803, pp. 143–159. Springer, Heidelberg (2014). https://doi.org/10.1007/978-3-662-45231-8_11

12. Katz, G., Peled, D.: Synthesizing, correcting and improving code, using model checking-based genetic programming. STTT **19**(4), 449–464 (2017)

13. Koza, J.R.: Complex adaptive systems. Genetic programming - on the Programming of Computers by Means of Natural Selection. MIT Press, Cambridge (1993)

14. Mnih, V., et al.: Human-level control through deep reinforcement learning. Nature **518**(7540), 529–533 (2015)

15. Neubig, G., et al.: Dynet: The dynamic neural network toolkit. CoRR (2017). arXiv:1701.03980

16. Peled, D.A., Vardi, M.Y., Yannakakis, M.: Black box checking. J. Automata, Lang. Comb. **7**(2), 225–246 (2002)

17. Pnueli, A., Rosner, R.: On the synthesis of a reactive module. In: Conference Record of the Sixteenth Annual ACM Symposium on Principles of Programming Languages, Austin, Texas, USA, 11–13 January 1989, pp. 179–190 (1989)

18. Silver, D., et al.: Mastering the game of go with deep neural networks and tree search. Nature **529**(7587), 484–489 (2016)

19. Silver, D., et al.: Mastering chess and shogi by self-play with a general reinforcement learning algorithm. CoRR (2017). arXiv:1712.01815

20. Wonham, W.M., Ramadge, P.J.: Modular supervisory control of discrete-event systems. MCSS **1**(1), 13–30 (1988)

21. Younes, H.L.S., Simmons, R.G.: Probabilistic verification of discrete event systems using acceptance sampling. In: Brinksma, E., Larsen, K.G. (eds.) CAV 2002. LNCS, vol. 2404, pp. 223–235. Springer, Heidelberg (2002). https://doi.org/10.1007/3-540-45657-0_17

Runtime Verification

The Cost of Monitoring Alone

Luca Aceto[1,2] , Antonis Achilleos[2](✉) , Adrian Francalanza[3] ,
Anna Ingólfsdóttir[2] , and Karoliina Lehtinen[4]

[1] Gran Sasso Science Institute, L'Aquila, Italy
luca.aceto@gssi.it
[2] Reykjavik University, Reykjavík, Iceland
{luca,antonios,annai}@ru.is
[3] University of Malta, Msida, Malta
adrian.francalanza@um.edu.mt
[4] University of Liverpool, Liverpool, UK
karoliina.lehtinen@liverpool.ac.uk

Abstract. We compare the succinctness of two monitoring systems
for properties of infinite traces, namely parallel and regular monitors.
Although a parallel monitor can be turned into an equivalent regular
monitor, the cost of this transformation is a double-exponential blowup
in the syntactic size of the monitors, and a triple-exponential blowup
when the goal is a deterministic monitor. We show that these bounds
are tight and that they also hold for translations between corresponding
fragments of Hennessy-Milner logic with recursion over infinite traces.

Keywords: Monitors · Runtime Verification ·
Hennessy Milner logic with recursion · State complexity ·
Determinization · Logical fragments

1 Introduction

Runtime Verification [8,13] is a lightweight verification technique where a computational entity that we call a monitor is used to observe a system run in order
to verify a given property. In this paper we formalize properties in Hennessy-
Milner logic with recursion (RECHML) [16] due to its ability to embed a variety
of widely used logics such as LTL and CTL, thus guaranteeing a good level of
generality for our monitorability and monitor synthesis results. Furthermore,
as RECHML has both branching- and linear-time semantics, we can use it to
express (and verify) a property either of a system behaviour as a whole [1,14],
or of the current system run, encoded as a trace of events [4]—see also, for
example, [9,11,17] for earlier work on the monitoring of trace properties, mainly
expressed in LTL.

This research was partially supported by the projects "TheoFoMon: Theoretical Foundations for Monitorability" (grant number: 163406-051) and "Epistemic Logic for Distributed Runtime Monitoring" (grant number: 184940-051) of the Icelandic Research
Fund, by the BMBF project "Aramis II" (project number: 01IS160253) and the EPSRC
project "Solving parity games in theory and practice" (project number: EP/P020909/1).

© Springer Nature Switzerland AG 2019
E. Bartocci et al. (Eds.): From Reactive Systems to Cyber-Physical Systems, LNCS 11500, pp. 259–275, 2019.
https://doi.org/10.1007/978-3-030-31514-6_15

To address the case of verifying trace properties, we introduced in [4] a class of monitors that consist of multiple parallel components that analyze the same system trace. These were called parallel monitors in [4] and were allowed to combine the respective verdicts reached at individual (parallel) monitors into one. In the same paper, it was determined that this monitoring system has the same monitoring power as its restriction to a single monitoring component, as used in [1,14], called regular monitors. However, the cost of the translation from the "parallel" monitoring system to the regular fragment, as given in [4], is doubly exponential with respect to the syntactic size of the monitors. Furthermore, if the goal is a deterministic regular monitor [2,3], then the resulting monitor is quadruply-exponentially larger than the original, parallel one, in [4].

In this paper, we show that the double-exponential cost for translating from parallel to equivalent regular monitors is tight. Furthermore, we improve on the translation cost from parallel monitors to equivalent deterministic monitors to a triple-exponential, and we show that this bound is tight. We define monitor equivalence in two ways, the first one stricter than the second. For the first definition, two monitors are equivalent when they reach the same verdicts for the same finite traces, while for the second one it suffices to reach the same verdicts for the same infinite traces. We prove the upper bounds for a transformation that gives monitors that are equivalent with respect to the stricter definition, while we prove the lower bounds with respect to transformations that satisfy the less strict definition. Therefore, our bounds hold for both definitions of monitor equivalence. This treatment allows us to derive stronger results, which yield similar bounds for the case of logical formulae, as well.

In [4], we show that, when interpreted over traces, MXHML, the fragment of RECHML that does not use least fixed points, is equivalent to the syntactically smaller safety fragment sHML. That is, every MXHML formula can be translated to a logically equivalent sHML formula. Similarly to the aforementioned translation of monitors, this translation of formulae results in formulae that are syntactically at most doubly-exponentially larger than the original formulae. We show that this upper bound is tight.

The first four authors have worked on the complexity of monitor transformations before in [2,3], where the cost of determinizing monitors is examined. Similarly to [2,3], in [4], but also in this paper, we use results and techniques from Automata Theory and specifically about alternating automata [10,12].

The case of monitors—parallel or regular—is interesting, as these are objects that are not quite (alternating) automata and not quite CCS processes, though they resemble, and can be represented as, both (see [2], Fig. 2 and Corollary 1). The most significant difference between CCS processes and monitors is due to the monitor *verdicts*, which lead to specific kinds of monitor equivalences. In contrast to finite automata, monitors can accept or reject an input string, or even reach no verdict, and furthermore, monitor verdicts persist for all extensions of the input. See also [2] for further discussion and comparisons between (regular) monitors and automata.

The Rest of the Paper is Structured as Follows: In Sect. 2, we introduce the necessary background on monitors and RECHML on infinite traces, as these were used in [4]. In Sect. 3, we describe the monitor translations that we mentioned above, and we provide upper bounds for these, which we prove to be tight in Sect. 4. In Sect. 5, we extrapolate these bounds to the case where we translate logical formulae, from MXHML to sHML. In Sect. 6, we conclude the paper. Omitted proofs can be found in the extended version [5].

2   Preliminaries

Monitors are expected to monitor for a specification, which, in our case, is written in RECHML. We use the linear-time interpretation of the logic RECHML, as it was given in [4]. According to that interpretation, formulae are interpreted over infinite *traces*.

2.1   The Model and the Logic

We assume a finite set of actions $\alpha, \beta, \ldots \in$ ACT with distinguished silent action τ. We also assume that $\tau \notin$ ACT and that $\mu \in$ ACT$\cup\{\tau\}$, and refer to the actions in ACT as *visible* actions (as opposed to the silent action τ). The metavariables $t, s \in$ TRC $=$ ACT$^\omega$ range over (infinite) sequences of visible actions, which abstractly represent system runs. We also use the metavariable $T \subseteq$ TRC to range over *sets of traces*. We often need to refer to *finite traces*, denoted as $u, r \in$ ACT*, to represent objects such as a finite prefix of a system run, or to traces that may be finite or infinite (*finfinite traces*, as they were called in [4]), denoted as $g, h \in$ ACT$^* \cup$ ACT$^\omega$. A trace (*resp.*, finite trace, *resp.*, finfinite trace) with action α at its head is denoted as αt (*resp.*, αu, *resp.*, αg). Similarly a trace with a prefix u is written ut.

Syntax

$$\varphi, \psi \in \text{RECHML} ::= \text{tt} \quad | \quad \text{ff} \quad | \quad \varphi \vee \psi \quad | \quad \varphi \wedge \psi$$
$$| \quad \langle \alpha \rangle \varphi \quad | \quad [\alpha]\varphi \quad | \quad \min X.\varphi \quad | \quad \max X.\varphi \quad | \quad X$$

Linear-Time Semantics

$$[\![\text{tt}]\!]_\rho \stackrel{\text{def}}{=} \text{TRC} \qquad\qquad\qquad [\![\text{ff}]\!]_\rho \stackrel{\text{def}}{=} \emptyset$$

$$[\![\varphi_1 \wedge \varphi_2]\!]_\rho \stackrel{\text{def}}{=} [\![\varphi_1]\!]_\rho \cap [\![\varphi_2]\!]_\rho \qquad [\![\varphi_1 \vee \varphi_2]\!]_\rho \stackrel{\text{def}}{=} [\![\varphi_1]\!]_\rho \cup [\![\varphi_2]\!]_\rho$$

$$[\![[\alpha]\varphi]\!]_\rho \stackrel{\text{def}}{=} \{\beta t \mid \beta \neq \alpha \text{ or } t \in [\![\varphi]\!]_\rho\} \qquad [\![\langle\alpha\rangle\varphi]\!]_\rho \stackrel{\text{def}}{=} \{\alpha t \mid t \in [\![\varphi]\!]_\rho\}$$

$$[\![\min X.\varphi]\!]_\rho \stackrel{\text{def}}{=} \bigcap \{T \mid [\![\varphi]\!]_{\rho[X \mapsto T]} \subseteq T\}$$

$$[\![\max X.\varphi]\!]_\rho \stackrel{\text{def}}{=} \bigcup \{T \mid T \subseteq [\![\varphi]\!]_{\rho[X \mapsto T]}\} \qquad [\![X]\!]_\rho \stackrel{\text{def}}{=} \rho(X)$$

Fig. 1. RECHML syntax and linear-time semantics

Syntax

$$m, n \in \text{Mon} ::= v \quad | \quad \alpha.m \quad | \quad m+n \quad | \quad \text{rec}\,x.m \quad | \quad x \quad | \quad m \otimes n \quad | \quad m \oplus n$$

$$v \in \text{Verd} ::= \text{no} \quad | \quad \text{yes} \quad | \quad \text{end}$$

Dynamics

Regular rules:

$$\text{Act} \frac{}{\alpha.m \xrightarrow{\alpha} m} \qquad \text{RecF} \frac{}{\text{rec}\,x.m \xrightarrow{\tau} m} \qquad \text{RecB} \frac{}{x \xrightarrow{\tau} p_x}$$

$$\text{Sel} \frac{m \xrightarrow{\mu} m'}{m+n \xrightarrow{\mu} m'} \qquad \text{Ver} \frac{}{v \xrightarrow{\alpha} v}$$

Parallel tracing rules:

$$\text{Par} \frac{m \xrightarrow{\alpha} m' \quad n \xrightarrow{\alpha} n'}{m \odot n \xrightarrow{\alpha} m' \odot n'} \qquad \text{TauL} \frac{m \xrightarrow{\tau} m'}{m \odot n \xrightarrow{\tau} m' \odot n}$$

Parallel evaluation rules:

$$\text{VrE} \frac{}{\text{end} \odot \text{end} \xrightarrow{\tau} \text{end}} \qquad \text{VrC1} \frac{}{\text{yes} \otimes m \xrightarrow{\tau} m} \qquad \text{VrC2} \frac{}{\text{no} \otimes m \xrightarrow{\tau} \text{no}}$$

$$\text{VrD1} \frac{}{\text{no} \oplus m \xrightarrow{\tau} m} \qquad \text{VrD2} \frac{}{\text{yes} \oplus m \xrightarrow{\tau} \text{yes}}$$

Fig. 2. Monitor syntax and semantics. We omit the obvious symmetric rules.

The logic RECHML [7,16], a reformulation of the μ-calculus [15], assumes a countable set LVAR (with $X \in$ LVAR) of logical variables, and is defined as the set of *closed* formulae generated by the grammar of Fig. 1. Apart from the standard constructs for truth, falsehood, conjunction and disjunction, the logic is equipped with possibility and necessity modal operators labelled by visible actions, together with recursive formulae expressing least or greatest fixpoints; formulae $\min X.\varphi$ and $\max X.\varphi$ bind free instances of the logical variable X in φ, inducing the usual notions of open/closed formulae and formula equality up to alpha-conversion.

We interpret RECHML formulae over traces, using an interpretation function $[\![-]\!]_\rho$ that maps formulae to sets of traces, relative to an environment $\rho : \text{LVAR} \to 2^{\text{FTRC}}$, which intuitively assigns to each variable X the set of traces that are assumed to satisfy it, as defined in Fig. 1. The semantics of a closed formula φ is independent of the environment ρ and is simply written $[\![\varphi]\!]$. Intuitively, $[\![\varphi]\!]$ denotes the set of traces satisfying φ. For a formula φ, we use $l(\varphi)$ to denote the length of φ as a string of symbols.

2.2   Two Monitoring Systems

We now present two monitoring systems, parallel and regular monitors, that were introduced in [1,4,14]. A monitoring system is a *Labelled Transition System*

(LTS) based on ACT, the set of actions, that is comprised of the monitor states, or monitors, and a transition relation. The set of monitor states, MON, and the monitor transition relation, $\longrightarrow \subseteq (\text{MON} \times (\text{ACT} \cup \{\tau\}) \times \text{MON})$, are defined in Fig. 2. There and elsewhere, $\odot$ ranges over both parallel operators $\oplus$ and $\otimes$. When discussing a monitor with free variables (an *open monitor*) m, we assume it is part of a larger monitor m' without free variables (a *closed monitor*), where every variable x appears at most once in a recursive operator. Therefore, we assume an injective mapping from each monitor variable x to a unique monitor p_x, of the form $\text{rec}\, x.m$ that is a submonitor of m'.

The suggestive notation $m \xrightarrow{\mu} n$ denotes $(m, \mu, n) \in \longrightarrow$; we also write $m \not\xrightarrow{\mu}$ to denote $\neg(\exists n.\ m \xrightarrow{\mu} n)$. We employ the usual notation for weak transitions and write $m \Longrightarrow n$ in lieu of $m(\xrightarrow{\tau})^* n$ and $m \overset{\mu}{\Longrightarrow} n$ for $m \Longrightarrow \cdot \xrightarrow{\mu} \cdot \Longrightarrow n$. We write sequences of transitions $m \overset{\alpha_1}{\Longrightarrow} \cdots \overset{\alpha_n}{\Longrightarrow} m_n$ as $m \overset{s}{\Longrightarrow} m_n$, where $s = \alpha_1 \cdots \alpha_n$. The monitoring system of *parallel monitors* is defined using the full syntax and all the rules from Fig. 2; *regular monitors* are parallel monitors that do not use the parallel operators $\otimes$ and $\oplus$. Regular monitors were defined and used already in [1] and [14], while parallel monitors were defined in [4]. We observe that the rules RECF and RECB are not the standard recursion rules from [1] and [14], but they are equivalent to these rules [2,4] and useful for our arguments.

A transition $m \xrightarrow{\alpha} n$ denotes that the monitor in state m can *analyse* the (external) action α and transition to state n. Monitors may reach any one of *three* verdicts after analysing a finite trace: *acceptance*, yes, *rejection*, no, and the *inconclusive* verdict end. We highlight the transition rule for verdicts in Fig. 2, describing the fact that from a verdict state any action can be analysed by transitioning to the same state; verdicts are thus *irrevocable*. Rule PAR states that *both* submonitors need to be able to analyse an external action α for their parallel composition to transition with that action. The rules in Fig. 2 also allow τ-transitions for the reconfiguration of parallel compositions of monitors. For instance, rules VRC1 and VRC2 describe the fact that, whereas yes verdicts are uninfluential in conjunctive parallel compositions, no verdicts supersede the verdicts of other monitors in a conjunctive parallel composition. The dual applies for yes and no verdicts in a disjunctive parallel composition, as described by rules VRD1 and VRD2. Rule VRE applies to both forms of parallel composition and consolidates multiple inconclusive verdicts. Finally, rules TAUL and its omitted dual TAUR are contextual rules for these monitor reconfiguration steps.

Definition 1 (Acceptance and Rejection). *We say that m rejects (resp., accepts) $u \in \text{ACT}^*$ when $m \overset{u}{\Longrightarrow} \text{no}$ (resp., $m \overset{u}{\Longrightarrow} \text{yes}$). We similarly say that m rejects (resp., accepts) $t \in \text{ACT}^\omega$ if $\exists u, s$ such that m rejects (resp., accepts) some prefix of t.*

Just like for formulae, we use $l(m)$ to denote the length of m as a string of symbols. In the sequel, for a finite nonempty set of indices I, we use $\sum_{i \in I} m_i$ to denote any combination of the monitors in $\{m_i \mid i \in I\}$ using the operator $+$. The notation is justified, because $+$ is commutative and associative with respect to the transitions that a resulting monitor can exhibit. For each $j \in I$, m_j is called a summand of $\sum_{i \in I} m_i$ (and the term $\sum_{i \in I} m_i$ is called a sum of m_j). The regular monitors in Fig. 2 have an important property, namely that their state space, *i.e.*, the set of reachable states, is finite (see Remark 1). On the other hand, parallel monitors can be infinite-state, but they are convenient when one synthesizes monitors. However, the two monitoring systems are equivalent (see Proposition 2). For a monitor m, reach(m) is the set of monitor states reachable through a transition sequence from m.

Lemma 1 (Verdict Persistence, [4,14]). $v \overset{u}{\Longrightarrow} m$ *implies* $m = v$.

Lemma 2. *Every submonitor of a closed regular monitor m can only transition to submonitors of m.*

Remark 1. An immediate consequence of Lemma 2 is that regular monitors are finite-state. This is not the case for parallel monitors, in general. For example, consider parallel monitor $m_\tau = \operatorname{rec} x.(x \otimes (a.\mathsf{yes} + b.\mathsf{yes}))$. We can see that there is a unique sequence of transitions that can be made from m_τ:

$$m_\tau \overset{\tau}{\longrightarrow} x \otimes (a.\mathsf{yes} + b.\mathsf{yes}) \overset{\tau}{\longrightarrow} m_\tau \otimes (a.\mathsf{yes} + b.\mathsf{yes})$$
$$\overset{\tau}{\longrightarrow} (x \otimes (a.\mathsf{yes} + b.\mathsf{yes})) \otimes (a.\mathsf{yes} + b.\mathsf{yes})$$
$$\overset{\tau}{\longrightarrow} (m_\tau \otimes (a.\mathsf{yes} + b.\mathsf{yes})) \otimes (a.\mathsf{yes} + b.\mathsf{yes}) \longrightarrow \cdots$$

One basic requirement that we maintain on monitors is that they are not allowed to give conflicting verdicts for the same trace.

Definition 2 (Monitor Consistency). *A monitor m is consistent when there is no finite trace s such that $m \overset{s}{\Longrightarrow} \mathsf{yes}$ and $m \overset{s}{\Longrightarrow} \mathsf{no}$.*

We identify a useful monitor predicate that allows us to neatly decompose the behaviour of a parallel monitor in terms of its constituent sub-monitors.

Definition 3 (Monitor Reactivity). *We call a monitor m reactive when for every $n \in$ reach(m) and $\alpha \in \mathrm{ACT}$, there is some n' such that $n \overset{\alpha}{\Longrightarrow} n'$.*

The following lemma states that parallel monitors behave as expected with respect to the acceptance and rejection of traces as long as the consitituent submonitors are reactive.

Lemma 3 ([4]). *For reactive m_1 and m_2:*

- $m_1 \otimes m_2$ *rejects t if and only if either m_1 or m_2 rejects t.*
- $m_1 \otimes m_2$ *accepts t if and only if both m_1 and m_2 accept t.*
- $m_1 \oplus m_2$ *rejects t if and only if both m_1 and m_2 reject t.*
- $m_1 \oplus m_2$ *accepts t if and only if either m_1 or m_2 accepts t.*

The following example, which stems from [4], indicates why the assumption that m_1 and m_2 are reactive is needed in Lemma 3.

Example 1. Assume that ACT $= \{a, b\}$. The monitors a.yes$+b$.no and rec $x.(a.x+$ b.yes) are both reactive. The monitor $m = a$.yes$\otimes b$.no, however, is *not* reactive. Since the submonitor a.yes can only transition with a, according to the rules of Fig. 2, m cannot transition with any action that is not a. Similarly, as the submonitor b.no can only transition with b, m cannot transition with any action that is not b. Thus, m cannot transition to any monitor, and therefore it cannot reject or accept any trace.

In general, we are interested in reactive parallel monitors, and the parallel monitors that we use will have this property.

2.3 Automata, Languages, Equivalence

In [4], we describe how to transform a parallel monitor to a verdict equivalent regular one. This transformation goes through alternating automata [10,12]. For our purposes, we only need to define nondeterministic and deterministic automata.

Definition 4 (Finite Automata). *A nondeterminitic finite automaton (NFA) is a quintuple $A = (Q, \text{ACT}, q_0, \delta, F)$, where Q is a finite set of states, ACT is a finite alphabet (here it coincides with the set of actions), q_0 is the starting state, $F \subseteq Q$ is the set of accepting, or final states, and $\delta \subseteq Q \times \text{ACT} \times Q$ is the transition relation. An NFA is deterministic (DFA) if δ is a function from $Q \times \text{ACT}$ to Q.*

Given a state $q \in Q$ and a symbol $\alpha \in$ ACT, δ returns a set of possible state where the NFA can transition, and we usually use $q' \in \delta(q, \alpha)$ instead of $(q, \alpha, q') \in \delta$. We extend the transition relation to $\delta^* : Q \times \text{ACT}^* \to 2^Q$, so that $\delta^*(q, \varepsilon) = \{q\}$ and $\delta^*(q, \alpha s) = \bigcup\{\delta^*(q', s) \mid q' \in \delta(q, \alpha)\}$. We say that the automaton *accepts* $s \in \text{ACT}^*$ when $\delta^*(q_0, s) \cap F \neq \emptyset$, and that it recognizes $L \subseteq \text{ACT}^*$ when L is the set of strings accepted by the automaton.

Definition 5 (Monitor Language Recognition). *A monitor m recognizes positively (resp., negatively) a set of finite traces (i.e., a language) $L \subseteq \text{ACT}^*$ when for every $s \in \text{ACT}^*$, $s \in L$ if and only if m accepts (resp., rejects) s. We call the set that m recognizes positively (resp., negatively) $L_a(m)$ (resp., $L_r(m)$). Similarly, we say that m recognizes positively (resp., negatively) a set of infinite traces $L \subseteq \text{ACT}^\omega$ when for every $t \in \text{ACT}^\omega$, $t \in L$ if and only if m accepts (resp., rejects) t.*

Observe that, by Lemma 1, $L_a(m)$ and $L_r(m)$ are suffix closed for each m.

Lemma 4. *The set of* infinite *traces that is recognized positively (resp., negatively) by m is exactly $L_a(m) \cdot \text{ACT}^\omega$ (resp., $L_r(m) \cdot \text{ACT}^\omega$).*

Proof. The lemma is a consequence of verdict-persistence (Lemma 1). □

To compare different monitors, we use a notion of monitor equivalence from [3] that focusses on how monitors can reach verdicts.

Definition 6 (Verdict Equivalence). *Monitors m and n are verdict equivalent, denoted as $m \simeq_v n$, if $L_a(m) = L_a(n)$ and $L_r(m) = L_r(n)$.*

One may consider the notion of verdict-equivalence, as defined in Definition 6 to be too strict. After all, verdict-equivalence is defined with respect to finite traces, so if we want to turn a parallel monitor into a regular or deterministic monitor, the resulting monitor not only needs to accept and reject the same infinite traces, but it is required to do so at the same time the original parallel monitor does. However, one may prefer to have a smaller, but not tight monitor, if possible, as long as it accepts the same infinite traces.

Definition 7 (ω-Verdict Equivalence). *Monitors m and n are ω-verdict equivalent, denoted as $m \simeq_\omega n$, if $L_a(m) \cdot \text{ACT}^\omega = L_a(n) \cdot \text{ACT}^\omega$ and $L_r(m) \cdot \text{ACT}^\omega = L_r(n) \cdot \text{ACT}^\omega$.*

From Lemma 4 we observe that verdict equivalence implies ω-verdict equivalence. The converse does not hold, because no $\simeq_\omega \sum_{\alpha \in \text{ACT}} \alpha.\text{no}$, but no $\not\simeq_v \sum_{\alpha \in \text{ACT}} \alpha.\text{no}$.

Definition 8 ([2]). *A closed regular monitor m is deterministic iff every sum of at least two summands that appears in m is of the form $\sum_{\alpha \in A} \alpha.m_\alpha$, where $A \subseteq \text{ACT}$.*

Example 21. *The monitor a.b.yes+a.a.no is not deterministic while the verdict equivalent monitor a.(b.yes + a.no) is deterministic.*

2.4   Synthesis

There is a tight connection between the logic from Sect. 2.1 and the monitoring systems from Sect. 2.2. Ideally, we would want to be able to synthesize a monitor from any formula φ, such that the monitor recognizes $[\![\varphi]\!]$ positively and $\text{TRC}\backslash[\![\varphi]\!]$ negatively. However, as shown in [4], neither goal is possible for all formulae. Instead, we identify the following fragments of RECHML.

Definition 9 (MAX and MIN Fragments of RECHML). *The greatest-fixed-point and least-fixed-point fragments of RECHML are, respectively, defined as:*

$$\varphi, \psi \in \text{MXHML} ::= \text{tt} \mid \text{ff} \mid \varphi \lor \psi \mid \varphi \land \psi \mid \langle \alpha \rangle \varphi \mid [\alpha]\varphi \mid \max X.\varphi$$
$$\varphi, \psi \in \text{MNHML} ::= \text{tt} \mid \text{ff} \mid \varphi \lor \psi \mid \varphi \land \psi \mid \langle \alpha \rangle \varphi \mid [\alpha]\varphi \mid \min X.\varphi$$

Definition 10 (Safety and co-Safety Fragments of RECHML). *The safety and co-safety fragments of RECHML are, respectively, defined as:*

$$\varphi, \psi \in \text{SHML} ::= \text{tt} \mid \text{ff} \mid \varphi \land \psi \mid [\alpha]\varphi \mid \max X.\varphi$$
$$\varphi, \psi \in \text{CHML} ::= \text{tt} \mid \text{ff} \mid \varphi \lor \psi \mid \langle \alpha \rangle \varphi \mid \min X.\varphi$$

The fragments SHML and CHML allow a much restricted syntax with respect to MXHML and MNHML. Whereas the second pair of logics allows both diamond and box modalities, and disjunctions as well as conjunctions, the fragments from Definition 10 allow only either boxes and conjunctions, or diamonds and disjunctions. Surprisingly, the two pairs of logical fragments can respectively express exactly the same trace properties [4], though the extended syntax provided by Definition 9 makes it easier to write such properties. For more on these fragments and how they relate to monitors and monitorability, we refer the reader to [14] and [4].

Theorem 1 (Monitorability and Maximality, [4]).

1. *For every $\varphi \in$ MXHML (resp., $\varphi \in$ MNHML), there is a reactive parallel monitor m, such that $l(m) = O(l(\varphi))$ and $L_r(m) \cdot \text{ACT}^\omega = \text{ACT}^\omega \backslash \llbracket \varphi \rrbracket$ (resp., $L_a(m) \cdot \text{ACT}^\omega = \llbracket \varphi \rrbracket$).*
2. *For every reactive parallel monitor m, there are $\varphi \in$ MXHML and $\psi \in$ MNHML, such that $l(\varphi), l(\psi) = O(l(m))$, $L_r(m) \cdot \text{ACT}^\omega = \text{ACT}^\omega \backslash \llbracket \varphi \rrbracket$, and $L_a(m) \cdot \text{ACT}^\omega = \llbracket \psi \rrbracket$.*
3. *For every $\varphi \in$ SHML (resp., $\varphi \in$ CHML), there is a regular monitor m, such that $l(m) = O(l(\varphi))$ and $L_r(m) \cdot \text{ACT}^\omega = \text{ACT}^\omega \backslash \llbracket \varphi \rrbracket$ (resp., $L_a(m) \cdot \text{ACT}^\omega = \llbracket \varphi \rrbracket$).*
4. *For every regular monitor m, there are $\varphi \in$ SHML and $\psi \in$ CHML, such that $l(\varphi), l(\psi) = O(m)$, $L_r(m) \cdot \text{ACT}^\omega = \text{ACT}^\omega \backslash \llbracket \varphi \rrbracket$, and $L_a(m) \cdot \text{ACT}^\omega = \llbracket \psi \rrbracket$.*

We say that a logical fragment is monitorable for a monitoring system, such as parallel or regular monitors, when for each of the fragment's formulae there is a monitor that detects exactly the satisfying or violating traces of that formula. One of the consequences of Theorem 1 is that the fragments defined in Definitions 9 and 10 are semantically the largest monitorable fragments of RECHML for parallel and regular monitors, respectively. As we will see in Sect. 3, every parallel monitor has a verdict equivalent regular monitor (Propositions 3 and 4), and therefore all formulae in MNHML and MXHML can be translated into equivalent CHML and SHML formulae respectively, as Theorem 4 later on demonstrates. However, Theorem 5 shows that the cost of this translation is significant.

3   Monitor Transformations: Upper Bounds

In this section we explain how to transform a parallel monitor into a regular or deterministic monitor, and what is the cost in monitor size of this transformation. The various relevant transformations, including some from [2] and [10,12], are summarized in Fig. 3, where each edge is labelled with the best-known worst-case upper bounds for the cost of the corresponding transformation in Fig. 3 (AFA abbreviates alternating finite automaton [10]). As we see in [2,3] and in Sect. 4, these bounds cannot be improved significantly.

Proposition 1 ([4]). *For every reactive parallel monitor m, there are an alternating automaton that recognizes $L_a(m)$ and one that recognises $L_r(m)$.*

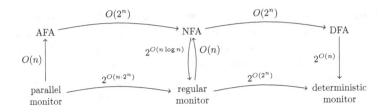

Fig. 3. Monitor transformations and costs

Proof. The construction from [4, Proposition 3.6] gives an automaton that has the submonitors of m as states. The automaton's transition function corresponds to the semantics of the monitor. As it is demonstrated in [4], the assumption that m is reactive is necessary. $\qquad\square$

Corollary 1 (Corollary 3.7 of [4]). *For every reactive and closed parallel monitor m, there are an NFA that recognises $L_a(m)$ and an NFA that recognises $L_r(m)$, and each has at most $2^{l(m)}$ states.*

Proposition 2. *For every reactive and closed parallel monitor m, there exists a verdict equivalent regular monitor n such that $l(n) = 2^{O\left(l(m)\cdot 2^{l(m)}\right)}$.*

Proof. Let A_m^a be an NFA for $L_a(m)$ with at most $2^{l(m)}$ states, and let A_m^r be an NFA for $L_r(m)$ with at most $2^{l(m)}$ states, which exist by Corollary 1. From these NFAs, we can construct regular monitors m_R^a and m_R^r, such that m_R^a recognizes $L_a(m)$ positively and m_R^r recognizes $L_r(m)$ negatively, and $l(m_R^a), l(m_R^r) = 2^{O\left(l(m)\cdot 2^{l(m)}\right)}$ [3, Theorem 2]. Therefore, $m_R^a + m_R^r$ is regular and verdict equivalent to m, and $l(m_R^a + m_R^r) = 2^{O\left(l(m)\cdot 2^{l(m)}\right)}$. $\qquad\square$

The constructions from [4] include a determinization result, based on [2].

Theorem 2 (Corollary 3 of [3]). *For every consistent closed regular monitor m, there is a deterministic monitor n such that $n \simeq_v m$ and $l(n) = 2^{2^{O(l(m))}}$.*

Proposition 3 (Proposition 3.11 of [4]). *For every consistent reactive and closed parallel monitor m, there is a verdict equivalent deterministic regular monitor n such that $l(n) = 2^{2^{2^{O\left(l(m)\cdot 2^{l(m)}\right)}}}$.*

However, the bound given by Proposition 3 for the construction of deterministic regular monitors from parallel ones is not optimal, as we promptly observe.

Proposition 4. *For every consistent reactive and closed parallel monitor m, there is a deterministic monitor n such that $n \simeq_v m$ and $l(n) = 2^{2^{2^{O(l(m))}}}$.*

In the following Sect. 4, we see that the upper bounds of Propositions 2 and 4 are tight, even for monitors that can only accept or reject, and even when the constructed regular or deterministic monitor is only required to be ω-verdict equivalent to the starting one, and not necessarily verdict equivalent, to the original parallel monitor. As we only need to focus on acceptance monitors, in the following we say that a monitor recognizes a language to mean that it recognizes the language positively.

4   Lower Bounds

We now prove that the transformations of Sect. 3 are optimal, by proving the corresponding lower bounds. For this, we introduce a family of suffix-closed languages $L_A^k \subseteq \{0, 1, e, \$, \#\}^*$. Each L_A^k is a variation of a language introduced in [10] to prove the $2^{2^{o(n)}}$ lower bound for the transformation from an alternating automaton to a deterministic one. In this section, we only need to consider closed monitors, and as such, all monitors are assumed to be closed.

A variation of the language that was introduced in [10] is the following:

$$L_V^k = \{u\#w\#v\$w \mid u, v \in \{0, 1, \#\}^*, \ w \in \{0,1\}^k\}.$$

An alternating automaton that recognizes L_V^k can nondeterministically skip to the first occurrence of w and then verify that for every number i between 0 and $k-1$, the i'th bit matches the i'th bit after the $\$$ symbol. This verification can be done using up to $O(k)$ states, to count the position i of the bit that is checked. On the other hand, a DFA that recognizes L_V^k must remember all possible candidates for w that have appeared before $\$$, and hence requires 2^{2^k} states. We can also conclude that any NFA for L_V^k must have at least 2^k states, because a smaller NFA could be determinized to a smaller DFA.

A Gap Language. For our purposes, we use a similar family L_A^k of suffix-closed languages, which are designed to be recognized by small parallel monitors, but such that each regular monitor recognizing L_A^k must be "large". We fix two numbers $l, k \geq 0$, such that $k = 2^l$. First, we observe that we can encode every string $w \in \{0, 1\}^k$ as a string $a_1\alpha_1 a_2\alpha_2 \cdots a_k\alpha_k \in \{0, 1\}^{(l+1) \cdot k}$, where $a_1 a_2 \cdots a_k$ is a permutation of $\{0, 1\}^l$ and for all i, $\alpha_i \in \{0, 1\}$. Then, $a_i\alpha_i$ gives the information that for j being the number with binary representation a_i, the j'th position of w holds bit α_i. Let $pos = \{i \mid 0 < i \leq k\}$, and

$$W = \left\{ a_1\alpha_1 \cdots a_k\alpha_k \in \{0,1\}^{(l+1)\cdot k} \ \middle| \ \begin{array}{l} \text{for all } 1 \leq i \leq k, \ \alpha_i \in \{0,1\} \text{ and} \\ a_i \in \{0,1\}^l, \text{ and } a_1 \cdots a_k \in \{0,1\}^{l!} \end{array} \right\}.$$

Let $w, w' \in W$, where $w = a_1\alpha_1 a_2\alpha_2 \cdots a_k\alpha_k$ and $w' = b_1\beta_1 b_2\beta_2 \cdots b_k\beta_k$, and for $1 \leq i \leq k$, $a_i, b_i \in \{0, 1\}^l$ and $\alpha_i, \beta_i \in \{0, 1\}$. We define $w \equiv w'$ to mean that for every $i, j \leq k$, $a_i = b_j$ implies $\alpha_i = \beta_j$. Let $a = \alpha_0 \ldots \alpha_{l-1} \in \{0, 1\}^l$; then, $enc(a) = bin(0)\alpha_0 \ldots bin(l-1)\alpha_{l-1}$ is the ordered encoding of a, where $bin(i)$ is the binary encoding of i. Then, $w \in W$ is called an encoding of a if $w \equiv enc(a)$.

Let $\Sigma = \{0, 1, \#\}$ and $\Sigma_\$ = \Sigma \cup \{\$\}$. Then,

$$L_A^k = \{u\#w\#v\$u'\#w'\#\$v' \mid u, v' \in \Sigma_\$^*, u', v \in \Sigma^*, \ w, w' \in W, \text{ and } w \equiv w'\}.$$

In other words, a finite trace is in L_A^k exactly when it has a substring of the form $\#w\#v\$u'\#w'\#\$$, where w and w' are encodings of the same string and there is only one $\$$ between them. Intuitively, $\#$ is there to delimit bit-strings that may be elements of W, and $\$$ delimits sequences of such bit-strings. So, the language asks if there are two such consecutive sequences where the last bit-string of the second sequence comes from W and matches an element from the first sequence. We observe that L_A^k is suffix-closed.

Lemma 5. $u \in L_A^k$ if and only if $\forall t.\ ut \in L_A^k \cdot \Sigma_\$^\omega$.

Conventions. For the conclusions of Lemma 3 to hold, monitors need to be reactive. However, a reactive monitor can have a larger syntactic description than an equivalent non-reactive one, e.g., α.yes vs α.yes $+$ β.end $+$ γ.end, when ACT $= \{\alpha, \beta, \gamma\}$. This last monitor is also verdict equivalent to α.yes $+$ end. In the following, for brevity and clarity, whenever we write a sum s of a monitor of the form $\alpha.m$, we will mean $s + $ end, which is reactive, so it can be safely used with a parallel operator, and is verdict equivalent to s. We use set-notation for monitors: for $A \subseteq$ ACT, $A.m$ stands for $\sum_{\alpha \in A} \alpha.m$ (or $\sum_{\alpha \in A} \alpha.m + $ end under the above convention). Furthermore, we define $\{0,1\}^0.m = m$ and $\{0,1\}^{i+1}.m = 0.\{0,1\}^i.m + 1.\{0,1\}^i.m$. Notice that $l(\{0,1\}^i.m) = 2^i \cdot l(m) + 5 \cdot (2^i - 1)$. We can also similarly define $T.m$ for $T \subseteq \{0,1\}^i$.

Auxiliary Monitors. We start by defining auxiliary monitors. Given a (closed) monitor m, let

$$skip_\#(m) := \mathsf{rec}\,x.((0.x + 1.x + \#.x)\oplus\#.m),$$
$$next_\#(m) := \mathsf{rec}\,x.(0.x + 1.x + \#.m),$$
$$next_\$(m) := \mathsf{rec}\,x.(0.x + 1.x + \#.x + \$.m), \quad \text{and}$$
$$skip\_last(m) := \mathsf{rec}\,x.(0.x + 1.x + \#.x + \#.(m\otimes\mathsf{rec}\,y.(0.y + 1.y + \#.\$.\mathsf{yes}))).$$

These monitors read the trace until they reach a certain symbol, and then they activate submonitor m. We can think that $skip_\#(m)$ nondeterministically skips to some occurrence of $\#$ that comes before the first occurence of $\$$; $next_\#(m)$ and $next_\$(m)$ respectively skip to the next occurence of $\#$ and $\$$; and $skip\_last(m)$ skips to the last occurence of $\#$ before the next occurence of $\#\$$.

Lemma 6. $skip_\#(m)$ accepts g iff there are u and h, such that $u\#h = g$, m accepts h, and $u \in \{0, 1, \#\}^*$.

The following lemmata are straightforward and explain how the remaining monitors defined above are used.

Lemma 7. $next_\#(m)$ accepts g iff there are u and h, such that $u\#h = g$, m accepts h, and $u \in \{0, 1\}^*$.

Lemma 8. $next_\$(m)$ accepts g iff there are u and h, such that $u\$h = g$, m accepts h, and $u \in \{0, 1, \#\}^*$.

Lemma 9. *skip_last(m) accepts g iff there are u, r, and h, such that u#r#$h = g, m accepts r#$h, r ∈ {0,1}*, and u ∈ {0, 1, #}*.*

The following monitors help us ensure that a bit-string from $\{0,1\}^{(l+1)\cdot k}$ is actually a member of W. Monitor *all* ensures that all bit positions appear in the bit-string; *no_more(u)* assures us that the bit position u does not appear any more in the remainder of the bit-string; and *unique* ensures that each bit position appears at most once. Monitor *perm* combines these monitors together.

$$all := \otimes\{\text{rec } x.(\{0,1\}^{l+1}.x \oplus u.\{0,1\}.\text{yes}) \mid u \in \{0,1\}^l\};$$

for $u \in \{0,1\}^l$,

$$no\_more(u) := \text{rec } x. \left(\#.\text{yes} + (\{0,1\}^l \setminus \{u\}).\{0,1\}.x \right);$$

$$unique := \text{rec } x. \left(\#.\text{yes} + \left(\{0,1\}^{l+1}.x \otimes \sum_{u \in \{0,1\}^l} u.\{0,1\}.no\_more(u) \right) \right); \text{ and}$$

$$perm := all \otimes unique.$$

The purpose of *perm* is to ensure that a certain block of bits before the appearance of the # symbol is a member of the set W: it accepts $w\#$ exactly when w is a sequence of blocks of bits with length exactly $l+1$ (by *unique*) and for every $a \in \{0,1\}^l$ there is some $\alpha \in \{0,1\}$ such that $a\alpha$ is one of these blocks (by *all*), and that for each such a only one block is of the form $a\alpha'$ (by *unique*).

Lemma 10. *perm accepts g iff w# is a prefix of g, for some w ∈ W.*

Lemma 11. $l(perm) = O(k^2)$.

Given a block u of $l+1$ bits, monitor $find(u)$ accepts a sequence of blocks of $l+1$ bits w exactly when u is one of the blocks of w:

$$find(u) := \text{rec } x.(u.\text{yes} + (\{0,1\}^{l+1} \setminus \{u\}).x).$$

Lemma 12. *For $u \in \{0,1\}^{l+1}$, $find(u)$ accepts g if and only if there is some $r \in (\{0,1\}^{l+1})^*$, such that ru is a prefix of g.*

For $u \in \{0,1\}^{l+1}$, $match(u)$ ensures that right before the second occurrence of \$, there is a $\#w\#$, where $w \in (\{0,1\}^{l+1})^+$ and u is a $(l+1)$-bit-block in w.

$$match(u) := next_\$(skip\_last(find(u))).$$

Lemma 13. *For $u \in \{0,1\}^{l+1}$, $match(u)$ accepts g if and only if there are $r\$r'\#w\#\$h = g$, such that $r, r' \in \Sigma^*$, $w \in \{0,1\}^*$, and there is a prefix $w'u$ of w, such that $w' \in (\{0,1\}^{l+1})^*$.*

Recognizing L_A^k with a Parallel Monitor. We can now define a parallel acceptance-monitor of length $O(k^2)$ that recognizes L_A^k. Monitor *matching* ensures that every one of the consecutive blocks of $l+1$ bits that follow, also appears in the block of bits that appears right before the occurrence of $\#\$$ that follows the next $\$$ (and that there is no other $\$$ between these $\$$ and $\#\$$). Therefore, if what follows from the current position in the trace and what appears right before that occurence of $\#\$$ are elements w, w' of W, *matching* ensures that $w \equiv w$. Then, m_A^k nondeterministically chooses an occurence of $\#$, it verifies that the block of bits that follows is an element w of W that ends with $\#$, and that what follows is of the form $v\$u'\#w'\#\$v'$, where $u', v \in \Sigma^*$, $w' \in W$, and $w \equiv w'$, which matches the description of L_A^k.

$$matching := \mathsf{rec}\, x. \sum_{u \in \{0,1\}^{l+1}} u.(x \otimes match(u))$$

$$m_A^k := skip_\# \, (perm \otimes next_\$(skip\_last(perm)) \otimes matching)$$

Lemma 14. m_A^k *recognizes* L_A^k *and* $l(m_A^k) = O(k^2)$.

Proof. The lemma follows from this section's previous lemmata and from counting the sizes of the various monitors that we have constructed. □

Lemma 15. *If m is a deterministic monitor that recognizes $L_A^k \cdot \Sigma_\$^\omega$, then*

$$|m| \geq \left((2^{2^{k-1}} - 1)!\right)^2 = 2^{\Omega\left(2^{2^{k-1}+k}\right)}.$$

Theorem 3 gathers our conclusions about L_A^k.

Theorem 3. *For every $k > 0$, L_A^k is recognized by an alternating automaton of $O(k^2)$ states and a parallel monitor of length $O(k^2)$, but by no DFA with $2^{o(2^k)}$ states and no deterministic monitor of length $2^{o\left(2^{2^{k-1}+k}\right)}$. $L_A^k \cdot \Sigma_\$^\omega$ is recognized by a parallel monitor of length $O(k^2)$, but by no deterministic monitor of length $2^{o\left(2^{2^{k-1}+k}\right)}$.*

Proof. Lemma 14 informs us that there is a parallel monitor m of length $O(k^2)$ that recognizes L_A^k. Therefore, it also recognizes $L_A^k \cdot \Sigma_\$^\omega$. Proposition 1 tells us that m can be turned into an alternating automaton with $l(m) = O(k^2)$ states that recognizes L_A^k. Lemma 15 yields that there is no deterministic monitor of length $2^{o\left(2^{2^{k-1}+k}\right)}$ that recognizes that language. From [3], we know that if there were a DFA with $2^{o(2^k)}$ states that recognizes L_A^k, then there would be a deterministic monitor of length $2^{2^{o(2^k)}}$ that recognizes L_A^k, which, as we argued, cannot exist. □

Hardness for Regular Monitors. Proposition 3 does not guarantee that the $2^{O(n \cdot 2^n)}$ upper bound for the transformation from a parallel monitor to a non-deterministic regular monitor is tight. To prove a tighter lower bound, let L_U^k be the language that includes all strings of the form $\#w_1\#w_2\#\cdots\#w_n\$w$ where for $i = 1,\ldots,n$, $w_i \in W$, and $w \in \{0,1,\#,\$\}^*$, and for every $i < n$, w_i encodes a string that is smaller than the string encoded by w_{i+1}, in the lexicographic order.

Lemma 16. $u \in L_U^k$ *if and only if* $\forall t. \; ut \in L_U^k \cdot \Sigma_\$^\omega$.

We describe how L_U^k can be recognized by a parallel monitor of size $O(k^2)$. The idea is that we need to compare the encodings of two consecutive blocks of $l + 1$ bits. Furthermore, a string is smaller than another if there is a position in these strings, where the first string has the value 0 and the second 1, and for every position that comes before that position, the bits of the two strings are the same. We define the following monitors:

$$smaller = \sum_{u\in\{0,1\}^l} \left(\begin{array}{c} find(u0) \otimes next_\#(find(u1)) \\ \otimes \\ \bigotimes_{r<u} \sum_{b\in\{0,1\}} (find(rb) \otimes next_\#(find(rb))) \end{array} \right)$$

$$last = \mathsf{rec}\, x.(0.x + 1.x + \$.\mathsf{yes})$$

$$m_U = \mathsf{rec}\, x.(next_\#(perm \otimes (last \oplus (smaller \otimes x))))$$

Proposition 5. m_U *recognizes* L_U^k *(and* $L_U^k \cdot \Sigma_\$^\omega$*) and* $|m_U| = O(k^2)$*. Every regular monitor that recognizes* L_U^k *or* $L_U^k \cdot \Sigma_\$^\omega$ *must be of length* $2^{\Omega(2^k)}$*.*

5   Logical Consequences

We now turn our attention back from the two monitoring systems to the corresponding logical fragments. We observe that the bounds that we have proved in the previous sections also apply when we discuss formula translations. A version of Theorem 4 was proven in [4], but without complexity bounds.

Theorem 4. *For every* $\varphi \in$ MNHML *(resp.,* $\varphi \in$ MXHML*), there is some* $\psi \in$ CHML *(resp.,* $\psi \in$ SHML*), such that* $l(\psi) = 2^{O(l(m)\cdot 2^{l(m)})}$ *and* $[\![\varphi]\!] = [\![\psi]\!]$*.*

Proof. We prove the case for $\varphi \in$ MNHML, as the case for $\varphi \in$ MXHML is similar. By Theorem 1, we know that there is a reactive parallel monitor m, such that $L_a(m) \cdot \mathrm{ACT}^\omega = [\![\varphi]\!]$ and $l(m) = O(l(\varphi))$. By Proposition 2, we know that there is a regular monitor n, such that $L_a(n) = L_a(m)$ and $l(n) = 2^{O(l(m)\cdot 2^{l(m)})}$. We can then see that $l(n) = 2^{O(l(\varphi)\cdot 2^{l(\varphi)})}$. According to Theorem 1, there is a formula $\psi \in$ CHML, such that $[\![\psi]\!] = L_a(n) \cdot \mathrm{ACT}^\omega = L_a(m) \cdot \mathrm{ACT}^\omega = [\![\varphi]\!]$, and $l(\psi) = O(l(n))$, yielding that $l(\psi) = 2^{O(l(\varphi)\cdot 2^{l(\varphi)})}$. $\qquad\square$

The cost of the construction in the proof of Theorem 4 is due to the regularization of the monitor. Our lower bounds—and specifically Proposition 5—demonstrate that this construction is optimal, because a better construction of ψ would lower the cost of regularization via the synthesis functions.

Theorem 5. *There is some* $\varphi \in$ MXHML, *such that for every* $\psi \in$ sHML, *if* $[\![\varphi]\!] = [\![\psi]\!]$, *then* $l(\psi) = 2^{\Omega\left(2^{\sqrt{l(\varphi)}}\right)}$.

Proof (Sketch). Otherwise, we could regularize m_U from Sect. 4 more efficiently than Proposition 5 allows, by first turning m_U to $\varphi \in$ MXHML, then to $\psi \in$ sHML, and finally to a regular monitor m.   □

Remark 2. We observe that to prove Theorem 5, it was necessary to prove Proposition 5 for regular monitors that are ω-*verdict equivalent*, and not just verdict equivalent, to m_U. The reason is that in the proof of Theorem 5, the monitor m that monitors for ψ is ω-verdict equivalent to m_U and there is no guarantee that it is, in fact, verdict equivalent to m_U.

Remark 3. In [2], the authors define a deterministic fragment of sHML, which they then show to be equivalent to the full sHML. We can claim analogous bounds for translating formulae into this smaller fragment, using similar arguments to those used above. We omit a full exposition of this claim.

6   Conclusion

We determined the cost of turning a parallel monitor into an equivalent regular, or deterministic, monitor. As a result, we saw that, over infinite traces, MXHML is doubly-exponentially more succinct than sHML.

Regular monitors were introduced in [14] to monitor for sHML over processes. The cost of determinization of regular monitors was examined in [2,3]. Aceto *et al.* in [6] used a similar determinization process on formulae in the context of enforcement.

In [4], we also synthesized *tight* monitors, which are monitors that reach a verdict as soon as they have analyzed enough information from the trace, and not later. It is often important to reach a verdict as soon as possible, but it is also important to not burden a monitored system with a very large monitor. Therefore, it would also be of interest to determine how much it costs to turn a parallel or regular monitor into a verdict-equivalent tight monitor. This is a topic that we leave for future work.

References

1. Aceto, L., Achilleos, A., Francalanza, A., Ingólfsdóttir, A.: Monitoring for silent actions. In: Lokam, S., Ramanujam, R. (eds.) FSTTCS. LIPIcs, vol. 93, pp. 7:1–7:14. Schloss Dagstuhl-Leibniz-Zentrum fuer Informatik, Dagstuhl, Germany (2017)
2. Aceto, L., Achilleos, A., Francalanza, A., Ingólfsdóttir, A., Kjartansson, S.Ö.: Determinizing monitors for HML with recursion. CoRR abs/1611.10212 (2016). http://arxiv.org/abs/1611.10212

3. Aceto, L., Achilleos, A., Francalanza, A., Ingólfsdóttir, A., Kjartansson, S.Ö.: On the complexity of determinizing monitors. In: Carayol, A., Nicaud, C. (eds.) CIAA 2017. LNCS, vol. 10329, pp. 1–13. Springer, Cham (2017). https://doi.org/10.1007/978-3-319-60134-2_1

4. Aceto, L., Achilleos, A., Francalanza, A., Ingólfsdóttir, A., Lehtinen, K.: Adventures in monitorability: from branching to linear time and back again. Proc. ACM Program. Lang. **3**, 52:1–52:29 (2019). https://doi.org/10.1145/3290365. https://dl.acm.org/citation.cfm?id=3290365

5. Aceto, L., Achilleos, A., Francalanza, A., Ingólfsdóttir, A., Lehtinen, K.: The cost of monitoring alone. CoRR abs/1902.05152 (2019). http://arxiv.org/abs/1902.05152

6. Aceto, L., Cassar, I., Francalanza, A., Ingólfsdóttir, A.: On runtime enforcement via suppressions. In: Schewe, S., Zhang, L. (eds.) 29th International Conference on Concurrency Theory (CONCUR 2018). Leibniz International Proceedings in Informatics (LIPIcs), vol. 118, pp. 34:1–34:17. Schloss Dagstuhl-Leibniz-Zentrum fuer Informatik, Dagstuhl, Germany (2018). https://doi.org/10.4230/LIPIcs.CONCUR.2018.34. http://drops.dagstuhl.de/opus/volltexte/2018/9572

7. Aceto, L., Ingólfsdóttir, A., Larsen, K.G., Srba, J.: Reactive Systems: Modelling, Specification and Verification. Cambridge Univ. Press, New York (2007). https://doi.org/10.1017/cbo9780511814105

8. Bartocci, E., Falcone, Y., Francalanza, A., Reger, G.: Introduction to runtime verification. In: Bartocci, E., Falcone, Y. (eds.) Lectures on Runtime Verification. LNCS, vol. 10457, pp. 1–33. Springer, Cham (2018). https://doi.org/10.1007/978-3-319-75632-5_1

9. Bauer, A., Leucker, M., Schallhart, C.: Runtime verification for LTL and TLTL. ACM Trans. Softw. Eng. Methodol. **20**(4), 1–64 (2011). https://doi.org/10.1145/2000799.2000800

10. Chandra, A.K., Kozen, D.C., Stockmeyer, L.J.: Alternation. J. ACM **28**(1), 114–133 (1981). https://doi.org/10.1145/322234.322243

11. Falcone, Y., Fernandez, J.C., Mounier, L.: What can you verify and enforce at runtime? Int. J. Softw. Tools Technol. Transf. **14**(3), 349–382 (2012). https://doi.org/10.1007/s10009-011-0196-8

12. Fellah, A., Jürgensen, H., Yu, S.: Constructions for alternating finite automata*. Int. J. Comput. Math. **35**(1–4), 117–132 (1990). https://doi.org/10.1080/00207169008803893

13. Francalanza, A., et al.: A foundation for runtime monitoring. In: RV, pp. 8–29 (2017). https://doi.org/10.1007/978-3-319-67531-2_2

14. Francalanza, A., Aceto, L., Ingolfsdottir, A.: Monitorability for the Hennessy-Milner logic with recursion. Form. Methods Syst. Des. **51**(1), 87–116 (2017). https://doi.org/10.1007/s10703-017-0273-z

15. Kozen, D.C.: Results on the propositional μ-calculus. Theor. Comput. Sci. **27**, 333–354 (1983). https://doi.org/10.1016/0304-3975(82)90125-6

16. Larsen, K.G.: Proof systems for satisfiability in Hennessy-Milner logic with recursion. Theor. Comput. Sci. (TCS) **72**(2), 265–288 (1990). https://doi.org/10.1016/0304-3975(90)90038-J. http://www.sciencedirect.com/science/article/pii/030439759090038J

17. Pnueli, A., Zaks, A.: PSL model checking and run-time verification via testers. In: Misra, J., Nipkow, T., Sekerinski, E. (eds.) FM 2006. LNCS, vol. 4085, pp. 573–586. Springer, Heidelberg (2006). https://doi.org/10.1007/11813040_38

Runtime Verification of Parametric Properties Using SMEDL

Teng Zhang$^{(\boxtimes)}$, Ramneet Kaur, Insup Lee, and Oleg Sokolsky

University of Pennsylvania, Philadelphia, PA 19104, USA
{tengz,ramneetk,lee,sokolsky}@cis.upenn.edu

Abstract. Parametric properties are typical properties to be checked in runtime verification (RV). As a common technique for parametric monitoring, trace slicing divides an execution trace into a set of sub traces which are checked against non-parametric base properties. An efficient trace slicing algorithm is implemented in *MOP*. Another RV technique, *QEA* further allows for nested use of universal and existential quantification over parameters. In this paper, we present a methodology for parametric monitoring using the RV framework SMEDL. Trace slicing algorithm in MOP can be expressed by execution of a set of SMEDL monitors. Moreover, the semantics of nested quantifiers is encoded by a hierarchy of monitors for aggregating verdicts of sub traces. Through case studies, we demonstrate that SMEDL provides a natural way to monitor parametric properties with more potentials for flexible deployment and optimizations.

Keywords: Runtime verification · Parametric property · Trace slicing · SMEDL

1 Introduction

Runtime verification (RV) is a technique for monitoring correctness of systems. The objective of RV is to use runtime monitors to check properties against a run of a system (referred as a target system) which can be abstracted as an event trace from the execution or the logging information. Usually, the event stream delivered to a monitor carries data bound to event parameters. The property may depend not only on event order in the trace but also on parameter values of events.

Example 1: unsafeMapIter [26]. An iterator of a collection created from a map is not allowed to be used after the map has been updated. The property that points out the violation of it can be described as a parametric regular expression: $createC(m, c)updateM(m)^*createI(c, i)useI(i)^*updateM(m)^+useI(i)$

This work is supported in part by the Air Force Research Laboratory (AFRL) and Defense Advanced Research Projects Agency (DARPA) under contract FA8750-16-C-0007 and by ONR SBIR contract N00014-15-C-0126.

© Springer Nature Switzerland AG 2019
E. Bartocci et al. (Eds.): From Reactive Systems to Cyber-Physical Systems, LNCS 11500, pp. 276–293, 2019.
https://doi.org/10.1007/978-3-030-31514-6_16

where $createC(m, c)$ denotes creation of a collection c, the key set of a map m; $createI(c, i)$ is creation of iterator i from c; $updateM(m)$ is update of m; and $useI(i)$ is use of i.

To monitor parametric properties, an efficient trace slicing algorithm is implemented in the MOP framework [26]. A parametric event trace is sliced into sub traces according to event parameters. Each sub trace is then checked against a non-parametric property. The property of the whole trace is obtained by aggregation of verdicts from all sub traces. QEA [4] further supports nested use of universal or existential quantifiers over parameters.

In [33], we presented a general RV framework SMEDL. A monitoring system in SMEDL is composed of a set of monitor instances communicating with each other using events, forming a *monitor network*. Instances can be created dynamically by binding monitor parameters with values. A scalable monitor network can not only describe multiple types of properties such temporal properties and numeric properties but also provides a flexible and intuitive way for monitor deployment [32], which is vital for balancing between the overhead of monitoring and timeliness of getting verdicts.

In this paper, we will further use SMEDL to describe and check parametric properties. We will present a transformation from MOP to SMEDL through an example of a MOP specification. The trace slicing algorithm can be represented by execution and evolution of a monitor network. We then will present that the semantics of nested quantifiers in QEA can be described by a hierarchy of SMEDL monitors aggregating verdicts from sub traces. Due to its flexibility in specifying monitors and communications, SMEDL may check parametric properties with more potentials for flexible deployment and optimizations.

The paper is organized as follows. Section 2 gives definitions of SMEDL and introduces MOP and QEA. Section 3 presents a transformation algorithm from MOP to SMEDL and illustrates how to check parametric properties using SMEDL monitors. Section 4 presents how to construct SMEDL monitors to express nested quantifiers in QEA. Section 5 presents the related work and Sect. 6 concludes the paper and presents the future work.

2   Preliminaries

2.1   Overview of SMEDL

A SMEDL specification contains a set of monitor specifications and an architecture description that captures patterns of communication between them. The relation between a SMEDL specification and a monitor network is illustrated in Fig. 1. During execution, each monitor can be instantiated as monitor instances multiple times with different parameters, either statically during startup of the target system or dynamically at runtime, in response to receiving *creation* events. The event communication and creation of instances within the monitor network is controlled by a *global wrapper* according to the architecture description.

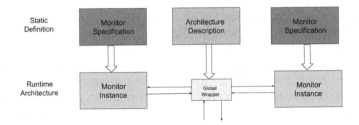

Fig. 1. SMEDL overview

Single Monitor. A SMEDL monitor is a collection of *scenarios*. Each scenario is an EFSM (Extended Finite State Machine) [33] in which the transitions are performed by reacting to events. Scenarios interact with each other using shared state variables or by triggering execution of other scenarios through raised events. There are three types of events: *imported, exported* and *internal*. Imported events, which are responsible for triggering the execution of a monitor, are raised from the target system or by other monitors; exported events are raised within the monitor and sent to other monitors; internal events are used to trigger transitions, but are only seen and processed within the monitor. Each transition is labeled with a triggering event and attached to a guard condition and a list of actions to be executed after the transition. Actions on transitions can raise events and update state variables. A monitor may have a set of typed parameters for identification. Multiple instances are created by binding parameters with actual values. The detailed syntax and semantics of a monitor was presented in [34].

Architecture Description and Monitor Network. The architecture description defines the event communication pattern among monitors, which consists of a set of *monitor interfaces* and *event connection specifications*. The interface of an monitor contains the name, parameter list, imported events and exported events of that monitor. If an imported event is labeled as a *creation* event, it can be used to create a instance of that monitor. When multiple instances exist, a finer control on delivery of events is desirable. For instance, we could specify that an event raised by an instance of monitor A is sent to instances of monitor B having the same value on the first parameter. This is achieved by *event connection specifications*.

An event connection specification is a tuple $(SrcMon, SrcEv, TarMon, TarEv, PatternExprs)$, which specifies how a source event $SrcEv$ exported from a source monitor $SrcMon$ is delivered to a target monitor $TarMon$ as its imported event $TarEv$. Note that $SrcMon$ is empty if $SrcEv$ is sent from the target system. Each parameter of a monitor or an event corresponds to an index according to its position in the parameter list, starting from 0. Each element of $PatternExpr$ is a tuple $(targetIdx, source, sourceIdx)$, meaning that the parameter value of $TarMon$ with index $targetIdx$ must be matched to the parameter value of $source$ with index $sourceIdx$. $source$ can be either $SrcMon$ or $SrcEv$.

For example, an event connection specification that describes event delivery from $e1(x, y)$ of $mon1\langle a\rangle$ to $e2(x', y')$ of $mon2\langle b, c\rangle$ is defined as $(mon1, e1, mon2, e2, ps)$ where ps is $\{(0, mon1, 0), (1, e1, 0)\}$. Note that (x, y) is the formal parameter list of $e1$; a is the formal parameter of $mon1$ and so on. When an event instance $e1(x1, y1)$ is sent from an monitor instance $mon1(a1)$, only one monitor instance of $mon2$, $mon2(a1, x1)$ receives it as $e2(x1, y1)$ as ps specifies that the first and second parameter of $mon2$ are respectively matched to the first parameter of $mon1$ and $e1$. $e2$ is instantiated by parameters of $e1$.

If there is no instance of $mon2$ parameterized with $(a1, x1)$ and $e2$ is a creation event for $mon2$, $mon2(a1, x1)$ will be created. Note that if $TarEv$ is a creation event, corresponding $PatternExprs$ must specify mapping relations to all parameters of $TarMon$. If $PatternExprs$ is empty, each raised $SrcEv$ is sent to all existing instances of $TarMon$.

The overall flow of event processing conducted by a monitor network is illustrated in Fig. 2. The global wrapper receives/outputs events from/to the environment and controls event dispatch to monitor instances and creation of instances using the architecture description. Two shared data structures, $InnerQueue$ and $OutputQueue$ are used to store events that are to be consumed within the monitor network and sent to the environment. The execution of the global wrapper begins with an event from the environment put into the $InnerQueue$. The global wrapper waits for the next incoming event from the environment after all events in the $InnerQueue$ have been consumed and events in the $OutputQueue$ have been sent to the environment.

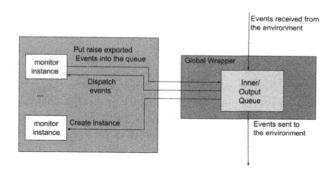

Fig. 2. Architecture of a monitor network

The pseudocode for the global wrapper is shown in Algorithm 1, parameterized by the architecture description. $monTypeList$ is the list of all monitors used for checking the property. Initially, an imported event e is sent from the environment into $InnerQueue$ to trigger the execution of the global wrapper. The global wrapper pulls out the event (denoted as $curE$) at the frontend of $InnerQueue$. $curE$ is mapped to the event in m (denoted as ev) in $matchIn$-$ComingEvent$ by looking up the architecture description. Monitors that cannot handle *curE* are filtered out before traversing *monTypeList*. Process *consume* dispatches *ev* to all compatible instances of *m*. The set of raised events *ies* and *oes* are then put into the *InnerQueue* and *OutputQueue* based on whether they are to be consumed within the monitor network. Note that all raised events carry the parameter information of corresponding instances which have raised them. If there is no compatible instance and *ev* is a creation event, an instance of *m* is created from *ev*. After all events in the *InnerQueue* have been handled, events in the *OutputQueue* will be sent to the environment or raised as alarms. It is worth noting that *consume* is an abstract representation of monitor execution. Moreover, we leave implementation flexibility in the algorithm. For instance, no order is defined in *monTypeList*. In Sect. 3, we impose a specific order among monitors in *monTypeList* to implement the trace slicing algorithm in MOP.

Algorithm 1. Global wrapper for parametric monitoring

1: $InnerQueue \leftarrow \{e\}, OutputQueue \leftarrow \{\}$
2: **procedure** GLOBALSTEP(archDescription)
3:       $monTypeList \leftarrow$ *monitors declared in archDescription*
4:       **while** $InnerQueue \neq \emptyset$ **do**
5:             $curE \leftarrow retrieveFromQueue(InnerQueue)$
6:             **for** $m \in filter(monTypeList, curE, archDescription)$ **do**
7:                   $ev \leftarrow matchInComingEvent(curE, m, archDescription)$
8:                   $(ies, oes) \leftarrow consume(m, archDescription, ev)$
9:                   $enQueue(InnerQueue, ies)$
10:                 $enQueue(OutputQueue, oes)$
11:     $sendEvents(OutputQueue)$

2.2   Overview of MOP

MOP is a monitoring framework supporting description of properties by multiple logical formalisms. In this paper, we only consider properties that are synthesized into FSMs (Finite State Machines). One can specify different ways of reporting verdicts and handling violations or validations of properties. A MOP monitor $M_{mop}\langle X_{mop}\rangle$ contains two parts. X_{mop} is the parameter set and M_{mop} is an finite state machine (FSM).

MOP implements an efficient trace slicing algorithm [11] for parametric monitoring, which is independent of the base monitor for checking the non-parametric property. The algorithm maintains a mapping Δ from bindings to current states in the base monitor. A *binding* is a partial function $X_{mop} \rightharpoonup Val$ from parameters to values. *Val* represents the set of all possible values for X_{mop}. Parameters of all parametric events are from X_{mop}. We denote $e\langle\theta\rangle$ as an event parameterized by the binding θ.

When an event $e\langle\theta\rangle$ arrives, the algorithm will update states of all existing bindings which has equal or more information than θ using e. If $dom(\theta_1)$ (the domain of θ_1) is the subset of $dom(\theta_2)$ and $\theta_1(x) = \theta_2(x)$ for all x $\in dom(\theta_1)$, we say θ_1 has equal or less information than θ_2, denoted as $\theta_1 \sqsubseteq \theta_2$.

If $\Delta(\theta)$ is undefined (and e is defined as a creation event in MOP), the algorithm will define $\Delta(\theta)$ using the state updated from $\Delta(\theta')$ by e where θ' is the largest binding in $dom(\Delta)$ that has less information than $\Delta(\theta)$. New bindings can also be created from extending existing bindings in Δ that are *compatible* with θ. Two bindings θ_1 and θ_2 are *compatible* with each other when $\theta_1(x)$ is equal to $\theta_2(x)$ for all $x \in dom(\theta_1) \cap dom(\theta_2)$. The *combination* between two bindings θ_1 and θ_2 is defined as follows: if θ_1 and θ_2 are compatible, $\theta_1 \sqcup \theta_2(x) = \theta_1(x)$ if $x \in dom(\theta_1)$; $\theta_1 \sqcup \theta_2(x) = \theta_2(x)$ if $x \in dom(\theta_2)$; $\theta_1 \sqcup \theta_2(x)$ is undefined if x is undefined in θ_1 and θ_2. The algorithm will always extend the binding with more information in e to generate the new binding. The detailed description for the slicing algorithm is in [11]. The notations introduced here will be reused in the rest of the paper.

SMEDL vs. MOP. In MOP, the mechanism for creating and updating parameter instances is controlled by the slicing algorithm which is independent of the monitor specification. Partially instantiated monitor instances are maintained in the algorithm. By contrast, SMEDL realizes parametric monitoring at the level of the semantics of monitor network. All monitor instances are created with full instantiation. In Sect. 3, we present a transformation from a MOP specification to a set of SMEDL monitors connecting through events. The idea is to analyze the structure of a parametric FSM in MOP and generate SMEDL monitors that are to be fully instantiated by creation events. The information of how to extend and update bindings is encoded in the single monitor specifications and the architecture description. The architecture description guarantees that events are only sent to compatible monitor instances.

2.3   Overview of QEA

QEA (Quantified Event Automata) is a formalism for parametric monitoring. A QEA is a pair $\langle \Lambda, E \rangle$ where E is an *Event Automaton* and $\Lambda \in (\{\forall, \exists\} \times vars(E) \times Guard)^*$ is a list of quantifiers with guards. An Event Automaton (EA) is an EFSM in which transitions are enriched with guard and assignments to variables; $vars(E)$ is the set of variable names appearing in E. In this paper, we focus on the semantics of nested quantifiers [4,27]. QEA also uses trace slicing to accomplish parametric monitoring. The acceptance for a parametric property for QEA is defined in [4], as illustrated below. In the terminology of QEA, a *ground* trace contains events of which all parameters are bound to concrete values; $Dom(\tau)(x)$ returns the derived domain for the parameter x in the trace τ; $\theta_1 \dagger \theta_2$ overrides the value in θ_1 by θ_2; $g(\theta)$ is the guard condition over the quantified variable; $E(\theta)$ is an event automaton E with its variables instantiated by θ; $\tau \downarrow_{E(\theta)}$ is the projection of a trace τ over $E(\theta)$; $L(E(\theta))$ is the set of traces accepted by $E(\theta)$.

Definition 1 (Acceptance in QEA). *A QEA accepts a ground trace τ if $\tau \models_{\langle\rangle} \Lambda.E$ where $\models_\theta$ is defined as*

$\tau \models_\theta (\forall x : g)\Lambda'.E$ iff $\forall\ d \in Dom(\tau)(x),$ if $g(\theta\dagger\langle x \to d\rangle)$ then $\tau \models_{\theta\dagger\langle x \to d\rangle} \Lambda'.E.$

$\tau \models_\theta (\exists x : g)\Lambda'.E$ iff there exists $d \in Dom(\tau)(x),$ if $g(\theta \dagger \langle x \to d\rangle)$ then
$\tau \models_{\theta\dagger\langle x \to d\rangle} \Lambda'.E.$

$\tau \models_\theta \epsilon.E$ iff $\tau \downarrow_{E(\theta)} \in L(E(\theta)).$

Bindings are generated by inductively traversing the derived domain of each variable in the nested quantifiers. When a full binding is created, the verdict is retrieved from the corresponding event automaton. The aggregation of the result is decided by which quantifier is used for a parameter variable. The interpretation of nested quantifiers in QEA leads to one significance difference between QEA and MOP in generating bindings: QEA records any binding that can be built from the derived domain that has a non-empty projection. For example, if $e(\theta)$ arrives where $\theta = \langle x \to x1, y \to y1\rangle$ and there is a binding $\theta_1 = \langle y \to y2, z \to z1\rangle$ ($y1 \neq y2$), a new binding $\theta' = \langle x \to x1, y \to y2, z \to z1\rangle$ would be created with e adding to its trace projection.

SMEDL vs. QEA. QEA has a uniform algorithm to handle the semantics of nested quantifiers. However, if the property indicates relations between quantified variables by events which cannot be described by the guard condition, bindings that do not comply with the relations may be generated. In Sect. 4, we will show that the semantics of nested quantifiers can be encoded through hierarchical *aggregation* monitors in SMEDL. Moreover, we will demonstrate that SMEDL can check the property involving the relation between quantified variables by properly generating monitor instances.

3   Implementation of Trace Slicing in SMEDL

This section presents how to use SMEDL to implement the trace slicing algorithm in MOP. Through an example, we first present a transformation from an FSM-based MOP monitor into a set of SMEDL monitors. Then, we propose the detailed design of the global wrapper mentioned in Sect. 2.1 and demonstrate that a monitor network in SMEDL controlled by the global wrapper can correctly monitor parametric properties.

We present a transformation from an FSM-based MOP monitor to a SMEDL specification based on the Example 1 in Sect. 1. Recall that Example 1 states a property *UnsafeMapIter* that an iterator of a collection must not be used after the corresponding map of that collection is updated. *UnsafeMapIter* has a parameter set with three variables: map(m), collection(c) and iterator(i). The FSM definition is illustrated in Fig. 3. The shaded states are accepting states, meaning there is no violation of the property. Note that the original FSM is complete (which means for each event in the alphabet of the FSM, there exists at least one transition triggered by the event from all states of that FSM) while self-looping transitions are omitted for clearer illustration. The process of constructing a set of SMEDL monitors corresponding to *UnsafeMapIter* are presented below.

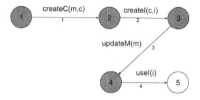

Fig. 3. FSM definition of *UnsafeMapIter*

Recall that when a SMEDL monitor instance is created, all its parameters should be bound to a value. As a result, multiple monitors with different parameters are necessary. In *UnsafeMapIter*, there are four events, $createC(m, c)$, $updateM(m)$, $createI(c, i)$ and $useI(i)$. All possible combinations of parameter variables include $\langle m \rangle$, $\langle i \rangle$, $\langle m, c \rangle$, $\langle c, i \rangle$, $\langle m, i \rangle$ and $\langle m, c, i \rangle$. Generally, a SMEDL monitor should be created for each combination. However, since $createC(m, c)$ is the only event that can start a trace [26], only two bindings $\langle m, c \rangle$ and $\langle m, c, i \rangle$ will be generated and maintained in MOP. Two SMEDL monitors, $mc\langle m, c \rangle$ and $mci\langle m, c, i \rangle$ are to be constructed.

The specifications of mc and mci are illustrated in Fig. 4. mc is responsible for storing all seen value pairs of (m, c) carried by $createC$. When mc receives $createI(c, i)$, $createM2(i)$ is raised to trigger creation of a new instance of mci carrying the value of (m, c, i). Note that $createM2(i)$ only carries i because mci knows which instance of mc has raised it. mci then checks whether $useI(i)$ happens after $updateM(m)$.

To construct SMEDL monitors from an FSM specification, the first step is to map states in the FSM into states in the SMEDL specifications. In *UnsafeMapIter*, m and c are bound in state 2 while i is further bound in state 3, 4 and 5. As a result, we map state 2 into mc and state 3, 4 and 5 into mci. In the rest of the paper, we assume that corresponding states between the FSM and the SMEDL specifications have the same name.

Then, the transitions in the FSM are mapped into SMEDL monitors. If the source and target state of a transition in the FSM carry the same parameter information, then it can be directly mapped to the corresponding SMEDL specification. For instance, transition 8 and 9 in mci are mapped from transition 3 and 4 in the FSM definition. If a transition $tr : s1 \rightarrow s2$ by an event e has the source and target state with different parameter information θ_1 and θ_2, there are two cases. If θ_1 is empty, a transition from the initial state s to $s2$ is generated in the SMEDL monitor $m\langle \theta_2 \rangle$. For instance, transition 5 in mc is mapped from transition 1 in the FSM. If θ_1 is not empty, two transitions are generated. One is in $m\langle \theta_1 \rangle$ from $s1$ to $s1$ triggered by e with raising an event re. Another one is in $m'\langle \theta_2 \rangle$ from the initial state s to $s2$, triggered by re. For instance, transition 6 in mc and transition 7 mci are generated from transition 2 in the FSM. Omitted transitions in the FSM are also mapped to mc and mci in the same way. We could also further optimize mc and mci by removing unnecessary transitions.

For instance, mc does not need to receive $useI$ or $updateM$ while mci does not need to receive $createI$ and $createC$.

Finally, the communication is specified in the architecture description. The communication between mc and mci is specified as: $\langle mc, createM2, mci,$ $createM2, ps \rangle$ where ps is $\{\langle 0, mc, 0 \rangle, \langle 1, mc, 1 \rangle, \langle 2, createM2, 0 \rangle\}$. Note that the two $createM2$ in the architecture description represent the exported event of mc and the imported event of mci and ps specifies that m and c of mci are from the first and second parameter of mc while i is from the first parameter of $createM2$. The communication between mc and the environment is defined as: (1) $\langle null, createC, mc, createC, ps1 \rangle$ where $ps1$ is $\{\langle 0, createC, 0 \rangle, \langle 1, createC, 1 \rangle\}$; (2) $\langle null, createI, mc, createI, \{\langle 1, createI, 0 \rangle\}\rangle$, respectively specifying how $createC$ and $createI$ are sent to mc.

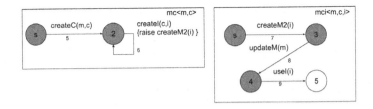

Fig. 4. SMEDL definition of *UnsafeMapIter*

The monitor design and connection specified in the architecture description statically describe how bindings are created or extended by other bindings. To fully implement the trace slicing algorithm, we need to impose an order to elements in $monTypeList$ in Algorithm 1 according to the relation $\sqsubseteq$ over monitor parameters: if $\theta_2 \sqsubseteq \theta_1$, $m\langle \theta_1 \rangle$ is placed before $m'\langle \theta_2 \rangle$ in $monTypeList$. Note that no two monitors in $monTypeList$ will have identical parameter list. A monitor with more parameter information (which means in the front of $monTypeList$) will be executed before the one with less parameter information. Corresponding raised events will also be placed in the $InnerQueue$ following this order. This ensures that an instance will be created by the creation event carrying the most parameter information, complying with the slicing algorithm that always creates a new binding by extending the most informative binding if possible.

We use an event trace $\tau : updateM\langle m_1 \rangle, createC\langle m_1, c_1 \rangle, createC\langle m_2, c_2 \rangle,$ $createI\langle c_1, i_1 \rangle, useI\langle i_1 \rangle$ [26] to illustrate the execution of the global wrapper. The state evolution of mc and mci is given in Table 1. Since $updateM$ is not the creation event of mc or mci, no instance is created. When $createC\langle m_1, c_1 \rangle$ and $createC\langle m_2, c_2 \rangle$ arrive, two instances of mc are created and transitioned to state 2. $createI\langle c_1, i_1 \rangle$ triggers the creation of $mci\langle m_1, c_1, i_1 \rangle$ by sending $createM2(i_1)$ to mci. $mci\langle m_1, c_1, i_1 \rangle$ is in state 3 after creation. $useI\langle i_1 \rangle$ is sent to $mci\langle m_1, c_1, i_1 \rangle$ and a self-looping transition is executed. It is worth noting that no instance of $mci\langle m_2, c_2, i_1 \rangle$ is created. This indicates that SMEDL can not only implement the trace slicing but provide a flexible way for optimization.

Table 1. State update of SMEDL monitors given τ

updateM(m_1)	createC(m_1,c_1)	createC(m_2,c_2)	createI(c_1,i_1)	useI(i_1)
$\emptyset$	$mc\langle m_1, c_1\rangle$:2	$mc\langle m_1, c_1\rangle$:2 $mc\langle m_2, c_2\rangle$:2	$mc\langle m_1, c_1\rangle$:2 $mc\langle m_2, c_2\rangle$:2 $mci\langle m_1, c_1, i_1\rangle$:3	$mc\langle m_1, c_1\rangle$:2 $mc\langle m_2, c_2\rangle$:2 $mci\langle m_1, c_1, i_1\rangle$:3

In the more general case, one monitor may have more than one creation event and a subset of them may be raised reacting to an incoming event. We modify the property *UnsafeMapIter*, changing the parameters of *createI* to $\langle m, c, i\rangle$ and trying to catching the illegal behavior that *createI* arrives before *createC*. The SMEDL specification is illustrated in Fig. 5(a). Suppose a setting in which there is an instance $mc\langle m_1, c_1\rangle$ and no instance $mci\langle m_1, c_1, i_1\rangle$. When $createI\langle m_1, c_1, i_1\rangle$ is sent to mc and mci, it will first trigger the execution of mci before mc because it has more parameter information than mc, as presented below. As a result, a new instance $mci\langle m_1, c_1, i_1\rangle$ is created and transitioned to state 5. However, it is not consistent with the semantics of the slicing algorithm, which would create $mci\langle m_1, c_1, i_1\rangle$ by *createM2* raised from $mc\langle m_1, c_1\rangle$ by $createI\langle m_1, c_1, i_1\rangle$. To achieve the desired result, the SMEDL specification is modified as shown in Fig. 5(b), which removes *createI* as a creation event of mci. Instead, *createI* is a creation event of mc, corresponding to transition 11. This modification guarantees that an instance of mci can always be created by the correct event.

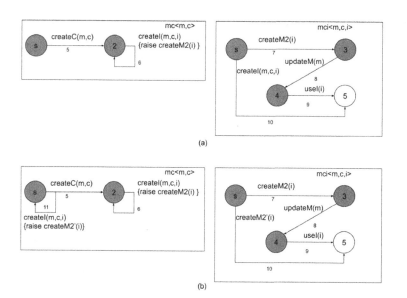

(a)

(b)

Fig. 5. Modification of SMEDL definition of *UnsafeMapIter*

We test the SMEDL specification in Fig. 5(b) using two traces $\tau_1 : createI$ $\langle m_1, c_1, i_1 \rangle$ and $\tau_2 : createC \langle m_1, c_1 \rangle, createI \langle m_1, c_1, i_1 \rangle$. For τ_1, $mc \langle m_1, c_1 \rangle$ and $mci \langle m_1, c_1, i_1 \rangle$ are created in state s and state 5. For τ_2, $mc \langle m_1, c_1 \rangle$ and $mci \langle m_1, c_1, i_1 \rangle$ are in state 2 and state 3.

4   Expressing Quantifiers in SMEDL

This section further explores expressing parametric properties with nested quantifiers introduced in QEA. We first propose a methodology to implement aggregation using a SMEDL monitor network through Example 2 below. Then we use a modified version of Example 2 to illustrate the flexibility of SMEDL to implement aggregation when the relation between parameters needs to be considered. The SMEDL specifications for Example 2 (also Example 4 below) are available online[1].

Example 2: candidateSelection [4]. For every voter there must exist a party that the voter is a member of, and the voter must rank all candidates for that party. The QEA specification is shown in Fig. 6, which contains two parts, the declaration of nested quantifiers and an event automaton (EA). There are three quantified variables, v(voter), c(candidate) and p(party) and three parametric events *member*, *candidate* and *rank*. The third parameter r of *rank* is an unquantified variable. The shaded circles in the EA represent accepting states. Self-looping transitions are omitted. To simplify the presentation, we impose a restriction on event order of traces: all *candidate* events always happen after all *member* events and all *rank* events happen after all *candidate* events.

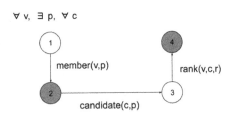

Fig. 6. QEA specification for candidate selection

The EA is transformed into a set of SMEDL monitors using the same process proposed in Sect. 3, as illustrated in Fig. 7. When fed with event trace τ_3 : $member(tom, red), member(ali, blue), candidate(jim, red), candidate(flo, red),$ $candidate(don, blue), \ rank(tom, jim, 1), rank(ali, don, 1)$, corresponding state evolution for the monitor network is shown in Table 2. Compared with bindings generated by execution of QEA in [4], fewer instances are generated.

---

[1] https://github.com/tengz2019/parametricSMEDL.

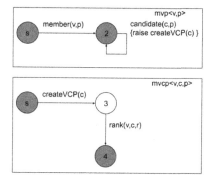

Fig. 7. SMEDL monitors for candidate selection

Table 2. State update of SMEDL monitors given τ_3

member(t,r)	member(a,b)	candidate(j,r)	candidate(f,r)	candidate(d,b)	rank(t,j,1)	rank(a,d,1)
$mvp\langle t,r\rangle{:}2$	$mvp\langle t,r\rangle{:}2$ $mvp\langle a,b\rangle{:}2$	$mvp\langle t,r\rangle{:}2$ $mvp\langle a,b\rangle{:}2$ $mvcp\langle t,j,r\rangle{:}3$	$mvp\langle t,r\rangle{:}2$ $mvp\langle a,b\rangle{:}2$ $mvcp\langle t,j,r\rangle{:}3$ $mvcp\langle t,f,r\rangle{:}3$	$mvp\langle t,r\rangle{:}2$ $mvp\langle a,b\rangle{:}2$ $mvcp\langle t,j,r\rangle{:}3$ $mvcp\langle t,f,r\rangle{:}3$ $mvcp\langle a,d,b\rangle{:}3$	$mvp\langle t,r\rangle{:}2$ $mvp\langle a,b\rangle{:}2$ $mvcp\langle t,j,r\rangle{:}4$ $mvcp\langle t,f,r\rangle{:}3$ $mvcp\langle a,d,b\rangle{:}3$	$mvp\langle t,r\rangle{:}2$ $mvp\langle a,b\rangle{:}2$ $mvcp\langle t,j,r\rangle{:}4$ $mvcp\langle t,f,r\rangle{:}3$ $mvcp\langle a,d,b\rangle{:}4$

For example, there is a binding $\langle v : a, p : r, c : j\rangle : candidate(j,r)$ in QEA (all values are abbreviated to the initial alphabet) but not in SMEDL. This binding does not influence the verdict of the property for τ_3 because *ali* is not a member of *red* and the property only requires the existence of a party.

The architecture is illustrated in Fig. 8. The high level idea is to use a hierarchy of *aggregation monitors* to implement the semantics of nested quantifiers. For each quantified variable, an aggregation monitor is constructed which receives checking results from other monitor instances and aggregates them using logical operations such as conjunction or disjunction. Each $mvcp\langle v,c,p\rangle$ instance checks whether the voter v belonging to the party p has ranked the candidate c in the trace and sends the result in *resultVCP* to *collectC*. Moreover, when a new instance of *mvcp* is created, a *countC* event is raised and sent to *collectC*. $collectC\langle v,p\rangle$ is the conjunction of all verdicts from instances of *mvcp* matching v and p to check whether all candidates of p have been ranked by v. By calculating disjunction on all verdicts from *collectC* matching v, $collectP\langle v\rangle$ further checks whether there exists a party to which v belongs that all candidates of p have been ranked by v. Finally, $collectV\langle\rangle$ is the conjunction of verdicts collected from all instances of *collectP* to compute the verdict for the property. Event *end* is used to trigger outputting verdicts from *mvcp*. It is also sent to *collectV* in case the trace is empty. From *mvcp* to *collectP*, each monitor sends two types of events to its downstream neighbor. One type is to count number of instances of the upstream monitor while another type carries the verdict for each instance. In this way, the downstream monitor knows whether it has already received all verdicts from its upstream monitor.

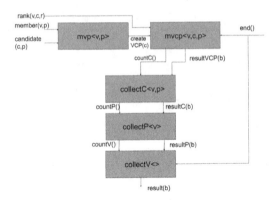

Fig. 8. Architecture for candidate selection

To justify the correctness of the structure above, we need to prove that (1) the generated *mvcp* instances are sufficient to check the property and (2) the structure of aggregation monitors correctly implement the semantics of nested quantifiers. For (1), instances of *mvcp* only contains all tuples of $\langle v, c, p \rangle$ satisfying the relation that v is a member of p and c is a candidate of p, which is sufficient for checking the property. For (2), *collectC* guarantees that given a voter and a party, the verdicts for all candidates belonging to the party are aggregated by conjunction, complying with the semantics of $\forall c$. Similarly, we could justify that *collectP* implements $\exists c$. For each voter, if there exist candidates for a party to which the voter belongs, *collectV* collects the verdict from the corresponding *collectP*. If all parties to which the voter belongs do not have candidate, *collectV* does not need to check that voter because no instance of *mvcp* is instantiated with the voter and *mvp* only contains accepting states. As a result, *collectV* implements $\forall v$ by conjunction over verdicts from all *collectP*. As mentioned above, fewer bindings are generated by SMEDL monitors than QEA, which illustrates that SMEDL has good efficiency in memory use.

Furthermore, by using the hierarchy structure, SMEDL can implement the semantics of nested quantifiers where quantified variables are related to each other using events. Two properties modified from *candidateSelection* are given below.

Example 3. For each voter and for each party that the voter is a member of, the voter must rank all candidates for that party.

Example 4. Each voter must belong to each party and he/she must rank all candidates for that party.

The same architecture illustrated in Fig. 8 can be used to monitor Example 3, except that *collectP* is a conjunction over verdicts from *collectC* instead of disjunction. Example 4 is different from Example 3 in the sense that the monitor needs to check whether each voter is bound with all parties appearing in the trace. The architecture for monitors checking Example 4 is shown in Fig. 9.

countPFront⟨*p*⟩ and *countP*⟨⟩ work together to count the domain of the party in the trace and send it to *collectPUniv*⟨*v*⟩ (conjunction version of *collectP*) to check whether *v* is the member of all parties. *collectC* is created using *createVP* because the monitor needs to check whether *member* is received for all parties given each voter. Moreover, *end* triggers the output of *countP*, which triggers *collectC* to send the verdict to *collectPUniv*. This order ensures that *collectPUniv* can get the number of parties before receiving verdicts from *collectC*.

Recall that the binding ⟨*v* : *a*, *p* : *r*, *c* : *j*⟩ : *candidate*(*j*, *r*) is generated in τ_3 for the original QEA specification. This would lead to violation of Example 3 even if the voter *ali* does not belong to *red*. To monitor it using QEA, apart from changing existential quantifier to universal one for *p*, we also need to add restriction to *p* in the guard condition or modify EA by setting state 1 as an accepting state.

Through examples presented above, we demonstrate that SMEDL is capable of describing and checking parametric properties with nested quantifiers while generating fewer bindings. Moreover, the hierarchy of aggregation monitors is flexible to describe relation between quantified variables. As a future work, we will propose a general process to generate aggregation monitors for parametric properties.

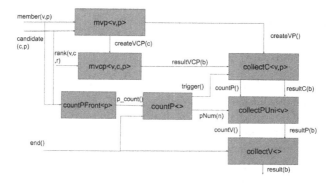

Fig. 9. Modification of architecture for candidate selection

5   Related Work

Apart from MOP and QEA, there have been a considerable number of studies about handling data in RV. In [1], Allan et al. present *Tracematches* in *AspectJ* [24] to support event matching with values of parameters. *RV-monitor* [25] and *Movec* [12] use the trace slicing algorithm proposed in [11] to support parametric monitoring. In [3], Ballarin presents a generalization of the slicing algorithm in [11] to support slicing with patterns and constraints. *Larva* [14] and its derived tool *polyLarva* [13] and *Valour* [2] support parametric monitoring by dynamic creation of monitor instances. But all parameters are quantified by universal quantifier.

Several formalisms of temporal logic have been proposed for parametric monitoring such as *JLO* [30], *LTL-FO*$^+$ [20], *LTL*^{FO} [10], *MFOTL* [9], *Monitor Modulo Theories* [16]. Rule-based RV technique is expressive to support data parameterization [5,8], from which a lot of tools and techniques have been derived such as *LogScope* [6], *TraceContract* [7], *LogFire* [22] and *data automata* [21]. There are also more research on exploring the relation between specification techniques for parametric monitoring. In [28] Reger et al. present a subset of syntactic fragments in first-order temporal logic that are sliceable and transform them into automata for slicing. In [29], a transformation from QEA to rule-based system is presented and differences between these two techniques with respect to parametric monitoring are highlighted.

In [18], Goubault-Larrecq and Olivain present *Orchids*, an intrusion detection tool. Monitors can by dynamically spawned reacting to possible beginnings of attacks. In [19], *TOPL automata* is presented based on register automata [23] for runtime verification of systems with unbounded resource generation. The key features of TOPL automata are use of registers and non-determinism. In [31], Yamagata et al. present a formalism CSP_E for monitoring concurrent systems. Parametric properties are expressed by recursive parametric processes. *Lola* [15] is a stream-based language for monitoring of synchronous systems. In [17], Lola 2.0 is presented for complex security properties. Parameterized stream templates and dynamic stream generation are added to the language to better support parametric monitoring.

6   Discussion and Conclusion

In this paper, we compared the approach to parametric monitoring adopted in SMEDL with well established frameworks of MOP and QEA. Through a transformation from MOP and QEA-inspired specification to SMEDL, we showed how SMEDL can reproduce monitoring behavior of these frameworks. In addition, SMEDL does not encode quantifiers in its semantics but rather implements them as additional aggregator monitors. We note that the size of monitoring specifications in SMEDL can grow as we avoid partial instantiations with multiple monitors. We believe that we can resort to monitor templates and automatic transformation to compensate for the increased specification size. In our future work we will study whether this affects the usability of our approach. Also note that communication between monitors is necessary in our approach, which may affect the efficiency of monitoring. At the same time, communicating monitors allow us to exploit the structure of the problem through distributed deployment of monitors, improving efficiency when monitoring large-scale systems. Carefully exploring this balance is also the subject of future work.

We are formalizing the transformation algorithm from MOP and QEA to SMEDL with correctness proof. We will also formally compare the expressiveness and parametric monitoring algorithm between SMEDL and MOP, QEA and other techniques. A preliminary prototype of the method presented in this paper has been completed. However, the work to implement the tools necessary to automatically generate and deploy the monitors is still in progress.

References

1. Allan, C., et al.: Adding trace matching with free variables to AspectJ. In: ACM SIGPLAN Notices, vol. 40, pp. 345–364. ACM (2005)
2. Azzopardi, S., Colombo, C., Ebejer, J.P., Mallia, E., Pace, G.J.: Runtime verification using VALOUR (2017)
3. Ballarin, C.: Two generalisations of Roşu and Chen's trace slicing Algorithm A. In: Bonakdarpour, B., Smolka, S.A. (eds.) RV 2014. LNCS, vol. 8734, pp. 15–30. Springer, Cham (2014). https://doi.org/10.1007/978-3-319-11164-3_3
4. Barringer, H., Falcone, Y., Havelund, K., Reger, G., Rydeheard, D.: Quantified event automata: towards expressive and efficient runtime monitors. In: Giannakopoulou, D., Méry, D. (eds.) FM 2012. LNCS, vol. 7436, pp. 68–84. Springer, Heidelberg (2012). https://doi.org/10.1007/978-3-642-32759-9_9
5. Barringer, H., Goldberg, A., Havelund, K., Sen, K.: Rule-based runtime verification. In: Steffen, B., Levi, G. (eds.) VMCAI 2004. LNCS, vol. 2937, pp. 44–57. Springer, Heidelberg (2004). https://doi.org/10.1007/978-3-540-24622-0_5
6. Barringer, H., Groce, A., Havelund, K., Smith, M.: Formal analysis of log files. J. Aerosp. Comput. Inf. Commun. **7**(11), 365–390 (2010)
7. Barringer, H., Havelund, K.: TRACECONTRACT: a Scala DSL for trace analysis. In: Butler, M., Schulte, W. (eds.) FM 2011. LNCS, vol. 6664, pp. 57–72. Springer, Heidelberg (2011). https://doi.org/10.1007/978-3-642-21437-0_7
8. Barringer, H., Rydeheard, D., Havelund, K.: Rule systems for run-time monitoring: from Eagle to RuleR. J. Log. Comput. **20**(3), 675–706 (2010)
9. Basin, D., Klaedtke, F., Müller, S., Zălinescu, E.: Monitoring metric first-order temporal properties. J. ACM (JACM) **62**(2), 15 (2015)
10. Bauer, A., Küster, J.-C., Vegliach, G.: From propositional to first-order monitoring. In: Legay, A., Bensalem, S. (eds.) RV 2013. LNCS, vol. 8174, pp. 59–75. Springer, Heidelberg (2013). https://doi.org/10.1007/978-3-642-40787-1_4
11. Chen, F., Roşu, G.: Parametric trace slicing and monitoring. In: Kowalewski, S., Philippou, A. (eds.) TACAS 2009. LNCS, vol. 5505, pp. 246–261. Springer, Heidelberg (2009). https://doi.org/10.1007/978-3-642-00768-2_23
12. Chen, Z., Wang, Z., Zhu, Y., Xi, H., Yang, Z.: Parametric runtime verification of C programs. In: Chechik, M., Raskin, J.-F. (eds.) TACAS 2016. LNCS, vol. 9636, pp. 299–315. Springer, Heidelberg (2016). https://doi.org/10.1007/978-3-662-49674-9_17
13. Colombo, C., Francalanza, A., Mizzi, R., Pace, G.J.: polyLARVA: runtime verification with configurable resource-aware monitoring boundaries. In: Eleftherakis, G., Hinchey, M., Holcombe, M. (eds.) SEFM 2012. LNCS, vol. 7504, pp. 218–232. Springer, Heidelberg (2012). https://doi.org/10.1007/978-3-642-33826-7_15
14. Colombo, C., Pace, G.J., Schneider, G.: Dynamic event-based runtime monitoring of real-time and contextual properties. In: Cofer, D., Fantechi, A. (eds.) FMICS 2008. LNCS, vol. 5596, pp. 135–149. Springer, Heidelberg (2009). https://doi.org/10.1007/978-3-642-03240-0_13
15. d'Angelo, B., et al.: LOLA: runtime monitoring of synchronous systems. In: 12th International Symposium on Temporal Representation and Reasoning, TIME 2005, pp. 166–174. IEEE (2005)
16. Decker, N., Leucker, M., Thoma, D.: Monitoring modulo theories. Int. J. Softw. Tools Technol. Transf. **18**(2), 205–225 (2016)

17. Faymonville, P., Finkbeiner, B., Schirmer, S., Torfah, H.: A stream-based specification language for network monitoring. In: Falcone, Y., Sánchez, C. (eds.) RV 2016. LNCS, vol. 10012, pp. 152–168. Springer, Cham (2016). https://doi.org/10.1007/978-3-319-46982-9_10

18. Goubault-Larrecq, J., Olivain, J.: A smell of ORCHIDS. In: Leucker, M. (ed.) RV 2008. LNCS, vol. 5289, pp. 1–20. Springer, Heidelberg (2008). https://doi.org/10.1007/978-3-540-89247-2_1

19. Grigore, R., Distefano, D., Petersen, R.L., Tzevelekos, N.: Runtime verification based on register automata. In: Piterman, N., Smolka, S.A. (eds.) TACAS 2013. LNCS, vol. 7795, pp. 260–276. Springer, Heidelberg (2013). https://doi.org/10.1007/978-3-642-36742-7_19

20. Hallé, S., Villemaire, R.: Runtime enforcement of web service message contracts with data. IEEE Trans. Serv. Comput. 5(2), 192–206 (2012)

21. Havelund, K.: Monitoring with data automata. In: Margaria, T., Steffen, B. (eds.) ISoLA 2014. LNCS, vol. 8803, pp. 254–273. Springer, Heidelberg (2014). https://doi.org/10.1007/978-3-662-45231-8_18

22. Havelund, K.: Rule-based runtime verification revisited. Int. J. Softw. Tools Technol. Transf. 17(2), 143–170 (2015)

23. Kaminski, M., Francez, N.: Finite-memory automata. Theor. Comput. Sci. 134(2), 329–363 (1994)

24. Kiczales, G., Hilsdale, E., Hugunin, J., Kersten, M., Palm, J., Griswold, W.G.: An overview of AspectJ. In: Knudsen, J.L. (ed.) ECOOP 2001. LNCS, vol. 2072, pp. 327–354. Springer, Heidelberg (2001). https://doi.org/10.1007/3-540-45337-7_18

25. Luo, Q., et al.: RV-Monitor: efficient parametric runtime verification with simultaneous properties. In: Bonakdarpour, B., Smolka, S.A. (eds.) RV 2014. LNCS, vol. 8734, pp. 285–300. Springer, Cham (2014). https://doi.org/10.1007/978-3-319-11164-3_24

26. Meredith, P.O., Jin, D., Griffith, D., Chen, F., Roşu, G.: An overview of the MOP runtime verification framework. Int. J. Softw. Tools Technol. Transf. 14(3), 249–289 (2012)

27. Reger, G.: Automata based monitoring and mining of execution traces. Ph.D. thesis, University of Manchester (2014)

28. Reger, G., Rydeheard, D.: From first-order temporal logic to parametric trace slicing. In: Bartocci, E., Majumdar, R. (eds.) RV 2015. LNCS, vol. 9333, pp. 216–232. Springer, Cham (2015). https://doi.org/10.1007/978-3-319-23820-3_14

29. Reger, G., Rydeheard, D.: From parametric trace slicing to rule systems. In: Colombo, C., Leucker, M. (eds.) RV 2018. LNCS, vol. 11237, pp. 334–352. Springer, Cham (2018). https://doi.org/10.1007/978-3-030-03769-7_19

30. Stolz, V., Bodden, E.: Temporal assertions using AspectJ. Electron. Notes Theor. Comput. Sci. 144(4), 109–124 (2006)

31. Yamagata, Y., et al.: Runtime monitoring for concurrent systems. In: Falcone, Y., Sánchez, C. (eds.) RV 2016. LNCS, vol. 10012, pp. 386–403. Springer, Cham (2016). https://doi.org/10.1007/978-3-319-46982-9_24

32. Zhang, T., Eakman, G., Lee, I., Sokolsky, O.: Flexible monitor deployment for runtime verification of large scale software. In: Margaria, T., Steffen, B. (eds.) ISoLA 2018. LNCS, vol. 11247, pp. 42–50. Springer, Cham (2018). https://doi.org/10.1007/978-3-030-03427-6_6

33. Zhang, T., Gebhard, P., Sokolsky, O.: SMEDL: combining synchronous and asynchronous monitoring. In: Falcone, Y., Sánchez, C. (eds.) RV 2016. LNCS, vol. 10012, pp. 482–490. Springer, Cham (2016). https://doi.org/10.1007/978-3-319-46982-9_32

34. Zhang, T., et al.: Correct-by-construction implementation of runtime monitors using stepwise refinement. In: Feng, X., Müller-Olm, M., Yang, Z. (eds.) SETTA 2018. LNCS, vol. 10998, pp. 31–49. Springer, Cham (2018). https://doi.org/10.1007/978-3-319-99933-3_3

Short Abstracts

Logic in the Time of Cancer: Causality and Clocks in Cancer

Bud Mishra[✉]

New York University, New York, NY, USA

Extended Abstract

A critical translational goal of cancer research is to prevent, control and cure cancer, and to do so by understanding cancer etiology better. The fact that cancer is a genomic disease with a progressive dynamics has been known for some time, but since the causal (etiological) explanations have shifted considerably over time, there is yet to emerge a consensus about how to tackle it. Were cancer a purely viral disease, it might have been possible to address it by identifying the (retro)virus and by preventing it, vaccinating against it or by interfering with the mechanisms at its disposal (e.g., reverse transcription). Were it a strictly genomic (mutational) disease, involving (driver) mutations in handful of key genes (e.g., functionalizing oncogenes or dysfunctionalizing tumor-suppressor genes), it might have been possible to formulate therapies by identifying such mutations, with drugs to control genomic instability (e.g., synthetic lethality or telomerase or topoisomerase involved in copying and disentangling genomes) or via gene-therapy. Were it simply endowed with a just a handful of possible trajectories consisting of succession of driver mutations, it might have been possible to find bottle-neck mutations (e.g., VEGF mutations involved with angiogenesis) and then inhibiting progression of these trajectories beyond a critical point, using one or combination of handful of drugs (e.g., Avastin) – or even better, to detect (non-invasively) the initiating mutations of these trajectories (e.g., EGFR or KRAS/NRAS) and treating the patient with suitable drugs (possibly universal therapies that work even when the tissue of origin remains unknown). Were the phenotypes (e.g., Cancer Hallmarks) associated with these driver mutations and their effects directly inferrable, it might have been possible to terminate or decelerate cancer's progression via appropriate drugs or immunotherapy in order to delay the arrival of metastatic phenotype–a fatal hallmark. Were the evolutionary landscapes of the phenotype-space to vary from patient to patient or tissue-type to tissue-type, it might have been possible to "cluster" individualized models by the germ-line genome, tumor genome, methylation patterns, HLA type and tissue of origin to personalize the therapy. Were the progression dynamics of cancer merely co-evolution of tumor and stroma, modulated by the host immune-system, it might have been completely prevented, contained and reversed by immune enhancement, immunotherapy, and cancer vaccines, targeting both adaptive and innate immune system, while avoiding adverse auto-immune response and immune resistance.

© Springer Nature Switzerland AG 2019
E. Bartocci et al. (Eds.): From Reactive Systems to Cyber-Physical Systems, LNCS 11500, pp. 297–298, 2019.
https://doi.org/10.1007/978-3-030-31514-6

While the logical analysis of such an etiological structure of the disease remains to be rigorously developed, it seems necessary that this logic must be able to address *time, heterogeneity* and *micro-environment*, involved in a reiterative selection processes, shifting balance (Haldane-Wright) in each stage. There are reasons to be optimistic as necessary ingredients for such a development are imminent, for following reasons: (1) Mathematical logic (namely, probabilistic propositional modal logic) is a mature field and the fragments that are needed are available along with rigorous and efficient decision and model checking algorithms. (2) Data sources (patient, model animal, organoid, cell-line, and in-silico data) are being made openly available and collected via single-cell, single-molecule genome and transcriptome mapping and sequencing at a high-throughput and inexpensively. (3) Systems-biology, data-science and so-called, artificial-intelligence (AI, ML, RL and statistical inference) tools can be made rigorous and reproducible in order to build models (e.g., Kripke Structures for Modal Logic) that could shed light on the underlying somatic evolution (e.g., using Suppes' prima-facie causality). (4) Literature on cancer can be mined to create annotations and ontologies (e.g., COSMIC) that can generate hypotheses that could be rigorously validate/refuted, further enriching not only the ontologies but also the epistemology of the models.

Towards Real-Time Program Analysis Based on Nested Timed Automata

Shoji Yuen[1]([✉]), Guoqiang Li[2], and Mizuhito Ogawa[3]

[1] Nagoya University, Nagoya, Japan
yuen@i.nagoya-u.ac.jp
[2] Shanghai Jiao Tong University, Shanghai, China
li-gq@cs.sjtu.edu.cn
[3] Japan Advanced Institute of Science and Technology, Nomi, Japan
mizuhito@jaist.ac.jp

We have been investigating a model called "Nested Timed Automata" [1], which is an extension of timed automata with recursive structure. A location may recursively invoke a new instance of timed automata with a transition labelled by push and resume with a pop transition. Besides global clocks common to all timed automata, each timed automaton may have local clocks. Local clocks are pushed and popped according to the nested structure of timed automata. The state reachability from the initial state is shown to be decidable [1] when local clocks work as regular clocks while in the stack. With a single global clock, the reachability problem is decidable even if local clocks are frozen in the stack [2]. Based on these results, a program with clocks local to a context can be analysed with respect to time passage. Moreover, even if the local clocks may be frozen while in the stack, we see how these results can be applied to the safety analysis of more structured real-time programs.

References

1. Li, G., Cai, X., Ogawa, M., Yuen, S.: Nested timed automata. In: Formal Modeling and Analysis of Timed Systems - 11th International Conference, FORMATS 2013, Buenos Aires, Argentina, 29–31 August 2013. Proceedings, pp. 168–182 (2013)
2. Li, G., Ogawa, M., Yuen, S.: Nested timed automata with frozen clocks. In: Formal Modeling and Analysis of Timed Systems - 13th International Conference, FORMATS 2015, Madrid, Spain, 2–4 September 2015, Proceedings, pp. 189–205 (2015)

© Springer Nature Switzerland AG 2019
E. Bartocci et al. (Eds.): From Reactive Systems to Cyber-Physical Systems, LNCS 11500, p. 299, 2019.
https://doi.org/10.1007/978-3-030-31514-6

Author Index

Printed in the United States
By Bookmasters